Samuel Thomas Morgan

U.S. Import Duties

under existing laws and decisions, and digest of the tariff laws, August 1, 1872 -

with an appendix containing tables of foreign moneys, weights and measures

Samuel Thomas Morgan

U.S. Import Duties
under existing laws and decisions, and digest of the tariff laws, August 1, 1872 - with an
appendix containing tables of foreign moneys, weights and measures

ISBN/EAN: 9783337351274

Printed in Europe, USA, Canada, Australia, Japan

Cover: Foto ©Suzi / pixelio.de

More available books at **www.hansebooks.com**

UNDER

EXISTING LAWS AND DECISIONS,

AND

DIGEST OF THE TARIFF LAW

AUGUST 1,

WITH AN APPENDIX CONTAINING TABLES OF
MEASURES, REDUCED TO U. S. STANDARD,
DRAWBACK, STANDARD WEIGHT OF
IMPORTANT REGULATIONS OF

COMPILED BY

SAMUEL T. M

CUSTOM HOUSE BROKER AND C

BALTIMORE.

Third Editio

BALTIMORE:
TURNBULL BROTHERS.   BAKER

BOSTON:
HOOPER, LEWIS & CO.   PHIL

1872.

PREFACE TO FIRST EDITION.

In presenting this Manual to the public, the compiler deems it only necessary to remark that an experience in the business of Custom-House Broker for upwards of Twelve Years, justifies his recommending it as a reliable work; and it may be readily inferred what amount of labor and research was required in its compilation, when it is considered that the provisions of the tariff laws, now in force, date back as far as the Act of August 30, 1842.

The Manual will be found to contain a Digest of the Tariff Laws from August 30, 1842, to date, thus covering the changes made at the last session of Congress, and a Schedule of the Rates of Duties, alphabetically arranged, (each article bearing reference to the paragraphs of the digest which prescribe the rate of duty,) and, in addition, numerous Extracts from Important Decisions of the Treasury Department and Explanatory Notes, with an Appendix of Tables of Foreign Moneys, Weights, and Measures, reduced to the United States standard, Rates of Tare, Rates of Drawback, and other important Regulations of the Customs, which cannot fail to prove of service, not only to the importer, but also to those dealing in imported articles and to the general business public.

See next page for the Plan of Compilation.

PREFACE TO THIRD EDITION.

The First and Second Editions of the Manual having met with such flattering success, the compiler has been encouraged to issue a Third Edition, which he presents to the public with full assurance of its reliability and correctness.

PLAN OF COMPILATION.

The Digest contains the various Tariff laws from 1842 to date; the portion *now in force* is printed in *large type*, while that which is repealed is in small type. When words are to be inserted in an act, by virtue of a subsequent act, the words are properly inserted with a foot note to explain. See paragraphs 3, 18, 23, 475, 610, 651, &c.

The articles in the Schedule of Duties, commencing page 129, are alphabetically arranged under the *noun*, the qualifying word following; and each article bears reference, by the numbers in the parenthesis, to the paragraphs of the Digest of the corresponding numbers, which paragraphs impose the duty. Extracts from important Decisions and Regulations of the Treasury Department are placed as foot-notes.

The comparative rates of duty on any article, as well as the phraseology of the law imposing the same, can be ascertained by tracing the article from the schedule through the various laws, as for example, liquors refer from the schedule to par. 652, that refers to 594, that to 577, that to 423, that to 192, that to 178, and that to 3, thus showing seven changes in the duty on this article within the last twelve years.

The term "Reg. of 1857" refers to the General Regulations of the Treasury Department issued 1857; "Rev. Reg." to the Revised Regulations issued 1869, and the "dec. of," to the Decisions rendered by the Department from 1857 to date.

CONTENTS.

PART I.

PART II.

APPENDIX.

DIGEST

OF THE

TARIFF LAWS.

———•+———

ACT OF AUGUST 30, 1842.

———

(From U. S. Statutes at Large, vol. 5, p. 548.)

———

AN ACT to provide Revenue from Imports, and to change and modify existing
Laws imposing Duties on Imports, and for other purposes.

*   *   *   *   *   *   *

1. **Sec. 20.** *And be it further enacted,* That there shall be levied,
collected, and paid, on each and every non-enumerated
article which bears a similitude, either in material, quality,
texture, or the use to which it may be applied, to any enumerated article chargeable with duty, the same rate of duty
which is levied and charged on the enumerated article
which it most resembles in any of the particulars before
mentioned ; and if any non-enumerated article equally resembles two or more enumerated articles, on which different rates of duty are chargeable, there shall be levied,
collected, and paid, on such non-enumerated article, the
same rate of duty as is chargeable on the article which it
resembles paying the highest duty ; and on all articles
manufactured from two or more materials, the duty shall
be assessed at the highest rates at which any of its component parts may be chargeable.†

*   *   *   *   *   *   *

---

†See section 24, Act of March 2, 1861, and section 22, Act of June 30, 1864.—Paragraphs Nos. 193
and 565.

ACT OF MARCH 2, 1861.

(From U. S. Statutes at Large, vol. 12, p. 178, &c.)

AN ACT to provide for the payment of outstanding Treasury Notes, to authorize a Loan, to regulate and fix the Duties on Imports, and for other purposes.

(Secs. 1, 2, 3 and 4 do not relate to import duties.)

Sec. 5. *And be it further enacted,* That from and after the first day of April, Anno Domini eighteen hundred and sixty-one, IN LIEU of the duties heretofore imposed by law on the articles hereinafter mentioned, and on such as may now be EXEMPT FROM DUTY, there shall be levied, collected, and paid, on the goods, wares, and merchandise herein enumerated and provided for, imported from foreign countries, the following duties and rates of duties, that is to say:

2. On raw sugar, commonly called Muscovado or brown sugar, not advanced beyond the raw state by claying or other process; and on syrup of sugar, or of sugar cane, and concentrated molasses, or concentrated melado, and on white and clayed sugars, when advanced beyond the raw state by claying, or other process, and not refined, three-fourths of one cent per pound; on refined sugars, whether loaf, lump, crushed, or pulverized, two cents per pound; on sugars, after being refined, when they are tinctured, colored, or in any way adulterated, and on sugar candy four cents per pound: *Provided,* That all syrups of sugar, or of sugar cane, concentrated molasses or melado, entered under the name of molasses, or any other name than syrup of sugar, or of sugar cane, concentrated molasses, or concentrated melado, shall be liable to forfeiture to the United States; on molasses, two cents per gallon; on confectionery of all kinds, not otherwise provided for, thirty per centum ad valorem.

Sec. 6. *And be it further enacted,* That from and after the day and year aforesaid, there shall be levied, collected, and paid, on the importation of the articles hereinafter mentioned, the following duties, that is to say:

3. On brandy, for first proof, one dollar per gallon; on other spirits manufactured or distilled from grain, for first proof, forty cents per gallon; on spirits from other materials, for first proof, forty cents per gallon; on cordials and (liquors) * liqueurs of all kinds, fifty cents per gallon; on arrack, absynthe, kirschenwasser, ratafia, and other similar spirituous beverages not otherwise provided for, fifty cents per gallon; on bay rum, twenty-five cents per gallon: *Provided,* That the duty upon brandy, spirits, and all other spirituous beverages herein enumerated, shall be collected upon the basis of first-proof, and so in proportion for any greater strength than the strength of first-proof; on wines of all kinds, forty per centum ad valorem: *Provided,* That all imitations of brandy, or s;irits, or of any of the said wines, and all wines imported by any names whatsoever, shall be subject to the duty provided for the genuine articles which it is intended to represent; *Provided also,* That no lower rate or amount of duty shall be levied, collected, and paid on brandy, spirits, and all other spirituous beverages, than that now fixed by law for the description of first-proof, but shall be increased in proportion for any greater strength than the strength of first-proof:† *Provided further,* That brandies or other spirituous liquors may be imported in bottles, when the package shall contain not less than one dozen, and all bottles shall pay a separate duty, according to the rate established by this Act, whether containing wines, brandies, or other spirtuous liquors, subject to

---

* The word "liquors" is stricken out, and the word "liqueurs" inserted by paragraph 183.

† The words "*Provided also,* That no lower rate or amount of duty shall be levied, collected, and paid on brandy, spirits, and all other spirituous beverages, than that now fixed by law for the description of first-proof, but shall be increased in proportion for any greater strength than the strength of first-proof," inserted here by paragraph 183.

duty as hereinbefore mentioned ; on ale, porter, and beer. In bottles, twenty-five cents per gallon; otherwise than in bottles, fifteen cents per gallon ; on all spirituous liquors not enumerated, thirty-three and one-third per centum ad valorem.

4. On cigars of all kinds, valued at five dollars or under per thousand, twenty cents per pound: over five dollars and not over ten, forty cents per pound; and over ten dollars, sixty cents per pound, and in addition thereto ten per centum ad valorem; on snuff, ten cents per pound: on un-manufactured tobacco, in leaf, twenty-five per centum ad valorem : on all other manufactured or unmanufactured tobacco, thirty per centum ad valorem (425).

Sec. 7. And be it further enacted, That from and after the day and year aforesaid there shall be levied, collected, and paid, on the importation of the articles hereinafter mentioned, the following duties. that is to say :

5. On bar iron, rolled or hammered, comprising flats not less than one inch, or more than seven inches wide, nor less than one-quarter of an inch or more than two inches thick ; rounds, not less than one-half an inch or more than four inches in diameter : and squares, not less than one-half an inch or more than four inches square, fifteen dollars per ton : Provided, That all iron in slabs, blooms, loops, or other forms less finished than iron in bars, and more advanced than pig iron, except castings, shall be rated as iron in bars, and pay a duty accordingly : And provided further, That none of the above iron shall pay a less rate of duty than twenty per centum ad valorem ; on all iron imported in bars for railroads or inclined planes, made to patterns and fitted to be laid down upon such roads or planes without farther manufacture, and not exceeding six inches high, twelve dollars per ton; on boiler plate iron. twenty dollars per ton (196) ; on iron wire drawn and finished, not more than one-fourth of one inch in diameter nor less than number sixteen wire gauge, seventy-five cents per one hundred pounds and fifteen per centum ad valorem: over number sixteen, not and not over number twenty-five wire gauge, one dollar and fifty cents per one hundred pounds, and in addition fifteen per centum ad valorem; over or finer than number twenty-five wire gauge, two dollars per one hundred pounds, and in addition fifteen per centum ad valorem (197) ; on all other descriptions of rolled or hammered iron, not otherwise provided for, twenty dollars per ton.

6. On iron in pigs, six dollars per ton : on vessels of cast iron, not otherwise provided for, and on sad irons, tailors' and hatters irons, stoves and stove plates, one cent per pound : on cast iron, steam, gas, and water pipe, fifty cents per one hundred pounds: on cast iron butts and hinges, two cents per pound : on hollow ware glazed or tinned, two cents and a half per pound ; on all other castings of iron, not otherwise provided for, twenty-five per centum ad valorem.

7. On old scrap iron, six dollars per ton : Provided, That nothing shall be deemed old iron that has not been in actual use, and fit only to be remanufactured.

8. On band and hoop iron, slit rods, not otherwise provided for, twenty dollars per ton ; on cut nails and spikes, one cent per pound . on iron cables or chains, or parts thereof, and anvils, one dollar and twenty-five cents per one hundred pounds: on anchors, or parts thereof, one dollar and fifty cents per one hundred pounds; on wrought board nails, spikes, rivets, and bolts, two cents per pound ; on bed screws and wrought hinges; one cent and a half per pound; on chains, trace chains, halter chains, and fence chains, made of wire or rods. one-half of one inch in diameter or over, one cent and a half per pound; under one-half of one inch in diameter and not under one-fourth of one inch in diameter, two cents per pound ; under one-fourth of one inch in diameter, and not under number nine wire gauge, two cents and a half per pound; under number nine wire gauge, twenty-five per centum ad valorem ; on blacksmiths' hammers and sledges, axles, or parts thereof, and malleable iron in castings not otherwise provided for, two cents per pound; on horse-shoe nails, three cents and a half per pound: on steam, gas, and water tubes and flues of wrought iron, two cents per pound; on wrought-iron railroad chairs, and on wrought-iron nuts and washers, ready punched, twenty-five dollars per ton; on cut tacks, brads, and sprigs, not exceeding sixteen ounces to the thousand, two cents per thousand ; exceeding sixteen ounces to the thousand, two cents per pound.

9. On smooth or polished sheet-iron, by whatever name designated, two cents per pound ; on other sheet-iron, common or black, not thinner than number twenty wire gauge, twenty dollars per ton; thinner than number twenty, and not thinner than number twenty-five wire gauge, twenty-five dollars per ton ; thinner than number twenty-five wire gauge, thirty dollars per ton ; on tin plates gal-vanized, galvanized iron, or iron coated with zinc, two cents per pound ; on mill irons and mill cranks

of wrought-iron, and wrought-iron for ships, locomotives, locomotive tire, or parts thereof, and steam engines, or parts thereof, weighing each twenty-five pounds or more, one cent and a half per pound ; on screws, commonly called wood screws, two inches or over in length, five cents per pound; less than two inches in length, eight cents per pound ; (on screws washed or plated, and all other screws of iron or any other metal),* on screws of any other metal than iron, thirty per centum ad valorem : on all manufactures of iron not otherwise provided for, thirty per centum ad valorem.

10. On all steel in ingots, bars, sheets, or wire, not less than one-fourth of one inch in diameter, valued at seven cents per pound or less, one and a half cent per pound; valued at seven cents per pound, and not above eleven cents per pound, two cents per pound ; steel in any form, not otherwise provided for, shall pay a duty of twenty per centum ad valorem ; on steel wire less than one-fourth of an inch in diameter, and not less than number sixteen wire gauge, two dollars per one hundred pounds, and in addition thereto, fifteen per centum ad valorem ; less or finer than number sixteen wire gauge, two dollars and fifty cents per one hundred pounds, and in addition thereto, fifteen per centum ad valorem ; on cross-cut saws, eight cents per lineal foot; on mill, pit, and drag saws, not over nine inches wide, twelve and a half cents per lineal foot: over nine inches wide, twenty cents per lineal foot (451); on skates costing twenty cents or less per pair, six cents per pair ; on those costing over twenty cents per pair, thirty per centum ad valorem ; on all manufactures of steel, or of which steel shall be a component part, not otherwise provided for, thirty per centum ad valorem: *Provided,* That all articles partially manufactured, not otherwise provided for, shall pay the same rate of duty as if wholly manufactured.

11. On bituminous coal, one dollar per ton of twenty-eight bushels, eighty pounds to the bushel ; on all other coal, fifty cents per ton of twenty-eight bushels, eighty pounds to the bushel ; on coke and culm of coal, twenty-five per centum ad valorem.

Sec. 8. *And be it further enacted,* That from and after the day and year aforesaid, there shall be levied, collected, and paid, on the importation of the articles hereinafter mentioned, the following duties, that is to say :

12. On lead in pigs and bars, one cent per pound ; on old scrap lead, fit only to be remanufactured, one cent per pound ; on lead in sheets, pipes, or shot, one cent and a half per pound ; on pewter, when old and fit only to be remanufactured, one cent per pound.

13. On copper in pigs, bars, or ingots, two cents per pound ; on copper when old and fit only to be remanufactured, one cent and a half per pound ; on sheathing copper, in sheets forty-eight inches long and fourteen inches wide, and weighing from fourteen to thirty-four ounces the square foot, two cents per pound (159) ; on copper rods, bolts, nails, spikes, copper bottoms, copper in sheets or plates, called braziers' copper, and other sheets of copper not otherwise provided for, twenty-five per centum ad valorem ; on zinc, spelter, or teutenegue, manufactured in blocks or pigs, one dollar per one hundred pounds; on zinc, spelter, or teutenegue in sheets, one cent and a half per pound.

Sec. 9. *And be it further enacted,* That from and after the day and year aforesaid, there shall be levied, collected, and paid, on the importation of the articles hereinafter mentioned, the following duties, that is to say :

14. On white lead and oxide of zinc, dry or ground in oil (295), red lead, and litharge, one cent and a half per pound ; on sugar of lead or acetate of lead and nitrate of lead, chromate and bichromate of potash, three cents per pound ; on hydriodate, and prussiate of potash and chromic acid, and salts of iodine, resublimed iodine, fifteen per centum ad valorem ; on whiting, twenty-five cents per one hundred pounds; on Paris white, pipe clay, and ochres or ochrey earth, not otherwise provided for, when dry, thirty-five cents per one hundred pounds, when ground in oil, one dollar and thirty-five cents per one hundred pounds: on umber, fifty cents per one hundred pounds ; on putty, one cent per pound : on linseed, flaxseed, hempseed, and

---

* The words " on screws washed or plated, and all other screws of iron or any other metal," stricken out, and the words "on screws of any other metal than iron" inserted instead, as per paragraph 183.

rapeseed oil, twenty cents per gallon (289); on kerosene oil, and all other coal oils, ten cents per gallon; on alum, alum substitute, sulphate of alumina and aluminous cake, fifty cents per one hundred pounds; on copperas, green vitriol, or sulphate of iron (288), twenty-five cents per one hundred pounds; on bleaching powders, fifteen cents per one hundred pounds; on refined camphor, six cents per pound (123); on refined borax, three cents per pound; on tallow, one cent per pound; on tallow candles, two cents per pound; on spermaceti or wax candles and tapers, and on candles and tapers of spermaceti and wax combined, eight cents per pound; on stearine candles, and all other candles and tapers, four cents per pound; on spirits of turpentine, ten cents per gallon; on opium, one dollar per pound; on morphine and its salts, one dollar per ounce; on liquorice paste or juice, three cents per pound.

Sec. 10. *And be it further enacted,* That from and after the day and year aforesaid, there shall be levied, collected, and paid, on the importation of the articles hereinafter mentioned, the following duties, that is to say:

15. On salt, four cents per bushel of fifty-six pounds: *Provided,* That salt, imported in bags, or not in bulk, shall pay a duty of six cents per bushel of fifty-six pounds; on bristles, four cents per pound; on honey, ten cents per gallon; on vinegar, six cents per gallon; on mackerel, two dollars per barrel; on herrings, pickled or salted, one dollar per barrel; on pickled salmon, three dollars per barrel; on all other fish pickled, in barrels, one dollar and fifty cents per barrel; on all other foreign caught fish imported otherwise than in barrels or half-barrels, or whether fresh, smoked, or dried, salted or pickled, not otherwise provided for, fifty cents per one hundred pounds.

16. On beef and pork, one cent per pound; on hams and bacon, two cents per pound; on cheese, four cents per pound; on wheat, twenty cents per bushel; on butter, four cents per pound; on lard, two cents per pound; on rye and barley, fifteen cents per bushel; on Indian corn or maize, ten cents per bushel; on oats, ten cents per bushel; on potatoes, ten cents per bushel; on cleaned rice, one cent per pound; on uncleaned rice, or paddy, fifty cents per one hundred pounds; on sago and sago flour, fifty cents per one hundred pounds; on flaxseed or linseed, sixteen cents per bushel of fifty-two pounds; on hemp and rapeseed, ten cents per bushel of fifty-two pounds; on raw hides and skins of all kinds whether dried, salted, or pickled, not otherwise provided for, five per centum ad valorem.

Sec. 11. *And be it further enacted,* That from and after the day and year aforesaid, there shall be levied, collected, and paid, on the importation of the articles hereinafter mentioned, the following duties, that is to say:

17. On cassia, four cents per pound; on cassia buds, eight cents per pound; on cloves, four cents per pound; on pepper, two cents per pound; on Cayenne pepper, three cents per pound; on ground Cayenne pepper, four cents per pound; on pimento, two cents per pound; on cinnamon, ten cents per pound; on mace and nutmegs, fifteen cents per pound; on prunes, two cents per pound; on plums one cent per pound; on dates, one-half of one cent per pound; on currants, two cents per pound; on figs, three cents per pound; on sultana, muscatel, and bloom raisins, either in boxes or jars, two cents per pound; on all other raisins, one cent per pound; on almonds, two cents per pound; on shelled almonds, four cents per pound; on all nuts not otherwise provided for, except those used for dyeing, one cent per pound.

Sec. 12. *And be it further enacted,* That from and after the day and year aforesaid, there shall be levied, collected, and paid, on the importation of the articles hereinafter mentioned, the following duties, that is to say :

18. On all wool unmanufactured, and all hair, of the alpaca, goat, and other like animals, un-manufactured, the value whereof at the last port or place from whence exported to the United States shall be (less than) * eighteen cents or less† per pound, five per centum ad valorem ; exceeding eighteen cents per pound, and not exceeding twenty-four cents per pound, there shall be levied, collected, and paid, a duty of three cents per pound; exceeding twenty-four cents per pound, there shall be levied, collected, and paid, a duty of nine cents per pound : *Provided,* That any wool of the sheep, or hair of the alpaca, the goat, and other like animal which shall be imported in any other than the ordinary condition, as now and heretofore practised, or which shall be changed in its character or condition for the purpose of evading the duty, or which shall be reduced in value by the admix-ture of dirt or any foreign substance to eighteen cents per pound or less, shall be subject to pay a duty of nine cents per pound, any thing in this Act to the contrary notwithstanding : *Provided also,* That when wool of different qualities is imported in the same bale, bag, or package, and the aggre-gate value of the contents of the bale, bag, or package shall be appraised by the appraisers at a rate exceeding twenty-four cents per pound, it shall be charged with a duty of nine cents per pound : *Provided further,* That if bales of different qualities are embraced in the same invoice at the same price whereby the average price shall be lessened more than ten per centum, the value of the whole shall be appraised according to the value of the bale of the best quality, and no bale or bales shall be liable to a less rate of duty in consequence of being invoiced with wool of lower value : *Provided also,* That sheep skins, raw or unmanufactured, imported with the wool on, washed or unwashed, shall be subject to a duty of fifteen per centum ad valorem.

Sec. 13. *And be it further enacted,* That from and after the day and year aforesaid, there shall be levied, collected, and paid, on the importation of the articles hereinafter mentioned, the following duties, that is to say :

19. On Wilton, Saxony, and Aubusson, Axminster patent velvet, Tournay velvet, and tapes-try velvet carpets and carpeting, Brussels carpets, wrought by the Jacquard machine, and all mo-dallion or whole carpets, valued at one dollar and twenty-five cents or under per square yard, forty cents per square yard ; valued at over one dollar and twenty-five cents per square yard, fifty cents per square yard : *Provided,* That no carpet or rugs of the above description shall pay a duty less than twenty-five per centum ad valorem ; on Brussels and tapestry Brussels carpets and carpeting, printed on the warp or otherwise, thirty cents per square yard ; on all treble-ingrain and worsted chain Ve-netian carpets and carpeting, twenty-five cents per square yard ; on hemp or jute carpeting, four cents per square yard ; on druggets, bockings, and felt carpets and carpeting, printed, colored, or otherwise, twenty cents per square yard ; on all other kinds of carpets and carpeting, of wool, flax, or cotton, or parts of either, or other material, not otherwise specified, a duty of thirty per centum ad valorem : *Provided,* That mats, rugs, screens, covers, hassocks, bedsides, and other portions of carpets or carpeting, shall pay the rate of duty herein imposed on carpets or carpeting of similar character : on all other mats, screens, hassocks, and rugs, a duty of thirty per centum ad valorem.

20. On woolen cloths, woolen shawls, and all manufactures of wool of every description, made wholly or in part of wool, not otherwise provided for, a duty of twelve cents per pound, and in ad-dition thereto twenty-five per centum ad valorem ; on endless belts for paper, and blanketing for printing machines, twenty-five per centum ad valorem : on all flannels, valued at thirty cents or less per square yard, twenty-five per centum ad valorem : valued above thirty cents per square yard, and on all flannels colored, printed, or plaided, and flannels composed in part of cotton or silk, thirty per centum ad valorem ; on hats of wool, twenty per centum ad valorem ; on woolen and worsted yarn, valued at fifty cents and not over one dollar per pound, twelve cents per pound, and in addi-tion thereto, fifteen per centum ad valorem : on woolen and worsted yarns, valued at over one dollar per pound, twelve cents per pound, and in addition thereto, twenty-five per centum ad valorem : on woolen and worsted yarns, or yarns for carpets, valued under fifty cents per pound, and not exceed-ing in fineness number fourteen, twenty-five per centum ad valorem : exceeding number fourteen, thirty per centum ad valorem : on clothing ready made, and wearing apparel of every description, composed wholly or in part of wool, made up or manufactured wholly or in part by the tailor, seamstress, or manufacturer, except hosiery,‡ twelve cents per pound, and in addition

---

* The words "less than" stricken out by paragraph 408.
† The words " or less " inserted here by paragraph 183.
‡ The words " except hosiery " inserted here by paragraph 183.

thereto, twenty-five per centum ad valorem; on blankets of all kinds, made wholly or in part of wool, valued at not exceeding twenty-eight cents per pound, there shall be charged a duty of six cents per pound, and in addition thereto, ten per centum ad valorem; on all valued above twenty-eight cents per pound, but not exceeding forty cents per pound, there shall be charged a duty of six cents per pound, and in addition thereto, twenty-five per centum ad valorem; on all valued above forty cents per pound there shall be charged a duty of twelve cents per pound, and in addition thereto, twenty per centum ad valorem; (on woolen shawls, or shawls of which wool shall be the chief component material, a duty of sixteen cents per pound, and in addition thereto, twenty per centum ad valorem).*

21. On all delaines, Cashmere delaines, muslin delaines, barege delaines, composed wholly or in part of (wool)† worsted, gray or uncolored, and on all other gray or uncolored goods of similar description, twenty-five per centum ad valorem; on bunting, and on all stained, colored, or printed, and on all other manufactures of (wool)† worsted, or of which (wool) † worsted shall be a component material, not otherwise provided for, thirty per centum ad valorem.

22. On oil cloth, for floors, stamped, painted, or printed, valued at fifty cents or less per square yard, twenty per centum ad valorem; valued at over fifty cents per square yard, and on all other oil cloth, thirty per centum ad valorem.

Sec. 14. *And be it further enacted,* That from and after the day and year aforesaid, there shall be levied, collected, and paid, on the importation of the articles hereinafter mentioned, the following duties, that is to say:

23. On all manufactures of cotton, not bleached, colored, stained, painted, or printed, and not exceeding one hundred threads to the square inch, counting the warp and filling, and exceeding in weight five ounces per square yard, one cent per square yard; on finer or lighter goods of like description, not exceeding one hundred and forty threads to the square inch, counting the warp and filling, two cents per square yard (339); on goods of like description, exceeding one hundred and forty threads, and not exceeding two hundred threads to the square inch, counting the warp and filling, three cents per square yard; on like goods exceeding two hundred threads to the square inch, counting the warp and filling, four cents per square yard; on all goods embraced in the foregoing schedules, if bleached, there shall be levied, collected, and paid, an additional duty of one-half of one cent per square yard; and if printed, painted, colored, or stained, there shall be levied, collected, and paid, a duty of ten per centum "ad valorem" ‡ in addition to the rates of duty provided in the foregoing schedules (339): *Provided,* That upon all plain woven cotton goods not included in the foregoing schedules, and upon cotton goods of every description, the value of which shall exceed sixteen cents per square yard, there shall be levied, collected, and paid, a duty of twenty-five per centum ad valorem : *And provided further,* That no cotton goods having more than two hundred threads to the square inch, counting the warp and filling, shall be admitted to a less rate of duty than is provided for goods which are of that number of threads (339).

24. On spool and other thread of cotton, thirty per centum ad valorem.

25. On shirts and drawers, wove or made on frames, composed wholly of cotton and cotton velvet, twenty-five per centum ad valorem; and on all manufactures composed wholly of cotton, bleached, unbleached, printed, painted or dyed, not otherwise provided for, thirty per centum ad valorem.

26. On all brown or bleached linens, ducks, canvas paddings, cot-bottoms, burlaps, drills, coatings, brown Hollands, blay linens, damasks, diapers, crash, huckabacks, handkerchiefs, lawns, or other manufactures of flax, jute, or hemp, [or of which flax, jute, or hemp] shall be the component material of chief value, being of the

---

*The words "on woolen shawls, or shawls of which wool shall be the chief component material, a duty of sixteen cents per pound, and in addition thereto, twenty per centum ad valorem," stricken out by paragraph 177.

† The word "wool" stricken out and the word "worsted" inserted in its stead. See paragraph 183.

‡ The words "ad valorem" inserted here by paragraph 183.

value of thirty cents and under per square yard, twenty-five per centum ad valorem ; valued about thirty cents per square yard, thirty per centum ad valorem (343) ; on flax or linen threads, twine and packthread and all other manufactures of flax or of which flax shall be the component material of chief value, and not otherwise provided for, thirty per centum ad valorem (343).

Sec. 15. *And be it further enacted,* That from and after the day and year aforesaid, there shall be levied, collected, and paid on the importation of the articles hereinafter mentioned, the following duties, that is to say :

27. On unmanufactured hemp, thirty-five dollars per ton ; on manilla, and other hemps of India, fifteen dollars per ton ; on jute, Sisal grass, sun hemp, coir, and other vegetable substances not enumerated, used for cordage, ten dollars per ton (344) ; on jute butts, five dollars per ton ; on codilla, or tow of hemp, ten dollars per ton ; on tarred cables or cordage, two cents and a half per pound ; on untarred Manilla cordage, two cents per pound ; on all other untarred cordage, three cents per pound ; on (hemp)* yarns, four cents per pound ; on coir yarns, one cent per pound ; on selnes, six cents per pound ; on cotton bagging, or any other manufacture not otherwise provided for, suitable for the uses to which cotton bagging is applied, whether composed in whole or in part of hemp, jute, or flax, or any other material valued at less than ten cents per square yard, one cent and a half per pound ; over ten cents per square yard, two cents per pound ; on sail duck, twenty-five per centum ad valorem ; on Russia and other sheetings of flax or hemp, brown and white, twenty-five per centum ad valorem ; and on all other manufactures of hemp,† or of which hemp shall be a component part, not otherwise provided for, twenty per centum ad valorem ; on unmanufactured flax, fifteen dollars per ton ; on tow of flax, five dollars per ton ; on grass cloth, twenty-five per centum ad valorem ; on (jute goods) ‡ jute yarns, fifteen per centum ad valorem ; on all other manufactures of jute or Sisal grass, not otherwise provided for, twenty per centum ad valorem.

Sec. 16. *And be it further enacted,* That from and after the day and year aforesaid, there shall be levied, collected, and paid on the importation of the articles hereinafter mentioned, the following duties, that is to say :

28. On silk in the gum, not more advanced in manufacture than singles, tram, and thrown or organzine, fifteen per centum ad valorem ; on all silks valued at not over one dollar per square yard, twenty per centum ad valorem ; on all silks valued at over one dollar per square yard, thirty per centum ad valorem ; on all silk velvets, or velvets of which silk is the component material of chief value, valued at three dollars per square yard, or under, twenty-five per centum ad valorem ; valued at over three dollars per square yard, thirty per centum ad valorem ; on floss silks, twenty per centum ad valorem ; on silk ribbons, galloons, braids, fringes, laces, tassels, buttons, button cloths, trimmings, and on silk twist, twist composed of mohair and silk, sewing silk in the gum or purified, and all other manufactures of silk, or of which silk shall be the component material of chief value, not otherwise provided for, thirty per centum ad valorem.

Sec. 17. *And be it further enacted,* That from and after the day and year aforesaid, there shall be levied, collected, and paid on the importation of the articles hereinafter mentioned, the following duties, that is to say :

29. On rough plate, cylinder, or broad window glass, not exceeding ten by fifteen inches, one cent per square foot; above that, and not exceeding sixteen by twenty-four inches, one cent and a half per square foot; above that, and not exceeding twenty-four by thirty inches, two cents per square foot; all above that, and not exceeding in weight one pound per square foot, three cents per

* The word " hemp" inserted here as per paragraph 183.
† The words " of flax or hemp" inserted here as per paragraph 183.
‡ The words "jute goods" stricken out and the words "jute yarns" inserted instead, as per paragraph 183.

square foot: *Provided,* That all glass imported in sheets or tables, without reference to size or form, shall pay the highest duty herein imposed: *And provided further,* That all rough plate cylinder, [or] broad glass, weighing over one hundred pounds per one hundred square feet, shall pay an additional duty on the excess: on crown, plate, or polish, and on all other window glass not exceeding ten by fifteen inches, one cent and a half per square foot; above that, and not exceeding sixteen by twenty-four inches, two cents and a half per square foot; above that, and not exceeding twenty-four by thirty inches, four cents per square foot; all above that, five cents per square foot: *Provided,* That all crown, plate, or polished, and all other window glass weighing over one hundred and fifty pounds per one hundred square feet, shall pay an additional duty on such excess of four cents per pound; on all plain and mould and press glassware, not cut, engraved, or painted, twenty-five per centum ad valorem; on all articles of glass cut, engraved, painted, colored, printed, stained, silvered, or gilded, thirty per centum ad valorem; on porcelain and Bohemian glass, glass crystals for watches, paintings on glass or glasses, pebbles for spectacles, and all manufactures of glass, or of which glass shall be a component material, not otherwise provided for, and all glass bottles or jars filled with sweetmeats, preserves or other articles, thirty per centum ad valorem.

30. On China and porcelain ware of all descriptions, thirty per centum ad valorem; on all brown earthen and common stone ware, twenty per centum ad valorem: on all other earthen, stone, or crockery ware, printed, white, glazed, edged, painted, dipped, or cream Colored, composed of earthy or mineral substances, twenty-five per centum ad valorem.

Sec. 18. *And be it further enacted,* That from and after the day and year aforesaid, there shall be levied, collected, and paid on the importation of the articles hereinafter mentioned, the following duties, that is to say:

31. On all books, periodicals and pamphlets, and all printed matter and illustrated books and papers, and on watches and parts of watches, and watch materials, and unfinished parts of watches, fifteen per centum ad valorem.

Sec. 19. *And be it further enacted,* That from and after the day and year aforesaid, there shall be levied, collected, and paid a duty of TEN PER CENTUM on the importation of the articles hereinafter mentioned and embraced in this section, that is to say:

32. Acids, nitric, yellow and white, oxalic and all other acids of every description used for medicinal purposes or in the fine arts, not otherwise provided for; aloes, amber, ammonia, sal ammonia, muriate and carbonate of ammonia; anise seed; arrow root; assafœtida (271);

33. Bamboos; barks of all kinds not otherwise provided for; beeswax (272); black lead, or plumbago; borate of lime; brass in pigs or bars, or when old and fit only to be remanufactured (230); Brazil paste; bronze liquor; building stones;

34. Cantharides; castor beans or seeds: chronometers, box or ship's, and parts thereof; cocculus indicus; compositions of glass or paste not set, intended for use by jewellers;* cornmeal;

35. Diamonds, glaziers', set or not set: Dutch and bronze metal in leaf;

36. Engravings or plates, bound or unbound; ergot;

37. Flocks, waste or shoddy (275); fruit, green, ripe, or dried, not otherwise provided for; furs, dressed or undressed, when on the skin; furs, hatters', dressed or undressed, when not on the skin:

---

* The words "compositions of glass or paste not set, intended for use by jewellers" stricken out by paragraph 183.

38. Gamboge; ginger, ground, preserved or pickled; glass plates or disks, unwrought, for optical instruments; goldbeaters' skin; green turtle; grindstones, wrought or finished; gum copal; gum substitute or burnt starch;

39. Hair of all kinds, cleaned, but unmanufactured, not otherwise provided for; hops, horns, horn-tips, bones, bone-tips, and teeth manufactured;

40. Iodine, crude; Ipecacuanha; iron liquor;

41. Jalap; juniper berries;

42. Lemon and lime juice; lime;

43. Manganese, manna; marrow and all other grease, and soap stocks and soap stuffs; mineral kermes; moss, Iceland; music printed with lines bound or unbound (280);

44. Oatmeal; oils, palm, seal, and cocoa-nut; olive oil in casks, other than salad oil; oranges, lemons and limes; orange and lemon peel (726);

45. Paintings (503) and statuary, not otherwise provided for; paving stones; pearl or hulled barley, Peruvian bark; plaster of Paris, when ground (283); Prussian blue;

46. Quicksilver;

47. Rhubarb; rye flour;

48. Saffron and saffron cake; saltpetre, or nitrate of soda, or potash, when refined, or partially refined; salts of tin; sarsaparilla; sepia; shaddock; sheathing paper; sponges; spunk; squills;

49. Tapioca; tagger's iron; teazels; terne tin in plates or sheets; tin foil; tin in plates or sheets;

50. Vanilla beans; vegetables, not otherwise provided for; verdigris;

51. Yams.

Sec. 20. *And be it further enacted,* That from and after the day and year aforesaid, there shall be levied, collected, and paid, a duty of TWENTY PER CENTUM on the importation of the articles hereinafter mentioned and embraced in this section, that is to say:

52. Antimony, tartrate of; acids, citric and tartaric;

53. Blank books, bound or unbound; blue or Roman vitriol, or sulphate of copper; boards, planks, laths, scantling, staves, spars, hewn and sawed timber, and timber used in building wharves; brick, fire-brick, and roofing and paving tile, not otherwise provided for; brimstone, in rolls; bronze powder; Burgundy pitch; burrstones, manufactured or bound up into millstones;

54. Calomel (273); castor oil; castorum; chickory root; chocolate; chromate of lead; corks; cotton laces; cotton insertings, cotton trimming laces, and cotton braids; cowhage down; cubebs;

55. Dried pulp; ether;

56. Feather beds, feathers for beds, and downs of all kinds; feldspar; fig blue; firewood; fish glue or isinglass; fish skins; flour of sulphur; Frankfort black; fulminates or fulminating powders;

57. Glue; gold and silver leaf; grapes; gunpowder;

58. Hair, curled, moss, seaweed, and all other vegetable substances used for beds or mattresses; hat bodies made of wool, or of which wool is the component material of chief value; hatters' plush, composed of silk and cotton, but of which cotton is the component material of chief value (384);

59. Lampblack; leather, tanned, bend, or sole; leather, upper of all kinds, except tanned calfskin, which shall pay twenty-five per centum ad valorem;

60. Magnesia: malt; mats of cocoa-nut (280); matting, China, and other floor matting (280), and mats made of flags, jute, or grass (280); mercurial preparations, not otherwise provided for; medicinal roots and leaves, and all other drugs and medicines in a crude state, not otherwise provided for; metals unmanufactured, not otherwise provided for; mineral and bituminous substances in a crude state, not otherwise provided for; musical instruments of all kinds (280), and strings for musical instruments of whip gut, catgut, and all other strings of the same material (280); mustard ground or unmanufactured;

61. Needles of all kinds for sewing, darning, and knitting (392);

62. Oils, neatsfoot and other animal oils; spermaceti; whale, and other fish oil, the produce of foreign fisheries; oils, volatile, essential or expressed, not otherwise provided for; osier or willow, prepared for basket-makers' use (282);

63. Paints, dry or ground in oil, not otherwise provided for; pitch; plaster of Paris calcined;

64. Quills;

65. Ratans and reeds manufactured or partially manufactured (398); red precipitate; Roman cement; rosin;

66. Sal soda, hyposulphate of soda, and all carbonates of soda by whatever name designated, not otherwise provided for; salts, Epsom, Glauber, Rochelle, and all other salts and preparations of salts not otherwise provided for; shoes or boots, and other articles, composed wholly of india-rubber, not otherwise provided for; skins, tanned, and dressed of all kinds (078); spices of all kinds, not otherwise provided for; spirits of turpentine; starch; stereotype plates (399); still bottoms; strychnine; sulphate of barytes, crude or refined; sulphate of magnesia; sulphate of quinine;

67. Tar; thread laces and insertings (286); type metal (400); types, new (400);

68. Varnish of all kinds; Vandyke brown; Venetian red; vermillon;

69. Whalebone, the produce of foreign fisheries; white vitriol or sulphate of zinc; wood unmanufactured, not otherwise provided for; woolen listings;

Sec. 21. *And be it further enacted,* That from and after the day and year aforesaid there shall be levied, collected and paid:

70. On copper ore and diamonds, cameos, mosaics, gems, pearls,

2

18 DIGEST OF THE TARIFF LAWS.

rubies, anu. other precious stones, when not set, a duty of five per centum au valorem on the same: when set in gold, silver, or other metal, or on imitations thereof, and all other jewelry, twenty-five per centum ad valorem ; on hair cloth and hair seatings, and all other manufactures of hair, not otherwise provided for, twenty-five per centum ad valorem (375).

Sec. 22. *And be it further enacted,* That from and after the day and year aforesaid there shall be levied, collected, and paid, a duty of THIRTY PER CENTUM on the importation of the articles hereinafter mentioned and embraced in this section, that is to say :

71. Alabaster and spar ornaments ; anchovies, sardines, and all other fish preserved in oil (540) ; Argentine, alabatta, or German silver, manufactured or unmanufactured (359) ; articles embroidered with gold, silver, or other metal (359) ;

72. Articles worn by men, women, or children, of whatever material composed, made up, or made wholly or in part by hand, not otherwise provided for (360) ; asses' skins ;

73. Balsams, cosmetics, essences, extracts, pastes, perfumes, and tinctures, used either for the toilet or for medicinal purposes ;

74. Baskets, and all other articles composed of grass, osier, palm leaf, straw, whalebone, or willow, not otherwise provided for (362) ;

75. Beads of amber, composition, or wax, and all beads : Benzoates ; Bologna sausages :

76. Bracelets, braids, chains, curls, or ringlets composed of hair, or of which hair is a component material (363) ;

77. Braces, suspenders, webbing, or other fabrics, composed wholly or in part of India rubber, not otherwise provided for (66 364) ;

78. Brooms and brushes of all kinds (364) ; buttons and button moulds of all kinds (688) ;

79. Canes and sticks for walking, finished or unfinished (365) ; capers, pickles, and sauces of all kinds, not otherwise provided for (273. 365) ;

80. Caps, hats, muffs and tippets of fur, and all other manufactures of fur, or of which fur shall be a component material (366) ;

81. Caps, gloves, leggins, mits, socks, stockings, wove shirts and drawers, and all similar articles made on frames of whatever material composed, worn by men, women, or children. and not otherwise provided for (367) ;

82. Carbonate of magnesia;

83. Card-cases, pocket-books, shell-boxes, souvenirs, and all similar articles, of whatever material composed (368); carriages and parts of carriages (368); clocks and parts of clocks (368);

84. Clothing, ready-made, and wearing apparel of every description, of whatever material composed, except wool, made up or manufactured wholly or in part by the tailor, seamstress, or manufacturer (20-369);

85. Coach and harness furniture of all kinds, saddlery, coach and harness hardware, silver-plated, brass, brass-plated or covered, common tinned, burnished or japanned, not otherwise provided for (370);

86. Combs of all kinds (371); composition of glass or paste, when set;* composition tops for tables, or other articles of furniture (114-371); comfits, sweetmeats, or fruits preserved in sugar, brandy, or molasses, not otherwise provided for (371); coral, cut or manufactured; cotton cords, gimps and galloons (371); cotton laces, colored (54-371); court plaster (371); crayons of all kinds; cutlery of all kinds (371);

87. Dolls and toys of all kinds (372);

88. Encaustic tiles (373); epaulets, galloons, laces, knots, stars, tassels, tresses and wings of gold, silver or other metal (373);

89. Fans and fire screens of every description, of whatever material composed (374); feathers and flowers, artificial or ornamental, and parts thereof, of whatever material composed; flats, braids, plaits, sparterre and willow squares, used for making hats and bonnets; firecrackers; frames and sticks for umbrellas, parasols, and sunshades, finished or unfinished (374); furniture, cabinet and household;

90. Hair pencils (375); hat bodies of cotton (375); hats and bonnets, for men, women, and children, composed of straw, chip, grass, palm leaf, willow, or any other vegetable substance, or of hair, whalebone, or other material not otherwise provided for; human hair, cleansed or prepared for use;

91. Ink and ink powder (376);

92. Japanned, patent, or enamelled leather or skins of all kinds; Japanned ware of all kinds, not otherwise provided for (278); jet and manufactures of jet, and imitations thereof (377);

93. Lead pencils;

94. Maccaroni, vermicelli, gelatine, jellies, and all similar preparations (379);

95. Manufactures of silk, or of which silk shall be a component material, not otherwise provided for;

96. Manufactures of the bark of the cork tree, except corks;

97. Manufactures of bone, shell, horn, ivory or vegetable ivory (380);

98. Manufactures, articles, vessels and wares not otherwise pro-

* The words " composition of glass or paste, when set" stricken out by paragraph 183

vided for, of brass, copper, gold, iron, lead, pewter, platina, silver, tin or other metal, or of which either of these metals or any other metal shall be the component material of chief value (383);

99. Manufactures, not otherwise provided for, composed of mixed materials, in part of cotton, silk, wool, or worsted, or flax (384);

100. Manufactures of cotton, linen, silk, wool, or worsted, if embroidered or tamboured, in the loom or otherwise, by machinery or with the needle, or other process, not otherwise provided for (385);

101. Manufactures of cedar wood, granadilla, ebony, mahogany, rosewood, and satin wood (386);

102. Marble in the rough or blocks, manufactures of marble, marble paving tiles, and all marble sawed, squared, dressed, or polished:

103. Manufactures and articles of leather, or of which leather shall be component part, not otherwise provided for (387);

104. Manufactures of paper, or of which paper is a component material, not otherwise provided for (381);

105. Manufactures, articles and wares, of papier mache (388);

106. Manufactures of goat's hair or mohair, or of which goat's hair or mohair shall be a component material, not otherwise provided for:

107. Manufactures of wood, or of which wood is the chief component part, not otherwise provided for (390);

108. Medicinal preparations, not otherwise provided for (280); metallic pens; mineral waters (550); muskets, rifles, and other fire-arms (391);

109. Oilcloth of every description, of whatever material composed, not otherwise provided for; olive salad oil; olives;

110. Paper boxes and all other fancy boxes (394); paper envelopes (394);

111. Paper hangings, and paper for screens or fire-boards; paper; antiquarian, demy, drawing, elephant, foolscap, imperial letter, and all other paper not otherwise provided for (395);

112. Parasols and sun shades; parchment: plated and gilt ware of all kinds (396); playing cards;

113. Prepared vegetables, meats, fish, poultry, and game, sealed or unsealed, in cans or otherwise (397); red chalk pencils;

114. Salmon, preserved; Scagliola tops, for tables or other articles of furniture (86-399); sealing wax (399); side arms of every description (399); silver-plated metal, in sheets or other form (399);

115. Slates, roofing slates (398), slate pencils, slate chimney pieces, mantels, slabs for tables, and all other manufactures of slate; soap, Castile, perfumed, Windsor, and all other kinds;

116. Twines and packthread, of whatever material composed, not otherwise provided for (400);

117. Umbrellas (112); unwrought clay, three dollars per ton *;

118. Vellum, velvet, when printed or painted (401); wafers: water colors (402);

119. Webbing, composed of wool, cotton, flax, or any other materials (403);

Sec. 23. *And be it further enacted,* That from and after the day and year aforesaid, the importation of the articles hereinafter mentioned and embraced in this section shall be EXEMPT FROM DUTY, that is to say:

120. Acids, acetic, acetous, benzolc, boracic, muriatic, sulphuric, and pyroligneous, and all acids of every description used for chemical and manufacturing purposes, not otherwise provided for; alcornoque;

121. All books, maps, charts, mathematical, nautical instruments, philosophical apparatus, and all other articles whatever, imported for the use of the United States; all philosophical apparatus (569), instruments (569), books, maps, and charts (615), statues, statuary, busts and casts of marble, bronze, alabaster, or plaster of Paris; paintings and drawings, etchings, specimens of sculpture, cabinets of coins, medals, regalia, gems, and all collections of antiquities: *Provided,* The same be specially imported, in good faith, for the use of any society incorporated or established for philosophical, literary or religious purposes, or for the encouragement of the fine arts, or for the use or by the order of any college, academy, school, or seminary of learning in the United States (730);

122. Ambergris; annatto, roncou or Orleans; animal carbon (bone black); animals, living, of all kinds; antimony, crude, or regulus of; argol, or crude tartar; arsenic; articles in a crude state used in dyeing or tanning (124), not otherwise provided for; asphaltum:

123. Bananas; bark, Peruvian, or bark quills; barilla, and soda ash; bells, old, and bell metal (714);

124. Berries, nuts, flowers, plants, and vegetables used exclusively in dyeing or in composing dyes; but no article shall be classed as such that has undergone any manufacture (122-713);

125. Birds, singing or other, and land and water fowls; bismuth; bitter apples; bolting cloths; bones, burnt, and bone-dust (39):

126. Books, maps, and charts, imported by authority of the Joint Library Committee of Congress for the use of the library of Congress: *Provided,* That if, in any case, a contract shall have been made with any bookseller, importer, or other person aforesaid, [and such person] shall have paid the duty or included the duty in said contract, in such case the duty shall [not] be remitted;†

127. Borax, crude, or tincal; boucho leaves; Brazil wood, brazilletto, and all other dyewoods, in sticks; breccia, in blocks or slabs;

---

*The words "unwrought clay, three dollars per ton," stricken out by paragraph 153.
†See Act of March 29, 1848, U. S. Statutes at Large, vol. 9, p. 217.

brimstone, crude, in bulk; brime ; bullion, gold and silver ; burrstones, wrought or unwrought, but unmanufactured, and not bound up into millstones (714) ;

128. Cabinets of coins, medals, and all other collections of antiquities (121-715) ; cadmium ; calamine ; camphor, crude (14); chalk, French chalk, and red chalk; cochineal ; cobalt; cocoa, cocoa shells, cocoa leaves, and cocoa nuts;

129. Coffee and tea, when imported direct from the place of their growth or production, in American vessels, or in foreign vessels entitled by reciprocal treaties to be exempt from discriminating duties, tonnage, and other charges; coffee, the growth or production of the possessions of the Netherlands, imported from the Netherlands in the same manner ;

130. Coins, gold, silver, and copper (128); copper, when imported for the United States mint (709) ; cotton ; cork-tree bark, unmanufactured ;

130. Cream of tartar; cudbear, vegetable, and orchil;

131. Divi-divi ; dragon's blood;

132. Emery, in lump or pulverized ; extract of indigo ; extract of madder ;

133. Extract and decoctions of logwoods, and other dye-woods, not otherwise provided for ;

134. Felt, adhesive, for sheathing vessels ; fish, fresh caught, for daily consumption (718) ; flints ; flint ground; fullers' earth;

135. Ginger root; gum, Arabic, Barbary, East India, Jedda, Senegal, Tragacanth, Benjamine or Benzoin, myrrh, and all other gums and resins in a crude state, not otherwise provided for ; gutta-percha, unmanufactured ; grindstones, rough or unfinished ;

136. Garden seeds, and all other seeds for agricultural, horticultural, medicinal, and manufacturing purposes, not otherwise provided for ;

137. Glass, when old, not in pieces which can be cut for use, and fit only to be remanufactured ;

138. Goods, wares, and merchandise, the growth, production, or manufacture of the United States, exported to a foreign country, and brought back to the United States in the same condition as when exported, upon which no drawback or bounty has been allowed : *Provided,* That all regulations to ascertain the identity thereof, prescribed by existing laws, or which may be prescribed by the Secretary of the Treasury, shall be complied with (710) ;

139. Guano;

140. Household effects, old, and in use of persons or families from foreign countries, if used abroad by them and not intended for any other person or persons, or for sale;

141. Hair of all kinds, uncleaned and unmanufactured (39); and all long horse hair, used for weaving, cleaned or uncleaned, drawn or undrawn ;

142. India rubber, in bottles, slabs, or sheets, unmanufactured; India rubber, milk of; indigo ; ice ; irridium; irris, orris-root ; ivory, unmanufactured; ivory nuts, or vegetable ivory;

143. Junk, old, and oakum ;

144. Kelp ;

145. Lac dye; lac spirits ; lac sulphur ;

ACT OF MARCH 2, 1861. 23

146. Lastings, mohair cloth, silk, twist, or other manufactures of cloth, cut in strips or patterns of the size and shape for shoes, slippers, boots, bootees, gaiters, and buttons, exclusively, not combined with India rubber:

147. Leeches; liquorice root:

148. Madder, ground or prepared, and madder root; manuscripts; marine coral, unmanufactured; medals, of gold, silver, or copper (130-713):

149. Machinery, suitable for the manufacture of flax and linen goods only, and imported for that purpose solely, but not including that which may be used for any other manufactures; maps and charts; mineral blue:

150. Models of inventions, and other improvements in the arts: *Provided,* That no article or articles shall be deemed a model or improvement which can be fitted for use;

151. Munjeet, or India madder:

152. Natron (178); nickel; nutgalls; nux vomica:

153. Oil, spermaceti, whale, and other fish, of American fisheries, and all other articles the produce of such fisheries; ores of gold and silver; * orpiment, or sulphuret of arsenic (267);

154. Paintings and statuary, the production of American artists residing abroad: (*Provided,* The same be imported in good faith as objects of taste, and not of merchandise†); *Provided,* the fact, as aforesaid, shall be certified by the artist, or by the Consul of the United States.

155. Palm leaf, unmanufactured; pearl, mother of; personal and household effects, not merchandise, of citizens of the United States dying abroad (731-162); pine apples; plantains; plaster of Paris, or sulphate of lime, unground; platina, unmanufactured; platina vases or retorts (734); polishing stones; pumice and pumice stones;

156. Quassia-wood;

157. Rags of whatever material, except wool; ratans and reeds, unmanufactured; rottenstone;

158. Safflower; saltpetre, or nitrate of soda, or potash, when crude; sandal-wood; seed-lac:

159. Sheathing metal, or yellow metal, not wholly of copper, nor wholly or in part of iron, ungalvanized, in sheets forty-eight inches long and fourteen inches wide, and weighing from fourteen to thirty-four ounces per square (yard) ‡ foot (13);

160. Shellac; shingle bolts and stave bolts; silk, raw, or as reeled from the cocoon, not being doubled, twisted, or advanced in manufacture any way, and silk cocoons and silk waste; smalts; specimens of natural history, mineralogy and botany; staves for pipes, hogsheads, or other casks; stoneware, not ornamented, above the capacity of ten gallons; substances expressly used for manure (139-719); sumac;

161. Terra japonica, catechu, or cutch; tin, in pigs, bars, or blocks; tortoise and other shell, unmanufactured; trees, shrubs, bulbs, plants, and roots not otherwise provided for; turmeric; types, old, and fit only to be remanufactured;

---

* The words " ores of gold and silver " inserted here by paragraph 408.
† The words "*Provided,* The same be imported in good faith as objects of taste, and not of merchandise " stricken out: the words " *Provided,* The fact, as aforesaid, shall be certified by the artist, or by the Consul of the United States " inserted instead, as per paragraph 408.
‡ The word " yard " stricken out and the word " foot " inserted in its stead by paragraph 183.

162. Wearing apparel in actual use, and other personal effects (not merchandise), professional books, implements, instruments, and tools of trade, occupation, or employment of persons arriving in the United States: *Provided,* That this exemption shall not be construed to include machinery, or other articles imported for use in any manufacturing establishment, or for sale (731) ;

163. Weld ; woad or pastel ;

164. Woods, namely : cedar, lignum vitæ, lancewood, ebony, box, granadilla, mahogany, rosewood, satinwood, and all cabinet woods, unmanufactured ;

165. Wool, unmanufactured, and all hair of the goat, alpaca, and other like animals, unmanufactured, the value whereof at the last port or place from whence exported to the United States shall be eighteen cents, or under, per pound.*

166. **Sec. 24.** *And be it further enacted,* That from and after the day and year aforesaid, there shall be levied, collected, and paid, on the importation of ALL RAW OR UNMANUFACTURED ARTICLES, NOT HEREIN ENUMERATED OR PROVIDED FOR, A DUTY OF TEN PER CENTUM AD VALOREM; and on ALL ARTICLES MANUFACTURED IN WHOLE OR IN PART, NOT HEREIN ENUMERATED OR PROVIDED FOR, A DUTY OF TWENTY PER CENTUM AD VALOREM.† See paragraphs No. 1 and 566.

167. **Sec. 25.** *And be it further enacted,* That all goods, wares, and merchandise which may be in the public stores on the day and year aforesaid, shall be subject to no other duty upon the entry thereof than if the same were imported respectively after that day (177).

168. **Sec. 26.** *And be it further enacted,* That whenever the word " ton " is used in this Act, in reference to weight, it shall be deemed and taken to be twenty hundred weight, each hundred weight being one hundred and twelve pounds avoirdupois.

169. **Sec. 27.** *And be it further enacted,* That railroad iron, partially or wholly worn, may be imported into the United States without payment of duty, under bond to be withdrawn and exported after the said railroad iron shall have been repaired or remanufactured ; and the Secretary of the Treasury is hereby authorized and directed to prescribe such rules and regulations as may be necessary to protect

---

* This paragraph is repealed by paragraph 176.

†" All articles entitled to entry free of duty are described or specified. All articles not named are liable to duty under this section, unless they can be assimilated, under the provisions of the 20th Section of the Act of August 30, 1842 (paragraph No. 1), to some enumerated article liable to duty. The said 20th section merely determines the rate at which duties shall be levied on enumerated articles, which are all dutiable by law, and does not authorize the transfer of any article from the unenumerated to the free list." (Decision of December 15, 1858).

the revenue against fraud, and secure the identity, character, and weight of all such importations when again withdrawn and exported, restricting and limiting the export and withdrawal to the same port of entry where imported, and also limiting all bonds to a period of time of not more than six months from the date of the importation. (See decision of March 22, 1870.)

170. **Sec. 28.** *And be it further enacted,* That in all cases where the duty upon any imports of goods, wares, or merchandise shall be subject to be levied upon the true market value of such imports in the principal markets of the country from whence the importation shall have been made, or at the port of exportation, the duty 'shall be estimated and collected upon the value on the day of actual shipment whenever a bill of lading shall be presented showing the date of shipment, and which shall be certified by a certificate of the United States Consul, Commercial Agent, or other legally authorized deputy (582).

171. **Sec. 29.** *And be it further enacted,* That the annual statistical accounts of the commerce of the United States with foreign countries, required by existing laws, shall hereafter be made up and completed by the Register of the Treasury, under the direction of the Secretary of the Treasury, so as to comprehend and include, in tabular form, the quantity by weight or measure, as well as the amount of value, of the several articles of foreign commerce, whether dutiable or otherwise ; and also a similar and separate statement of the commerce of the United States with the British Provinces, under the late, so-called, reciprocity treaty with Great Britain

172. **Sec. 30.** *And be it further enacted,* That from and after the day and year aforesaid, there shall be allowed a drawback on foreign hemp, manufactured into cordage in the United States and exported therefrom, equal in amount to the duty paid on the foreign hemp from which it shall be manufactured, to be ascertained under such regulations as shall be prescribed by the Secretary of the Treasury, and no more : *Provided,* That ten per centum on the amount of all drawbacks so allowed shall be retained for the use of the United States by the collectors paying such drawbacks respectively (181).

173. **Sec. 31.** *And be it further enacted,* That all Acts and parts
of Acts repugnant to the provisions of this Act be, and the
same are hereby repealed : *Provided,* That the existing laws
shall extend to, and be in force for, the collection of the
duties imposed by this Act; for the prosecution and punishment of all offences, and for the recovery, collection,
distribution, and remission of all fines, penalties, and forfeitures, as fully and effectually as if every regulation,
penalty, forfeiture, provision, clause, matter, and thing to
that effect, in the existing laws contained, had been inserted
in and re-enacted by this Act.

174. **Sec. 32.** *And be it further enacted,* That when merchandise of the same material or description, but of different
values, are invoiced at an average price, and not otherwise
provided for, the duty shall be assessed upon the whole
invoice at the rate the highest valued goods in such invoice
are subject to under this Act.   The words value and valued,
used in this Act, shall be construed and understood as
meaning the true market value of the goods, wares, and
merchandise in the principal markets of the country from
whence exported at the date of exportation (582-602).

175. **Sec. 33.** *And be it further enacted,* That all goods, wares, and merchandise actually
on shipboard and bound to the United States, within fifteen days after the passage of
this Act and all goods, wares, and merchandise in deposit in warehouse or public store
on the first day of April, eighteen hundred and sixty-one, shall be subject to pay such
duties as provided by law before and at the time of the passage of this Act; and all goods
in warehouse at the time this Act takes effect, on which the duties are lessened by its
provisions, may be withdrawn on payment of the duties herein provided.

JOINT RESOLUTION OF MARCH 2, 1861.

(From U. S. Statutes at Large, vol. 12, p. 252.)

A RESOLUTION to correct certain errors in the Act entitled "An Act to
'provide for the payment of outstanding Treasury Notes, to authorize
a Loan, to regulate and fix the duties on Imports and for other purposes," approved the second of March, eighteen hundred and sixty-
one.

176. *Resolved by the Senate and House of Representatives of the United States of America in
Congress assembled,* That the Act entitled " An Act to provide for the payment of outstanding treasury notes, to authorize a loan, to regulate and fix the duties on imports and
for other purposes," approved the second March, eighteen hundred and sixty-one, shall
be so far altered and corrected as to strike from said Act the following words, that is to

say, from the list of articles exempt from duty "wool, unmanufactured, and all hair of the goat, alpaca, and other like animals, unmanufactured, the value whereof, at the last port or place from whence exported to the United States shall be eighteen cents, or under, per pound," (166) from section twenty-four, as follows:

177. **Sec. 24.** *And be it further enacted*, That all goods, wares, and merchandise, which may be in the public stores on the day and year aforesaid, shall be subject to no other duty upon entry thereof than if the same were imported respectively after that day (167): and from section thirteen, as follows: " On woollen shawls, or shawls of which wool shall be the chief component material, a duty of sixteen cents per pound, and in addition thereto, twenty per centum ad valorem " (20).

ACT OF AUGUST 5, 1861.

(From U. S. Statutes at Large, vol. 12, p. 292, &c.

AN ACT to provide increased Revenue from Imports, to pay Interest on the Public Debt, and for other purposes.

Be it enacted by the Senate and House of Representatives of the United States of America in Congress assembled, That from and after the date of the passage of this Act, IN LIEU of the duties heretofore imposed by law on the articles hereinafter mentioned, and on such as may now be exempt from duty, there shall be levied, collected, and paid, on the goods, wares, and merchandise herein enumerated and provided for, imported from foreign countries, the following duties and rates of duty, that is to say:

178. On raw sugar (2), commonly called Muscovado or brown sugar, and on sugars not advanced above number twelve, Dutch standard, by claying, boiling, clarifying, or other process, and on syrup of sugar or of sugar cane and concentrated molasses, or concentrated melado, two cents per pound: and on white and clayed sugar, when advanced beyond the raw state, above number twelve, Dutch standard, by clarifying or other process, and not yet refined, two and a half cents per pound; on refined sugars, whether loaf, lump, crushed, or pulverized, four cents per pound; on sugars after being refined, when they are tinctured, colored, or in any way adulterated, and on sugar candy, six cents per pound (2); on molasses, five cents per gallon (2): *Provided*, That all syrups of sugar or sugar-cane, concentrated molasses or melado, entered under the name of molasses, or any other name than syrup of sugar or of sugar-cane, concentrated molasses, or concentrated melado, shall be liable to forfeiture to the United States (2). On all teas, fifteen cents per pound (20): on almonds, four cents per pound (17): shelled almonds, six cents per pound (17); on brimstone, crude, three dollars per ton (127): on brimstone, in rolls, six dollars per ton (53): on coffee of all kinds, four cents per pound (123); on cocoa, three cents per pound (128); on cocoa leaves and cocoa shells, two cents per pound (128): on cocoa prepared or manufactured, eight cents per pound (128) · on chickory root, one cent per pound: and on chickory ground, two cents per pound (54); on chocolate, six cents per pound (54); on cassia, ten cents per pound (17): cassia buds, fifteen cents per pound (17): on cinnamon, twenty cents per pound (17); on cloves, eight cents per pound (17); on cayenne pepper, six cents per pound (17); on cayenne pepper, ground, eight cents per pound (17); on currants, five cents per pound (17); on argol, three cents per pound (122); on cream tartar, six cents per pound (130); on tartaric acid (32), tartar emetic (52), and rochelle salts (66), ten cents per pound; on dates, two cents per pound (17); on figs, five cents per pound (17); on ginger root, three cents per pound (135); on ginger, ground, five cents per pound (88); on liquorice paste and

juice, five cents per pound (14); liquorice root, one cent per pound (147); on mace (17), and nutmegs (17), twenty-five cents per pound on nuts of all kinds, not otherwise provided for, two cents per pound (17); on pepper, six cents per pound (17); on pimento six cents per pound (17); on plums, five cents per pound (17); prunes, five cents per pound (17); on raisins, five cents per pound (17); on unmanufactured Russia hemp, forty dollars per ton (27); on Manilla and other hemps of India, twenty-five dollars per ton (27); on lead, in pigs or bars, one dollar and fifty cents per one hundred pounds (12); in sheets, two dollars and twenty-five cents per one hundred pounds (12); on white lead, dry, or ground in oil, and red lead, two dollars and twenty-five cents per one hundred pounds (14); on salt, in sacks, eighteen cents per one hundred pounds (15); and in bulk, twelve cents per one hundred pounds (15); on soda ash, one-half cent per pound (123); on bicarbonate of soda, one cent per pound (66-290); on sal soda, one-half cent per pound (66); on caustic soda, one cent per pound (66-290); on chlorate of lime, thirty cents per one hundred pounds (14); on saltpetre, crude, one cent per pound (158); refined, or partially refined, two cents per pound (43) · spirits of turpentine, ten cents per gallon (14); on oil of cloves, seventy cents per pound (62); on brandy, one dollar and twenty-five cents per gallon (3); on spirits distilled from grain, or other materials fifty cents per gallon (3); on gum copal, and other gums or resinous substances used for the same or similar purposes as gum copal, ten cents per pound (38-240).

Sec. 2. *And be it further enacted,* That from and after the day and year aforesaid, there shall be levied, collected, and paid, on the importation of the articles hereinafter mentioned, the following duties, that is to say :

179. On arrowroot, twenty per centum ad valorem (32); on ginger, preserved or pickled, thirty per centum ad valorem (38); on limes (44), lemons (44), oranges (44), bananas (123), and plantains (155), twenty per centum ad valorem; on Peruvian bark, fifteen per centum ad valorem (45-123); on quinine, thirty per centum ad valorem (66); on rags, of whatever material, ten per centum ad valorem (157-612½); on gunpowder, thirty per centum ad valorem (57); on feathers and downs, thirty per centum ad valorem (56); on hides, ten per centum ad valorem (16); on sole and bend leather, thirty per centum ad valorem (59); on India rubber, raw or unmanufactured, ten per centum ad valorem (142); on India-rubber shoes and boots, thirty per centum ad valorem (66); on ivory, unmanufactured, and on vegetable ivory, ten per centum ad valorem (142); on wines of all kinds, fifty per centum ad valorem (3); on silk in the gum, not more advanced in the manufacture than single tram and thrown or organzine, twenty-five per centum ad valorem (28); on all silks valued at not over one dollar per square yard, thirty per centum ad valorem (28); on all silks valued over one dollar per square yard, forty per centum ad valorem (28); on all silk velvets, or velvets of which silk is the component material of chief value (28), valued at three dollars per square yard, or under, thirty per centum ad valorem (28); valued at over three dollars per square yard, forty per centum ad valorem (28); on floss silks, thirty per centum ad valorem (28); on silk ribbons, galloons, braids, fringes, laces, tassels, buttons, button-cloths, trimmings (28), and on silk twist, twist composed of mohair and silk (28), sewing silk in gum or purified (28), and all other manufactures of silk, or of which silk shall be the component material of chief value, not otherwise provided for, forty per centum ad valorem (28).   ·

180. **Sec. 3.** *And be it further enacted,* That all articles, goods, wares, and merchandise, imported from beyond the Cape of Good Hope in foreign vessels, not entitled by reciprocal treaties to be exempt from discriminating duties, tonnage, and other charges, and all other articles, goods, wares, and merchandise not imported direct from the place of their growth or production, or in foreign vessels, entitled by reciprocal treaties to be exempt from discriminating duties, tonnage, and other charges, shall be subject to pay, in addition to the duties imposed by this Act, ten per centum ad valorem : *Provided,* That this rule shall not apply to goods, wares, and merchandise imported from beyond the Cape of Good Hope in American vessels (562).

181. **Sec. 4.** *And be it further enacted,* That from and after the passage of this Act, there shall be allowed, on all articles wholly manufactured of materials imported, on which duties have been paid when exported, a drawback, equal in amount to the duty paid on such materials and no more, to be ascertained under such regulations as shall be prescribed by the Secretary of the Treasury : *Provided,* That ten per centum on the amount of all drawbacks, so allowed, shall be retained for the use of the United States by the collectors paying such drawbacks, respectively (172-421-873).

182. **Sec. 5.** *And be it further enacted,* That all goods, wares, and merchandise, actually on shipboard and bound to the United States, and all goods, wares, and merchandise on deposit in warehouses or public stores at the date of the passage of this Act, shall be subject to pay such duties as provided by law before and at the time of the passage of this Act : *Provided,* That all goods deposited in public store or bonded warehouse after this Act takes effect and goes into operation, if designed for consumption in the United States, must be withdrawn therefrom, or the duties thereon paid in three months after the same are deposited, and goods designed for exportation and consumption in foreign countries may be withdrawn by the owner at any time before the expiration of three years after the same are deposited, such goods, if not withdrawn in three years, to be regarded as abandoned to the Government, and sold under such regulations as the Secretary of the Treasury may prescribe, and the proceeds paid into the Treasury : *Provided,* That merchandise upon which the owner may have neglected to pay duties within three months from the time of its deposit may be withdrawn and entered for consumption at any time within two years of the time of its deposit, upon the payment of the legal duties, with an addition of twenty-five per centum thereto : *Provided also,* That merchandise upon which duties have been paid, if exported to a foreign country, within three years shall be entitled to return duties, proper evidence of such merchandise having been landed abroad to be furnished to the collector by the importer, one per centum of said duties to be retained by the Government (410).

183. **Sec. 6.** *And be it further enacted,* That the Act entitled "An Act to provide for the payment of outstanding Treasury Notes, to authorize a loan, to regulate and fix the duties on imports, and for other purposes," approved March two, eighteen hundred and sixty-one, be and the same is hereby amended, as follows : That is to say, First, in section six, article first, after the words " on cordials and," strike out " liquors," and insert " liquors ' (3) ; Second, in the same section, after the word " represent," insert, "*Provided also,* That no lower rate or amount of duty shall be levied, collected, and paid on brandy, spirits, and all other spirituous beverages, than that now fixed by law for the description of first proof, but shall be increased in proportion for any greater strength than the strength of first proof" (3) ; Third, in section seventh, clause fifth, the words, " on screws, washed or plated, and all other screws, of iron or any other metal," shall be stricken out, and the words " on screws, of any other metal than iron," shall be inserted (9) ; Fourth, section twelve, article first, after the words " eighteen cents," where the first occur, insert, " or less " (18) ; Fifth, section thirteen, article second, after the word " manufacturer," insert " except hosiery ' (20) ; Sixth, in the same section, article third, strike out " wool " wherever it occurs, and insert in each place " worsted " (21) ; Seventh, in section fourteen, article first, after the words " ten per centum," insert " ad valorem " (23) ; Eighth, in section fifteen, before the word " yarns " insert " hemp "; in the same section, after the word " sheetings," insert " of flax or hemp "; and strike out " jute goods," and in lieu thereof insert " jute yarns " (27) ; Ninth, in section twenty-two, strike out the words " unwrought clay, three dollars per ton " (117) ; Tenth, in section nineteen, strike out " compositions of glass or paste, not set; intended for use by jewellers " (34) ; Eleventh, in section twenty-two, strike out "compositions of glass or paste, when set" (86); Twelfth, in section twenty-three, article sheathing metal, strike out " yard," and insert "foot " (159).

184. **Sec. 7.** *And be it further enacted,* That all Acts and parts of

Acts repugnant to the provisions of this Act be and the same are hereby repealed: *Provided*, That the existing laws shall extend to, and be in force for, the collection of the duties imposed by this Act, for the prosecution and punishment of all offences, and for the recovery, collection, distribution and remission of all fines, penalties, and forfeitures, as fully and effectually as if every regulation, penalty, forfeiture, provision, clause, matter, and things to that effect in the existing laws contained, had been inserted in and reenacted by this Act.

(The other sections do not relate to import duties).

ACT OF DECEMBER 24, 1861.

(From U. S. Statutes at Large, vol. 12, p. 330.)

AN ACT to increase the duties on Tea, Coffee, and Sugar.

Be it enacted by the Senate and House of Representatives of the United States of America in Congress assembled, That from and after the date of the passage of this Act, in lieu of the duties heretofore imposed by law on articles hereinafter mentioned, there shall be levied, collected, and paid, on the goods, wares, and merchandise herein enumerated and provided for, imported from foreign countries, the following duty and rates of duty, that is to say:

185.   On all teas, twenty cents per pound (178) ; on coffee of all kinds, five cents per pound (178) ; on raw sugar, commonly called Muscovada (Muscovado) or brown sugar, and on sugars not advanced above number twelve, Dutch standard, by claying, boiling, clarifying, or other process, and on syrup of sugar or of sugar cane, and concentrated molasses or concentrated melado, two cents and a half per pound ; and on white and clayed sugar, when advanced beyond the raw state, above number twelve, Dutch standard, by clarifying or other process, and not yet refined, three cents per pound ; on refined sugars, whether loaf, lump, crushed, or pulverized, five cents per pound ; on sugars, after being refined, when they are tinctured, colored, or in any way adulterated, and on sugar candy, eight cents per pound (178) ; on molasses, six cents per gallon (178) : *Provided*, That all syrups of sugar or of sugar cane, concentrated molasses or concentrated melado, entered under the name of molasses, or any other name than syrup of sugar or of sugar cane, concentrated molasses or concentrated melado, shall be liable to forfeiture to the United States, and the same shall be forfeited (178).

ACT OF JULY 14, 1862.

(From U. S. Statutes at Large, vol. 12, page 543, &c.)

AN ACT increasing, temporarily, the duty on imports, and for other purposes.

Be it enacted by the Senate and House of Representatives of the United States of America in Congress assembled, That from and after the first day of August, Anno Domini, eighteen hundred and sixty-two, IN LIEU of the duties heretofore imposed by law on the articles hereinafter mentioned, there shall be levied, collected, and paid, on the goods, wares and merchandise herein enumerated and provided for, imported from foreign countries, the following duties and rates of duty, that is to say :

186. On syrup of sugar, or of sugar cane, or concentrated molasses, or concentrated melado, two cents per pound (185);

187. On all sugar not above number twelve, Dutch standard in color, two and one-half cents per pound (185); on all sugar above number twelve, and not above number fifteen, Dutch standard in color. three cents per pound (185); on all sugar above number fifteen, not stove-dried, and not above number twenty, Dutch standard in color, three and one-half cents per pound (185); on all refined sugar in form of loaf, lump, crushed, powdered, pulverized, or granulated, and all stove-dried or other sugar above number twenty, Dutch standard in color, four cents per pound (185) : *Provided,* That the standards by which the color and grades of sugars are to be regulated shall be selected and furnished to the collectors of such ports of entry as may be necessary, by the Secretary of the Treasury, from time to time, and in such manner as he may deem expedient.

188. On sugar candy, not colored, six cents per pound ; on all other confectionery, made wholly or in part of sugar. and on sugars, after being refined, when tinctured, colored, or in any way adulterated, ten cents per pound (185);

189. On molasses. six cents per gallon (185) : *Provided,* That all syrups of sugar or sugar cane, concentrated molasses or concentrated melado, entered under the name of molasses, or any other name than syrup of sugar, or of sugar cane, concentrated molasses, or concentrated melado, shall be liable to forfeiture to the United States, and the same shall be forfeited (185).

190. On cigars of all kinds, valued at five dollars or less per thousand, thirty-five cents per pound · valued at over five dollars and not over ten dollars per thousand, sixty cents per pound ; valued at over ten and not over twenty dollars per thousand, eighty cents per pound ; valued at over twenty dollars per thousand, one dollar per pound; and in addition thereto on all cigars valued at over ten dollars per thousand. ten per centum ad valorem : *Provided,* That paper-cigars, or cigarettes. including wrappers. shall be subject to the same duties imposed on cigars (4) ;

191. On snuff, thirty-five cents per pound (4) : on tobacco, in leaf, unmanufactured and not stemmed. twenty-five cents per pound (4) ; on stemmed, and tobacco manufactured of all descriptions, not otherwise provided for, thirty-five cents per pound (4).

Sec. 2. *And be it further enacted,* That from and after the day and year aforesaid, IN ADDITION to the duties heretofore imposed by law on the articles hereinafter mentioned and included in this section, there shall be levied, collected, and paid, on the goods, wares, and merchandise herein enumerated and provided for, imported from foreign countries, the following duties and rates of duty, that is to say :

192. On brandy, for first proof, twenty-five cents per gallon (173) ; on other spirits, manufactured or distilled from grain or other materials, for first proof, fifty cents per gallon (173) ; on cordials and liquors of all kinds, and arrack, absynthe, kirschenwasser, ratafia, and other similar spirituous beverages not otherwise provided for, twenty-five cents per gallon (3) ; on bay rum, twenty-five cents per gallon (3) ; on ale, porter, and beer, in bottles or otherwise, five cents per gallon (3) ;

193. On all spirituous liquors not otherwise enumerated, sixteen and two-thirds per centum ad valorem (3) : *Provided,* That no lower rate or amount of duty shall be levied, collected, and paid, on brandy, spirits, and all other spirituous beverages, than that fixed by law for the description of first proof, but shall be increased in proportion for any greater strength than the strength of first proof: *And provided further,* That bottles containing wines subject to ad valorem duties shall be liable to and pay the same rate of duty as that fixed upon the wines therein contained (3).

Sec. 3. *And be it further enacted,* That from and after the day and year aforesaid, IN ADDITION to the duties heretofore imposed by law on the articles hereinafter mentioned and included in this section, there shall be levied, collected, and paid, on the goods, wares, and merchandise herein enumerated and provided for, imported from foreign countries, the following duties and rates of duty, that is to say :

194. On bar iron, rolled or hammered, comprising flats not less than one inch or more than seven inches wide, nor less than one-quarter of an inch or more than two inches thick; rounds not less than one-half an inch nor more than four inches in diameter; and squares not less than one-half an inch nor more than four inches square, not exceeding in value the sum of fifty dollars per ton, two dollars per ton ; exceeding in value the sum of fifty dollars per ton, three dollars per ton (5) :

195. On bar iron, rolled or hammered, comprising flats, less than one-quarter of an inch thick or more than seven inches wide, rounds less than one-half an inch or more than four inches in diameter, and squares less than one-half an inch or more than four inches square, five dollars per ton (5) ;

196. On all iron imported in bars for railroads and inclined planes made to patterns and fitted to be laid down on such roads or planes without further manufacture, one dollar and fifty cents per ton (5) · on boiler or other plate iron, five dollars per ton (5) ;

197. On iron wire, drawn and finished, not more than one-fourth of an inch in diameter nor less than number sixteen, wire gauge, one dollar per one hundred pounds ; over number sixteen and not over number twenty-five, wire gauge, one dollar and fifty cents per one hundred pounds; over or finer than number twenty-five, wire gauge, two dollars per one hundred pounds: *Provided,* That wire covered with cotton, silk, or other material, shall pay five cents per pound in addition to the foregoing rates (5) ;

198. On hollow ware, glazed or tinned, one-half cent per pound (6) ;

199. On sadirons, tailors' and hatters' irons, stoves, and stove-plates, one-fourth of one cent per pound (6-296) :

200. On band and hoop iron and slit rods, and all other descriptions of rolled or hammered iron. not otherwise provided for, five dollars per ton (5) ;

201. On cut nails and spikes, one-fourth of one cent per pound (8) ;

202. On iron cables or cable chains, or parts thereof, seventy-five cents per one hundred pounds: *Provided,* That no chains made of wire or rods of a diameter less than one-half of one inch shall be considered a chain cable (8) ;

203. On anvils, one dollar per one hundred pounds (8) ;

204. On anchors, or parts thereof, fifty cents per one hundred pounds (8) ;

205. On wrought board nails, spikes, rivets, bolts, bed-screws, and wrought hinges, one-fourth of one cent per pound (8);'

206. On chains, trace chains, halter chains, and fence chains, made of wire or rods, not under one-fourth of an inch in diameter, one-fourth of one cent per pound; under one-fourth of one inch in diameter and not under number nine, wire gauge, one-half of one cent per pound; under number nine, wire gauge, five per centum ad valorem (8);

207. On blacksmiths' hammers, and sledges, and axles, or parts thereof, one-half of one cent per pound (8);

208. On horseshoe nails, one cent per pound (8);

209. On steam, gas, and water tubes, and flues of wrought iron, one-fourth of one cent per pound (8);

210. On wrought iron railroad chairs, and wrought iron nuts and washers, ready punched, five dollars per ton (8);

211. On smooth or polished sheet iron, by whatever name designated, one-half cent per pound (9);

212. On sheet iron, common or black, not thinner than number twenty, wire gauge, three dollars per ton: thinner than number twenty, and not thinner than number twenty-five, wire gauge, four dollars per ton: thinner than number twenty-five, wire gauge, five dollars per ton (9);

213. On tin plates galvanized, galvanized iron, or iron coated with any metal by electric batteries, one-half cent per pound (9);

214. On locomotive tire, or parts thereof, one cent per pound (9);

215. On mill irons, and mill-cranks of wrought iron, and wrought iron for ships, steam-engines, and locomotives, or parts thereof, weighing each twenty-five pounds or more, one-fourth of one cent per pound (9);

216. On screws, commonly called wood screws, one cent and a half per pound (9);

217. On screws, washed or plated, and all other screws of iron, except wood-screws, five per centum ad valorem (9);

218. On all manufactures of iron, not otherwise provided for, five per centum ad valorem (9);

219. On cast iron, steam, gas, and water pipes, twenty-five cents per one hundred pounds (6); on all other castings of iron, not otherwise provided for, nor exempted from duty, five per centum ad valorem (6): *Provided,* That the following descriptions of iron, manufactures of iron, and manufactures of steel, shall not be subject to any additional duty or rates of duty under the provisions of this Act, that is to say: Iron in pigs; cast iron butts and hinges; old scrap iron; malleable iron, and malleable iron castings, not otherwise provided for; cut-tacks, brads, and sprigs; cross-cut, mill, pit, and drag saws;

220. On steel in ingots, bars, sheets, or wire, not less than one-fourth of an inch in diameter, valued at seven cents per pound or less, one-fourth of one cent per pound; valued at above seven cents per pound, and not above eleven cents per pound, one-half cent per pound; valued above eleven cents per pound, and on steel wire and steel in any form, not otherwise provided for, five per centum ad valorem (10);

221. On skates valued at twenty cents or less per pair, two cents per pair; when valued at over twenty cents per pair, five per centum ad valorem (10);

222. On iron squares, marked on one side, two cents and a half per pound; on all other squares made of iron or steel, five cents per pound (9-10);

223. On files, rasps, and floats, of all descriptions, two cents per pound, and in addition thereto, five per centum ad valorem (10);

224. On all manufactures of steel, or of which steel shall be a component part, not otherwise provided for, five per centum ad valorem (10): *Provided,* That no allowance or reduction of duties for partial loss or damage shall be hereafter made in consequence of rust of iron or steel, or upon the manufactures of iron or steel, except on polished Russia sheet iron; *

* " Four cases of needles were submerged in sea water on the voyage of importation, being entirely worthless, the whole duties assessed were remitted ". (Dec. of July 15, 1869, see also decisions of Nov. 18, 1864, June 30, 1869, and Dec. 7, 1858).

3

225. On bituminous coal, ten cents per ton of twenty-eight bushels, eighty pounds to the bushel : on all other coal, ten cents per ton of twenty-eight bushels, eighty pounds to the bushel (11); on coke and culm of coal, five per centum ad valorem (11).

Sec. 4. *And be it further enacted,* That from and after the day and year aforesaid, IN ADDITION to the duties heretofore imposed by law on the articles hereinafter mentioned and included in this section, there shall be levied, collected, and paid, on the goods, wares, and merchandise herein enumerated and provided for, imported from foreign countries, the following duties and rates of duty, that is to say :

226. On copper rods, bolts, nails, spikes, copper bottoms, copper in sheets or plates, called braziers' copper, and other sheets and manufactures of copper, not otherwise provided for, five per centum ad valorem (13) :

227. On zinc, spelter, and teutenegue, unmanufactured, in blocks or pigs, twenty-five cents per one hundred pounds (13) ;

228. On zinc, spelter, and teutenegue, in sheets, one-half of one cent per pound (13) ;

229. On lead, in pipes and shot, three-fourths of one cent per pound (178) ;

230. On brass, in bars or pigs, and old brass, fit only to be remanufactured, five per centum ad valorem (33).

Sec. 5. *And be it further enacted,* That from and after the day and year aforesaid, IN LIEU of the duties heretofore imposed by law on the articles hereinafter mentioned, and on such as may now be exempt from duty, there shall be levied, collected, and paid, on the goods, wares, and merchandise enumerated and provided for in this section, imported from foreign countries, the following duties and rates of duty, that is to say :

231. Acid, boracic, five cents per pound (120); citric, ten cents per pound (52) ; oxalic, four cents per pound (32) ; sulphuric, one cent per pound (120) ; tartaric, twenty cents per pound (178) ; gallic, fifty cents per pound (32) ; tannic, twenty-five cents per pound (32) ;

232. Alum, patent alum, alum substitute, sulphate of alumina, and aluminous cake, sixty cents per one hundred pounds (14) ;

233. Argols, or crude tartar, six cents per pound (178) ; cream tartar, ten cents per pound (178) ; asphaltum, three cents per pound (122) ;

234. Balsam copavia, twenty cents per pound (73) ; Peruvian, fifty cents per pound (73) ; tolu, thirty cents per pound (73) ; blanc fixe, enamelled white, satin white, or any combination of barytes and acids, two cents and a half per pound (63); barytes and sulphate of barytes, five mills per pound (66); burning fluid, fifty cents per gallon (166); bitter apples, coloçynth, or coloquintida, ten cents per pound (135); borax, crude, or tincal, five cents per pound (127); refined, ten cents per pound (14); borate of lime, five cents per pound (33) ; buchu leaves, ten cents per pound (127) ;

235. Camphor, crude, thirty cents per pound (128) ; refined, forty cents per pound (128) ; cantharides, fifty cents per pound (34) ; cloves, fifteen cents per pound (178) ; cassia, fifteen cents per pound (178) ; cassia buds, twenty cents per pound (178) ; cinnamon, twenty-five cents per pound (178) ; cayenne pepper, twelve cents per pound ; ground, fifteen cents per pound ; black pepper, twelve cents

per pound; ground, fifteen cents per pound; white pepper, twelve cents per pound; ground, fifteen cents per pound (178) : cocculus indicus, ten cents per pound (34) ; cuttle-fish bone, five cents per pound (48) · cubebs, ten cents per pound (54) :

236. Dragon's blood, ten cents per pound (131) :

237. Emery, ore or rock, six dollars per ton (132) ; manufactured, ground, or pulverized, one cent per pound (132) ; ergot, twenty cents per pound (36) : epsom salts, one cent per pound (66) ; glauber salts, five mills per pound (66) ; rochelle salts, fifteen cents per pound (178) :

238. Fruit ethers, essences or oils of apple, pear, peach, apricot, strawberry, and raspberry, made of fusil oil or of fruit, or imitations thereof, two dollars and fifty cents per pound (62) ;

239. French green (63), Paris green (63), mineral green (63), carmine lake (63), wood lake (63), dry carmine (63), Venetian red (68), vermilion (68), mineral blue (149). Prussian blue (45), chrome yellow (54), rose pink (63), extract of resin or analine colors (100), Dutch pink (63), and paints and painters' colors (63), (except white and red lead and oxide of zinc,) dry or ground in oil, and moist water colors, used in the manufacture of paper-hangings and colored papers and cards, not otherwise provided for, twenty-five per centum ad valorem (63) ;

240. Ginger root, five cents per pound (176) ; ginger ground, eight cents per pound (178) : on gold leaf, one dollar and fifty cents per package of five hundred leaves (57) ; on silver leaf, seventy-five cents per package of five hundred leaves (57) ; gum aloes, six cents per pound (32) ; benzoin, ten cents per pound (135) ; sandarac. ten cents per pound (135) ; shellac, ten cents per pound (160) ; mastic, fifty cents per pound (135) : copal (178-38), kowrie (135), damar (135), and all gums used for like purposes, ten cents per pound (178) ;

241. Honey, fifteen cents per gallon (15) :

242. Iodine, crude, fifty cents per pound (40) ; resublimed, seventy-five cents per pound (14) ; ipecacuanha, or ipecac, fifty cents per pound (40) :

243. Jalap, fifty cents per pound (41) :

244. Licorice root, one cent per pound (173) ; paste or juice, five cents per pound (178) ;

245. Litharge, two and one-fourth cents per pound (14) ;

246. Magnesia, carbonate, six cents per pound (82); calcined, twelve cents per pound (60) ; manna, twenty-five cents per pound (43) :

247. Nitrate of soda, one cent per pound (46-202) ;

248. Morphine and its salts, two dollars per ounce (14) ; mace (178) and nutmeg (178), thirty cents per pound ;

249. Ochres and ochrey earths, not otherwise provided for, when dry, fifty cents per one hundred pounds ; when ground in oil, one dollar and fifty cents per one hundred pounds (14) ;

250. Oils, fixed or expressed, croton, fifty cents per pound (62); almonds, ten cents per pound (62); bay or laurel, twenty cents per pound (62) ; castor, fifty cents per gallon (51); mace, fifty cents per pound (62); olive, not salad, twenty-five

cents per gallon (44); salad, fifty cents per gallon (109): mustard, not salad, twenty-five cents per gallon (62); salad, fifty cents per gallon (62-109);

251. Oils, essential or essence, anise, fifty cents per pound (62): almonds, one dollar and fifty cents per pound (62); amber, crude, ten cents per pound (62): rectified, twenty cents per pound (62) bay leaves, seventeen dollars and fifty cents per pound (62); bergamot, one dollar per pound (62); cajeput, twenty-five cents per pound (62); caraway, fifty cents per pound (62): cassia. one dollar per pound (62): cinnamon, two dollars per pound (62): cloves, one dollar per pound (178): citronella, fifty cents per pound (62); cognac or œnanthic ether, two dollars per ounce (62): cubebs, one dollar per pound (62); fennel, fifty cents per pound (62) Juniper twenty-five cents per pound (62); lemons, fifty cents per pound (62); orange, fifty cents per pound (62); origanum, or red thyme, twenty-five cents per pound (62): roses, or otto, one dollar and fifty cents per ounce (62); thyme, white, thirty cents per pound (63): valerian, one dollar and fifty cents per pound (62); all other essential oils, not otherwise provided for, fifty per centum ad valorem (62);

252. Opium, two dollars per pound (14): opium prepared for smoking, eighty per centum ad valorem (14):

253. Paraffine, ten cents per pound (166); Paris white, when dry, sixty cents per one hundred pounds (14): when ground in oil, one dollar and fifty cents per one hundred pounds (14); pimento, twelve cents per pound (178); when ground, fifteen cents per pound (178);

254. Potash, bichromate, three cents per pound (14); hydriodate (14), iodate (14), iodide (14), and acetate (32-48), seventy-five cents per pound; prussiate, yellow, five cents per pound (14); prussiate, red, ten cents per pound (14); chlorate, six cents per pound (66);

255. Petroleum and coal illuminating oil, crude, ten cents per gallon; refined, or kerosene, produced from the distillation of coal, asphaltum, shale, peat, petroleum, or rock oil, or other bituminous substances, used for like purposes, twenty cents per gallon (14);

256. Putty, one dollar and fifty cents per one hundred pounds (14);

257. Quinine, sulphate of, and other salts of quinine, forty-five per centum ad valorem (179);

258. Rhubarb. fifty cents per pound (47); rose leaves, fifty cents per pound (166); rum essence or oil, and bay rum essence or oil, two dollars per ounce (62):

259. Saltpetre, or nitrate of potash, crude, two cents per pound (178); refined, three cents per pound (178):

260. Seeds, anise, five cents per pound (32); star anise, ten cents per pound (32): canary, one dollar per bushel of sixty pounds (166); caraway, three cents per pound (136) · cardamom, fifty cents per pound (136); cummin, five cents per pound (136); coriander, three cents per pound (136); fennel, two cents per pound (136): fe[n]ugreek, two cents per pound (136): hemp, one-half cent per pound (16); mustard, brown, three cents per pound (136): white, three cents per pound (136); rape, one cent per pound (16); castor seeds or beans, thirty cents per bushel (34);

261. Sugar of lead, four cents per pound (14):

262. Tartar emetic, fifteen cents per pound (178);

263. Varnish, valued at one dollar and fifty cents or less per gallon, fifty cents per gallon, and twenty per centum ad valorem; valued at above one dollar and fifty cents per gallon, fifty cents per gallon, and twenty five per centum ad valorem (68);

264. Vanilla beans, three dollars per pound (50); verdigris, six cents per pound (50);

265. Whiting, when dry, fifty cents per one hundred pounds; when ground in oil, one dollar and fifty cents per one hundred pounds (14):

266. Acetous (120), benzoic (120), muriatic (120), and pyroligneous (120) acids, cutch or catechu (161), orchil (130) and cudbear (130), safflower (158), and sumac (160), ten per centum ad valorem;

267. Arsenic in all forms (122), ammonia (32), and sulphate and carbonate of ammonia (32); bark, cinchona (123), Peruvian (179), Lima (123), calisaya (123), quilla (123), and all other medicinal barks, flowers, leaves, plants, roots, and seeds, not otherwise provided for (60-136); cobalt, and oxide of cobalt (128); gums, amber (32), Arabic (135), Jedda (135), Senegal (135), tragacanth (135), myrrh (135); and all other gums and gum resins not otherwise provided for (135-240); quassia wood (156), smalts (160), sarsaparilla (48), tapioca (49), tonqua beans (166) and sponges (48), twenty per centum ad valorem; acetic acid, twenty-five per centum ad valorem (120);

268. Santonine (108) and glycerine (108), thirty per centum ad valorem;

269. On all pills, powders, tinctures, troches or lozenges, syrups, cordials, bitters, anodynes, tonics, plasters, liniments, salves, ointments, pastes, drops, waters, essences, spirits, oils, or other medicinal preparations or compositions, recommended to the public as proprietary medicines, or prepared according to some private formula or secret art as remedies or specifics for any disease or diseases or affections whatever affecting the human or animal body, fifty per centum ad valorem (73-594);

270. On all essences, extracts, toilet waters, cosmetics, hair oils, pomades, hair dressings, hair restoratives, hair dyes, tooth washes, dentifrices, tooth pastes, aromatic cachous, or other perfumeries or cosmetics, by whatsoever name or names known, used or applied as perfumes or applications to the hair, mouth, or skin, fifty per centum ad valorem (73-520-594).

Sec. 6. *And be it further enacted,* That from and after the day and year aforesaid, IN ADDITION to the duties heretofore imposed by law on the articles hereinafter mentioned, and on such as may now be exempt from duty, there shall be levied, collected, and paid on the goods, wares, and merchandise enumerated and provided for in this section, imported from foreign countries, a duty of ten per centum ad valorem, that is to say:

271. Antimony, crude (122); assafœtida (32);

272. Beeswax (33); blacking of all descriptions (166); building stones of all descriptions not otherwise provided for (33);

273. Calomel (54); catsup (79); civet, oil of (62-608); cobalt ores (128);

274. Extract of indigo (132-504); extract of madder (132); extract and decoctions of logwood, and other dyewoods (133);

275. Flints and flint, ground (134); flocks, waste or shoddy (37-612½); furs, dressed, when not on the skin (37);

276. Garancine (133-274): ginger. preserved or pickled (179); green turtle (38); grind-stones, unwrought. or wrought or finished (88-135): gutta percha, unmanufactured (135);

277. Isinglass or fish glue (56).

278. Japanned ware of all kinds not otherwise provided for (92);

279. Lastings, monair cloth, silk, twist, or other manufacture of cloth woven or made in patterns or such size. shape and form, or cut in such manner as to be fit for shoes, slippers, boots, bootees, gaiters and buttons, exclusively, not combined with India-rubber (146);

280. Mats of cocoa-nut (30); matting, China, and other floor matting, and mats made of flags, jute, or grass (60); manufactures of gutta percha (166 mlik of India rubber (179) medicinal preparations not otherwise provided for (108); music, printed with lines, bound or unbound (43); musical instruments of all kinds (60), and strings for musical instruments of whipgut or catgut, and all other strings of the same material (60);

281. Nickel (152):

282. Osier or willow, prepared for basket-makers' use (62);

283. Philosophical apparatus and instruments (98); plaster of Paris, when ground (45);

284. Quills (64):

285. Strychnine (66): staves for pipes, hogsheads, or other casks (160);

286. Teeth, manufactured (39): thread lace and insertings (67);

287. Woollen listings (69).

Sec. 7. *And be it further enacted,* That, IN ADDITION to the duties heretofore imposed by law on the articles hereinafter mentioned and provided for in this section, there shall be levied, collected and paid, on the goods, wares and merchandise herein enumerated, imported from foreign countries, the following duties and rates of duty, that is to say:

288. On chocolate and cocoa prepared. one cent per pound (178); on copperas, green vitriol, or sulphate of iron, one-fourth cent per pound (14);

289. On linseed. flax-seed. hemp-seed, and rape-seed oil, three cents per gallon (14);

290. On saleratus, and bicarbonate of soda, one half-cent per pound (178); on caustic soda, one-half cent per pound (178);

291. On salt, in sacks. barrels, other packages, or in bulk, six cents per one hundred pounds (178):

292. On soap, fancy, scented. honey, cream, transparent, and all descriptions of toilet and shaving soap, two cents per pound: all other soaps, five per centum ad valorem (113);

293. On spirits of turpentine, five cents per gallon (178); on starch of all descriptions, one-half cent per pound (66);

294. On white and red lead, dry or ground in oil, fifteen cents per one hundred pounds (178):

295. On oxide of zinc, dry or ground in oil, twenty-five cents per one hundred pounds (14).

Sec. 8. *And be it further enacted,* That from and after the day and year aforesaid, IN LIEU of the duties heretofore imposed by law on the articles hereinafter mention[ed], and on such as may now be exempt from duty, there shall be levied, collected, and paid on the goods, wares, and merchandise enumerated and provided for in this section, imported from foreign countries, the following duties and rates of duty, that is to say:

296. On anchovies preserved in salt, thirty per centum ad valorem (71); on andirons, made of cast iron, one cent and one fourth per pound (6-199):

297. On barley, pearl or hulled, one cent per pound (45);

298. On bonnets, hats, and hoods for men, women and children, composed of straw, chip, grass, palm-leaf, willow, or any other vegetable substance, or of silk (483), hair (785), whalebone, or other material not otherwise provided for, forty per centum ad valorem (90);

299. On braids, plaits, flats, laces, trimmings, sparterre (858), tissues, willow sheets and squares, used for making or ornamenting hats, bonnets and hoods, composed of straw, chip, grass, palm-leaf, willow, or any other vegetable substance, or of hair (785), whalebone, or other material, not otherwise provided for, thirty per centum ad valorem (89);

300. On books (31). periodicals (31), pamphlets (31), blank-books (53), bound or unbound, and all printed matter (31) engravings (36), bound or unbound, illustrated books and papers (31), and maps (149) and charts (149), twenty per centum ad valorem: *Provided*, That all imported cotton and linen rags for the manufacture of paper shall be free of duty (157); on bristles, ten cents per pound (15):

301. On candles and tapers, stearine and adamantine, five cents per pound; on spermaceti, paraffine and wax candles and tapers, pure or mixed, eight cents per pound; on all other candles and tapers, two and one-half cents per pound (14);

302. On chickory root, two cents per pound; on chickory ground, burnt, or prepared, three cents per pound (175);

303. On acorn coffee and dandelion root, raw or prepared, and all other articles used or intended to be used as coffee, or a substitute for coffee, and not otherwise provided for, three cents per pound (166);

304. On coloring for brandy, fifty per centum ad valorem (166); on cork wood, unmanufactured thirty per centum ad valorem (130); on corks, fifty per centum ad valorem (54); on cotton, one-half cent per pound (136):

305. On feathers and downs for beds or bedding, of all descriptions, thirty per centum ad valorem (179):

306. On ostrich, vulture, cock and other ornamental feathers, crude or not dressed, colored or manufactured twenty per centum ad valorem; when dressed, colored, or manufactured, forty per centum ad valorem (85):

307. On feathers and flowers artificial and parts thereof, of whatever material composed, no' otherwise provided for, forty per centum ad valorem (89);

308. On fire-crackers, fifty cents per box of forty packs, not exceeding eighty to each pack, and in the same proportion for a greater number (89);

309. On fruit, shade, lawn, and ornamental trees, shrubs, plants, and bulbous roots and flower seeds, not otherwise provided for, thirty per centum ad valorem (136-161);

310. On gloves, made of skins or leather, forty per centum ad valorem (81-84);

311. On gunpowder, and all explosive substances used for mining, blasting, artillery or sporting purposes, valued at less than twenty cents per pound, six cents per pound; valued at twenty cents or over per pound, six cents per pound, and twenty per centum ad valorem in addition thereto (170);

312. On garden seeds, and all other seeds for agricultural and horticultural purposes, not otherwise provided for, thirty per centum ad valorem (136);

313. On hides raw and skins of all kinds, whether dried, salted, or pickled, ten per centum ad valorem (179);

314. On hollow-ware and vessels of cast iron, not otherwise provided for, one cent and one-fourth per pound (6-199);

315. On hops, five cents per pound (39);

316. On human hair, raw, uncleaned, and not drawn, twenty per centum ad valorem; when cleaned or drawn, but not manufactured, thirty per centum ad valorem; when manufactured, forty per centum ad valorem (90);

317. On lead ore, one dollar per one hundred pounds (166);

318. On marble, white statuary, in block, rough, or squared, seventy-five cents per cubic foot; veined marble, and marble of all other descriptions, not otherwise provided for, in block, rough, or squared, forty per centum ad valorem (102);

319. On all manufactures of marble, marble slabs, marble paving tiles, and marble sawed, dressed, or polished, fifty per centum ad valorem (102);

320. On manufactures of bladders, thirty per centum ad valorem (166);

321. On manufactures of India-rubber and silk, or of India-rubber and silk and other materials, fifty per centum ad valorem (364-179-486);

322. On mustard, ground, in bulk, twelve cents per pound; when enclosed in glass or tin, sixteen cents per pound (60);

323. On plates engraved, of steel, copper (640), wood, or any other material, twenty-five per centum ad valorem (98); on plumbago or black lea'), ten dollars per ton (33); on potatoes, twenty-five cents per bushel (16);

324. On percussion caps (98), fulminates, fulminating powders, and all articles used for like purposes, not otherwise provided for, thirty per centum ad valorem (56);

325. On playing cards, valued at twenty-five cents or less per pack, fifteen cents per pack; valued above twenty-five cents per pack, twenty-five cents per pack (113); on pens, metallic, ten cents per gross (98); on pen-holder tips, metallic, ten cents per gross (98); on pen-holders, complete, ten cents per dozen (107); on lead pencils, one dollar per gross (93);

326. On rice, cleaned, one cent and a half per pound (16); paddy, three-quarters of one cent per pound (16); uncleaned rice, one cent per pound (16);

327. On sago and sago flour, one cent and a half per pound (16);

328. On sheathing copper, and sheathing metal or yellow metal not wholly of copper nor wholly or in part of iron, ungalvanized, in sheets forty-eight inches long and fourteen inches wide, and weighing from fourteen to thirty-four ounces per square foot, three cents per pound (159);

329. On tin in pigs, bars, or blocks, fifteen per centum ad valorem (161); on tin in plates or sheets, terne, and tagger tin, twenty-five per centum ad valorem (49); on oxide (66), muriatic (66), and salts of tin (48) and tin foil (49), thirty per centum ad valorem.

Sec. 9. *And be it further enacted,* That IN ADDITION to the duties heretofore imposed by law on the articles hereinafter mentioned and included in this section, there shall be levied, collected, and paid, on the goods, wares, and merchandise herein enumerated and provided for, imported from foreign countries, the following duties and rates of duty, that is to say :

330. On Wilton, Saxony and Aubusson, Axminster, patent velvet, Tournay velvet, and tapestry velvet carpets and carpeting, Brussels carpets wrought by the Jacquard machine, and all medallion or whole carpets, five cents per square yard ; on Brussels and tapestry Brussels carpets and carpeting, printed on the warp or otherwise, three cents per square yard ; on all treble-ingrain and worsted chain Venetian carpets and carpeting, three cents per square yard ; on hemp or jute carpeting, two cents per square yard; on all other kinds of carpets and carpeting, of wool, flax, or cotton, or parts of either or other material, (except druggets, bockings, and felt carpets and carpetings,) not otherwise provided for, five per centum ad valorem: *Provided,* That mats, rugs, screens, covers, hassocks, bedsides, and other portions of carpets or carpeting, shall pay the rate of duty herein imposed on carpets and carpeting of similar character; on all other mats, screens, hassocks and rugs, five per centum ad valorem (19) ;

331. On woollen cloths, woollen shawls, and all manufactures of wool, of every description, made wholly or in part of wool, not otherwise provided for, a duty of six cents per pound, and in addition thereto, five per centum ad valorem (20) ;

332. On goods of like description, when valued at over one dollar per square yard, or weighing less than twelve ounces per square yard, a duty of six cents per pound, and in addition thereto, ten per centum ad valorem (20) ;

333. On endless belts or felts for paper, and blanketing for printing machines, five per centum ad valorem (20) : on flannels, of all descriptions, five per centum ad valorem (20) ; on hats of wool, ten per centum ad valorem (20) ; on woollen and worsted yarn, of all descriptions, five per centum ad valorem (20) ;

334. On clothing ready made, and wearing apparel of every description, composed wholly or in part of wool, made up or manufactured wholly or in part by the tailor, seamstress, or manufacturer, six cents per pound, and in addition thereto, five per centum ad valorem (20) : *Provided,* That Balmoral skirts, or goods of like description, or used for like purposes, made wholly or in part of wool, shall be subjected to the same duties that are levied upon ready-made clothing (20) ;

335. On blankets of all kinds, made wholly or in part of wool, five per centum ad valorem (20) ;

336. On all delaines, cashmere delaines, muslin delaines, barege delaines, composed wholly or in part of worsted, wool, mohair, or goat's hair, and on all goods of similar description, not exceeding in value forty cents per square yard, two cents per square yard (21) ;

337. On bunting, worsted yarns, and on all other manufactures of worsted, or of which worsted shall be a component material, not otherwise provided for, five per centum ad valorem (21) ;

338. On oil-cloth for floors, stamped or printed, of all descriptions, five per centum ad valorem (22) : on coir floor matting and carpeting, five per centum ad valorem (60).

Sec. 10. *And be it further enacted,* That from and after the day and year aforesaid, IN ADDITION to the duties heretofore imposed by law on the articles hereinafter mentioned and provided for in this section, there shall be levied, collected, and paid, on the goods, wares, and merchandise herein enumerated, imported from foreign countries, the following duties and rates of duty, that is to say:

539. On all manufactures of cotton, bleached or unbleached, and not colored, stained, painted or printed, and not exceeding one hundred threads to the square inch, counting the warp and filling, and exceeding in weight five ounces per square yard, one-fourth of one cent per square yard: on finer or lighter goods of like description, not exceeding one hundred and forty threads to the square inch, counting the warp and filling, one-half cent per square yard; on goods of like description, exceeding one hundred and forty threads and not exceeding two hundred threads to the square inch, counting the warp and filling, three-fourths of one cent per square yard: on like goods, exceeding two hundred threads to the square inch, counting the warp and filing, one cent per square yard; on all goods embraced in the foregoing schedules, (except jeans, denimes, drillings, bedtickings, ginghams, plaids, cottonades, pantaloon stuffs, and goods of like description, not exceeding in value the sum of sixteen cents per square yard), if printed, painted, colored, or stained, they shall be considered to have been bleached goods, and there shall be levied, collected, and paid a duty of one cent per square yard, in addition to the rates of duty provided for bleached goods (23): *Provided*, That upon all plain woven cotton goods not included in the foregoing schedules, and upon cotton goods of every description, the value of which shall exceed sixteen cents per square yard, there shall be levied, collected, and paid a duty of five per centum ad valorem: *And provided further*, That no cotton goods having more than two hundred threads to the square inch, counting the warp and filling, shall be admitted to a less rate of duty than is provided for goods which are of that number of threads (23);

540. On spool and other thread of cotton, ten per centum ad valorem (24);

541. On shirts and drawers, wove or made on frames, composed wholly of cotton, and cotton velvet, five per centum ad valorem (25);

542. On all cotton jeans, denimes, drillings, bedtickings, ginghams, plaids, cottonades, pantaloon stuffs, and goods of like description, not exceeding in value the sum of sixteen cents per square yard, two cents per square yard, and on all manufactures composed wholly of cotton, bleached, unbleached, printed, painted, or dyed, not otherwise provided for, five per centum ad valorem (23);

543. On all brown or bleached linens, ducks, canvas paddings, cot-bottoms, burlaps, drills, coatings, brown hollands, blay linens, damasks (26-482), diapers, crash, huckabacks, handkerchiefs, lawns, or other manufactures of flax, jute, or hemp, (or of which flax, jute, or hemp shall be the component material of chief value), five per centum ad valorem; on flax or linen threads, twine and packthread, and all other manufactures of flax, or of which flax shall be the component material of chief value, and not otherwise provided for, five per centum ad valorem (26-182).

Sec. 11. *And be it further enacted,* That from and after the day and year aforesaid, IN ADDITION to the duties heretofore imposed by law on the articles hereinafter mentioned and provided for in this section, there shall be levied, collected, and paid, on the goods, wares, and merchandise herein enumerated, imported from foreign countries, the following duties and rates of duty, that is to say:

544. On jute, Sisal grass, sun hemp, coir, and other vegetable substances not enumerated (except flax, tow of flax, Russia and Manilla hemp, and codilla, or tow of hemp), five dollars per ton (27-166);

345. On Jute butts, one dollar per ton (27); on tarred cables, or cordage, one-fourth of one cent per pound (27); on untarred Manilla cordage, one-fourth of one cent per pound (27); on all other untarred cordage, one-half cent per pound (27); on hemp yarn, one cent per pound (27); on coir yarn, one cent per pound (27); on seines, one-half cent per pound (27);

346. On cotton bagging, or other manufactures not otherwise provided for, suitable for the uses to which cotton bagging is applied, whether composed in whole or in part of hemp, jute, or flax, or any other material valued at less than ten cents per square yard, three-fourths of one cent per pound; over ten cents per square yard, one cent per pound (27);

347. On sail duck, five per centum ad valorem (27); on Russia and other sheetings, made of flax or hemp, brown and white, five per centum ad valorem (27); and on all other manufactures of hemp, or of which hemp shall be a component part, not otherwise provided for, five per centum ad valorem (27); on grass cloth, five per centum ad valorem (27); on jute yarns, five per centum ad valorem (27); on all other manufactures of jute or Sisal grass not otherwise provided for, five per centum ad valorem (27); *Provided,* That all hemp, or preparations of hemp used for naval purposes by the Government of the United States, shall be of American growth or manufacture: *Provided, further,* The same can be obtained of as good quality and at as low a price.

Sec. 12. *And be it further enacted,* That from and after the day and year aforesaid, IN LIEU of the duties heretofore imposed by law on the articles hereinafter mentioned, and on such as may now be exempt from duty, there shall be levied, collected, and paid, on the goods, wares, and merchandise enumerated and provided for in this section, imported from foreign countries, the following duties and rates of duty, that is to say:

348. On all brown earthenware and common stoneware, gas retorts, stoneware not ornamented (30), and stoneware above the capacity of ten gallons, twenty per centum ad valorem (160);

349. On China and porcelain ware, gilded, ornamented, or decorated in any manner, forty per centum ad valorem (30);

350. On China and porcelain ware, plain white, and not decorated in any manner, and all other earthen, stone, or crockery ware, white, glazed, edged, printed, painted, dipped, or cream colored, composed of earthy or mineral substances, and not otherwise provided for, thirty-five per centum ad valorem (30);

351. Slates, slate pencils, slate chimney-pieces, mantels, slabs for tables, and all other manufactures of slate, forty per centum ad valorem (115); on unwrought clay, pipe clay, fire clay, and kaoline, five dollars per ton (14-117); on fuller's earth, three dollars per ton (134);

352. On white chalk, four dollars per ton; on red and French chalk, ten per centum ad valorem; on chalk of all descriptions, not otherwise provided for, twenty-five per centum ad valorem (123);

353. On all plain and mould and press glassware, not cut, engraved, or painted, thirty per centum ad valorem (29);

354. On all articles of glass, cut, engraved, painted, colored, printed, stained, silvered or gilded, not including plate-glass silvered, or looking-glass plates, thirty-five per centum ad valorem (29);

355. On fluted, rolled, or rough plate-glass, not including crown, cylinder, broad, or common window glass, not exceeding ten by fifteen inches, seventy-five cents per one hundred square feet; above that, and not exceeding sixteen by twenty-four inches, one cent per square foot, above that, and not exceeding twenty-four by thirty inches, one cent and a half per square foot; all above that, two cents per square foot: *Provided,* That all fluted, rolled, or rough plate-glass, weighing over one hundred pounds per one hundred square feet, shall pay an additional duty on the excess at the same rates herein imposed (29

356. On all cast polished plate-glass, unsilvered, not exceeding ten by fifteen inches, three cents per square foot: above that, and not exceeding sixteen by twenty-four inches, five cents per square foot; above that, and not exceeding twenty-four by thirty inches, eight cents per square foot; above that, and not exceeding twenty-four by sixty inches, twenty-five cents per square foot; and all above that, fifty cents per square foot (29):

357. On all cast polished plate-glass, silvered, or looking-glass plates, exceeding ten by fifteen inches, four cents per square foot; above that, and not exceeding sixteen by twenty-four inches, six cents per square foot: above that. and not exceeding twenty-four by thirty inches, ten cents per square foot; above that- and not exceeding twenty-four by sixty inches, thirty-five cents per square foot; all above that, sixty cents per square foot: *Provided.* That no looking-glass plates, or plate-glass, silvered, when framed shall pay a less rate of duty than that imposed upon similar glass, of like description. not framed, but shall be liable to pay, in addition thereto, thirty per centum ad valorem upon such frames (29):

358. On porcelain and Bohemian glass, glass crystals for watches, paintings on glass or glasses, pebbles for spectacles and all manufactures of glass, or of which glass shall be a component material, except crown. cylinder. and other window glass, not otherwise provided for, and all glass bottles or jars filled with sweetmeats. preserves, thirty-five per centum ad valorem (29).

Sec. 13. *And be it further enacted,* That from and after the day and year aforesaid, IN ADDITION to the duties heretofore imposed by law on the articles hereinafter mentioned, there shall be levied, collected, and paid, on the goods, wares, and merchandise enumerated and provided for in this section, imported from foreign countries, a duty of FIVE PER CENTUM AD VALOREM, that is to say:

359. Argentine, alabatta, or German silver, manufactured (511) or unmanufactured (71); articles embroidered with gold, silver, or other metal (71);

360. Articles worn by men, women, or children, of whatever material composed, made up, or made wholly or in part by hand, not otherwise provided for (72-578-613);

361. Britannia ware (98);

362. Baskets, and all other articles composed of grass, osier, palm-leaf, straw, whalebone, or willow, not otherwise provided for (74);

363. Bracelets, braids, chains, curls, or ringlets composed of hair, or of which hair is a component material (76-685);

364. Braces, suspenders, webbing, or other fabrics composed wholly or in part of India-rubber, not otherwise provided for (77-321); brooms and brushes of all kinds (78-524);

365. Canes and sticks for walking, finished or unfinished (79-864); capers, pickles, and sauces of all kinds, not otherwise provided for (79-273);

366. Caps, hats, muffs, and tippets of fur, and all other manufactures of fur, or of which fur shall be a component material (80);

367. Caps, gloves, leggins, mits, socks, stockings, wove shirts and drawers, and all similar articles made on frames. of whatever

material composed, worn by men, women, and children, and not otherwise provided for (81-486-613) ;

368. Card cases, pocket books, shell boxes, souvenirs, and all similar articles, of whatever material composed (83); carriages and parts of carriages (83); clocks and parts of clocks (83) ;

369. Clothing, ready made, and wearing apparel of whatever description, of whatever material composed, except wool, made up or manufactured wholly or in part by the tailor, seamstress, or manufacturer (84-334-578-618) ;

370. Coach and harness furniture of all kinds, saddlery, coach and harness hardware, silvef plated, brass plated, or covered, common tinned, burnished, or japanned, not otherwise provided for (85-640);

371. Combs of all kinds (86); compositions of glass or paste, when set (70-86); composition tops for tables, or other articles of furniture (86-114); comfits, sweetmeats, or fruits preserved in sugar, brandy, or molasses, not otherwise provided for (86); cotton cords, gimps, and galloons (86); cotton laces, cotton insertings, cotton trimming laces; and cotton braids, colored or uncolored (54-86); court-plaster (86); cutlery of all kinds (86-455);

372. Dolls and toys of all kinds (87-543);

373. Encaustic tiles (88); epaulets, galloons, laces, knots, stars, tassels, tresses, and wings, of gold, silver, or other metal (88-785) ;

374. Fans and fire-screens of every description, of whatever material composed (89-826); frames and sticks for umbrellas, parasols, and sunshades, finished or unfinished (89-802); furniture, cabinet and household (89); furs, dressed (37) ;

375. Hair pencils (90-685); hat bodies of cotton (90) or wool, or of which wool is the component material of chief value (613); hair cloth, hair seatings, and all other manufactures of hair, not otherwise provided for (70-684) ;

376. Ink, printers' ink, and ink powder (91) ;

377. Japanned, patent or enamelled leather, or skins of all kinds (92-66); jet and manufactures of jet, and imitations thereof (92) ;

378. Leather, tanned, of all descriptions (179-66-59) ;

379. Maccaroni, vermicelli, gelatine, jellies (542), and all similar preparations (94) ;

380. Manufactures of bone, shell, horn, ivory or vegetable ivory (97) ;

381. Manufactures of paper, or of which paper is a component material, not otherwise provided for (104) ;

382. Manufactures of the bark of the cork tree, except corks (96-304) ;

383. Manufactures, articles, vessels, and wares, not otherwise provided for, of gold (511), silver (311), copper (640), brass, iron, steel (458), lead,

pewter, tin, or other metal, or of which either of these metals or
any other metal shall be the component material of chief value (98);

384. Manufactures not otherwise provided for, composed of
mixed materials, in part of cotton, silk, wool (613), or worsted, hemp,
jute (184), or flax (58-99);

385. Manufactures of cotton, linen, silk, wool (613), or worsted, if
embroidered or tamboured, in the loom or otherwise, by machinery
or with the needle or other process, not otherwise provided for (100);

386. Manufactures of cedar wood, granadilla, ebony, mahogany,
rosewood, and satin wood (101-390);

387. Manufactures and articles of leather, or of which leather
shall be a component part, not otherwise provided for (103);

388. Manufactures, articles, and wares, of papier mache (105);

389. Manufactures of goats' hair or mohair, or of which goats' hair or mohair shall be a
component material, not otherwise provided for (21);

390. Manufactures of wood, or of which wood is the chief component part, not otherwise provided for (107-386);

391. Morocco skins (59); muskets, rifles, and other fire-arms (108);

392. Needles, - sewing, darning, knitting, and all other descriptions (61-456);

393. Oil-cloth of every description, of whatever materia. composed, not otherwise provided
for (338);

394. Paper boxes, and all other fancy boxes (110); paper
envelopes (110);

395. Paper-hangings, and paper for screens or fire-boards; paper,
antiquarian, demy, drawing, elephant, foolscap, imperial, letter,
and all other paper, not otherwise provided for (111-381-419-48);

396. Pins, solid head or other (98); plated and gilt ware of all
kinds (112);

397. Prepared vegetables, meat, fish, poultry, and game, sealed
or unsealed, in cans or otherwise (113);

398. Ratans and reeds, manufactured or partially manufactured (65); roofing slates (115);

399. Scagliola tops for tables or other articles of furniture
(114-371); sealing-wax (114); side arms of every description
(114-679); silver-plated metal, in sheets or other form (114);
stereotype plates (66); still bottoms (13-66-226);

400. Twines and packthread, of whatever material composed, not
otherwise provided for (116); type metal (67); types, new (67);

401. Umbrellas, parasols, and sunshades (117-112); velvet, when printed or
painted (118);

402. Wafers (118); water-colors (118); watches and parts of watches, and watch
materials, and unfinished parts of watches (31);

403. Webbing, composed of wool (618). cotton, flax, or any other materials, not otherwise provided for (119).

404. **Sec. 14.** *And be it further enacted,* That from and after the day and year aforesaid, there shall be levied, collected, and paid, on all goods, wares, and merchandise of the growth or produce of countries beyond the Cape of Good Hope, when imported from places this side of the Cape of Good Hope, a duty of ten per cent. ad valorem, and in addition to the duties imposed on any such articles when imported directly from the place or places of their growth or production (363-416).

404½ **Sec. 15.** *And be it further enacted,* That upon all ships, vessels, or steamers, which, after the thirty-first day of December, eighteen hundred and sixty-two, shall be entered at any custom-house in the United States, from any foreign port or place, or from any port or place in the United States, whether ships or vessels of the United States, or belonging wholly or in part to subjects of foreign powers, there shall be paid a tax or tonnage duty of ten cents per ton of the measurement of said vessel, in addition to any tonnage duty now imposed by law. *Provided,* That the said tax or tonnage duty shall not be collected more than once in each year on any ship, vessel or steamer having a license to trade between the different districts of the United States, or to carry on the bank, whale or other fisheries, whilst employed therein, or on any ship, vessel, or steamer, to or from any port or place in Mexico, the British provinces of North America, or any of the West India Islands : *Provided, also,* That nothing in this Act contained shall be deemed in anywise to impair any rights and privileges which have been or may be acquired by any foreign nation under the laws and treaties of the United States relative to the duty on tonnage of vessels : *Provided, further,* That so much of the Act of August eighteen, eighteen hundred and fifty-six, entitled "An Act to authorize protection to be given to citizens of the United States who may discover deposits of guano," as prohibits the export thereof, is hereby suspended for one year from and after the passage of this Act (418-579).

405. **Sec. 16.** *And be it further enacted,* That from and after the passage of this Act, in estimating the allowance for tare on all chests, boxes, cases, casks, bags, or other envelope or covering of all articles imported liable to pay any duty, where the original invoice is produced at the time of making entry thereof, and the tare shall be specified therein, it shall be lawful for the collector, if he shall see fit, or for the col-

lector and naval officer, if such officer there be, if they shall see fit, with the consent of the consignees, to estimate the said tare according to such invoice; but in all other cases the real tare shall be allowed, and may be ascertained under such regulations as the Secretary of the Treasury may from time to time prescribe, but in no case shall there be any allowance for draft.

406. **Sec. 17.** *And be it further enacted,* That from and after the first day of November, eighteen hundred and sixty-two, no goods, wares, or merchandise subject to ad valorem or specific duty, whether belonging to a person or persons residing in the United States or otherwise, or whether acquired by the ordinary process of bargain and sale, or otherwise, shall be admitted to entry, unless the invoice of such goods, wares, or merchandise be verified by the oath of the owner, or one of the owners, or, in the absence of the owner, one of the party who is authorized by the owner to make the shipment and sign the invoice of the same, certifying that the invoice annexed contains a true and faithful account, if subject to ad valorem duty and obtained by purchase, of the actual cost thereof, and of all charges thereon, and that no discounts, bounties, or drawbacks are contained in the said invoice but such as have actually been allowed on the same; and when consigned or obtained in any manner other than by purchase, the actual market value thereof, and if subject to specific duty, of the actual quantity thereof; which said oath shall be administered by the consul or commercial agent of the United States in the district where the goods are manufactured, or from which they are sent; and if there be no consul or commercial agent of the United States in the said district, the verification hereby required shall be made by the consul or commercial agent of the United States at the nearest point, or at the port from which the goods are shipped, in which case the oath shall be administered by some public officer, duly authorized to administer oaths, and transmitted, with a copy of the invoice, to the consul or commercial agent, for his authentication; and this Act shall be construed only to modify, and not repeal, the Act of March first, eighteen hundred and twenty-three, entitled "An Act supplementary to, and to amend an Act entitled 'An Act to regulate the collection of duties on imports and tonnage,' passed second March, one thousand seven hundred and ninety-nine, and for other purposes," and the forms of

the oaths therein set forth shall be modified accordingly.
And there shall be paid to the said consul, vice-consul, or
commercial agent, by the person or persons by or in behalf
of whom the said invoices are presented and deposited, one
dollar for each and every invoice verified, which shall be
accounted for by the officers receiving the same, in such
manner as is now required by the laws regulating the fees
and salaries of consuls and commercial agents: *Provided,*
That nothing herein contained shall be construed to require
for goods imported under the reciprocity treaty with Great
Britain, signed June fifth, eighteen hundred and fifty-four,
any other consular certificate than is now required by law:
And provided, further, That the provisions of this section
shall not apply to invoices of goods, wares, and merchandise,
imported into the United States from beyond Cape Horn
and the Cape of Good Hope, until the first day of April,
one thousand eight hundred and sixty-three: *And provided,
further,* That the provisions of this section shall not apply
to countries where there is no consul, vice-consul, or commercial agent of the United States (170-582-602).

407. **Sec. 18.** *And be it further enacted,* That from and after the
date aforesaid, it shall be the duty of consuls and commercial agents of the United States, having any knowledge or
belief of any case or practice of any person or persons who
obtain or should obtain verification of invoices as described
in the preceding section, whereby the revenue of the United
States is or may be defrauded, to report the facts to the collector of the port where the revenue is or may be defrauded,
or to the Secretary of the Treasury of the United States.

408. **Sec. 19.** *And be it further enacted,* That, from and after the
passage of this Act, the Act entitled "An Act to provide for
the payment of outstanding treasury notes, to authorize a
loan, to regulate and fix the duties on imports, and for other
purposes," approved March two, eighteen hundred and
sixty-one, be, and the same is hereby amended as follows,
that is to say: First, in section twelve, before the word
"eighteen," where it first occurs, strike out "less than" (18);
Second, in section twenty-three, after the words, "artists
residing abroad," strike out, "provided the same be imported in good faith as objects of taste and not of merchandise," and insert, "provided the fact, as aforesaid, shall be
certified by the artist, or by a Consul of the United States."

4

154); and in tne same section, before the word "orvi-
ment," insert, " ores of gold and silver " (153).

409. **Sec. 20.** *Ana be it further enactea,* That the sixth section
of an Act entitled " An Act to extend the warehousing
system by establishing private bonded warehouses, and for
other purposes," be, and the same is hereby amended so
that the additional duty of one hundred per centum shall
not apply to the invoice or appraised value of the merchandise withdrawn, but shall be so consstued as to require for
failure to transport and deliver within the time limited a
duty to be levied and collected of double the amount which
said goods, wares, and merchandise would be liable upon
the original entry thereof.

410. **Sec. 21.** *And be it further enacted,* That all goods, wares,
merchandise, which may be in public stores or bonded
warehouses on the first day of August, eighteen hundred
and sixty-two, may be withdrawn for consumption upon
payment of the duties now imposed thereon by law : *Pro-*
vided, The same shall be so withdrawn within three months
from the date of original importation ; but all goods, wares,
and merchandise which shall remain in the public stores or
bonded warehouses for more than three months from the
date of original importation, if withdrawn for consumption,
and all goods on shipboard on the first day of August,
eighteen hundred and sixty-two, shall be subject to the
duties prescribed by this Act *Provided,* That all goods
which now are or may be deposited in public stores or
bonded warehouse after this Act takes effect and goes into
operation, must be withdrawn therefrom, or the duties
thereon paid within one year from the date of original importation, but may be withdrawn by the owner for exportation to foreign countries, or may be transhipped to any port
of the Pacific or western coast of the United States at any
time before the expiration of three years from the date of
original importation ; such goods on arrival at a Pacific or
western port, as aforesaid, to be subject to the same rules and
regulations as if originally imported there; any goods remaining in public store or bonded warehouse beyond three
years shall be regarded as abandoned to the Government,
and sold under such regulations as the Secretary of the
Treasury may prescribe, and the proceeds paid into the
treasury : *Provided, further,* That merchandise upon which

duties nave been paid may remain in warehouse in custody of the officers of the customs at the expense and risk of the owners of said merchandise, and if exported directly from said custody to a foreign country within three years, shall be entitled to return duties, proper evidence of such merchandise having been landed abroad to be furnished to the collector by the importer, one per centum of said duties to be retained by the Government: *And provided, further,* That all drugs, medicines, and chemical preparations, entered for exportation and deposited in warehouse or public store, may be exported by the owner or owners thereof in the original package, or otherwise, subject to such regulations as shall be prescribed by the Secretary of the Treasury: *And provided, further,* That the third or last proviso to the fifth section of an Act entitled "An Act to provide increased revenue from imports, to pay interest on the public debt, and for other purposes," approved the sixth [fifth] day of August, eighteen hundred and sixty-one, be, and the same is hereby repealed (182) ; and no return of the duties shall be allowed on the export of any merchandise after it has been removed from the custody and control of the Government; but nothing herein contained shall be held to apply to or repeal section thirty (172) of the Act entitled "An Act to provide for the payment of outstanding treasury notes, to authorize a loan, to regulate and fix the duties on imports, and for other purposes," approved March second, eighteen hundred and sixty-one, or section four of an Act entitled "An Act to provide increased revenue from imports, to pay interest on the public debt, and for other purposes," approved August fifth, eighteen hundred and sixty-one (181-589-603).

411. **Sec. 22.** *And be it further enacted,* That the privilege of purchasing supplies from the public warehouses, duty free, be extended under such regulations as the Secretary of the Treasury shall prescribe to the vessels-of-war of any nation in ports of the United States, which may reciprocate such privilege towards the vessels of war of the United States in its ports.

412. **Sec. 23.** *And be it further enacted,* That all Acts and parts of Acts repugnant to the provisions of this Act be, and the same are hereby repealed : *Provided,* That the existing laws shall extend to, and be in force for, the collection of the duties imposed by this Act, for the prosecution and

punishment of all offences, and for the recovery, collection, distribution, and remission of all fines, penalties, and forfeitures, as fully and effectually as if every regulation, penalty, forfeiture, provision, clause, matter, and thing to that effect, in the existing laws contained, had been inserted in and re-enacted by this Act.

413. **Sec. 24.** 'This section does not relate to import duties.)

414. **Sec. 25.** (This section does not relate to import duties.

———————

ACT OF MARCH 3, 1863.

(From U. S. Statutes at Large, vol. 12, p. 742, &c.)

AN ACT to modify existing Laws imposing Duties on Imports, and for other Purposes.

415. *Be it enacted by the Senate and House of Representatives of the United States of America in Congress assembled,* That all goods, wares, and merchandise now in public stores or bonded warehouses, on which duties are unpaid, having been in bond more than one year and less than three years, when the Act entitled "An Act increasing temporarily the duties on imports, and for other purposes," approved July fourteenth, eighteen hundred and sixty-two, went into effect, may be entered for consumption and the bonds cancelled, at any time before the first day of June next, on payments of duties at the rates prescribed by the Act aforesaid, and all Acts, and parts of Acts, inconsistent with the provisions of this act, are hereby repealed.

416. **Sec. 2.** *And be it further enacted,* That section fourteen of an Act entitled "An Act increasing temporarily the duties on imports, and for other purposes," approved July fourteen, eighteen hundred and sixty-two, be, and the same hereby is, modified so as to allow cotton and raw silk as reeled from the cocoon, of the growth or produce of countries beyond the Cape of Good Hope, to be exempt from any additional duty when imported from places this side of the Cape of Good Hope, for two years from and after the passage of this Act (404).

417. **Sec. 3.** *And be it further enacted,* That so much of an Act entitled "An Act to authorize protection to be given to citizens of the United States, who may discover deposits of guano," approved August eighteen, eighteen hundred and fifty-six, as prohibits the export thereof, is hereby suspended in relation to all persons who have complied with the provisions of section second of said Act for two years from and after July fourteenth, eighteen hundred and sixty-three (583).

418. **Sec. 4.** *And be it further enacted,* That the proviso in section fifteen of an Act entitled "An act increasing temporarily the duties on imports, and for other purposes," approved July fourteen, eighteen hundred and sixty-two, shall be construed

to include any ship, vessel, or steamer to or from any port or place south of Mexico down to and including Aspinwall and Panama (404½-579).

419. **Sec. 5.** *And be it further enacted,* That in lieu of the duties now imposed by law, there shall be levied and collected upon printing paper (395) unsized, used for books and newspapers exclusively, twenty per centum ad valorem; upon seedlac and sticklac the same duties now imposed upon gum shellack (240-158); upon polishing powders, of all descriptions (166), Frankfort black (56), and Berlin, Chinese, Fig and wash blue (56), twenty-five per centum ad valorem.

420. **Sec. 6.** *And be it further enacted,* That from and after the passage of this Act, the duty on petroleum and coal illuminating oil, crude and not refined, when imported from foreign countries in a crude state, shall be twenty per centum ad valorem, and no more (14-255).

421. **Sec. 7.** *And be it further enacted,* That from and after the passage of this Act, there shall be allowed a drawback on foreign saltpetre, manufactured into gunpowder in the United States and exported therefrom, equal in amount to the duty paid on the foreign saltpetre from which it shall be manufactured, to be ascertained under such regulations as shall be prescribed by the Secretary of the Treasury, and no more: *Provided,* That ten per centum on the amount of all drawbacks so allowed shall be retained for the use of the United States by the collectors paying such drawbacks respectively (181-743½).

JOINT RESOLUTION OF APRIL 29, 1864.

(From U. S. Statutes at Large, vol. 13, p. 405).

JOINT RESOLUTION to increase temporarily the Duties on Imports.

421½. *Resolved by the Senate and House of Representatives of the United States of America in Congress assembled,* That until the end of sixty days from the passage of this resolution, fifty per cent. of the rates of duties and imports now imposed by law on all goods, wares, merchandise, and articles imported, shall be added to the present duties and imposts now charged on the importation of such articles: *Provided,* That printing paper unsized, used for books and newspapers exclusively, shall be exempt from the operation of this resolution (419-564-573½).

ACT OF JUNE 30, 1864.*

(From U. S. Statutes at Large, vol. 13, p. 202, &c.)

AN ACT to increase duties on imports and for other purposes

Be it enacted by the Senate and House of Representatives of the United States of America in Congress assembled, That on and after the first day of July, Anno Domini eighteen hundred and sixty-four, IN LIEU of the duties heretofore imposed by law on the articles hereinafter mentioned, there shall be levied, collected, and paid, on goods, wares, and merchandise herein enumerated and provided for, imported from foreign countries, the following duties and rates of duty, that is to say :

422. On teas of all kinds, twenty-five cents per pound (185). On all sugar not above number twelve, Dutch standard in color, three cents per pound (187). On all sugar above number twelve, and not above number fifteen, Dutch standard in color, three cents and a half per pound. On all sugar above number fifteen, not stove-dried, and not above number twenty, Dutch standard in color, four cents per pound. On all refined sugar in forms of loaf, lump, crushed, powdered, pulverized, or granulated, and all stove-dried or other sugar above number twenty, Dutch standard in color, five cents per pound (187): *Provided,* That the standard by which the color and grades of sugar are to be regulated shall be selected and furnished to the collectors of such ports of entry as may be necessary by the Secretary of the Treasury, from time to time. and in such manner as he may deem expedient (187).

422½. On sugar candy, not colored, ten cents per pound (188). On all other confectionery, not otherwise provided for, made wholly or in part of sugar, and on sugars, after being refined, when tinctured, colored, or in any way adulterated, valued at thirty cents per pound or less, fifteen cents per pound. On all confectionery valued above thirty cents per pound, or when sold by the box, package, or otherwise than by the pound, fifty per centum ad valorem (188). On molasses from sugar cane, eight cents per gallon (189). On syrup of sugar-cane juice, melado, concentrated melado, or concentrated molasses, two cents and a half per pound (186): *Provided,* That all syrups of sugar or sugar cane, cane juice, concentrated molasses, or concentrated melado, entered under the name of molasses, or any other name than syrup of sugar, or of sugar cane, cane juice, concentrated molasses, or concentrated melado, shall be liable to forfeiture to the United States. and the same shall be forfeited (189-646).

Sec. 2. *And be it further enacted,* That on and after the day and

---

* The general clauses of this Act cannot be construed to embrace any articles specifically enumerated or mentioned in it or former tariff Acts. (Dec. of Sep. 22. 1864. or Feb. 13. 1865.)

year aforesaid, IN LIEU of the duties heretofore imposed by law on the articles hereinafter mentioned, there shall be levied, collected, and paid, on the goods, wares, and merchandise enumerated and provided for in this section, imported from foreign countries, the following duties and rates of duty, that is to say:

423. On brandy, for first proof, two dollars and fifty cents per gallon (192). On other spirits, manufactured or distilled from grain or other materials, for first proof, two dollars per gallon (192). On cordials, and liqueurs of all kinds, and arrack, absynthe, kirschenwasser, ratifia, and other similar spirituous beverages, not otherwise provided for, two dollars per gallon (192). On bay rum, one dollar and fifty cents per gallon (193-594). On wines of all kinds, valued at not over fifty cents per gallon, twenty cents per gallon and twenty-five per centum ad valorem: valued at over fifty cents and not over one dollar per gallon, fifty cents per gallon and twenty-five per centum ad valorem: valued at over one dollar per gallon, one dollar per gallon and twenty-five per cent. ad valorem (179): *Provided,* That no champagne or sparkling wines, in bottles, shall pay a less rate of duty than six dollars per dozen bottles, each bottle containing not more than one quart and more than one pint, or six dollars per two dozen bottles, each bottle containing not more than one pint (193).

423½. On all spirituous liquors, not otherwise enumerated, one hundred per centum ad valorem (193): *Provided,* That no lower rate or amount of duty shall be levied, collected, and paid, on brandy, spirits, and other spirituous beverages, than that fixed by law for the description of first proof, but shall be increased in proportion for any greater strength than the strength of first proof (193); and no brandy, spirits, or other spirituous beverages under first proof shall pay a less rate of duty than fifty per centum ad valorem: *Provided, further,* That all imitations of brandy, or spirits, or of wines imported by any names whatever, shall be subject to the highest rate of duty provided for the genuine articles respectively intended to be represented, and in no case less than one dollar per gallon (3): *And provided, further,* That brandies, or other spirituous liquors, may be imported in bottles when the packages shall contain not less than one dozen; and all bottles shall pay a separate duty of two cents each, whether containing wines, brandies, or other spirituous liquors subject to duty as hereinbefore mentioned (192).

424. On ale, porter, and beer, in bottles, thirty-five cents per gallon; otherwise than in bottles, twenty cents per gallon (192).

424½. On cigars (190) of all kinds, valued at fifteen dollars or less per thousand, seventy-five cents per pound and twenty per centum ad valorem: valued at over fifteen dollars and not over thirty dollars per thousand, one dollar and twenty-five cents per pound and thirty per centum ad valorem: valued at over thirty dollars and not over forty-five dollars per thousand, two dollars per pound and fifty per centum ad valorem: valued at over forty-five dollars per thousand, three dollars per pound and sixty per centum ad valorem: *Provided,* That paper cigars or cigarettes, including wrappers, shall be subject to the same duties imposed on cigars (190).

425. On snuff and snuff flour, manufactured of tobacco, ground, dry, or damp, and pickled, scented, or otherwise, of all descriptions, fifty cents per pound (191). On tobacco in leaf, unmanufactured and not stemmed, thirty-five cents per pound (191). On tobacco manufactured, of all descriptions, and stemmed tobacco not otherwise provided for, fifty cents per pound (191).

Sec. 3. *And be it further enacted,* That on and after the day and year aforesaid, IN LIEU of the duties heretofore imposed by

law on the articles hereinafter mentioned, there shall be
levied, collected, and paid, on the goods, wares, and merchandise herein enumerated and provided for, imported
from foreign countries, the following duties and rates of
duty, that is to say:

426. On bar iron, rolled or hammered, comprising flats not less
than one inch or more than six inches wide, nor less than three-
eighths of an inch or more than two inches thick; rounds not less
than three-fourths of an inch nor more than two inches in diameter;
and squares not less than three-fourths of an inch nor more than
two inches square, one cent per pound. On bar iron, rolled or
hammered, comprising flats less than three-eighths of an inch or
more than two inches thick or less than one inch or more than six
inches wide; rounds less than three-fourths of an inch or more
than two inches in diameter; and squares less than three-fourths
of an inch or more than two inches square, one cent and one-half
per pound: *Provided*, That all iron in slabs, blooms, loops, or
other forms, less finished than iron in bars, and more advanced
than pig iron, except castings, shall be rated as iron in bars, and
pay a duty accordingly: *And provided, further*, That none of the
above iron shall pay a less rate of duty than thirty-five per centum
ad valorem (194-195).

427. On all iron imported in bars for railroads and inclined
planes, made to patterns and fitted to be laid down on such roads
or planes without further manufacture, sixty cents per one hundred pounds (196). On boiler or other plate iron not less than
three-sixteenths of an inch in thickness, one cent and a half per
pound (196). On iron wire, bright, coppered, or tinned, drawn and
finished, not more than one-fourth of an inch in diameter, nor less
than number sixteen, wire gauge, two dollars per one hundred
pounds, and in addition thereto fifteen per centum ad valorem;
over number sixteen and not over number twenty-five, wire gauge,
three dollars and fifty cents per one hundred pounds, and in addition thereto fifteen per centum ad valorem (197): *Provided*, That
wire covered with cotton, silk, or other material, shall pay five cents
per pound in addition to the foregoing rates (197). On smooth or
polished sheet iron, by whatever name designated, three cents per
pound (211). On sheet iron, common or black, not thinner than
number twenty, wire gauge, one cent and one-fourth of one cent
per pound; thinner than number twenty, and not thinner than
number twenty-five, wire gauge, one cent and a half per pound;
thinner than number twenty-five, wire gauge, one cent and three-
fourths of one cent per pound (212).

428. On tin plates, and iron galvanized or coated with any metal by electric batteries, or otherwise, two cents and a half per pound (213).

429. On all band, hoop, and scroll iron, from one-half to six inches in width, not thinner than one-eighth of an inch, one and one-fourth cent per pound (200). On all band, hoop, and scroll iron, from one-half to six inches wide, under one-eighth of an inch in thickness, and not thinner than number twenty, wire gauge, one and one-half cent per pound (200). On all band, hoop, and scroll · iron, thinner than number twenty, wire gauge, one and three-fourths cent per pound (200).

430. On slit rods one cent and one-half per pound, and on all other descriptions of rolled or hammered iron not otherwise provided for, one cent and one-fourth per pound (200). On locomotive tire, or parts thereof, three cents per pound (214). On mill irons and mill cranks of wrought iron, and wrought iron for ships, steam-engines, and locomotives, or parts thereof, weighing each twenty-five pounds or more, two cents per pound (215). On anvils and on iron cables, or cable chains, or parts thereof, two cents and a half per pound (203-202).

431. On chains, trace chains, halter chains, and fence chains, made of wire or rods, not less than one-fourth of an inch in diameter, two cents and a half per pound; less than one-fourth of one inch in diameter, and not under number nine, wire gauge, three cents per pound; under number nine, wire gauge, thirty-five per centum ad valorem (206).

432. On anchors, or parts thereof, two cents and one-fourth per pound (204). On blacksmiths' hammers (207) and sledges (207), axles (207), or parts thereof, and malleable iron in castings, not otherwise provided for, two cents and a half per pound (8-219).

433. On wrought iron railroad chairs, and wrought iron nuts and washers, ready punched, two cents per pound (210).

434. On bed-screws and wrought iron hinges, two cents and a half per pound (205).

435. On wrought board-nails, spikes, rivets and bolts, two and one-half cents per pound (205).

436. On cut nails and spikes, one and a half cent per pound (201). On horseshoe nails, five cents per pound (208).

437. On cut tacks, brads or sprigs, not exceeding sixteen ounces to the thousand, two and one-half cents per thousand; exceeding sixteen ounces to the thousand, three cents per pound (8-219).

438. On steam, gas, and water *tubs* [tubes] and flues, of wrought iron, two cents and a half per pound (209). ·

439. On screws, commonly called wood-screws, two inches or

over in length, eight cents per pound; less than two inches in length, eleven cents per pound (216). On screws of any other metal than iron, and all other screws of iron, except wood-screws, thirty-five per centum ad valorem (217).

440. On Iron in pigs, nine dollars per ton (6-219).

441. On vessels of cast iron, not otherwise provided for, and on andirons (296), sadirons, tailors' and hatters' irons, stoves and stove plates, of cast iron, one and one-half cent per pound (199).

442. On cast iron, steam, gas, and water-pipe, one and one-half cent per pound (219). On cast iron butts and hinges, two and a half cents per pound (6-219). On hollow ware, glazed or tinned, three and one-half cents per pound (198-314).

443. On all other castings of iron, not otherwise provided for, thirty per centum ad valorem (6-219).

444. On all manufactures of iron, not otherwise provided for, thirty-five per centum ad valorem (218).

445. On old scrap iron, eight dollars per ton: *Provided*, That nothing shall be deemed old iron that has not been in actual use, and fit only to be remanufactured (7-219).

446. On steel, ingots, bars, coils, sheets, and steel wire, not less than one-fourth of one inch in diameter, valued at seven cents per pound or less, two cents and one-fourth per pound; valued at above seven cents, and not above eleven cents per pound, three cents per pound; valued at above eleven cents per pound, three cents and a half per pound, and ten per centum ad valorem (220).

447. On steel wire less than one-fourth of an inch in diameter, and not less than number sixteen, wire gauge, two and one-half cents per pound, and in addition thereto, twenty per centum ad valorem; less or finer than number sixteen, wire gauge, three cents per pound, and in addition thereto twenty per centum ad valorem (220).

448. On steel in any form, not otherwise provided for, thirty per centum ad valorem (220).

449. On skates costing twenty cents or less per pair, eight cents per pair; costing over twenty cents per pair, thirty-five per centum ad valorem (221).

450. On cross-cut saws, ten cents per lineal foot (10-219).

451. On mill, pit, and drag saws, not over nine inches wide, twelve and a half cents per lineal foot (10-219).

452. On all hand-saws not over twenty-four inches in length, seventy-five cents per dozen, and in addition thereto thirty per centum ad valorem; over twenty-four inches in length, one dollar per dozen; and in addition thereto thirty per centum ad valorem (224).

453. On all back-saws not over ten inches in length, seventy-five cents per dozen, and in addition thereto thirty per centum ad valorem; over ten inches in length, one dollar per dozen, and in addition thereto thirty per centum ad valorem (224).

454. On files, file blanks, rasps, and floats of all descriptions, not exceeding ten inches in length, ten cents per pound, and in addition thereto thirty per centum ad valorem; exceeding ten inches in length, six cents per pound, and in addition thereto thirty per centum ad valorem (223).

455. On pen knives, jack knives, and pocket knives of all kinds, fifty per centum ad valorem (371).

456. On needles for knitting or sewing machines, one dollar per thousand, and in addition thereto thirty-five per centum ad valorem (392).

457. On iron squares marked on one side, three cents per pound, and in addition thereto thirty per centum ad valorem; on all other squares of iron or steel, six cents per pound. and thirty per centum ad valorem (222).

458. On all manufactures of steel, or of which steel shall be a component part, not otherwise provided for, forty-five per centum ad valorem (224) : *Provided*, That all 'articles of steel partially manufactured, or of which steel shall be a component part, not otherwise provided for, shall pay the same rate of duty as if wholly manufactured (10-224).

459. On bituminous coal, and shale, one dollar and twenty-five cents for a ton of twenty-eight bushels, eighty pounds to the bushel; on all other coal, forty cents per ton of twenty-eight bushels, eighty pounds to the bushel (225-715). On coke and culm of coal, twenty-five per centum ad valorem (225).

460. On lead, in pigs and bars, two cents per pound (178). On old scrap lead, fit only to be remanufactured, one cent and one-half per pound (12). On' lead in sheets, pipes, or shot, two and three-quarter cents per pound (229).

461. On pewter. when old and fit only to be remanufactured, two cents per pound (12).

462. On lead ore, one and a half cent per pound (317). On copper in pigs, bars, or ingots, two and a half cents per pound (13).

463. On sheathing copper, in sheets forty-eight inches long and fourteen inches wide, weighing from fourteen to thirty-four ounces per square foot, three and a half cents per pound (328-640).

464. On copper rods, bolts, nails, spikes, copper bottoms, copper in sheets or plates, called braziers' copper. and other sheets of copper not otherwise provided for, thirty-five per centum ad valorem (13-66-226).

465. On zinc, spelter, or teutenegue, manufactured in blocks or pigs, one and a half cent per pound (227). On zinc, spelter, or teutenegue in sheets, two and one-quarter cents per pound (228).

466. On diamonds, cameos, mosaics, gems, pearls, rubies, and

other precious stones when not set, a duty of ten per centum ad valorem (70).

Sec. 4. *And be it further enacted,* That on and after the day and year aforesaid, there shall be levied, collected, and paid, on the importation of the articles hereinafter mentioned, the following duties, that is to say :

467. On all wool, unmanufactured, and all hair of the alpaca, goat, and other like animals, unmanufactured, the value whereof at the last port or place from whence exported to the United States, exclusive of charges in such ports, shall be twelve cents or less per pound, three cents per pound ; exceeding twelve cents and not exceeding twenty-four cents per pound, six cents per pound; exceeding twenty-four cents per pound, and not exceeding thirty-two cents, ten cents per pound, and in addition thereto ten per centum ad valorem ; exceeding thirty-two cents per pound, twelve cents per pound, and in addition thereto ten per centum ad valorem: *Provided,* That any wool of the sheep, or hair of the alpaca, the goat, and other like animals, which shall be imported in any other than the ordinary condition, as now and heretofore practised, or which shall be changed in its character or condition for the purpose of evading the duty, or which shall be reduced in value by the admixture of dirt or of any foreign substance, shall be subject to pay a duty of twelve cents per pound and ten per centum ad valorem, anything in this Act to the contrary notwithstanding: *Provided, further,* That when wool of different qualities is imported in the same bale, bag or package, and the aggregate value of the contents of the bale, bag or package shall be appraised by the appraisers at a rate exceeding twenty-four cents per pound, it shall be charged with a duty of ten cents per pound and ten per centum ad valorem ; and when bales of different qualities are embraced in the same invoice at the same price, whereby the average price shall be lessened more than ten per centum, the value of the whole shall be appraised according to the value of the bale of the best quality; and no bale, bag or package shall be liable to a less rate of duty in consequence of being invoiced with wool of lower value: *And provided, further,* That wool which shall be imported scoured, shall pay, in lieu of the duties herein provided, three times the amount of such duties (18).

468. On sheepskins, raw or unmanufactured, imported with the wool on, washed or unwashed, shall be subject to a duty of twenty per centum ad valorem (18) ; and on flocks, waste or shoddy, three cents per pound (275).

Sec. 5. *And be it further enacted,* That on and after the day and year aforesaid, there shall be levied, collected, and paid, on the importation of the articles hereinafter mentioned, the following duties, that is to say :

469. On Wilton, Saxony, and Aubusson, Axminster, patent velvet, Tournay velvet, and tapestry velvet carpets and carpeting, Brussels carpets wrought by the Jacquard machine ; and all medallion or whole carpets, valued at one dollar and twenty-five cents or under per square yard, seventy cents per square yard ; valued at over one dollar and twenty-five cents per square yard, eighty cents per square yard: *Provided,* That no carpeting, carpets, or rugs, of the foregoing description, shall pay a duty of less than fifty per centum ad valorem. On Brussels and tapestry Brussels carpets and carpetings, printed on the warp or otherwise, fifty cents per square yard (330). On all treble ingrain, three-ply and worsted chain Venetian carpets and carpeting, forty cents per square yard. On yarn Venetian and two-ply ingrain carpets and carpeting, thirty-five cents per square yard. On hemp or jute carpeting, six and a half cents per square yard. On druggets, bockings, and felt carpets and carpetings, printed, colored, or otherwise, twenty-five cents per square yard. On carpets and carpeting of wool, flax or cotton, or parts of either, or other material not otherwise specified, forty per centum ad valorem: *Provided,* That mats, rugs, screens, covers, hassocks, bedsides, and other portions of carpets or carpetings, shall be subject to the rate of duty herein imposed on carpets or carpeting of like character or description, and on all other mats, screens, hassocks and rugs, forty-five per centum ad valorem (330).

470. On woollen cloths, woollen shawls, and all manufactures of wool of every description, made wholly or in part of wool; not otherwise provided for, twenty-four cents per pound, and in addition thereto forty per centum ad valorem (331). On goods of like description, when valued at over two dollars per square yard, a duty, in addition to the foregoing rates, of five per centum ad valorem: *Provided,* That goods of like description, composed of worsted, the hair of the alpaca,

goat, or other like animals, and weighing over eight ounces to the square yard, shall be subject to pay the same duty and rates of duty herein provided for woollen cloths. On endless belts or felts for paper, and blanketing for printing machines, twenty cents per pound, and in addition thereto thirty-five per centum ad valorem (833). On flannels (333), uncolored, valued at thirty cents or less per square yard, twenty-four cents per pound, and thirty per centum ad valorem; valued at above thirty cents per square yard, and on all flannels, colored, printed or plaided, not otherwise provided for, and flannels composed in part of cotton, twenty-four cents per pound, and thirty-five per centum ad valorem. On flannels composed in part of silk, fifty per centum ad valorem. On hats of wool (333), twenty-four [cents] per pound, and in addition thereto thirty-five per centum ad valorem. On woollen and worsted yarn (333), valued at fifty cents and not over one dollar per pound, twenty cents per pound, and in addition thereto twenty-five per centum ad valorem; valued at over one dollar per pound, twenty-four cents per pound, and in addition thereto thirty per centum ad valorem. On woollen and worsted yarn, valued at less than fifty cents per pound, and not exceeding in fineness number fourteen, sixteen cents per pound, and in addition thereto twenty-five per centum ad valorem. On clothing, ready made, and wearing apparel of every description, composed wholly or in part of wool, made up or manufactured wholly or in part by the tailor, seamstress or manufacturer, except hosiery, twenty-four cents per pound, and in addition thereto forty per centum ad valorem (334-369). On blankets of all kinds (335), made wholly or in part of wool, valued at not exceeding twenty-eight cents per pound, twelve cents per pound, and in addition thereto twenty per centum ad valorem; valued at above twenty-eight cents and not exceeding forty cents per pound, twenty-four cents per pound and twenty-five per centum ad valorem; valued above forty cents per pound, twenty-four cents per pound and thirty per centum ad valorem. On Balmorals, and goods of a similar description, or used for like purposes, composed of wool, worsted, or any other material, twenty-four cents per pound, and in addition thereto thirty-five per centum ad valorem (334-614).

471. On women's and children's dress goods, composed wholly or in part of wool, worsted, mohair, alpaca or goats' hair, gray or uncolored, not exceeding in value the sum of thirty cents per square yard, four cents per square yard, and in addition thereto twenty-five per centum ad valorem ; exceeding in value thirty cents per square yard, six cents per square yard, and in addition thereto thirty per centum ad valorem (336-20).

472. On all goods of the last mentioned description, if stained, colored or printed, not exceeding in value the sum of thirty cents per square yard, four cents per square yard, and thirty per centum ad valorem ; exceeding in value thirty cents per square yard, six cents per square yard, and in addition thereto thirty-five per centum ad valorem (336-20).

473. On shirts, drawers, and hosiery, of wool, or of which wool shall be a component material, not otherwise provided for, twenty cents per pound, and in addition thereto thirty per centum ad valorem (20-334).

474. On bunting (337), and on all other manufactures of worsted, mohair, alpaca, or goats' hair, or of which worsted, mohair, alpaca, or goats' hair shall be a component material, not otherwise provided for, fifty per centum ad valorem (337).

475. On lastings, mohair cloth, silk, twist, or other manufacture of cloth, woven or made, in patterns of such size, shape and form, or cut in such manner as to be fit for shoes, slippers, boots, bootees, gaiters and buttons, exclusively, not combined with India-rubber, ten per centum ad valorem (146-179).*

476. On oil-cloths for floors, stamped, painted or printed, valued at fifty cents or less per square yard, thirty per centum ad valorem ; valued at over fifty cents per square yard, and on all other oil-cloths, except silk oil-cloth, forty per centum ad valorem (393).

Sec. 6. *And be it further enacted,* That on and after the day and year aforesaid, there shall be levied, collected, and paid, on the importation of the articles hereinafter mentioned, the following duties, that is to say :

477. On cotton, raw or unmanufactured, two cents per pound (304). On all manufactures of cotton, (except jeans, denims, drillings, bed tickings, ginghams, plaids, cottonades, pantaloon stuffs

---

* This paragraph repealed by paragraph 608, and re-enacted by paragraph 629.

and goods of like description,) not bleached, colored, stained, painted or printed, and not exceeding one hundred threads to the square inch, counting the warp and filling, and exceeding in weight five ounces per square yard, five cents per square yard ; if bleached, five cents and a half per square yard ; if colored, stained, painted or printed, five cents and a half per square yard, and in addition thereto ten per centum ad valorem. On finer and lighter goods of like description, exceeding one hundred threads and not exceeding two hundred threads to the square inch, counting the warp and filling, unbleached, five cents per square yard ; if bleached, five and a half cents per square yard ; if colored, stained. painted or printed, five and a half cents per square yard, and in addition thereto twenty per centum ad valorem. On goods of like description. exceeding two hundred threads to the square inch, counting the warp and filling, unbleached, five cents per square yard ; if bleached, five and a half cents per square yard : if colored, stained. painted or printed, five and a half cents per square yard, and in addition thereto twenty per centum ad valorem (339).

478. On all cotton jeans. denims, drillings, bed tickings, ginghams, plaids, cottonades, pantaloon stuffs and goods of like description, or for similar use, if unbleached, and not exceeding one hundred threads to the square inch, counting the warp and filling, and exceeding five ounces to the square yard, six cents per square yard ; if bleached, six and a half cents per square yard ; if colored, stained, painted or printed, six and a half cents per square yard, and in addition thereto ten per centum ad valorem. On finer or lighter goods of like description, exceeding one hundred threads and not exceeding two hundred threads to the square inch, counting the warp and filling, if unbleached, six cents per square yard ; if bleached, six and a half cents per square yard ; if colored, stained, painted or printed, six and a half cents per square yard, and in addition thereto fifteen per centum ad valorem. On goods of like description, exceeding two hundred threads to the square inch, counting the warp and filling, if unbleached, seven cents per square yard ; if bleached, seven and a half cents per square yard ; if colored, stained, painted or printed, seven and a half cents per square yard, and in addition thereto fifteen per centum ad valorem : *Provided,* That upon all plain woven cotton goods, not included in the foregoing schedules, unbleached, valued at over sixteen cents per square yard, bleached, valued at over twenty cents per square yard, colored, valued at over twenty-five cents per square yard, and cotton jeans, denims and drillings, unbleached, valued at over twenty cents per square yard, and all other cotton goods, of every description, the value of which shall exceed twenty-five cents per square yard, there shall be levied, collected, and paid, a duty of thirty-five per centum ad valorem : *And provided, further,* That no cotton goods having more than two hundred threads to the square inch, counting the warp and filling, shall be admitted to a less rate of duty than is provided for goods which are of that number of threads (339).

479. On spool thread of cotton, six cents per dozen spools, containing on each spool not exceeding one hundred yards of thread, and in addition thereto thirty per centum ad valorem ; exceeding one hundred yards, for every additional hundred yards of thread on each spool, or fractional part thereof in excess of one hundred yards, six cents per dozen, and thirty per centum ad valorem (340).

480. On cotton shirts and drawers, woven or made on frames, and on all cotton hosiery, thirty-five per centum ad valorem (341).

481. On cotton velvet, thirty-five per centum ad valorem (341-401). On cotton braids, insertings, lace, trimming or bobbinet, and all other manufactures of cotton, not otherwise provided for, thirty-five per centum ad valorem (371-25). ·

Sec. 7. *And be it further enacted,* That on and after the day and year aforesaid, IN LIEU of the duties heretofore imposed by law on the articles hereinafter mentioned, there shall be levied, collected, and paid, on the goods, wares, and merchandise enumerated and provided for in this section, imported from foreign countries, the following duties and rates of duty, that is to say :

482. On brown and bleached linens, ducks, canvas, paddings, cotton bottoms, burlaps (783), diapers, crash, huckabacks, handkerchiefs, lawns or other manufactures of flax, jute or hemp, or of which flax, jute or hemp shall be the component material of chief value, not

otherwise provided for, valued at thirty cents or less per square yard, thirty-five per centum ad valorem; valued at above thirty cents per square yard, forty per centum ad valorem (343-783). On flax or linen yarn for carpets, not exceeding number eight Lea, and valued at twenty-four cents or less per pound, thirty per centum ad valorem (343). On flax or linen yarns valued at above twenty-four cents per pound, thirty-five per centum ad valorem (343). On flax or linen thread, twine and pack thread, and all other manufactures of flax, or of which flax shall be the component material of chief value, not otherwise provided for, forty per centum ad valorem (343-26-783).

483. On tarred cables or cordage, three cents per pound (345). On untarred Manilla cordage, two and a half cents per pound (345). On all other untarred cordage, three and a half cents per pound (345). On hemp yarns, five cents per pound (345). On coir yarn, one and a half cent per pound (315). On seines, six and a half cents per pound (345).

484. On gunny cloth, gunny bags,* and cotton bagging (674-783), or other manufactures not otherwise provided for, suitable for the uses to which cotton bagging is applied, composed in whole or in part of hemp, jute, flax or other material, valued at ten cents or less per square yard, three cents per pound; over ten cents per square yard, four cents per pound (346). On sail duck or canvas for sails, thirty per centum ad valorem (347). On Russia and other sheetings of flax or hemp, brown and white, thirty-five per centum ad valorem (347). On all other manufactures of hemp, or of which hemp shall be the component material of chief value, not otherwise provided for, thirty per centum ad valorem (347). On grass cloth, thirty per centum ad valorem (347). On jute yarns, twenty-five per centum ad valorem (347). On all other manufactures of jute or Sisal grass, not otherwise provided for, thirty per centum ad valorem (347).

Sec. 8. *And be it further enacted,* That on and after the day and year aforesaid, IN LIEU of the duties heretofore imposed by law on the articles hereinafter mentioned, there shall be levied, collected, and paid, on the goods, wares and merchandise enumerated and provided for in this section, imported from foreign countries, the following duties and rates of duty, that is to say :

485. On spun silk for filling in skeins or cops, twenty-five per centum ad valorem. On silk in the gum not more advanced than singles, tram, and thrown or organzine, thirty-five per centum ad valorem (179). On floss silks, thirty-five per centum ad valorem (179). On sewing silk in the gum, or purified, forty per centum ad

---

* Gunny cloth and gunny bags suitable to the uses to which cotton bagging is applied, pay as cotton bagging under paragraph 674.

valorem (179). On all dress and piece silks, ribbons, and silk velvets, or velvets of which silk is the component material of chief value, sixty per centum ad valorem (179).

486. On silk vestings, pongees, shawls, scarfs, mantillas, pelerines, handkerchiefs, veils, laces, shirts, drawers, bonnets, hats, caps, turbans, chemisettes, hose, mitts, aprons, stockings, gloves, suspenders, watch chains, webbing, braids, fringes, galloons, tassels, cords, and trimmings, sixty per centum ad valorem (179-321).

487. On all manufactures of silk, or of which silk is the component material of chief value, not otherwise provided for, fifty per centum ad valorem (179).

Sec. 9. *And be it further enacted*, That from and after the day and year aforesaid, IN LIEU of the duties heretofore imposed by law on the articles hereinafter mentioned, there shall be levied, collected, and paid, on the goods, wares, and merchandise enumerated and provided for in this section, imported from foreign countries, the following duties and rates of duty; that is to say:

488. On all brown earthenware and common stoneware, gas retorts, stoneware not ornamented, twenty-five per centum ad valorem (348).

489. On China, porcelain, and Parian ware, gilded, ornamented, or decorated in any manner, fifty per centum ad valorem (349).

490. On China, porcelain, and Parian ware, plain white, and not decorated in any manner, forty-five per centum ad valorem; on all other earthen, stone, or crockery ware, white, glazed, edged, printed, painted, dipped, or cream-colored, composed of earthy or mineral substances, not otherwise provided for, forty per centum ad valorem (350).

491. On slates, slate pencils, slate chimney pieces, mantels, slabs for tables, and all other manufactures of slate, forty per centum ad valorem (351).

492. On unwrought clay, pipe clay, fire clay, and kaoline, five dollars per ton (351).

493. On fullers' earth, three dollars per ton (351).

494. On white chalk and cliff stone, ten dollars per ton. On red and French chalk, twenty per centum ad valorem. On chalk of all descriptions, not otherwise provided for, twenty-five per centum ad valorem (352-540).

495. On whiting (265) and Paris white (253), one cent per pound. On whiting ground in oil, two cents per pound (265).

496. On all plain and mould and press glass not cut, engraved, or painted, thirty-five per centum ad valorem (353).

497. On all articles of glass cut, engraved, painted, colored, printed, stained, silvered, or gilded, not including plate glass silvered, or looking-glass plates, forty per centum ad valorem (354).

498. On all unpolished cylinder, crown, and common window glass, not exceeding ten by fifteen inches square, one cent and a half per pound; above that and not exceeding sixteen by twenty-four inches square, two cents [per] pound; above that, and not exceeding twenty-four by thirty inches square, two cents and a half per pound; all above that, three cents per pound (29).

499. On cylinder and crown glass, polished, not exceeding ten by fifteen inches square, two and one-half cents per square foot; above that, and not exceeding sixteen by twenty-four inches square, four cents per square foot; above that, and not exceeding twenty-four by thirty inches square, six cents per square foot; above that, and not exceeding twenty-four by sixty inches, twenty cents per square foot; all above that, forty cents per square foot (29).

500. On fluted, rolled, or rough plate glass, not including crown, cylinder, or common window glass, not exceeding ten by fifteen inches square, seventy-five cents per one hundred square feet; above that, and not exceeding sixteen by twenty-four inches square, one cent per square foot; above that, and not exceeding twenty-four by thirty inches square, one cent and a half per square foot; all above that, two cents per square foot: *Provided,* That all fluted, rolled, or rough plate glass, weighing over one hundred pounds per one hundred square feet, shall pay an additional duty on the excess at the same rates herein imposed (355).

501. On all cast polished plate glass, unsilvered, not exceeding ten by fifteen inches square, three cents per square foot; above that, and not exceeding sixteen by twenty-four inches square, five cents per square foot; above that, and not exceeding twenty-four by thirty inches square, eight cents per square foot; above that, and not exceeding twenty-four by sixty inches square, twenty-five cents per square foot; all above that, fifty cents per square foot (356).

502. On all cast polished plate glass, silvered, or looking-glass plates not exceeding ten by fifteen inches square, four cents per square foot; above that, and not exceeding sixteen by twenty-four inches square, six cents per square foot; above that, and not exceeding twenty-four by thirty inches square, ten cents per square foot; above that, and not exceeding twenty-four by sixty inches square, thirty-five cents per square foot; all above that, sixty cents

5

per square foot: *Provided*, That no looking-glass plates or plate glass, silvered, when framed, shall pay a less rate of duty than that imposed upon similar glass of like description not framed, but shall be liable to pay in addition thereto thirty per centum ad valorem upon such frames (357).

503. On porcelain and Bohemian glass, glass crystals for watches (358-693), paintings on glass or glasses (45), pebbles for spectacles, and all manufactures of glass, or of which glass shall be a component material, not otherwise provided for (497-354-358), and all glass bottles or jars filled with sweetmeats or preserves, not otherwise provided for, forty per centum ad valorem (358-29).

Sec. 10. *And be it further enacted*, That on and after the day and year aforesaid, IN LIEU of the duties heretofore imposed by law on the articles hereinafter mentioned, and on such as may now be exempt from duty, there shall be levied, collected, and paid on the goods, wares, and merchandise enumerated and provided for in this section, imported from foreign countries, the following duties and rates of duties, that is to say :

504. On annatto seed (267), extract of annatto (166), nitrate of barytes (234), carmined indigo (247), crude tien (60), extract of safflower (166), finishing powder (166), gold size (166) and patent size (166), cobalt, oxide of cobalt (128), smalt (160), zaffre (128), and terra alba (14), twenty per centum ad valorem ; on nickel, fifteen per centum ad valorem (281).

505. On albumen (166), asbestos (60), asphaltum (233), crocus colcottra (166), blue or Roman vitriol or sulphate of copper (53), bone or ivory drop black (122), murexide (122), ultramarine (63), Indian red (63), and Spanish brown (14), twenty-five per centum ad valorem.

Sec. 11. *And be it further enacted*, That on and after the day and year aforesaid, IN LIEU of the duties heretofore imposed by law on the articles hereinafter mentioned, there shall be levied, collected, and paid, on goods, wares, and merchandise enumerated and provided for in this section, imported from foreign countries, the following duties and rates of duty, that is to say :

506. On acetic acid, acetous or concentrated vinegar, or pyroligneous acid, exceeding the specific gravity of 1.040, eighty cents per pound; not exceeding the specific gravity of 1.040, known as number eight, twenty-five cents per pound (266-267).

507. On acetate or pyrolignite of ammonia, seventy cents per pound; of baryta, forty cents per pound; of iron, strontia, and zinc, fifty cents per pound; of lead, twenty cents per pound (361); of magnesia and soda, fifty cents per pound ; of lime, twenty-five per centum ad valorem (166).

508. On aniline dyes, one dollar per pound and thirty-five per centum ad valorem (239).

509. On blanefixe (234), enamelled white (234), satin white (234), lime white (239), and all combinations of barytes with acids or water, three cents per pound (234) ; on carmine lake, dry or liquid (239), thirty-five per centum ad valorem ; on French green (239), Paris green (239), mineral green (239), mineral blue (239), and Prussian blue (239), dry or moist, thirty per centum ad valorem.

510. On almonds, six cents per pound; shelled, ten cents per pound (178).

511. On articles not otherwise provided for, made of gold, silver, German silver, or platina, or of which either of these metals shall be a component part, forty per centum ad valorem (383-359).

512. On antimony, crude, and regulus of antimony, ten per centum ad valorem (122).

513. On opium, two dollars and fifty cents per pound (252). On opium prepared for smoking, and the extract of opium, one hundred per centum ad valorem (252).

514. On morphine and its salts, two dollars and fifty cents per ounce (248). On arrow-root, thirty per centum ad valorem (179).

515. On brimstone, crude, six dollars per ton (178). On brimstone, in rolls, or refined, ten dollars per ton (178).

516. On castor beans or seeds, per bushel of fifty pounds, sixty cents (260).

517. On chicory root, four cents per pound; ground, burnt, or prepared, five cents per pound (602).

518. On cassia, twenty cents per pound (235). On cassia buds and ground cassia, twenty-five cents per pound (235). On cinnamon, thirty cents per pound (235). On chloroform, one dollar per pound (108).

519. On collodion and ethers of all kinds, not otherwise provided for, and etherial preparations or extracts, fluid, one dollar per pound (55).

520. On cologne water and other perfumery, of which alcohol forms the principal ingredient, three dollars per gallon, and fifty per centum ad valorem (270-594).

521. On cloves, twenty cents per pound; on clove stems, ten cents per pound (235).

522. On fusel oil, or amylic alcohol, two dollars per gallon (251). On Hoffman's anodyne and spirits of nitric ether, fifty cents per pound (280).

523. On bristles, fifteen cents per pound (300); on hogs' hair, one cent per pound (39) ; on istle or Tampico fibre, one cent per pound (344).

524. On brushes of all kinds, forty per centum ad valorem (364). On honey, twenty cents per gallon (241).

525. On lead, white or red, and litharge, dry or ground in oil,

three cents per pound (294-245). On percussion caps, forty per centum ad valorem (324).

526. On lemons (179), oranges (179), pine apples (155), plantains (179), cocoa-nuts (128) and fruits preserved in their own juice, and fruit juice, twenty-five per centum ad valorem (166).

527. On liquorice root, two cents per pound (244); on liquorice paste or liquorice in rolls, ten cents per pound (244).

528. On nutmegs, fifty cents per pound (248). On mace, forty cents per pound (248).

529. On oils, croton, one dollar per pound (250); olive, in flasks or bottles, and salad, one dollar per gallon (250); castor, one dollar per gallon (250).; cloves, two dollars per pound (251); cognac or œnanthic ether, four dollars per ounce (251).

530. On peanuts, or ground beans, one cent per pound; shelled, one and a half cent per pound (178). On filberts and walnuts, of all kinds, three cents per pound (178).

531. On petroleum and coal illuminating oil, crude, ten cents per gallon (420). On illuminating oil and naphtha, benzine and benzole, refined or produced from the distillation of coal, asphaltum, shale, peat, petroleum, or rock oil, or other bituminous substances used for like purposes, thirty cents per gallon (255).

532. On pimento, and black, white, and red, or cayenne pepper, fifteen cents per pound; on ground pimento and pepper of all kinds, eighteen cents per pound (253-235).

533. On spirits of turpentine, thirty cents per gallon (293). On sulphur, flour of, twenty dollars per ton and fifteen per centum ad valorem (56).

534. On tannin, tannic acid, two dollars per pound (231); on gallic acid, one dollar and fifty cents per pound (231). On santonine, five dollars per pound (268).

535. On salt in sacks, barrels, and other packages, twenty-four cents per one hundred pounds; on salt in bulk, eighteen cents per one hundred pounds (291).

536. On crude saltpetre, two and one-half cents per pound (259). On strychnine and its salts, one dollar and one-half per ounce (285). On taggar's iron, thirty per centum ad valorem (49). On vinegar, ten cents per gallon (15). On watches, gold or silver, twenty-five per centum ad valorem (402).

537. On wood pencils, filled with lead or other materials, fifty cents per gross, and in addition thereto thirty per centum ad valorem (325-113).

538. On ostrich, vulture, cock and other ornamental feathers, crude or not dressed, colored or manufactured, twenty-five per centum ad valorem; when dressed, colored or manufactured, fifty per centum ad valorem (306).

539. On playing cards, costing not over twenty-five cents per pack, twenty-five cents per pack; costing over twenty-five cents per pack, thirty-five cents per pack (325).

Sec. 12. *And be it further enacted,* That on and after the day and year aforesaid, there shall be levied, collected, and paid, a duty of FIFTY PER CENTUM AD VALOREM on the importation of the articles hereinafter mentioned and embraced in this section, that is to say:

540. Anchovies and sardines, preserved in oil or otherwise (71-296). Artificial and ornamental feathers and flowers, or parts thereof, of whatever material composed, not otherwise provided for (307), beads and bead ornaments (75). Billiard chalk (494).

541. Ginger, preserved or pickled (276).

542. Ivory or bone dice, draughts, chess men, chess balls and bagatelle balls (380). Jellies of all kinds (379).

543. On kid or other leather gloves of all descriptions, for men's, women's or children's wear (310). On wooden and other toys for children (372).

Sec. 13. *And be it further enacted,* That on and after the day and year aforesaid, IN LIEU of the duties heretofore imposed by law on the articles hereinafter mentioned, there shall be levied, collected, and paid, on the goods, wares, and merchandise enumerated and provided for in this section, imported from foreign countries, the following duties and rates of duty, that is to say:

544. On books, periodicals, pamphlets, blank-books, bound or unbound, and all printed matter, engravings, bound or unbound, illustrated books and papers, and maps and charts, twenty-five per centum ad valorem (300).

545. On cork, bark or wood, unmanufactured, thirty per centum ad valorem (301). On cork and cork bark, manufactured, fifty per centum ad valorem (301-332).

546. On hatters' furs, not on the skin, and dressed furs on the skin, twenty per centum ad valorem (275). Furs on the skin, undressed, ten per centum ad valorem (37).

547. On fire-crackers, one dollar per box of forty packs, not exceeding eighty to each pack, and in the same proportion for any greater number (308-69). On gutta percha, manufactured, forty per centum ad valorem (280).

548. On gunpowder, and all explosive substances used for mining, blasting, artillery, or sporting purposes, when valued at twenty cents or less per pound, a duty of six cents per pound, and in addition thereto twenty per centum ad valorem; valued above twenty cents per pound, a duty of ten cents per pound, and in addition thereto twenty per centum ad valorem (311).

549. On marble, white statuary, brocatella, sienna and verd-antique, in block, rough or squared, one dollar per cubic foot, and in addition thereto twenty-five per centum ad valorem. On veined marble and marble of all other descriptions, not otherwise provided

for, in block, rough or squared, fifty cents per cubic foot, and in addition thereto twenty per centum ad valorem (318).

550. On mineral or medicinal waters, or waters from springs impregnated with minerals, for each bottle or jug containing not more than one quart, three cents, and in addition thereto twenty-five per centum ad valorem; containing more than one quart, three cents for each additional quart, or fractional part thereof, and in addition thereto twenty-five per centum ad valorem (108-844).

551. On palm-leaf fans, one cent each (374). On pipes, clay, common or white, thirty-five per centum ad valorem (350).

552. On meerschaum, wood, porcelain, lava, and all other tobacco-smoking pipes and pipe-bowls, not herein otherwise provided for, one dollar and fifty cents per gross, and in addition thereto seventy-five per centum ad valorem (390-350).

553. On pipe cases, pipe stems, tips, mouth-pieces and metallic mountings for pipes, and all parts of pipes or pipe fixtures, and all smoker's articles, seventy-five per centum ad valorem (390-383).

554. On pen-tips and pen-holders, or parts thereof, thirty-five per centum ad valorem (325). On pens, metallic, ten cents per gross, and in addition thereto twenty-five per centum ad valorem (325).

555. On soap, fancy, perfumed, honey, transparent, and all descriptions of toilet and shaving soap, ten cents per pound, and in addition thereto twenty-five per centum ad valorem (292). On all soap not otherwise provided for, one cent per pound, and in addition thereto thirty per centum ad valorem (292).

556. On starch, made of potatoes or corn, one cent per pound, and twenty per centum ad valorem (293). On starch, made of rice, or any other material, three cents per pound, and twenty per centum ad valorem (293).

557. On rice, cleaned, two and a half cents per pound; on uncleaned, two cents per pound (326). On paddy, one cent and a half per pound (326).

558. **Sec. 14.** *And be it further enacted,* That on the entry of any vessel, or of any goods, wares, or merchandise, the decision of the collector of customs at the port of importation and entry, as to the rate and amount of duties to be paid on the tonnage of such vessel or on such goods, wares, or merchandise, and the dutiable costs and charges thereon, shall be final and conclusive against all persons interested therein, unless the owner, master, commander, or consignee of such vessel, in the case of duties levied on tonnage, or the owner.

importer, consignee, or agent of the merchandise, in the case of duties levied on goods, wares, or merchandise, or the costs and charges thereon, shall, within ten days after the ascertainment and liquidation of the duties by the proper officers of the customs, as well in cases of merchandise entered in bond, as for consumption, give notice in writing to the collector on each entry, if dissatisfied with his decision, setting forth therein, distinctly and specifically, the grounds of his objection thereto, and shall within thirty days after the date of such ascertainment and liquidation, appeal therefrom to the Secretary of the Treasury, whose decision on such appeal shall be final and conclusive; and such vessel, goods, wares, or merchandise, or costs and charges, shall be liable to duty accordingly, any Act of Congress to the contrary notwithstanding, unless suit shall be brought within ninety days after the decision of the Secretary of the Treasury on such appeal for any duties which shall have been paid before the date of such decision on such vessel, or on such goods, wares, or merchandise, or costs or charges, or within ninety days after the payment of duties paid after the decision of the Secretary. And no suit shall be maintained in any court for the recovery of any duties alleged to have been erroneously or illegally exacted, until the decision of the Secretary of the Treasury shall have been first had on such appeal, unless said decision of the Secretary shall be delayed more than ninety days from the date of such appeal in case of an entry at any port east of the Rocky Mountains, or more than five months in case of an entry west of those mountains (559-560-600).*

559. **Sec. 15.** *And be it further enacted,* That the decision of the respective collectors of customs as to all fees, charges, and exactions of whatever character, other than those mentioned in the next preceding section, claimed by them, or by any of the officers under them, in the performance of their official duty, shall be final and conclusive against all persons interested in such fees, charges, or exactions, unless the like notice that an appeal will be taken from such decision to the Secretary of the Treasury shall be given within ten days from the making of such decision, and unless such appeal shall actually be taken within thirty

* The protest must be in writing, and filed with the Collector within "ten" days after the ascertainment and liquidation of the duties. Failure to protest and not properly followed by appeal will be fatal to a claim for any illegal charges or exactions, and is not excused by the non-receipt of notice of liquidation, when such notice was properly posted in the Custom House, although not seen by the importer. (Decisions of Sept. 17, 1863, Feb. 24, 1868, Dec. 15, 1868, and Oct. 10, 1870.)

days from the making of such decision; and the decision
of the Secretary of the Treasury shall be final and conclusive upon the matter so appealed, unless suit shall be
brought for the recovery of such fees, charges, or exactions,
within the period as provided for in the next preceding
section in regard to duties. And no suit shall be maintained in any court for the recovery of any such fees,
costs, and charges, alleged to have been erroneously or
illegally exacted, until the decision of the Secretary of the
Treasury shall have been first had on such appeal, unless
such decision of the Secretary shall be delayed more than
ninety days from the date of such appeal in case of an entry
at any port east of the Rocky Mountains, nor more than five
months in case of an entry west of those mountains (558-
560-600).

560. **Sec. 16.** *And be it further enacted,* That whenever it shall
be shown to the satisfaction of the Secretary of the Treasury that, in any case of unascertained duties, or duties or
other moneys paid under protest and appeal, as hereinbefore
provided, more money has been paid to the collector, or
person acting as such, than the law requires should have
been paid, it shall be the duty of the Secretary of the
Treasury to draw his warrant upon the Treasury in favor
of the person or persons entitled to the over-payment,
directing the said Treasurer to refund the same out of any
money in the Treasury not otherwise appropriated (559).

561. **Sec. 17.** *And be it further enacted,* That a discriminating
duty of ten per centum ad valorem, in addition to the
duties imposed by law, shall be levied, collected, and paid
on all goods, wares, and merchandise which, on and after
the day this Act shall take effect, shall be imported in ships
or vessels not of the United States: *Provided,* That this
discriminating duty shall not apply to goods, wares, and
merchandise which shall be imported, on and after the day
this Act takes effect, in ships or vessels not of the United
States, entitled, by treaty or any Act or Acts of Congress, to
be entered in the ports of the United States on payment of
the same duties as shall then be paid on goods, wares, and
merchandise imported in ships or vessels of the United
States.*

---

* Chapter 8, part 3, page 65, of Revised Regulations specifies such vessels as are exempt from
such duty. See also Decision of Feb. 25, 1870, and Proclamation of Feb. 25, 1871. (Int. Rev. Rec.
of March 4, 1871.)

562. **Sec. 18.** *And be it further enacted,* That on and after the day and year this Act shall take effect, there shall be levied, collected, and paid on all goods, wares, and merchandise of the growth or produce of countries east of the Cape of Good Hope, (except raw cotton,) when imported from places west of the Cape of Good Hope, a duty of ten per centum, ad valorem, in addition to the duties imposed on any such articles when imported directly from the place or places of their growth or production (581) : *Provided,* That section three of the Act approved August five, eighteen hundred and sixty-one, entitled "An Act to provide increased revenue from imports, to pay interest on the public debt, and for other purposes," and section fourteen of the Act approved July fourteen, eighteen hundred and sixty-two, entitled "An Act increasing temporarily the rates of duties on imports, and for other purposes," be, and the same are hereby, repealed (180-404-416).

563. **Sec. 19.** *And be it further enacted,* That all goods, wares, and merchandise which may be in the public stores or bonded warehouses on the day and year this Act shall take effect shall be subjected to no other duty upon the entry thereof for consumption than if the same were imported respectively after that day, and so much of the Act of August sixth, eighteen hundred and forty-six, or any other Act, as requires the sale of fire-crackers, or prohibits their deposit in bonded warehouse, is hereby repealed.

564. **Sec. 20.** *And be it further enacted,* That the joint resolution " to increase temporarily the duties on imports," approved April twenty-ninth, eighteen hundred and sixty-four, shall not be deemed to have taken effect until after the thirtieth day of April, eighteen hundred and sixty-four, and shall be and remain in force until and including the thirtieth day of June, eighteen hundred and sixty-four, and any duties which shall have been exacted and received, contrary to the provisions of this section, shall be refunded by the Secretary of the Treasury (421½-573½).

565. **Sec. 21.** *And be it further enacted,* That, during the period of one year from the passage of this Act, there may be imported into the United States, free of duty, any machinery designed for and adapted to the manufacture of woven fabrics from the fibre of flax or hemp, including all the preliminary processes requisite therefor; and that steam agricultural machinery and implements may be imported free from duty for one year from the passage of this Act (149-586).

566. **Sec. 22.** *And be it further enacted,* That all Acts and parts of Acts repugnant to the provisions of this Act be and the same are hereby repealed : *Provided,* That the existing laws shall extend to and be in force for the collection of the duties imposed by this Act for the prosecution and punishment of all offences, and for the recovery, collection, distribution, and remission of all fines, penalties, and forfeitures, as fully and effectually as if every regulation, penalty, forfeiture, provision, clause, matter, and thing to that effect in the existing laws contained, had been inserted in, and re-enacted by this Act : *And provided, further,* THAT THE DUTIES UPON ALL GOODS, WARES, AND MERCHANDISE IMPORTED FROM FOREIGN COUNTRIES NOT PROVIDED FOR IN THIS ACT, SHALL BE AND REMAIN AS THEY WERE, ACCORDING TO EXISTING LAWS PRIOR TO THE TWENTY-NINTH OF APRIL, EIGHTEEN HUNDRED AND SIXTY-FOUR (166).*

* The general clauses of this Act cannot be construed to embrace any articles specifically enumerated or mentioned in it or former tariff Acts. (Decision of September 22, 1864, or February 13, 1865).

567. **Sec. 23.** *And be it further enacted,* That, on and after the day and year this Act shall take effect, it shall be lawful for the owner, consignee, or agent of any goods, wares, or merchandise which shall have been actually purchased, or procured otherwise than by purchase, at the time when he shall produce his original invoice, or invoices, to the collector, and make and verify his written entry of his goods, wares, and merchandise, as provided by section thirty-six of the Act of March two, seventeen hundred and ninety-nine, entitled, " An Act to regulate the collection of duties on imports and tonnage," and not afterwards, to make such addition in the entry to the cost or value given in the invoice as, in his opinion, may raise the same to the true market value of such goods, wares, and merchandise in the principal markets of the country whence they shall have been imported, and to add thereto all costs and charges which, under existing laws, would form part of the true value at the port where the same may be entered, upon which the duties should be assessed. And it shall be the duty of the collector, within whose district the same may be imported, or entered, to cause the dutiable value of such goods, wares, and merchandise to be appraised, estimated, and ascertained, in accordance with the provisions of existing laws. And if the •appraised value thereof shall exceed, by ten per centum, or more, the value so declared on the entry, then, in addition to the duties imposed by law on the same, there shall be levied, collected, and paid a duty of twenty per centum ad valorem on such appraised value : *Provided,* That the duty shall not be assessed upon an amount less than the invoice or entered value, any law of Congress to the contrary notwithstanding : *And provided, further,* That, on and after the day and year aforesaid, the eighth section of the Act entitled "An Act reducing the duty on imports, and for other purposes,"_ approved July thirty, eighteen hundred and forty-six, and the Act amendatory thereof, approved March three, eighteen hundred and fifty-seven, be, and the same are hereby, repealed (602-582).

568. **Sec. 24.** *And be it further enacted,* That in determining the valuation of goods imported into the United States from foreign countries, except as hereinbefore provided, upon which duties imposed by any existing laws are to be assessed, the actual value of such goods on shipboard at the last place of shipment to the United States shall be deemed the

dutiable value. And such value shall be ascertained by
adding to the value of such goods at the place of growth,
production, or manufacture, the cost of transportation, shipment, and transhipment, with all the expenses included, from
the place of growth, production, or manufacture, whether by
land or water, to the vessel in which shipment is made to
the United States, the value of the sack, box, or covering
of any kind, in which such goods are contained, commission
at the usual rate, in no case less than two and one-half per
centum, brokerage, and all export duties, together with all
costs and charges, paid or incurred for placing said goods
on shipboard, and all other proper charges specified by
law (170-602).

569. **Sec. 25.** *And be it further enacted*, That so much of section
twenty-three of the Act entitled "An Act to provide for
the payment of outstanding Treasury notes, to authorize a
loan, to regulate and fix the duties on imports, and for other
purposes," approved March two, eighteen hundred and sixty-
one, as exempts from duty all philosophical apparatus and
instruments imported for the use of any society incorporated
for philosophical, literary, or religious purposes, or for the
encouragement of the fine arts, or for the use, or by the
order of any college, academy, school, or seminary of learning in the United States, is hereby repealed. And the
same shall be subject to a duty of fifteen per centum ad
valorem (121-730).

570. **Sec. 26.** *And be it further enacted*, That when any cask,
barrel, carboy, or other vessel of American manufacture,
exported or sent out of the country, filled with the products
of the United States, shall be returned to the United States
empty, the same shall be admitted free of duty, under such
rules and regulations as may be prescribed by the Secretary
of the Treasury (805).

571. **Sec. 27.** *And be it further enacted*, That on and after
January first, eighteen hundred and sixty-five, the invoices
of all goods, wares, and merchandise, imported into the
United States, shall be made out in the weights or measures
of the country or place from which the importations shall
be made, and shall contain a true statement of the actual
weights or measures of such goods, wares, and merchandise,
without any respect to the weights or measures of the United
States.

572. **Sec. 28.** (This section does not relate to import duties.)

573. **Sec. 29.** *And be it further enacted,* That any baggage or personal effects arriving in the United States in transit to any foreign country, may be delivered by the parties having it in charge to the collector of customs, to be by him retained, without the payment or exaction of any import duty, and to be delivered to such parties on their departure for their foreign destination, under such rules, regulations, and fees as the Secretary of the Treasury may prescribe.

JOINT RESOLUTION OF JUNE 27, 1864.

(From U. S. Statutes at Large, vol. 13, p. 411.)

JOINT RESOLUTION to continue in force the Joint Resolution entitled "Joint Resolution to increase temporarily the Duties on Imports," approved April twenty-ninth, eighteen hundred and sixty-four.

573½. *Be it resolved by the Senate and House of Representatives of the United States of America in Congress assembled,* That the joint resolution increasing the duties on imports, approved April twenty-ninth, eighteen hundred and sixty-four, be, and is hereby, continued in force until the first day of July next (421½-564).

ACT OF MARCH 3, 1865.

(From U. S. Statutes at Large, vol. 13, p. 491, &c.)

AN ACT amendatory of certain Acts imposing Duties upon Foreign Importations.

Be it enacted by the Senate and House of Representatives of the United States of America in Congress assembled, That section six of an Act entitled "An Act to increase the duties on imports, and for other purposes," approved June thirty, eighteen hundred and sixty-four, be amended, so that paragraphs second, third, and fourth, of section six of said Act, shall read as follows:

574. On all manufactures of cotton (except jeans, denims, drillings, bed-tickings, ginghams, plaids, cottonades, pantaloon stuff, and goods of like description) not bleached, colored, stained, painted, or printed, and not exceeding one hundred threads to the square inch, counting the warp and filling, and exceeding in weight five ounces per square yard, five cents per square yard; if bleached, five cents and a half per square yard; if colored, stained, painted, or printed, five cents and a half per square yard, and. in addition thereto, ten per centum ad valorem. On finer and lighter goods of like description, not exceeding two hundred threads to the square inch, counting the warp and filling, unbleached, five cents per square yard; if bleached, five and a half cents per square yard; if colored, stained, painted, or printed, five and a half cents per square yard, and, in addition thereto, twenty per centum ad valorem. On goods of like description, exceeding two hundred threads to the square inch, counting the warp and filling, unbleached, five cents per square yard; if bleached, five and a half cents per square yard; if colored, stained, painted, or printed, five and a half cents per square yard, and, in addition thereto, twenty per centum ad valorem (477).

575. On all cotton jeans, denims, drillings, bed-tickings, ginghams, plaids, cottonades, pantaloon stuffs, and goods of like description, or for similar use, if unbleached, and not exceeding one hundred threads to the square inch, counting the warp and filling, and exceeding five ounces to the square yard, six cents per square yard; if bleached, six cents and a half per square yard; if colored, stained, painted, or printed, six cents and a half per square yard, and, in addition thereto, ten per centum ad valorem. On finer or lighter goods of like description, not exceeding two hundred threads to the square inch, counting the warp and filling, if unbleached, six cents per square yard; if bleached, six and a half cents per square yard; if colored, stained, painted, or printed, six and a half cents per square yard, and, in addition thereto, fifteen per centum ad valorem. On goods of lighter description, exceeding two hundred threads to the square inch, counting the warp and filling, if unbleached, seven cents per square yard; if bleached, seven and a half cents per square yard; if colored, stained, painted, or printed, seven and a half cents per square yard, and, in addition thereto, fifteen per centum ad valorem: *Provided*, That upon all plain woven cotton goods, not included in the foregoing schedule, unbleached, valued at over sixteen cents per square yard, bleached, valued at over twenty cents per square yard, colored, valued at over twenty-five cents per square yard, and cotton jeans, denims, and drillings, unbleached, valued at over twenty cents per square

yard, and all other cotton goods of every description, the value of which shall exceed twenty-five cents per square yard, there shall be levied, collected, and paid a duty of thirty-five per centum ad valorem : *And provided further*, That no cotton goods having more than two hundred threads to the square inch, counting the warp and filling, shall be admitted to a less rate of duty than is provided for goods which are of that number of threads (478).

576. On spool thread of cotton, six cents per dozen spools, containing on each spool not exceeding one hundred yards of thread, and, in addition thereto, thirty per centum ad valorem ; exceeding one hundred yards, for every additional hundred yards of thread on each spool or fractional part thereof, in excess of one hundred yards, six cents per dozen, and thirty-five per centum ad valorem (479).

On cotton thread or yarn when advanced beyond single yarn, by twisting two or more strands together, if not wound upon spools, four (4) cents per skein or hank of eight hundred and forty (840) yards, and thirty per cent. ad valorem (479).

Sec. 2. *And be it further enacted,* That from and after the day when this Act takes effect, IN ADDITION to the duties heretofore imposed by law on the importation of the articles mentioned in this section, there shall be levied, collected, and paid the following duties and rates of duty, that is to say :

577. On brandy, rum, gin, and whiskey, and on cordials, liquors, [liqueurs] arrack, absynthe, and all other spirituous liquors and spirituous beverages, fifty cents per gallon, of first proof and less strength, and shall be increased in proportion for any greater strength that [than] the strength of first proof (423). On spun silk for filling in skins [skeins] or cops, ten per centum ad valorem (485). On iron bars for railroads or inclined planes, ten cents per one hundred pounds (427). On wrought-iron tubes. one cent per pound (438).

Sec. 3. *And be it further enacted,* That from and after this Act takes effect, IN LIEU of the duties heretofore imposed by law on the importation of the articles mentioned in this section, there shall be levied, collected, and paid the following duties and rates of duty, that is to say :

578. On cotton, five cents per pound (477). On illuminating oil and naphtha, benzine, and benzole, refined or produced from the distillation of coal, asphaltum, shale, peat, petroleum, or rock oil, or other bituminous substances used for like purposes, forty cents per gallon (531). On crude petroleum, or rock oil, twenty cents per gallon (531) ; on crude coal oil, fifteen cents per gallon (531). On tobacco stems, fifteen cents per pound (425). On ready-made clothing of silk, or of which silk shall be a component material of chief value, sixty per centum ad valorem (487-369) On quicksilver, fifteen per centum ad valorem (46).

579. Sec. 4. *And be it further enacted,* That section fifteen of an Act entitled "An Act increasing temporarily the duties on imports, and for other purposes," approved July fourteen, eighteen hundred and sixty-two, be, and the same hereby is, amended so as to impose a tax or tonnage duty of thirty cents per ton, IN LIEU of "ten cents," as therein mentioned: *Provided,* That the receipts of vessels paying tonnage duty shall not be subject to the tax provided in section one hundred and three of "An Act to provide internal revenue to support the government, to pay interest on the public debt, and for other purposes," approved June thirtieth, eighteen hundred and sixty-four, nor by any Act amendatory thereof: *Provided further,* That no ship, vessel, or steamer, having a license to trade between different districts of the United States, or to carry on the bank, whale, or other fisheries, or [nor] on any ship, vessel, or steamer to or from any port or place in Mexico, the British Provinces of North America, or any of the West India Islands, or in all these trades, shall be required to pay the tonnage duty, contemplated by this Act, more than once a year (595-404½-418).

580. Sec. 5. *And be it further enacted,* That the term "statuary," as used in the laws now in force imposing duties on foreign importations, shall be understood to include professional productions of a statuary or of a sculptor only. (See decision of December 15, 1869).

581. Sec. 6. *And be it further enacted,* That there shall be hereafter collected and paid on all goods, wares, and merchandise of the growth or produce of countries [east] of the Cape of Good Hope, (except raw cotton and raw silk, as reeled from the cocoon, or not further advanced than tram, thrown, or organzine,) when imported from places west of the Cape of Good Hope, a duty of ten per centum ad valorem, in addition to the duties imposed on any such article when imported directly from the place or places of their growth or production (562-782).*

582. Sec. 7. *And be it further enacted,* That in all cases where there is or shall be imposed any ad valorem rate of duty on any goods, wares, or merchandise imported into the United States, and in all cases where the duty imposed by law shall be regulated by, or directed to be estimated or based upon, the value of the square yard, or of any specified quantity or parcel of such goods, wares, or merchandise, it shall be the duty of the collector, within whose district the same shall be imported or entered, to cause the actual market value, or wholesale price thereof, at the period of the exportation to the United States, in the principal markets of the country from which the same shall have been imported into the United States, to be appraised, and such appraised value shall be considered the value upon which duty shall be assessed That it shall be lawful for the owner, consignee, or agent of any goods, wares, or merchandise, which shall have been actually purchased, or procured otherwise than by purchase, at the time, and not afterwards, when he shall produce his original invoice, or invoices, to the collector and make and verify his written entry of his goods, wares, or merchandise, as provided by section thirty-six of the Act of March two, seventeen hundred and ninety-nine, entitled "An Act to regulate the collection of duties on imports and tonnage," to make such addition in the entry to the cost or value given in the invoice as in his opinion may raise the same to the actual market value or wholesale price of such goods, wares, or merchandise, at the period of exportation to the United States, in the principal markets of the country from which the same shall have been imported; and it shall be the duty of the collector, within whose district the same may be imported or entered, to cause such actual market value or wholesale price to be appraised in accordance with the provisions of existing laws, and if such appraised value shall exceed by ten per centum or more the value so declared in the entry, then, in addition to the duties imposed by law on the same, there shall be levied, collected, and paid a duty of twenty per centum ad valorem on such appraised value: *Provided*, That the duty shall not be assessed upon an amount less than the invoice or entered value, any Act of Congress to the contrary notwithstanding: *And provided further*, That the sections twenty-third and twenty-fourth of the Act approved June thirtieth, eighteen hundred and sixty-four, entitled "An Act to increase duties on imports, and for other purposes," and all Acts and parts of Acts requiring duties to be assessed upon commissions, brokerage, costs of transportation, shipment, transhipment, and other like costs and charges incurred in placing any goods, wares, or merchandise on shipboard, and all Acts or parts of Acts inconsistent with the provisions of this Act, are hereby repealed (170-174-406-567-568-602).

583. **Sec. 8.** *And be it further enacted*, That so much of an Act entitled "An Act to authorize protection to be given to citizens of the United States who may discover deposits of guano," approved August eighteen, eighteen hundred and fifty-six, as prohibits the exports thereof, is hereby suspended in relation to all persons who have complied with the provisions of section second of said Act for two years from and after July fourteenth, eighteen hundred and sixty-five (417-596).

584. **Sec. 9.** *And be it further enacted*, That this Act shall take effect on and after the first day [of] April, eighteen hundred and sixty-five.

585. **Sec. 10.** *And be it further enacted*, That so much of sections thirty-nine, forty, forty-one, forty-two, forty-three, and forty-four of the Act entitled "An Act to regulate the [collection of] duties on imports and tonnage," approved March second, seventeen hundred and ninety-nine, as requires the branding or marking and certifying of casks, chests, vessels, and cases containing distilled spirits, or teas, be and the same is hereby revived, to be executed under such rules and regulations as shall be prescribed by the Secretary of the Treasury.

586. **Sec. 11.** *And be it further enacted*, That flax and hemp machinery and steam agricultural machinery, as designated in section 21 [twenty-one] of the Act "to increase duties on imports, and for other purposes," approved June thirtieth, eighteen hundred and sixty-four, may be imported free from duty for one year from the passage of this Act (565).

587. **Sec. 12.** *And be it further enacted*, That in all proceedings brought by the United States in any court for due recovery as well of duties upon imports alone as of penalties for the non-payment thereof, the judgment shall recite that the same is rendered for duties, and such judgment, interest, and costs shall be payable in the coin by law receivable for duties, and the execution issued on such judgment shall set forth that the recovery is for duties, and shall require the marshal to satisfy the same in the coin by law receivable for duties; and in case of levy upon and sale of the property of the judgment debtor, the marshal shall refuse payment from any purchaser at such sale in any other money than that specified in the execution.

588. **Sec. 13.** *And be it further enacted*, That the eighth section of the Act of March twenty-third, [eight] eighteen hundred and fifty-four, "to extend the warehousing system by estab-

6

lishing private bonded warehouses, and for other purposes," which authorized the Secretary of the Treasury, in case of the actual injury or destruction of goods, wares, or merchandise by accidental fire or other casualty, while in warehouse under bond, &c., to abate or refund the duties paid or accruing thereon, be extended so as to include goods, wares, or merchandise injured or destroyed in like manner while in the custody of the officers of the customs, and not in bond, and also to goods, wares, and merchandise so injured or destroyed after their arrival within the limits of any port of entry of the United States, and before the same have been *bonded* [landed] under the *suspension* [supervision] of the officers of the customs: *Provided,* That this Act shall apply only to cases arising from and after its passage, and to cases where the duties have not already been paid.

ACT OF MARCH 14, 1866.

(From U. S. Statutes at Large, vol. 14, page 8, &c.)

AN ACT to extend the time for the withdrawal of goods for consumption from public store and bonded warehouse, and for other purposes.

589. *Be it enacted by the Senate and House of Representatives of the United States of America in Congress assembled,* That on and after the passage of this Act, and until the first day of May, eighteen hundred and sixty-six, any goods, wares, or merchandise under bond, in any public or private bonded warehouse, upon which the duties are unpaid, may be withdrawn for consumption, and the bonds cancelled, on payment of the duties and charges prescribed by law; and any goods, wares, or merchandise deposited in bond, in any public or private bonded warehouse, on and after the first day of May aforesaid, and all goods, wares, or merchandise remaining in warehouse, under bond, on said first day of May, may be withdrawn for consumption within one year from the date of original importation, on payment of the duties and charges to which they may be subject by law at the time of such withdrawal; and after the expiration of

one year from the date of original importation, and until the expiration of three years from said date, any goods, wares, or merchandise, in bond as aforesaid, may·be withdrawn for consumption on payment of the duties assessed on the original entry and charges, and an additional duty of ten per centum of the amount of such duties and charges (410-603).* (Decision of March 28, 1868).

590. **Sec. 2.** *And be it further enacted,* That neither this nor any other Act shall operate to prevent the exportation of bonded goods, wares, or merchandise from warehouse within three years from the date of original importation, nor their transportation in bond from the port into which they were originally imported to any other port or ports for the purpose of exportation; and all Acts and parts of Acts inconsistent with the provisions of this Act are hereby repealed.

ACT OF MARCH 16, 1866.

(From U. S. Statutes at Large, vol. 14, p. 9.)

AN ACT further to secure American citizens certain privileges under the Treaty of Washington.

590½. *Be it enacted by the Senate and House of Representatives of the United States of America in Congress assembled,* That the produce of the forests of the State of Maine upon the Saint John river and its tributaries, owned by American citizens, and sawed or hewed in the Province of New Brunswick by American citizens, (the same being unmanufactured in whole or in part,) which is now admitted into the ports of the United States free of duty, shall continue to be so admitted under such regulations as the Secretary of the Treasury shall from time to time prescribe (591½).

Sec. 2. *And be it further enacted,* That this Act shall take effect from and after the seventeenth day of March, eighteen hundred and sixty-six.

*Goods in bonded warehouse are at the risk and expense of the owner. (Dec. of Nov. 25, 1870, Jan. 28, 1870, and Jan. 25, 1870.)

ACT OF MAY 16, 1866.

(From U. S. Statutes at Large, vol. 14, p. 48.)

AN ACT imposing a duty on live animals.

591. *Be it enacted by the Senate and House of Representatives of the United States of America in Congress assembled,* That on and after the passage of this Act, there shall be levied, collected, and paid, on all horses, mules, cattle, sheep, hogs, and other live animals imported from foreign countries, a duty of twenty per centum ad valorem (122): *Provided,* That any such animals now bona fide owned by resident citizens of the United States, and now in any of the provinces of British America, may be imported into the United States free of duty until the expiration of ten days next after the passage of this Act.

ACT OF JUNE 1, 1866.

(From U. S. Statutes at Large, vol. 14, p. 56.)

AN ACT to protect American citizens engaged in Lumbering on the St. Croix river, in the State of Maine.

591½. *Be it enacted by the Senate and House of Representatives of the United States of America in Congress assembled,* That the produce of the forests of the State of Maine upon the St. Croix river and its tributaries, owned by American citizens, and sawed in the province of New Brunswick by American citizens, (the same being unmanufactured in whole, or part,) and having paid the same taxes as other American lumber on that river, shall be admitted into the ports of the United States free of duty, under such regulations as the Secretary of the Treasury shall from time to time prescribe (590½).

Sec. 2. *And be it further enacted,* That this Act shall take effect from and after its passage.

ACT OF JULY 28, 1866.

(From U. S. Statutes at Large, vol. 14, p. 328, &c.)

AN ACT to protect the Revenue, and for other purposes.

Be it enacted by the Senate and House of Representatives of the United States of America in Congress assembled, That from and after the tenth day of August, eighteen hundred and sixty-six, IN LIEU of the duties now imposed by law on the articles mentioned and embraced in this section, there shall be levied, collected, and paid, on all goods, wares, and merchandise imported from foreign countries, the duties *heretofore* [hereinafter] provided, viz.:

592. On cigars, cigarettes, and cheroots of all kinds, three dollars per pound, and, in addition thereto, fifty per centum ad valorem (421½): *Provided,* That paper cigars and cigarettes, including wrappers, shall be subject to the same duties as are herein imposed upon cigars: *And provided further,* That on and after the first day of August, eighteen hundred and sixty-six, no cigars shall be imported unless the same are packed in boxes of not more than five hundred cigars in each box ; and no entry of any imported cigars shall be allowed of less quantity than three thousand in a single package ; and all cigars on importation shall be placed in public store or bonded warehouse, and shall not be removed therefrom until the same shall have been inspected and a stamp affixed to each box indicating such inspection, with the date thereof. And the Secretary of the Treasury is hereby authorized to provide the requisite stamps, and to make all necessary regulations for carrying the above provisions of law into effect ;

593. On cotton, three cents per pound (578):

594. On all compounds or preparations of which distilled spirits is a component part of chief value, there shall be levied a duty not less than that imposed upon distilled spirits : *Provided,* That brandy and other spirituous liquors may be imported in casks or other packages of any capacity not less than thirty gallons; and that wine in bottles may be imported in boxes containing not less than one dozen bottles of not more than one quart each ; and wine, brandy, or other spirituous liquor imported into the United States, and shipped after the first day of October, eighteen hundred and sixty-six, in any less quantity than herein provided for, shall be forfeited to the United States (577).

595. **Sec. 2.** *And be it further enacted,* That, the second proviso in section four of an Act entitled " An Act amendatory of

certain Acts imposing duties upon foreign importations,"
approved March three, eighteen hundred and sixty-five,
shall be construed to include any ship, vessel, or steamer to
or from any port in the Sandwich Islands or Society
Islands (579).

596. **Sec. 3.** *And be it further enacted,* That so much of an Act entitled "An Act to authorize protection to be given to citizens of the United States who may discover deposits of
guano," approved August eighteen, eighteen hundred and fifty-six, as prohibits the export
thereof, is hereby suspended in relation to all persons who have complied with the provisions of section second of said Act, for five years from and after the fourteenth day of
July, eighteen hundred and sixty-seven (583). (This section continued in force for "ten
years " from and after July 14, 1867, by Act of April 2, 1872.)

597. **Sec. 4.** *And be it further enacted,* That all laws and parts
of laws allowing fishing bounties to vessels hereafter
licensed to engage in the fisheries be, and the same are
hereby, repealed : *Provided,* That, from and after the date
of the passage of [t]his Act, vessels licensed to engage in
the fisheries may take on board imported salt in bond to be
used in curing fish, under such regulations as the Secretary
of the Treasury shall prescribe, and upon proof that said
salt has been used in curing fish, the duties on the same
shall be remitted (875).

598. **Sec. 5.** *And be it further enacted,* That, from and after the
passage of this Act, all goods, wares, or merchandise arriving
at the ports of New York, Boston, and Portland, or any other
port of the United States which may be specially designated
by the Secretary of the Treasury, and destined for places
in the adjacent British provinces, or arriving at the port of
Point Isabel, Texas, or any other port of the United States
which may be specially designated by the Secretary of the
Treasury, and destined for places in the republic of Mexico,
may be entered at the custom-house, and conveyed, in transit, through the territory of the United States, without the
payment of duties, under such rules, regulations, and conditions for the protection of the revenue as the Secretary
of the Treasury may prescribe.

599. **Sec. 6.** *And be it further enacted,* That imported goods,
wares, or merchandise in bond, or duty-paid, and products
or manufactures of the United States, may, with the consent
of the proper authorities of the provinces or republic aforesaid, be transported from one port or place in the United
States to another port or place therein, over the territory
of said provinces or republic, by such routes, and under

such rules, regulations and conditions as the Secretary of
the Treasury may prescribe; and the goods, wares, and
merchandise, so transported, shall, upon arrival in the
United States from the provinces or republic aforesaid, be
treated in regard to the liability to or exemption from
duty, or tax, as if the transportation had taken place
entirely within the limits of the United States.*

600. **Sec. 7.** *And be it further enacted,* That whenever it shall
be shown to the satisfaction of the Secretary of the
Treasury that more moneys have been paid to the collector
of customs, or others acting as such, than the law requires,
and the parties have failed to comply with the requirements
of the fourteenth and fifteenth sections of the Act entitled
"An Act to increase the duties on imports, and for other
purposes," approved June thirtieth, eighteen hundred and
sixty-four, and the Secretary of the Treasury shall be satisfied that said non-compliance with the requirements as
above stated was owing to circumstances beyond the control
of the importer, consignee, or agent making such payments,
he may draw his warrant upon the Treasurer in favor of the
person or persons entitled to the overpayment, directing the
said Treasurer to refund the same out of any money in the
Treasury not otherwise appropriated (558-559-560).

601. **Sec. 8.** (This section does not relate to import duties).

602. **Sec. 9.** *And be it further enacted,* That in determining the
dutiable value of merchandise hereafter imported, there
shall be added to the cost, or to the actual wholesale price
or general market value at the time of exportation in the
principal markets of the country from whence the same
shall have been imported into the United States, the cost
of transportation,† shipment, and transhipment, with all
the expenses included from the place of growth, production,
or manufacture, whether by land or water, to the vessel in
which shipment is made to the United States; the value
of the sack, box, or covering of any kind in which such
goods are contained; commission at the usual rates, but in
no case less than two and a half per centum;‡ brokerage,
export duty, and all other actual or usual charges for
putting up, preparing, and packing for transportation or
shipment. And all charges of a general character incurred
in the purchase of a general invoice shall be distributed

---

*See Act of June 4, 1872. † Decision of March 28, 1868, March 9, 1870. ‡ Decision of Aug. 8, 1868.

pro rata among all parts of such invoice; and every part thereof charged with duties based on value shall be advanced according to its proportion, and all wines or other articles paying specific duty by grades shall be graded and pay duty according to the actual value so determined : *Provided,* That all additions made to the entered value of merchandise for charges shall be regarded as part of the actual value of such merchandise, and if such addition shall exceed by ten per centum the value so declared in the entry, in addition to the duties imposed by law, there shall be levied, collected, and paid a duty of twenty per centum on such value : *Provided,* That the duty shall in no case be assessed upon an amount less than the invoice or entered value : *Provided further,* That nothing herein contained shall apply to long-combing or carpet wools costing twelve cents or less per pound, unless the charges so added shall carry the cost above twelve cents per pound, in which case, one cent per pound duty shall be added (170-174-406-582-567-568).*

603. **Sec. 10.** *And be it further enacted,* That the second proviso in section twenty-one of an Act entitled "An Act increasing temporarily the duties on imports, and for other purposes," approved July fourteen, eighteen hundred and sixty-two, which provides that any goods remaining in public store or bonded warehouse beyond three years shall be regarded as abandoned to the Government, and sold under such regulations as the Secretary of the Treasury may prescribe, and the proceeds paid into the treasury, be, and the same is hereby, amended so as to authorize the Secretary of the Treasury, in case of any sale under the said provision, to pay to the owner, consignee, or agent of such goods, the proceeds thereof, after deducting duties, charges, and expenses, in conformity with the provision of the first section of the warehouse Act of August six, eighteen hundred and forty-six (589).

---

* "Consular fees for verification of invoices are not dutiable charges." (Rev. Reg. part 4, page 47.)

"The usual rate of commission on cutlery from Sheffield is not less than 5 per ct., the addition of but 2½ per ct. to the invoice by the importer, is insufficient."—(Dec. of March 20, 1869.)

"Bill brokerage, or the charge made by a broker for selling a bill of exchange to pay for goods purchased, and the cost of stamps upon such bills under foreign revenue laws are not dutiable charges."—(Dec. of Sept. 30, 1870.)

"The dutiable value of malt imported from Canada will, hereafter, be taken at its value in bond in that country; the same rule will be held applicable to tea, coffee, wine, &c., exported from England to the United States, which are chargeable with duty on their entry into consumption in that country, but which is not exacted on the exportation thereof from bond, and also to any other importation similarly situated."—(Dec. of Jan. 5, 1871.)

"Cost of telegrams is not a dutiable charge."—(Dec. of Nov. 14, 1870.)

"The usual rate of commission on French goods is 3 per ct., except on such articles as bronzes, and dec'd china ware, on which the commission is generally 5 per ct."—(Dec. of July 23, 1870.)

604. **Sec. 11.** *And be it further enacted,* That during [the] period of one year from the passage of this Act, there may be imported into the United States, free of duty, any machinery designed solely for and adapted to the manufacture of sugar from beets, including all the preliminary processes requisite therefor, but not including any machinery which may be used for any other manufactures (608½).

605. **Sec. 12.** *And be it further enacted,* That upon the re-importation of articles once exported of the growth, product, or manufacture of the United States, upon which no internal tax has been assessed or paid, or upon which such tax has been paid and refunded by allowance or drawback, there shall be levied, collected, and paid, a duty equal to the tax imposed by the internal revenue laws upon such articles (138-710).

606. **Sec. 13.** (This section does not relate to import duties.)

607. **Sec. 14.** (This section does not relate to import duties.)

----·•·----

JOINT RESOLUTION OF MARCH 2, 1867.

(From U. S. Statutes at Large, vol. 14, p. 571, &c.)

JOINT RESOLUTION to amend section five of an Act entitled "An Act to increase duties on imports and for other purposes," approved June thirtieth, one thousand eight hundred and sixty-four.

608. *Be it resolved by the Senate and House of Representatives of the United States of America in Congress assembled,* That the paragraph of section five of an Act entitled "An Act to increase duties on imports, and for other purposes," approved June thirtieth, eighteen hundred and sixty-four, as follows, to wit: "on lastings, mohair cloth, silk, twist, wool, or other manufactured cloth woven or made in patterns of such size, shape, and form, or cut in such manner as to be fit for shoes, slippers, bootees, gaiters and buttons exclusively, not combined with India-rubber, ten per cent. ad valorem," be, and the same is hereby, repealed (475-629).

608½. **Sec. 2.** *And be it further resolved,* That from and after the passage of this resolution, machinery for the manufacture of beet sugar, and imported for that purpose solely, shall be exempted from duty (604).

ACT OF MARCH 2, 1867.

(From U. S. Statutes at Large, vol. 14, p. 559.)

AN ACT to provide increased revenue from imported wool, and for other purposes.

Be it enacted by the Senate and House of Representatives of the United States of America in Congress assembled, That from and after the passage of this Act, IN LIEU of the duties now imposed by law on the articles mentioned and embraced in this section, there shall be levied, collected, and paid on all unmanufactured wool, hair of the alpaca, goat, and other like animals, imported from foreign countries, the duties hereinafter provided. All wools, hair of the alpaca, goat, and other like animals, as aforesaid, shall be divided, for the purpose of fixing the duties to be charged thereon, into three classes, to wit:—

CLASS 1.—CLOTHING WOOL.

609. That is to say, merino, mestiza, metz, or metis wools, or other wools of merino blood, immediate or remote; down clothing wools, and wools of like character with any of the preceding, including such as have been heretofore usually imported into the United States from Buenos Ayres, New-Zealand, Australia, Cape of Good Hope, Russia, Great Britain, Canada, and elsewhere, and also including all wools not hereinafter described or designated in classes two and three.

CLASS 2.—COMBING WOOLS.

610. That is to say, Leicester, Cotswold, Lincolnshire, down combing wools, Canada long wools,* or other like combing wools of English blood, and usually known by the terms herein used; and also all hair of the alpaca, goat, and other like animals.

CLASS 3.—CARPET WOOLS, AND OTHER SIMILAR WOOLS.

611. Such as Donskoi, native South American, Cordova, Valparaiso, native Smyrna, and including all such wools of like character as have been heretofore usually imported into the United States from Turkey, Greece, Egypt, Syria, and elsewhere.

612. For the purpose of carrying into effect the classification herein provided, a sufficient number of distinctive samples of the

---

* The words "Canada long wools" inserted in class 2 by virtue of paragraph 623.

various kinds of wool or hair embraced in each of the three classes
above named, selected and prepared under the direction of the
Secretary of the Treasury, and duly verified by him, (the standard
samples being retained in the Treasury Department,) shall be deposited in the custom-houses and elsewhere, as he may direct, which
samples shall be used by the proper officers of the customs to determine the classes above specified, to which all imported wools
belong. And upon wools of the first class, the value whereof at
the last port or place whence exported to the United States, excluding charges in such port, shall be thirty-two cents or less per
pound, the duty shall be ten cents per pound, and, in addition
thereto, eleven per centum ad valorem; upon wools of the same
class, the value whereof at the last port or place whence exported
to the United States, excluding charges in such port, shall exceed
thirty-two cents per pound, the duty shall be twelve cents per
pound, and, in addition thereto, ten per centum ad valorem. Upon
wools of the second class, and upon all hair of the alpaca, goat, and
other like animals, the value whereof at the last port or place whence
exported to the United States, excluding charges in such port, shall
be thirty-two cents or less per pound, the duty shall be ten cents
per pound, and, in addition thereto, eleven per centum ad valorem;
upon wools of the same class, the value whereof at the last port or
place whence exported to the United States, excluding charges in
such port, shall exceed thirty-two cents per pound, the duty shall
be twelve cents per pound, and in addition thereto, ten per centum
ad valorem. Upon wools of the third class, the value whereof at
the last port or place whence exported into the United States, excluding charges in such port, shall be twelve cents or less per
pound, the duty shall be three cents per pound; upon wools of the
same class, the value whereof at the last port or place whence exported to the United States, excluding charges in such port, shall
exceed twelve cents per pound, the duty shall be six cents per
pound: *Provided*, That any wool of the sheep, or hair of the
alpaca, goat, and other like animals, which shall be imported in
any other· than the ordinary condition as now and heretofore
practised, or which shall be changed in its character or condition,
for the purpose of evading the duty, or which shall be reduced in
value by the admixture of dirt, or any other foreign substance,
shall be subject to pay twice the amount of the duty to which it
would be otherwise subjected, anything in this Act to the contrary
notwithstanding: *Provided further*, That when wool of different
qualities is imported in the same bale, bag, or package, it shall be
appraised by the appraiser, to determine the rate of duty to which
it shall be subjected, at the average aggregate value of the contents

of the bale, bag, or package; and when bales of different qualities are embraced in the same invoice at the same prices whereby the average price shall be reduced more than ten per centum below the value of the bale of the best quality, the value of the whole shall be appraised according to the value of the bale of the best quality; and no bale, bag, or package shall be liable to a less rate of duty in consequence of being invoiced with wool of lower value: *And provided further*, That the duty upon wool of the first class which shall be imported washed shall be twice the amount of duty to which it would be subjected if imported unwashed, and that the duty upon wool of all classes which shall be imported scoured shall be three times the amount of the duty to which it would be subjected if imported unwashed (467).

612½. On sheep skins and Angora goat skins, raw or unmanufactured, imported with the wool on, washed or unwashed, the duty shall be thirty per centum ad valorem (468); and on woollen rags (179-468), shoddy, mungo, waste, and flocks, the duty shall be twelve cents per pound (468).

Sec. 2. *And be it further enacted*, That IN LIEU of the duties heretofore imposed by law on the articles hereinafter mentioned, and on such as may now be exempt from duty, there shall be levied, collected, and paid on the goods, wares, and merchandise herein enumerated and provided for, imported from foreign countries, the following duties and rates of duty, that is to say:

613. On woollen cloths, woollen shawls, and all manufactures of wool of every description made wholly or in part of wool, not herein otherwise provided for, fifty cents per pound, and, in addition thereto, thirty-five per centum ad valorem (470).

614. On flannels, blankets, hats of wool, knit goods, balmorals, woollen and worsted yarns, and all manufactures of every description composed wholly or in part of worsted, the hair of the alpaca, goat, or other like animals, except such as are composed in part of wool, not otherwise provided for, valued at not exceeding forty cents per pound, twenty cents per pound; valued at above forty cents per pound and not exceeding sixty cents per pound, thirty cents per pound; valued at above sixty cents per pound and not exceeding eighty cents per pound, forty cents per pound; valued at above eighty cents per pound, fifty cents per pound; and, in addition thereto, upon all the above-named articles, thirty-five per centum ad valorem (470-473).

615. On endless belts or felts for paper or printing machines, twenty cents per pound and thirty-five per centum ad valorem (470).

616. On bunting, twenty cents per square yard, and, in addition thereto, thirty-five per centum ad valorem (474).

617. On women's and children's dress goods and real or imitation Italian cloths, composed wholly or in part of wool, worsted, the hair of the alpaca, goat, or other like animals, valued at not exceeding twenty cents per square yard, six cents per square yard, and, in addition thereto, thirty-five per centum ad valorem; valued at above twenty cents the square yard, eight cents per square yard, and, in addition thereto, forty per centum ad valorem: *Provided*, That on all goods weighing four ounces and over per square yard, the duty shall be fifty cents per pound, and, in addition thereto, thirty-five per centum ad valorem (471-472).

618. On clothing ready made, and wearing apparel of every description, and balmoral skirts and skirting, and goods of similar description, or used for like purposes, composed wholly or in part of wool, worsted, the hair of the alpaca, goat, or other like animals, made up or manufactured wholly or in part by the tailor, seamstress, or manufacturer, except knit goods, fifty cents per pound, and, in addition thereto, forty per centum ad valorem (470).

619. On webbings, beltings, bindings, braids, galloons, fringes, gimps, cords, cords and tassels, dress-trimmings, head-nets, buttons or barrel buttons, or buttons of other forms for tassels or ornaments, wrought by hand or braided by machinery, made of wool, worsted, or mohair, or of which wool, worsted, or mohair is a component material, [unmixed with silk,*] fifty cents per pound, and, in addition thereto, fifty per centum ad valorem (470).

620. On Aubusson and Axminster carpets, and carpets woven whole for rooms, fifty per centum ad valorem; on Saxony, Wilton, and Tournay velvet carpets wrought by the Jacquard machine, seventy cents per square yard, and, in addition thereto, thirty-five per centum ad valorem; on Brussels carpets wrought by the Jacquard machine, forty-four cents per square yard, and, in addition thereto, thirty-five per centum ad valorem; on patent velvet and tapestry velvet carpets, printed on the warp or otherwise, forty cents per square yard, and, in addition thereto, thirty-five per centum ad valorem; on tapestry Brussels carpets printed on the warp or otherwise, twenty-eight cents per square yard, and, in addition thereto, thirty-five per centum ad valorem; on treble ingrain, three-ply, and worsted chain Venetian carpets, seventeen cents per square yard, and, in addition thereto, thirty-five per centum ad valorem; on yarn Venetian and two-ply ingrain carpets, twelve cents per square yard, and, in addition thereto, thirty-five per centum ad valorem; on druggets and bockings, printed, colored, or

---

* The words " unmixed with silk " repealed by paragraph 628.

otherwise, twenty-five cents per square yard, and, in addition
thereto, thirty-five per centum ad valorem; on hemp or jute carpeting, eight cents per square yard; on carpets and carpetings of
wool, flax, or cotton, or parts of either, or other material not otherwise herein specified, forty per centum ad valorem : *Provided,* That
mats, rugs, screens, covers, hassocks, bedsides, and other portions
of carpets or carpeting shall be subjected to the rate of duty herein
imposed on carpets or carpeting of like character or description,
and that the duty on all other mats, (not exclusively of vegetable
material,) screens, hassocks, and rugs, shall be forty-five per centum
ad valorem (469).

621. On oil cloths for floors, stamped, painted, or printed, valued
at fifty cents or less per square yard, thirty-five per centum ad
valorem; valued at over fifty cents per square yard, and on all
other oil cloth, (except silk oil cloth,) and on water-proof cloth, not
otherwise provided for, forty-five per centum ad valorem; on oil
silk cloth, sixty per centum ad valorem (476).

JOINT RESOLUTION OF MARCH 22, 1867.

(From U. S. Statutes at Large, vol. 15, p. 21.)

JOINT RESOLUTION to supply an omission in the enrollment of the
"Act to provide increased revenue from imported Wool, and for other
purposes."

622. *Whereas,* in the enrollment of the bill entitled "An Act to
provide increased revenue from imported wool, and for
other purposes," approved March second, eighteen hundred
and sixty-seven, the words "Canada long wools" were in-
advertently omitted from the paragraph designated under
the heading "Class 2—Combing Wools;" *and whereas,* said
words are in the engrossed bill, and were intended as a part
of the Act aforesaid, as passed by the thirty-ninth Congress;
therefore,

623. *Be it resolved by the Senate and House of Representatives of the
United States of America in Congress assembled,* That the
"Act to provide increased revenue from imported wool, and
for other purposes," aforesaid, be, and is hereby, amended
by inserting after the words "Down combing wools," in the
paragraph headed "Class 2—Combing Wools" the words
"Canada long wools" (610).

JOINT RESOLUTION OF MARCH 25, 1867.

(From U. S. Statutes at Large, vol. 15, p. 22.)

JOINT RESOLUTION fixing the rate of duty on Umbrellas, and on Wire Spiral Furniture Springs.

624. *Be it resolved by the Senate and House of Representatives of the United States of America in Congress assembled,* That from and after the passage of this joint resolution, there shall be levied, collected, and paid upon umbrellas, parasols, and sunshades, imported from foreign countries, when made of silk, no lower rate of duty than that now imposed upon piece and dress silks, namely, sixty per centum ad valorem; and when made of other materials than silk, the duty shall be fifty per centum ad valorem (401); and that wire spiral furniture springs, imported from foreign countries, manufactured of iron wire, shall be required to pay the same rate of duty as now imposed on iron wire, namely, two cents per pound, and fifteen per centum ad valorem (427).

JOINT RESOLUTION OF MARCH 26, 1867.

(From U. S. Statutes at Large, vol. 15, p. 23.)

JOINT RESOLUTION providing for the importation into the United States of certain works of art duty free, and for other purposes.

625. *Be it resolved by the Senate and House of Representatives of the United States of America in Congress assembled,* That from and after the passage of this joint resolution, any object of art imported by any individual or association of individuals for presentation, as a gift, to the United States government, or to any State, county, or municipal government, shall be admitted free of duty, under such rules and regulations as the Secretary of the Treasury may prescribe.

626. **Sec. 2.** *And be it further resolved,* That the Secretary of the Treasury be, and he hereby is, authorized to refund the duties paid on any steam agricultural machinery imported into the United States during the current fiscal year as models or for experimental purposes, and to remit the duties on any steam machinery of like description which may be imported for such purpose prior to the thirtieth of June, eighteen hundred and sixtyeight: *Provided,* That this section shall apply only to steam ploughs.*

627. **Sec. 3.** (This section does not relate to import duties.)

* The provisions of this Resolution extended for one year from the 30th June, 1868. (See Joint Resolution of July 23, 1868.)

JOINT RESOLUTION OF MARCH 29, 1867.

(From U. S. Statutes at Large, vol. 15, p. 24.)

JOINT RESOLUTION to amend an Act entitled "An Act to provide increased revenue from imported Wool, and for other purposes."

628. *Be it resolved by the Senate and House of Representatives of the United States of America in Congress assembled,* That the Act entitled "An Act to provide increased revenue from imported wool and for other purposes," approved March second, eighteen hundred and sixty-seven, be amended by striking out in the paragraph commencing with the words "on webbings, beltings, bindings, braids," the following words, viz: "unmixed with silk" (619).

629. **Sec. 2.** *And be it further resolved,* That the joint resolution of March second, eighteen hundred and sixty-seven, to amend section five of an Act entitled "An Act to increase the duties on imports and for other purposes," approved June thirtieth, eighteen hundred and sixty-four, shall not be construed to apply to lasting, mohair cloth, silk, twist, or other manufactures of cloth woven or made in patterns of such size, shape, and form, or cut in such manner as to be fit for buttons exclusively (608-475).

ACT OF FEBRUARY 3, 1868.

(From U. S. Statutes at Large, vol. 15, p. 34.)

AN ACT to provide for the exemption of Cotton from Internal Tax.

630. *Be it enacted by the Senate and House of Representatives of the United States of America in Congress assembled,* That all cotton grown in the United States after the year eighteen hundred and sixty-seven shall be exempt from internal tax; and cotton imported from foreign countries on and after November first, eighteen hundred and sixty-eight, shall be exempt from duty (593).

EXTRACT OF ACT OF JULY 20, 1868.

(From U. S. Statutes at Large, vol. 15, p. 125, &c.)

AN ACT imposing taxes on distilled Spirits and Tobacco, and for other purposes.

*   *   *   *   *   *

631. **Sec. 2.** *And be it further enacted,* That proof spirits shall be held and taken to be that alcoholic liquor which contains one half its volume of alcohol of a specific gravity of seven thousand nine hundred and thirty-nine ten thousandths (.7939) at sixty degrees Fahrenheit (651);

*   *   *   *   *   *

632. **Sec. 61.** * * * On snuff, manufactured of tobacco or any substitute for tobacco, ground, dry, damp, pickled, scented, or otherwise, of all descriptions, when prepared for use, a tax of thirty-two cents per pound. And snuff flour * * * shall be taxed as snuff (425-633); * * * on all chewing tobacco, * * * a tax of thirty-two cents per pound. * * * On all smoking tobacco * * * a tax of sixteen cents per pound (876).

*   *   *   *   *   *

633. **Sec. 77.** * * * All manufactured tobacco and snuff (not including cigars) imported from foreign countries, after the passage of this Act, shall, IN ADDITION to the import duties imposed on the same, pay the tax prescribed in this Act for like kinds of tobacco and snuff manufactured in the United States, and have the same stamps respectively affixed (632).

*   *   *   *   *   *

634. **Sec. 81.** * * * On cigars, of all descriptions, made of tobacco or any substitute therefor, five dollars per thousand; on cigarettes weighing not exceeding three pounds per thousand, one dollar and fifty cents per thousand; when weighing exceeding three pounds per thousand, five dollars per thousand (635-637).

*   *   *   *   *   *

635. **Sec. 82.** * * * Cigarettes and cheroots shall be held to be cigars under the meaning of this Act (634).

*   *   *   *   *   *

7

636. **Sec. 85.** *And be it further enacted,* That from and after the passage of this Act all cigars shall be packed in boxes, not before used for that purpose, containing, respectively, twenty-five, fifty, one hundred, two hundred and fifty, or five hundred cigars each (638);

　　　*　　　*　　　*　　　*　　　*　　　*

637. **Sec. 87.** *　*　* That from and after the passage of this Act, the duty on all cigars imported into the United States from foreign countries shall be two dollars and fifty cents [per] pound, and twenty-five per centum ad valorem (592-636-634-638).

　　　*　　　*　　　*　　　*　　　*　　　*

638. **Sec. 93.** *And be it further enacted,* That all cigars imported from foreign countries after the passage of this Act, shall, IN ADDITION to the import duties imposed on the same, pay the tax prescribed in this Act for cigars manufactured in the United States, and have the same stamps affixed (637-634). Such stamps shall be affixed and cancelled by the owner or importer of cigars while they are in the custody of the proper custom house officers; and such cigars shall not pass out of the custody of such officers until the stamps have been affixed and cancelled, but shall be put up in boxes containing quantities as prescribed in this Act for cigars manufactured in the United States before such stamps are affixed (636).

　　　*　　　*　　　*　　　*　　　*　　　*

ACT OF FEBRUARY 19, 1869.

(From U. S. Statutes at Large, vol. 15, p. 271.)

AN ACT to authorize the Importation of Machinery, for Repair only, free of Duty.

639. *Be it enacted by the Senate and House of Representatives of the United States of America in Congress assembled,* That machinery for repair may be imported into the United States without payment of duty, under bond to be given in double the appraised value thereof, to be withdrawn and exported after said machinery shall have been repaired; and

the Secretary of the Treasury is hereby authorized and directed to prescribe such rules and regulations as may be necessary to protect the revenue against fraud, and secure the identity and character of all such importations when again withdrawn and exported, restricting and limiting the export and withdrawal to the same port of entry where imported, and also limiting all bonds to a period of time not more than six months from the date of the importation. (See decision of May 12, 1870).

———•••———

ACT OF FEBRUARY 24, 1869.

(From U. S. Statutes at Large, vol. 15, p. 274.)

AN ACT regulating the duties on imported Copper and Copper Ores.

Be it enacted by the Senate and House of Representatives of the United States of America in Congress assembled, That from and after the passage of this Act, IN LIEU of the duties heretofore imposed by law on the articles hereinafter mentioned, there shall be levied, collected, and paid on the articles herein enumerated and provided for, imported from foreign countries, the following specified duties and rates of duty, that is to say:

640. On all copper imported in the form of ores, three cents on each pound of fine copper contained therein (70); on all regulus of copper, and on all black or coarse copper, four cents on each pound of fine copper contained therein (70); on all old copper, fit only for re-manufacture, four cents per pound (13); on all copper in plates, bars, ingots, pigs, and in other forms not manufactured or herein enumerated (462), including sulphate of copper or blue vitriol (505), five cents per pound; on copper in rolled plates called braziers' copper, sheets, rods, pipes, and copper bottoms (463-464), eyelets (665), and all manufactures of copper * (383), or of which copper shall be a component of chief value, not otherwise herein provided for, forty-five per centum ad valorem: *Provided,* That the increased duty imposed by this Act shall not apply to any of the articles therein enumerated which shall have been in course of transit to the United States, and actually on shipboard on the nineteenth of January, eighteen hundred and sixty-nine.

---

* See note to manufactures of copper in the schedule.

ACT OF JULY 14, 1870.

(From U. S. Statutes at Large, vol. 16, p. 256, &c.)

AN ACT to reduce Internal Taxes, and for other purposes.

(The first twenty sections do not relate to import duties.)

Sec. 21. *And be it further enacted,* That after the thirty-first day of December, eighteen hundred and seventy, IN LIEU of the duties now imposed by law on the articles hereinafter enumerated or provided for, imported from foreign countries, there shall be levied, collected, and paid the following duties and rates of duties, that is to say:

641. On teas of all kinds, fifteen cents per pound (423).

642. On coffee of all kinds, three cents per pound (185).

643. On cacao, or cocoa, two cents per pound (178). On cocoa leaves or shells, one cent per pound (173).

644. On ground or prepared cacao, or cocoa, five cents per pound; and on chocolate, seven cents per pound (288).

645. On all molasses, five cents per gallon (422½).

646. On tank-bottom syrup of sugar-cane juice, melada, concentrated melada, and concentrated molasses, one and one-half cents per pound (750-422½).

647. On all raw or muscovado sugar not above number seven, Dutch standard in color, one and three-quarter cents per pound. On all raw or muscovado sugar above number seven, Dutch standard in color, and on all other sugars not above number ten, Dutch standard in color, two cents per pound. On all other sugars above number ten, Dutch standard in color, and not above number thirteen, Dutch standard in color, two and one-quarter cents per pound. On all other sugars above number thirteen, Dutch standard in color, and not above number sixteen, Dutch standard in color, two and three-quarter cents per pound. On all other sugars above number sixteen, Dutch standard in color, and not above number twenty, Dutch standard in color, three and one-quarter cents per pound. On all sugar above number twenty, Dutch standard in color, and on all refined loaf, lump, crushed, powdered, and granulated sugar, four cents per pound: *Provided,* That the Secretary of the Treasury shall, by regulations, prescribe and require that samples shall be taken by inspectors from the hogsheads, box, or other package, in such a manner as to represent a true average of the contents of the package, and from a sufficient number of packages of the same mark in each and every invoice, so that the samples on which the classification is made shall be a fair average in quality of the sugar imported under that mark, and the classification shall be adjudged on the entire mark accordingly; and the weights of sugar imported in casks or boxes shall be marked distinctly by the custom house weigher by scoring the figures indelibly on each package: *Provided,* That all syrup of sugar, syrup of sugar-cane juice, melado, concentrated melado, or concentrated molasses entered under the name of molasses, shall be forfeited to the United States (422-422½).

648. On all wines imported in casks, containing not more than twenty-two per centum of alcohol, and valued at not exceeding forty cents per gallon, twenty-five cents per gallon; valued at over forty cents, and not over one dollar per gallon, sixty cents per gallon; valued at over one dollar per gallon, one dollar per gallon, and in addition thereto twenty-five per centum ad valorem (423).

649. On wines of all kinds, imported in bottles, and not otherwise herein provided for, the same rate per gallon as wines imported in casks, but all bottles containing one quart or less than one quart, and more than one pint, shall be held to contain one quart, and all bottles containing one pint or less shall be held to contain one pint, and shall pay in addition three cents for each bottle (423½-594).

650. On champagne and all other sparkling wines, in bottles, six dollars per dozen bottles containing each not more than one quart and more than one pint; and three dollars per dozen bottles containing not more than one pint each, and more than one half-pint; and one dollar and fifty cents per dozen bottles, containing one-half pint each, or less; and in bottles containing more than one quart each, shall pay, in addition to six dollars per dozen bottles, at the rate of two dollars per gallon on the quantity in excess of one quart per bottle: *Provided*, That any liquors containing more than twenty-two per centum of alcohol, which shall be entered under the name of wine, shall be forfeited to the United States: *And provided further*, That wines, brandy, and other spirituous liquors imported in bottles shall be packed in packages containing not less than one dozen bottles in each package; and all such bottles shall pay an additional duty of three cents for each bottle; no allowance shall be made for breakage unless such breakage is actually ascertained by count, and certified by a custom-house appraiser; and so much of section fifty-nine of an Act entitled "An Act to regulate the collection of duties on imports and tonnage," approved March two, seventeen hundred and ninety-nine, as provided for allowance for leakage and breakage, is hereby repealed (423-423½-594).

651. On brandy and other spirits manufactured or distilled from grain or other materials, and not otherwise herein * provided for, two dollars per proof gallon (577-594): *Provided*, That each and every gauge or wine gallon of measurement shall be counted as at least one proof gallon; and the standard for determining the proof of brandy and other spirits, and of wine or liquors of any kind imported, shall be the same as that which is defined in the second section of the "Act imposing taxes on distilled spirits and tobacco, and for other purposes," approved July twenty, eighteen hundred and sixty-eight (631).

652. On cordials, liqueurs, arrack, absynthe, kirshwasser, vermutb, ratafia, and other similar spirituous beverages, or bitters containing spirits, and not otherwise herein † provided for, two dollars per

---

* The word "herein" inserted in this paragraph by virtue of the resolution of January 30, 1871. (See paragraph 752).
† The word "herein" inserted in this paragraph by virtue of the resolution of July 30, 1871. (See paragraph 752.)

proof gallon (577-594): *Provided*, That any brandy or other spirituous liquors imported in casks of less capacity than fourteen gallons shall be forfeited to the United States (594).

653. On pimento and on black, white, and red or Cayenne pepper, five cents per pound (532).

654. On ground pimento and on ground pepper of all kinds, ten cents per pound (532).

655. On ginger root, two cents per pound (240).

656. On ginger, ground, five cents per pound (240).

657. On cinnamon (518) and on nutmegs (528), twenty cents per pound.

658. On mace, twenty-five cents per pound (528).

659. On cloves, five cents per pound (521).

660. On clove stems, three cents per pound (521).

661. On cassia and cassia vera, ten cents per pound (518).

662. On cassia buds and ground cassia, twenty cents per pound (518).

663. On all other spices, twenty cents per pound; ground or prepared, thirty cents per pound (66).

664. On corsets, or manufactured cloth, woven or made in patterns of such size, shape, and form, or cut in such manner as to be fit for corsets, when valued at six dollars per dozen or less, two dollars per dozen; when valued over six dollars per dozen, thirty-five per centum ad valorem (360).

665. On eyelets of every description, six cents per thousand (640).

666. On ultramarine, six cents per pound (505).

667. On wools on the skin, the same rates as on other wools, the quantity and value to be ascertained under such rules as the Secretary of the Treasury may prescribe (612½).

668. On flax straw, five dollars per ton (27).

669. On flax not hackled or dressed, twenty dollars per ton (27); on flax hackled, known as "dressed line," forty dollars per ton (27).

670. On hemp, manilla, and other like substitutes for hemp, not otherwise herein * provided for, twenty-five dollars per ton (178).

671. On the tow of flax or hemp, ten dollars per ton (27).

672. On jute, sunn, coir, and Sisal grass, fifteen dollars per ton (344).

673. On jute buts, six dollars per ton (345).

---

* The word "herein" inserted in this paragraph by virtue of the Resolution of January 30, 1871. (See paragraph 752).

674. On cotton bagging, or other manufactures, not otherwise herein * provided for, suitable for the uses to which cotton bagging is applied, composed in whole or in part of hemp, jute, flax, gunny bags, gunny cloth, or other material, and valued at seven cents or less per square yard, two cents per pound; valued at over seven cents per square yard, three cents per pound (484).

675. On iron in pigs, seven dollars per ton (440).

676. On cast scrap-iron of every description, six dollars per ton (445).

677. On wrought scrap-iron of every description, eight dollars per ton : *Provided,* That nothing shall be deemed scrap-iron except waste or refuse iron that has been in actual use, and is fit only to be remanufactured (445).

678. On sword blades, thirty-five per centum ad valorem (458).

679. On swords, forty-five per centum ad valorem (371).

680. On steel railway bars, one and one-quarter cent per pound ; and on all railway bars made in part of steel, one cent per pound (458) : *Provided,* That metal converted, cast, or made from iron by the Bessemer or pneumatic process; of whatever form or description, shall be classed as steel : *And provided further,* That round iron in coils, three-sixteenths of an inch or less in diameter, whether coated with metal or not so coated, and all descriptions of iron wire, and wire of which iron is a component part, not otherwise specifically enumerated and provided for, shall pay the same duty as iron wire, bright, coppered, or tinned (427) : *And provided further,* That steel, commercially known as crinoline, corset, and hat steel wire, shall pay duty at the rate of nine cents per pound and ten per centum ad valorem (446).

681. On rough or unfinished grindstones, one dollar and fifty cents per ton ; on finished grindstones, two dollars per ton (276).

682. On freestone, sandstone, granite, and all building or monumental stone, except marble, one dollar and fifty cents per ton (272).

683. On all sawed, dressed, or polished marble, marble slabs, and marble paving tiles, thirty per centum ad valorem, and in addition twenty-five cents per superficial square foot not exceeding two inches in thickness; if more than two inches in thickness, ten cents per foot, in addition to the above rates for each inch or fractional part thereof in excess of two inches in thickness : *Provided,* That if exceeding six inches in thickness, such marble shall be subject to the duty now imposed upon marble blocks (549-319).

* The word "herein" inserted in this paragraph by virtue of the Resolution of January 30,. 1871. (See paragraph 752).

684. On hair cloth of the description known as hair seating, eighteen inches wide or over, forty cents per square yard; less than eighteen inches wide, thirty cents per square yard (375).

685. On hair cloth known as crinoline cloth, and on all other manufactures of hair not otherwise herein * provided for, thirty per centum ad valorem (375).

686. On hair pins, made of iron wire, fifty per centum ad valorem (396).

687. On aniline dyes and colors, by whatever name known, fifty cents per pound, and thirty-five per centum ad valorem (508).

688. On buttons and on ornaments for dresses and outside garments made of silk, or of which silk is the component material of chief value, and containing no wool, worsted, or goat's hair, fifty per centum ad valorem (179).

689. On silicate of soda, or other alkaline silicates, a half a cent per pound (66).

690. On sporting gun-wads of all descriptions, thirty-five per centum ad valorem (381 or 613).

691. On nickel, thirty cents per pound (504).

692. On nickel oxide and alloy of nickel with copper, twenty cents per pound (166).

693. On watches (536), watch cases (402), watch movements (402), parts of watches (503-402), and watch materials (402), twenty-five per centum ad valorem.

694. On watch jewels, ten per centum ad valorem (402).

695. On live animals, twenty per centum ad valorem (591): *Provided*, That animals specially imported for breeding purposes from beyond the seas shall be admitted free, upon proof thereof satisfactory to the Secretary of the Treasury, and under such regulations as he may prescribe: *And provided further*, That teams of animals, including their harness and tackle, actually owned by persons immigrating to the United States with their families from foreign countries, and in actual use for the purposes of such immigration, shall also be admitted free of duty, under such regulations as the Secretary of the Treasury may prescribe: *And provided further*, That all animals brought into the United States temporarily and for a period not exceeding six months, for the purpose of exhibition or competition for prizes offered by any agricultural or racing association, shall be admitted free of duty upon bond being first given, in accordance with regulations to be prescribed by the Secretary of the Treasury, with condition that the full duty herein-

---

* The word "herein" inserted in this paragraph by virtue of the Resolution of January 30, 1871. (See paragraph 752).

before imposed shall be paid in case of the sale of any such animals in the United States (807).

696. On oranges (526), lemons (526), pineapples (526), and grapes (57), twenty per centum ad valorem; and on limes (179), bananas (179), plantains (526), shaddocks (48), mangoes (50), and cocoanuts (526), ten per centum ad valorem: *Provided*, That no allowance shall be made for loss by decay on the voyage, unless the said loss shall exceed twenty-five per centum of the quantity, and the allowance then made shall be only for the amount of loss in excess of twenty-five per centum of the whole quantity.

697. On Zante, or other currants, and prunes and plums, two and one-half cents per pound (178).

698. On neat's-foot oil, and all animal, whale, seal, and fish oils, twenty per centum ad valorem (44-62).

699. On oil made of linseed or flaxseed, thirty cents per gallon, seven pounds and a half of weight to be estimated as a gallon (289).

700. On hempseed (260) and rapeseed (16), and other oil seeds of like character other than linseed or flaxseed, one-half cent per pound.

701. On linseed or flaxseed, twenty cents per bushel of fifty-six pounds weight (16): *Provided*, That no drawback shall be allowed on oil cake made from imported seed.

702. On sesame seed oil or Cenne oil, and cotton seed oil, thirty cents per gallon (62).

703. On sesame seed, ten per centum ad valorem (136).

704. On opium, one dollar per pound (513).

705. On opium prepared for smoking, and on all other preparations of opium not otherwise herein* provided for, six dollars per pound (513): *Provided*, That opium prepared for smoking, and other preparations of opium, deposited in bonded warehouse, shall not be removed therefrom for exportation without payment of duties, and such duties shall not be refunded.

706. On morphia, and on all salts of morphia, one dollar per ounce (514).

707. On cotton thread, yarn, warps, or warp yarn, not wound upon spools, whether single or advanced beyond the condition of single by twisting two or more single yarns together, whether on beams or in bundles, skeins, or cops, or in any other form, valued at not exceeding forty cents per pound, ten cents per pound; valued at over forty cents per pound and not exceeding sixty cents per

---

*The word "herein" inserted in this paragraph by virtue of the Resolution of January 30, 1871. (See paragraph 752).

pound, twenty cents per pound; valued at over sixty cents per pound and not exceeding eighty cents per pound, thirty cents per pound; valued at over eighty cents per pound, forty cents per pound; and in addition to said rates of duty twenty per centum ad valorem (576).

Sec. 22. *And be it further enacted,* That after the thirty-first day of December, eighteen hundred and seventy, IN ADDITION to imported articles now by law EXEMPT FROM DUTY, and not herein otherwise provided for, the following articles hereinafter enumerated and provided for shall also be free.

708. Acid, arsenious, crude (32). Acid, nitric, not chemically pure (32). Acid, muriatic (266). Acid, oxalic (231). Acid, picric, and nitro-picric (32): *Provided,* That carboys containing acids shall be subject to the same duty as if empty. Arsenic (267). Aconite, root, leaf, and bark (267). Agaric (166). Alkanet root (267). Alkckengi (166). Albumen (505) and lactarine (280). Amber, gum (267). Aloes (240). Aniline oil, crude (166). Ammonia, crude (267). Annato seed (504). Argols, crude (233). Asbestos, not manufactured (505).

709. Articles imported for the use of the United States : *Provided,* That the price of the same did not include the duty (121-126).

710. Articles the growth, produce, and manufacture of the United States when returned in the same condition as exported : *Provided,* That proof of the identity of such articles be made under regulations to be prescribed by the Secretary of the Treasury ; and if such articles were subject to internal tax at the time of exportation, such tax shall be proved to have been paid before exportation and not refunded. And all Acts and parts of Acts heretofore passed prescribing regulations in regard to such importations are hereby repealed (138-605).

711. Bamboos, unmanufactured (33).

712. Barks, viz: Quilla, Peruvian, Lima, calisaya, and all cinchona barks, Canella alba, pomegranate, croton, cascarilla, and all other barks not otherwise provided for (267).

713. Belladonna, root and leaf (267). Bromine (280). Bitter apples, colocynth, coloquinitida (234). Berries, nuts, and vegetables for dyeing, or used for composing dyes, not otherwise provided for in this Act (124).

714. Bells broken and bell metal broken, and fit only to be re-manufactured (123). Bones, crude, not manufactured, bones ground and calcined, bone dust (125) and bone ash for manufacture of phosphates and fertilizers (160). Books which have been printed and manufactured more than twenty years (544).

Brimstone, crude (515). Burrstone in blocks, rough or unmanufactured, and not bound up into millstones (127). Buchu leaves (234).

715. Citrate of lime (166). Colombo root (267). Cantharides (235). Castor or castoreum (54). Catechu or cutch (266). Catgut or whip gut, unmanufactured (166). Coal, anthracite (459). Coc[c]ulus indicus (235). Conian cicuta, or hemlock, seed and leaf (267). Cudbear (266). Collections of antiquity, specially imported, and not for sale (128). Chalk and cliff stone, unmanufactured (494). Cork wood, or cork bark, unmanufactured (545). Carnelian, unmanufactured (166). Cuttle-fish bone (235).

716. Diamond dust or bort (166). Dragon's blood (236).

717. Eggs (166). Emory ore or rock, not pulverized, not ground (237). Esparto, or Spanish grass, and other grasses and pulp of, for the manufacture of paper (166-344).

718. Fibrin, in all forms (166-344). Fish, fresh, for immediate consumption (134). Fish for bait (134). Flint and ground flint stones (275). Foliæ digitalis (267). Fashion plates engraved on steel or on wood, colored, plain (323). Fur skins of all kinds not dressed in any manner (546).

719. Glass, broken in pieces, which cannot be cut for use, and fit only to be remanufactured (137). Guano (139), and other animal manures (160). Gums, Arabic (267), Jeddo (267), Senegal (267), Barbary (135), East India (135), Cape (267), Australia (267), gum benzoin or benjamin (240), gum copal (240), sandarac (240), damar (240), gamboge (38), cowrie (240), mastic (240), shellac (240), tragacanth (267), olebanum (267), guiac (267), myrrh (267), bdellium (267), garbanum (267), and all gums not otherwise provided for (267-708-240). Gutta-percha, crude (276). Goat skins, raw (612½).

720. Horse and cow hair, not cleaned and dressed (141). Hoofs, horns, and horn tips (39). Hide cuttings, raw and in the hair, for glue stock (166). Hemlock bark (267). Hyoscyamus, or henbane leaf (267).

721. Iodine, crude (242). Ipecac (242). India-rubber, crude, and milk of (280). Ivory and vegetable ivory, unmanufactured (179).

722. Jalap (243). Jet, unmanufactured (377). Juniper (41) and laurel berries (267).

723. Kryolite (60).

724. S. Lac, crude (145), seed (419), button, stick (419), shell or dye (145). Lava, unmanufactured (60). Leeches (147). Life-boats and life-saving apparatus, specially imported by societies incorporated or established to encourage the saving of human life.

108   DIGEST OF THE TARIFF LAWS.

Liquorice root (527). Litmus and all lichens, prepared or not prepared (166). Logs and round unmanufactured timber not otherwise provided for, and ship timber (843). Madder root, of all kinds, ground, and ground munget, or Indian madder (148). Manna (246). Moss, Iceland, and other mosses, crude (43). Musk and civet, crude, in natural pod (166).

725. Nitrate of soda, or cubic niter (247).

726. Oak bark (122). Ore of antimony, or crude sulphuret of (66). Orange and lemon peel, not preserved, candied, or otherwise prepared (44). Orchill, or archill, in the weed or liquid (266).

727. Palm nuts and palm-nut kernels (178). Palm and cocoa-nut oil (44).

728. Paintings, statuary, fountains, and other works of art, the production of American artists: *Provided,* That the fact of such production be verified by the certificate of any consul or minister of the United States indorsed upon the written declaration of the artist (154): *And provided further,* That all paintings, statuary, fountains, and other works of art, the production and property of an American artist, now held for payment of duties in any custom-house in the United States, shall be surrendered to such artist without payment of duties or charge, upon his affidavit filed in the Department of the Secretary of the Treasury that the same are the production of such artist.

729. Paintings, statuary, fountains, and other works of art, imported expressly for presentation to national institutions or to any State, or to any municipal corporation (625).

730. Philosophical and scientific apparatus, instruments, and preparations, statuary, casts of marble, bronze, alabaster, or plaster of Paris, paintings, drawings, and etchings, specially imported in good faith, for the use of any society or institution incorporated or established for philosophical, educational, scientific, or literary purposes, or encouragement of the fine arts, and not intended for sale (569-121-815).

731. Household effects of persons and families returning or emigrating from foreign countries, which have been in actual use abroad by them, and not intended for any other person or persons or for sale, not exceeding the value of five hundred dollars (155-102-817).

732. Phosphates, crude or native, for fertilizing purposes (160).

733. Plants, trees, shrubs, roots, seed-cane, and seeds imported by the Department of Agriculture, or the United States Botanic Garden (121).

734. Platinum vases or retorts for chemical uses, or parts thereof (155).

735. Potassa, muriate of (166 or 160).

736. Quassia wood (267).

737. Rags, of cotton, linen, jute, and hemp, and paper waste, or waste or clippings of any kind fit only for the manufacture of paper, including waste rope and waste bagging (300).

738. Rhubarb (258). Resins, crude, not otherwise provided for (135). Rose leaves (258).

739. Saffron (48) and safflower (266). Sarsaparilla, crude (267). Seaweed, not otherwise provided for (58-166). Scammony, or resin of scammony (267). Sandal wood (158). Seeds: cardamon (260), caraway (260), coriander (260), fenugreek (260), fennel (260), cummin (260), andother seeds not otherwise provided for (136-267-608). Senna, in leaves (267). Shells of every description, not manufactured (155-161). Shrimps, or other shell fish (166). Skeletons, and other preparations of anatomy (380). Silk-worm eggs (166). Specimens of natural history, botany, and mineralogy, when imported for cabinets as objects of taste or science, and not for sale (160). Squills, or silla (48). Sweepings of silver or gold (127).

740. Tapioca, cassava, or cassada (267). Tea plants (309). Turtles (276).

741. Verdigris, or subacetate of copper (264).

742. Wood ashes, and lye of, and beet-root ashes (166). Woods, viz: poplar or other woods for the manufacture of paper. Worm seed, Levant (267). Xylonite, or Xylotile (60).

743. **Sec. 23.** *And be it further enacted,* That for the term of two years from and after the passage of this Act, and no longer, machinery and apparatus designed only for, and adapted to be used for, steam-towage on canals, and not now manufactured in the United States, may be imported by any State, or by any person duly authorized by the legislature of any State, free of duty, subject to such regulations as may be prescribed by the Secretary of the Treasury. And also that for the term of two years from and after the passage of this Act, and no longer, steam-plow machinery, adapted to the cultivation of the soil, may be imported by any person for his own use, free of duty, subject to such regulations of the Secretary of the Treasury as before provided (626-871).

744. **Sec. 24.** *And be it further enacted,* That the word "saltpetre," as used in section seven of the Act of March three, eighteen hundred and sixty-three, allowing drawback of duty on foreign saltpetre manufactured into gunpowder in the United States, and exported therefrom, shall be construed to mean the element of nitre so used, whether it be the nitrate of potash or nitrate of soda (421).

745. **Sec. 25.** *And be it further enacted,* That section fifteen of the Act approved July fourteen, eighteen hundred and sixty-two, entitled "An Act increasing, temporarily, the duties on imports, and for other purposes," and section four

of the Act in amendment thereof, approved March three, eighteen hundred and sixty-five, be, and the same are hereby, so amended, that no ship, vessel, steamer, boat, barge, or flat belonging to any citizen of the United States, trading from one port or point within the United States, to another port or point within the United States, or employed in the bank, whale, or other fisheries, shall hereafter be subject to the tonnage tax or duty provided for in said Acts; and the proviso in section one hundred and three of the "Act to provide internal revenue to support the Government and to pay the interest on the public debt, and for other purposes," approved June thirty, eighteen hundred and sixty-four, requiring an annual special tax to be paid by boats, barges, and flats, is hereby repealed (404½-579).

746. **Sec. 26.** *And be it further enacted,* That all imported goods, wares, and merchandise which may be in the public stores or bonded warehouses on the day and year this Act shall take effect, shall be subjected to no other duty upon the entry thereof for consumption than if the same were imported respectively after that day; and all goods, wares, and merchandise remaining in bonded warehouses on the day and year this Act shall take effect, and upon which the duties shall have been paid, shall be entitled to a refund of the difference between the amount of duties paid and the amount of duties said goods, wares, and merchandise would be subject to if the same were imported respectively after that day (751).

Sec. 27. (This section does not relate to import duties.)

Sec. 28. (This section does not relate to import duties.)

Sec. 29. *And be it further enacted,* That whenever any merchandise, except wine, distilled spirits, and perishable or explosive articles, or articles in bulk, imported at the ports of New York, in the State of New York; Philadelphia, in the State of Pennsylvania; Boston, in the State of Massachusetts; Baltimore, in the State of Maryland; Portland, in the State of Maine; Port Huron, in the State of Michigan; New Orleans, in the State of Louisiana; and San Francisco, in the State of California, shall appear by the invoice or bill of lading and by the manifest to be consigned to and destined for either of the ports specified in section thirty-five of this Act, the collector at the port of arrival shall permit the owner, agent, or consignee to make entry thereof for warehouse or immediate transportation, in triplicate, setting forth the particulars in such entry and the route by which such goods are to be forwarded, whether by land or water. The entry having been compared with the invoice and duly sworn to, and such an examination of the goods and merchandise having been made as will satisfy the customs officers that the same corresponds with the manifest and invoice, and the duties estimated on the value and quantity of the invoice, and on the execution of a bond as hereinafter provided, the collector shall deliver the same to be immediately transported to such port of destination, at the sole cost and risk of such owner, agent, or consignee. And goods and merchandise imported to any of the aforesaid ports of entry, and designed for any port designated by the thirty-fifth section of this Act, the collector of said port shall give priority in time to the examination of said goods and merchandise for the purpose of forwarding the same to their port of destination, and said examination shall not necessitate the transportation of said goods and merchandise to the warehouse or appraiser's office; and such merchandise so entered for immediate transportation shall not be subject to appraisement and liquidation of duties at the port of first arrival aforesaid, but shall undergo such examination as the Secretary of the Treasury shall deem necessary to verify the invoice and entry, and the same examination and appraisement thereof shall be required and had at the said port of destination as would have been required at the port of original importation if such merchandise had been entered for consumption or warehouse at such port.

Sec. 30. *And be it further enacted,* That the bond required by the foregoing section shall be in a penal sum of at least double the invoice value of the merchandise, with the duties added, and in such form, and with such number of sureties (not less than two) as shall be prescribed by the Secretary of the Treasury; and the said sureties shall justify, by affidavit taken before the collector of customs and attached to the said bond, in an amount at least double the penalty of the bond, and the said collector shall certify to their sufficiency; and the said bond may be executed at the port of final destination, and transmitted to the collector at the port of first arrival, as provided by the Act of March two, eighteen hundred and thirty-one.

Sec. 31. *And be it further enacted,* That merchandise so entered for transportation shall be delivered to and transported by common carriers, to be designated for this purpose by the Secretary of the Treasury, and to or by none others; and such carriers shall be responsible to the United States as common carriers for the safe delivery of such merchandise to the collector at the port of its destination; and before any such carriers shall be permitted to receive and transport any such merchandise they shall become bound to the United States in bonds of such form and amount, and with such conditions (not inconsistent with law) and such security as the Secretary of the Treasury shall require.

Sec. 32. *And be it further enacted,* That merchandise transported under the provisions of this Act shall be conveyed in cars, vessels, or vehicles, securely fastened with locks or seals, under the exclusive control of the officers of customs; and inspectors shall be stationed at proper points along the designated routes, or upon any car, vessel, vehicle, or train, at the discretion of the said Secretary, and at the expense of the said companies respectively. And such merchandise shall not be unladen or tran[s]hipped between the ports of first arrival and final destination. (See Act of April 5, 1872.)

Sec. 33. *And be it further enacted,* That merchandise so destined for immediate transportation as aforesaid, except the packages designated for examination, shall be transferred, under proper supervision, directly from the importing vessel to the cars, vessel, or vehicles in which the same is to be transported to its final destination; and if transferred from the importing vessel to any bonded or other warehouse, or to any other place than such car, vessel, or vehicle, it shall be taken possession of by the collector as unclaimed, and deposited in public store, and shall not be removed from such store without entry and appraisement, as in ordinary cases. But the Secretary of the Treasury may, in his discretion, and with such precaution as he shall deem proper, authorize the establishment of bonded warehouses especially and exclusively appropriated to the reception of such merchandise in cases where its immediate transfer to the transporting car, vessel, or vehicle shall be impracticable. But merchandise remaining in such warehouse more than ten days shall be deprived of the privileges conferred by this Act, and shall be taken possession of by the collector as unclaimed, and held until regularly entered and appraised.

Sec. 34. *And be it further enacted,* That the Secretary of the Treasury shall prescribe forms of entries, oaths, bonds, and other papers to be required, and all needful rules. and regulations, not inconsistent with law, to be observed in the execution of this Act, which shall have the force and effect of law.

Sec. 35. *And be it further enacted,* That the privilege of this Act shall extend to the ports of New York, in the State of New York; Boston, in the State of Massachusetts; Providence, in the State of Rhode Island; Philadelphia, in the State of Pennsylvania; Baltimore, in the State of Maryland; Norfolk, in the State of Virginia; Charleston, in the State of South Carolina; Savannah, in the State of Georgia; New Orleans, in the State of Louisiana; Portland, in the State of Maine; Buffalo, in the State of New York; Chicago, in the State of Illinois; Cincinnati, in the State of Ohio; Saint Louis, in the State of Missouri; Evansville, in the State of

Indiana; Milwaukee, in the State of Wisconsin; Louisville, in the State of Kentucky; Cleveland, in the State of Ohio; San Francisco, in the State of California; Portland, in the State of Oregon; Memphis, in the State of Tennessee; and Mobile, in the State of Alabama; and to importations from or to Europe, and from or to Asia, or the islands adjacent thereto, via the United States.*

Sec. 36. *And be it further enacted,* That at each of said ports, for which an appraiser of imported merchandise is not now provided for by law, there shall be appointed an appraiser of imported merchandise, at a salary of three thousand dollars per annum, and also such number of weighers, gaugers, measurers, and inspectors as may be necessary to execute the provisions of this Act, who shall receive the ordinary legal compensation of such officers.

Sec. 37. *And be it further enacted,* That any person maliciously opening, breaking, or entering, by any means whatever, any car, vessel, vehicle, warehouse, or package containing any such merchandise delivered for transportation as aforesaid, removing, injuring, breaking, or defacing any lock or seal placed upon such car, vessel, vehicle, warehouse, or package, or aiding, abetting, or encouraging any other person or persons so to remove, break, injure, or deface such locks or seals, or to open, break, or enter such car, vessel, or vehicle, with intent to remove or cause to be removed unlawfully any merchandise therein, or in any manner to injure or defraud the United States; and any person receiving any merchandise unlawfully removed from any such car, vessel, or vehicle, knowing it to have been so unlawfully removed, shall be guilty of felony, and in addition to any penalties heretofore prescribed shall, on conviction, be imprisoned not less than six months nor more than two years; and any person swearing wilfully false in any oath prescribed in this Act, or by the Secretary of the Treasury in pursuance of authority to make all needful regulations conferred upon him by this Act, shall be guilty of wilful and corrupt perjury.

Sec. 38. *And be it further enacted,* That sections twenty-nine, thirty, thirty-one, thirty-two, thirty-three, thirty-four, thirty-five, thirty-six, and thirty-seven of this Act shall take effect on the first day of October, eighteen hundred and seventy.

---

* The privileges of this Act shall extend to the port of Toledo, in the State of Ohio. (Act of March 5, 1872.)

The privileges of this Act shall extend to the port of Pittsburgh, in the State of Pennsylvania. (Act of March 18, 1872.)

8

ACT OF DECEMBER 22, 1870.

(From U. S. Statutes at Large, vol. 16, p. —.)

AN ACT to amend an Act entitled "An Act to reduce Internal Taxes, and for other purposes," approved July 14, 1870.

Be it enacted by the Senate and House of Representatives of the United States of America in Congress assembled, That so much of section twenty-one, of the Act to reduce internal taxes, and for other purposes, approved July fourteenth, eighteen hundred and seventy, as relates to sugar, be AMENDED so it will read:

746½. On all sugar not above number seven, Dutch standard in color, one and three-quarter cents per pound (647).

747. On all sugar above number seven, and not above number ten, Dutch standard in color, two cents per pound (647).

747½. On all sugar above number ten, and not above number thirteen, Dutch standard in color, two and one-quarter cents per pound (647).

748. On all sugar above number thirteen, and not above number sixteen, Dutch standard in color, two and three-quarter cents per pound (647).

749. On all sugar above number sixteen, and not above number twenty, Dutch standard in color, three and one-quarter cents per pound (647).

750. On all sugar above number twenty, Dutch standard in color, and on all refined loaf, lump, crushed, powdered and granulated sugar, four cents per pound: *Provided,* That the Secretary of the Treasury shall, by regulation, prescribe and require that samples from packages of sugar shall be taken by the proper officers, in such manner as to ascertain the true quality of such sugar; and the weights of sugar imported in casks or boxes shall be marked distinctly by the custom-house weigher, by scoring the figures indelibly on each package: *And provided further,* That all syrup of sugar, syrup of sugar-cane juice, melada, concentrated melada, or concentrated molasses, entered under the name of molasses, shall be forfeited to the United States (646-647).

JOINT RESOLUTION OF JANUARY 30, 1871.

(From U. S. Statutes at Large, vol. 16, p.   .)

JOINT RESOLUTION declaratory of the meaning of the Act entitled "An Act to reduce Internal Taxes, and for other purposes," approved July 14, 1870.

751. *Be it resolved by the Senate and House of Representatives of the United States of America in Congress assembled,* That all foreign merchandise which arrived at a port of the United States on or before the thirty-first day of December, eighteen hundred and seventy, and not entered or transferred to a public store or bonded warehouse, shall be entitled to the benefits of the twenty-sixth section of an Act entitled, "An Act to reduce internal taxes, and for other purposes," approved July fourteen, eighteen hundred and seventy, the same as such merchandise would have been entitled to, had it actually been in public store or bonded warehouse on or prior to the thirty-first day of December, eighteen hundred and seventy : *Provided,* That the owner of such merchandise shall, within thirty days from the passage of this resolution, make application therefor in writing to the collector of the port at which such merchandise arrived (746).

752. **Sec. 2.** *And be it further enacted,* That the said Act is hereby further amended by inserting the word "herein" in the twenty-first section thereof, between the words "otherwise" and "provided," wherever the said words occur together in the said section, and this amendment shall take effect from and after January first, eighteen hundred and seventy-one (651-652-670-674-685-705).

ACT OF MAY 1, 1872.

(From U. S. Statutes at Large, vol. 16, p.   .)

AN ACT repealing the duty on Tea and Coffee.

753. *Be it enacted by the Senate and House of Representatives of the United States of America in Congress assembled,* That on and after the first day of July next tea and coffee shall be

placed on the free list, and no further import duties shall
be collected upon the same. And all tea and coffee which
may be in the public stores or bonded warehouses on said
first day of July shall be subject to no duty upon the entry
thereof for consumption, and all tea and coffee remaining
in bonded warehouses on said first day of July, upon which
the duties shall have been paid, shall be entitled to a refund
of the duties paid (641-642).

ACT OF JUNE 6, 1872.

(From U. S. Statutes at Large, vol. 16, p.   .)

AN ACT to reduce duties on imports, and to reduce internal taxes, and for
other purposes.

*Be it enacted by the Senate and House of Representatives of the
United States of America in Congress assembled,* That on
and after the first day of August, eighteen hundred and
seventy-two, IN LIEU of the duties heretofore imposed by
law on the articles hereinafter enumerated or provided
for, imported from foreign countries, there shall be levied,
collected, and paid the following duties and rates of duty,
that is to say :

754. On all slack coal or culm, such as will pass through a
half-inch screen, forty cents per ton of twenty-eight bushels, eighty
pounds to the bushel (459). On all bituminous coal and shale,
seventy-five cents per ton of twenty-eight bushels, eighty pounds
to the bushel (459).

755. On salt, in bulk, eight cents per one hundred pounds (535).
On salt, in bags, sacks, barrels, or other packages, twelve cents per
one hundred pounds (535).

756. On oat-meal, one half cent per pound (44). On potatoes,
fifteen cents per bushel (323).

757. On bend or belting leather, and on Spanish or other sole
leather, fifteen per centum ad valorem (378).

758. On calf-skins, tanned, or tanned and dressed, twenty-five
per centum ad valorem (378).

759. On upper leather of all other kinds, and on skins dressed
and finished of all kinds, not herein otherwise provided for, twenty
per centum ad valorem (391-377-378).

760. On all skins for morocco tanned, but unfinished, ten per centum ad valorem (391).

761. On chiccory root, ground or unground, one cent per pound (517).

762. On all timber, squared or sided, not otherwise provided for, one cent per cubic foot (53) ;

763. On sawed boards, plank, deals, and other lumber of hemlock, white-wood, sycamore, and bass-wood, one dollar per thousand feet board measure (53) ;

764. On all other varieties of sawed lumber, two dollars per thousand feet board measure (53) : *Provided,* That when lumber of any sort is planed or finished, in addition to the rates herein provided, there shall be levied and paid, for each side so planed or finished, fifty cents per thousand feet; and if planed on one side and tongued and grooved, one dollar per thousand feet; and if planed on two sides and tongued and grooved, one dollar and fifty cents per thousand feet.

765. On hubs for wheels, posts, last-blocks, wagon blocks, oar blocks, gun blocks, heading blocks, and all like blocks or sticks, rough-hewn or sawed only, twenty per centum ad valorem (53-69).

766. On pickets and palings, twenty per centum ad valorem (53-69). On laths, fifteen cents per thousand pieces (53). On all shingles, thirty-five cents per thousand (390).

767. On pine clapboards, two dollars per thousand. On spruce clapboards, one dollar and fifty cents per thousand (390-69).

768. On house or cabinet furniture, in pieces or rough, and not finished, thirty per centum ad valorem (374). On cabinet wares and house furniture, finished, thirty-five per centum ad valorem (374).

769. On casks and barrels, empty, and on sugar-box shooks, and packing-boxes of wood, not otherwise provided for, thirty per centum ad valorem (390).

770. On fruit, shade, lawn, and ornamental trees, shrubs, plants, and flower-seeds, not otherwise provided for, twenty per centum ad valorem (309).

771. On garden-seeds, and all other seeds for agricultural and horticultural purposes, not otherwise provided for, twenty per centum ad valorem (312).

772. On ginger, ground, three cents per pound (656). On ginger, preserved or pickled, thirty-five per centum ad valorem (541). On ginger, essence of, thirty-five per centum ad valorem (251).

773. On chocolate, five cents per pound, and on cocoa, prepared or manufactured, two cents per pound (644).

Sec. 2. That on and after the first day of August, eighteen hundred and seventy-two, IN LIEU of the duties imposed by law on the articles in this section enumerated, there shall be levied, collected, and paid on the goods, wares, and merchandise in this section enumerated and provided for, imported from foreign countries, NINETY PER CENTUM OF THE SEVERAL DUTIES AND RATES OF DUTY NOW IMPOSED BY LAW UPON SAID ARTICLES SEVERALLY, it being the intent of this section to reduce existing duties on said articles TEN PER CENTUM OF SUCH DUTIES, that is to say:

774. On all manufactures of cotton of which cotton is the component part of chief value.

775. On all wools, hair of the alpaca goat, and other animals, and all manufactures wholly or in part of wool or hair of the alpaca, and other like animals, except as hereinafter provided.*

776. On all iron and steel, and on all manufactures of iron and steel, of which such metals or either of them shall be the component part of chief value, excepting cotton machinery.

777. On all metals not herein otherwise provided for, and on all manufactures of metals of which either of them is the component part of chief value, excepting percussion caps, watches, jewelry, and other articles of ornament: *Provided*, That all wire-rope and wire strand or chain made of iron-wire, either bright, coppered, galvanized, or coated with other metals, shall pay the same rate of duty that is now levied on the iron wire of which said rope or strand or chain is made; and all wire-rope and wire strand or chain made of steel wire, either bright, coppered, galvanized, or coated with other metals, shall pay the same rate of duty that is now levied on the steel wire of which said rope or strand or chain is made.

778. On all paper, and manufactures of paper, excepting unsized printing paper, books and other printed matter, not herein specifically provided for.†

779. On all manufactures of India-rubber, gutta-percha, or straw, and on oil-cloths of all descriptions.

780. On glass and glassware,‡ and on unwrought pipe-clay, fine clay, and fuller's earth.

---

* " The question has been presented to the Department whether, under the second section of the Act approved June 6, 1872, which provides for ten per cent. reduction on all manufactures wholly or in part of wool or hair, of the alpaca and other like animals, worsted goods are to be entitled to the benefits of this reduction.
    The Department's decision is to consider, for the purpose of this Act, worsted goods as manufactures of wool, and to allow worsted goods the benefits of said reduction.
    This information is communicated to you in advance of the law going into effect, for the benefit of the numerous importers who have applied for its decision in regard thereto." (Dec. June 24, 1872.)
    † " Books and other printed matter are entitled to the ten per cent. reduction." (Dec. of July 30, 1872.)
    ‡ " The terms Glass and Glassware should be understood as referring only to such articles as are commercially known by those terms." (Dec. of August 5, 1872.)

781. On all leather not otherwise herein provided for, and on all manufactures of skins, bone, ivory, horn, and leather, except gloves and mittens, and of which either of said articles is the component part of chief value ; and on liquorice paste or liquorice juice.

782. **Sec. 3.** That on and after the first day of October next there shall be collected and paid on all goods, wares, and merchandise of the growth or produce of countries east of the Cape of Good Hope, (except wool, raw cotton, and raw silk as reeled from the cocoon, or not further advanced than tram, thrown, or organzine,) when imported from places west of the Cape of Good Hope, a duty of ten per centum ad valorem, in addition to the duties imposed on any such article when imported directly from the place or places of their growth or production (581).*

Sec. 4. That on and after the first day of August, eighteen hundred and seventy-two, IN LIEU of the duties heretofore imposed by law on the articles mentioned in this section, there shall be levied, collected, and paid on the goods, wares, and merchandise in this section enumerated, imported from foreign countries, the following duties and rates of duty, that is to say :

783. On all burlaps (482), and like manufactures of flax, jute, or hemp, or of which flax, jute, or hemp shall be the component material of chief value, excepting such as may be suitable for bagging for cotton, thirty per centum ad valorem (482) ; on all oilcloth foundations or floor-cloth canvas, made of flax, jute, or hemp, or of which flax, jute, or hemp shall be the component material of chief value, forty per centum ad valorem (482) ; on all bags, cotton bags, and bagging, and all other like manufactures, not herein otherwise provided for, except bagging for cotton, composed wholly or in part of flax, hemp, jute, gunny-cloth, gunny-bags, or other material, forty per centum ad valorem (484-674).

784. On insulators for use exclusively in telegraphy, except those made of glass, twenty-five per centum ad valorem (503).

785. On bouillons or cannetille, and metal threads, filé or gespinst, twenty-five per centum ad valorem (373).

786. On emery ore, six dollars a ton (717) ; and on emery grains, two cents a pound (237).

787. On corks and cork bark, manufactured, thirty per centum ad valorem (545).

---

788. On acids, namely, acetic, acetous, and pyroligneous of specific gravity of 1.047, or less, five cents per pound (506); acetic, acetous, and pyroligneous of specific gravity over 1.047, thirty cents. per pound (506); carbolic, liquid, ten per centum ad valorem (32); gallic, one dollar per pound (534); sulphuric, fuming, (Nordhausen,) one cent per pound (231); tannic, one dollar per pound (534); tartaric, fifteen cents per pound (231).

789. On acetates of ammonia, twenty-five cents per pound (507); baryta, twenty-five cents per pound (507); copper, ten cents per pound (166); iron, twenty-five cents per pound (507); lead, brown, five cents per pound (507); white, ten cents per pound (507); potassia, twenty-five cents per pound (254); soda, twenty-five cents per pound (507); strontia, twenty-five cents per pound (507); zinc, twenty-five cents per pound (507).

790. On blue vitriol, four cents per pound (640); on camphor, refined, five cents per pound (235); on sulphate of quinine, twenty per centum ad valorem (257); on chlorate of potash, three cents per pound (254); on Rochelle salts, five cents per pound (237); on sal-soda, and soda ash, one-fourth of one cent per pound (178); on santonine, three dollars per pound (534); on strychnia, one dollar per ounce (536);

791. On bay-rum or bay-water, whether distilled or compounded, one dollar per gallon of first proof, and in proportion for any greater strength than first proof (423).

792. On rum essence or oil, and bay-rum essence or oil, fifty cents per ounce (258).

793. On all sized or glued paper, suitable only for printing-paper, twenty-five per centum ad valorem (395-419);

794. On vermuth, the same duty as on wines of the same cost (652);

795. On mustard, ground, in bulk, ten cents per pound; when enclosed in glass or tin, fourteen cents per pound (322);

796. On Zante or other currants, one cent per pound (697); on figs, two and one-half cents per pound (178); on raisins, two and one-half cents per pound (178); on dates (178) and prunes (197), one cent per pound;

797. On preserved or condensed milk, twenty per centum ad valorem (166);

798. On fire-crackers, one dollar per box of forty packs, not exceeding eighty to each pack, and in the same proportion for any greater or less number (547).

799. On tin, in plates or sheets, terne, and taggers tin, fifteen per centum ad valorem (329).

800. On iron and tin-plates galvanized or coated with any metal by electric batteries, two cents per pound (428).

801. On Moisic iron, made from sand ore by one process, fifteen dollars per ton.

802. On umbrella and parasol ribs and stretchers, frames, tips, runners, handles, or other parts thereof, when made in whole or chief part of iron, steel, or any other metal, a duty of forty-five per centum ad valorem (374): *Provided,* That the rate of duty upon umbrellas, parasols, and sunshades, when covered with silk or alpaca, shall be sixty per centum ad valorem; all other umbrellas shall be forty-five per centum ad valorem (624);

803. On saltpetre, crude, one cent per pound (536); refined and partially refined, two cents per pound (178-259).

Sec. 5. That on and after the first day of August next the importation of the articles enumerated and described in this section shall be EXEMPT FROM DUTY, that is to say:

804. Acid, boracic and sulphuric (231); agates, unmanufactured (466); almond shells (739); aluminium, or aluminum (60); amber beads (540) and amber gum (708);

805. American manufactures, the following, to wit, casks, barrels, or carboys, and other vessels, and grain-bags, the manufacture of the United States, if exported, containing American produce, and declaration be made of intent to return the same empty, under such regulations as shall be prescribed by the Secretary of the Treasury (570);

806. Angelica root (267);

807. Animals brought into the United States temporarily and for a period not exceeding six months, for the purpose of exhibition or competition for prizes offered by any agricultural or racing association: *Provided,* That bond be first given, in accordance with the regulations to be prescribed by the Secretary of the Treasury, with the condition that the full duty to which such animals would otherwise be liable shall be paid in case of their sale in the United States, or if not re-exported within said six months (695);

808. Annato, roncou, rocou, or orleans, and all extracts of (122); annatto-seed (708); antimony, ore, and crude sulphuret of (726); aqua fortis (32); argal-dust (166); arseniate of aniline (166);

809. Balm of Gilead (280); balsams, viz: copavia, fir or Canada, Peru and Tolu (73-234);

810. Bamboo reeds, not further manufactured than cut into suitable lengths for walking-sticks or canes, or for sticks for umbrellas, parasols, or sunshades (711-374);

811. Bamboos, unmanufactured (711); bezoar stones (166); bed feathers and downs (305); birds, stuffed (166); black salts (166); black tares (166);

812. Bladders, crude, and all integuments of animals not otherwise provided for (166); Bologna sausages (75); bones, crude and not manufactured; bones, burned, calcined, ground, or steamed (714); borax, crude (234); borate of lime (234);

813. Books which shall have been printed and manufactured more than twenty years at the date of importation (714);

814. Books, maps, and charts imported by authority for the use of the United States or for the use of the library of Congress : *Provided,* That the duty shall not have been included in the contract or price paid (709-126);

815. Books, maps, and charts specially imported, not more than two copies in any one invoice, in good faith for the use of any society incorporated or established for philosophical, literary, or religious purposes, or for the encouragement of the fine arts, or for the use, or by the order, of any college, academy, school, or seminary of learning in the United States (121);

816. Books, professional, of persons arriving in the United States (162);

817. Books, household effects, or libraries, or parts of libraries, in use of persons or families from foreign countries, if used abroad by them not less than one year, and not intended for any other person or persons, nor for sale (155-162-731);

818. Brazil paste (33); Brazil pebbles for spectacles, and pebbles for spectacles, rough (503); Burgundy pitch (53);

819. Camphor, crude (235); cat-gut strings, or gut-cord, for musical instruments (280); chamomile flowers (267); charcoal (166); China root (267); cinchona root (712); chloride of lime (178);

820. Coal-stores of American vessels : *Provided,* That none shall be unloaded ;

821. Cobalt, ore of (273); cocoa or cocao, crude, and fiber, leaves, and shells of (643); coir (672) and coir yarn (483); colcothar, dry, or oxide of iron (60); coltsfoot, (crude drug) (267); contrayerva root (267);

822. Copper, old, taken from the bottom of American vessels compelled by marine disaster to repair in foreign ports ;

823. Cowage down (54); cow or kine pox, or vaccine virus (166); cubebs (235); curling-stones or quoits (166); curry and curry powders (166); cyanite or kyanite (166);

824. Diamonds, rough or uncut, including glazier's diamonds

(466-35); dried bugs (166); dried blood (166); dried and prepared flowers (540);

825. Elecampane-root (267) ; ergot (237);

826. Fans, common palm-leaf (551); farina (166);

827. Flowers, leaves, plants, roots, barks, and seeds, for medicinal purposes, in a crude state, not otherwise provided for (267);

828. Firewood (56); flint, flints, and ground flint-stones (718-275); fossels (166);

829. Fruits, plants, tropical and semi-tropical, for the purpose of propagation or cultivation (309);

830. Galanga, or galangal (60-267); garancine (276); gentian-root (267); ginger-root (655); ginseng-root (267); goldbeaters' molds and goldbeaters' skins (38); gold-size (504);

831. Grease, for use as soap-stock only, not otherwise provided for (43-857);

832. Gunny-bags and gunny-cloth, old or refuse, fit only for remanufacture (166);

833. Gut and worm-gut, manufactured or unmanufactured, for whip and other cord; guts, salted (60-166-715);

834. Hair, all horse, cattle, cleaned or uncleaned, drawn or undrawn, but unmanufactured (720); hair of hogs, curled, for beds and mattresses, and not fit for bristles (58-523);

835. Hellebore-root (267); hide cuttings, raw, with or without the hair on, for glue-stock (720); hide-rope (166);

836. Hides, namely, Angora goat-skins, raw, without the wool, unmanufactured (719); asses' skins, raw, unmanufactured (72); hides, raw or uncured, whether dry, salted, or pickled, and skins, except sheep-skins with the wool on (313);

837. Hones and whetstones (166); hop-roots for cultivation (309); horn-strips (720);

838. Indian hemp, (crude drug) (60);

839. Indio or Malacca joints, not further manufactured than cut into suitable lengths for the manufactures into which they are intended to be converted (365);

840. Iridium (142); isinglass, or fish glue (277); istle, or Tampico fiber (523);

841. Jalap (722); josstick or josslight (166); jute butts (673);

842. Leather, old scrap (166); leaves, all, not otherwise provided for (267); lithographic stones, not engraved (166); loadstones (166);

843. Logs, and round unmanufactured timber not otherwise provided for, and ship timber (724);

844. Macaroni and vermicella (379); madder and munject, ground or prepared (724), and all extracts of (274); magnets (166); manganese, oxide and ore of (43); marrow, crude (43); marsh-mallows (267); matico leaf (267); meerchaum, crude or raw (60); mica and mica waste (60); mineral waters, all, not artificial (550);

845. Moss, sea-weed, and all other vegetable substances used for beds and mattresses (58);

846. Murexide, (a dye) (505); musk, crude (724); mustard-seed, brown and white (260);

847. Nuts, cocoa (696) and Brazil or cream (178); nux vomica (152);

848. Oil, essential, fixed or expressed, viz: Almonds (250); amber, crude and rectified (251); ambergris (251); anise, or anise-seed (251); anthos, or rosemary (251); bergamont (251); cajeput (251); caraway (251); cassia (251); cedrat (251); chamomile (251); cinnamon (251); citronella, or lemon-grass (251); civet (273); fennel (251); jasmine, or jessamine (251); juglandium (251); juniper (251); lavender (251); mace (250); ottar of roses (251); poppy (62); sesame, or sesamum-seed, or bene (702); thyme, red, or origanum (251); thyme, white (251); valerian (251);

849. Oil-cake (166); olives, green or prepared (109); orange buds and flowers (267); orpiment (153); osmium (60); oxidizing paste (166);

850. Palladium (60);

851. Paper-stock, crude, of every description, including all grasses, fibers, rags other than wool, waste, shavings, clippings, old paper, rope ends, waste rope, waste bagging, gunny-bags and gunny-cloth, old or refuse, to be used in making and fit only to be converted into paper, and unfit for any other manufacture, and cotton waste, whether for paper-stock or other purposes (742-737);

852. Pellitory root (267); persis, or extract of archil (726), and cudbear (715); Peruvian bark (712); pewter and britannia metal, old, and fit only to be remanufactured (461-60); phanglein (166); plumbago (323); polypodium (60); pulu (58);

853. Quick-grass root (166-344); quills, prepared or unpre-pared (284);

854. Railroad ties, of wood (69); ratan and reeds, unmanu-factured (157); rennets, raw or prepared (166); root flour (267);

855. Saffron (739) and safflower (739) and extract of (504); saffron cake (48); sago, crude (327); sago and sago-flour (327); Saint John's beans (50); salacine (280); salep, or saloup (166); sassafras, bark and root (267); sauerkraut (397); sausage-skins (166);

856. Seeds, namely, anise (260), anise star (260), canary (260), chia (267), sesamum (703), sugar-cane (309), and seeds of forest-trees (309);

857. Shark-skins (166); snails (166); soap-stocks (43-831);

858. Sparterre, for making or ornamental hats (299);

859. Spunk (48); stavesacre, crude (267); storax, or styrax (73); straw, unmanufactured (166);

860. Strontia, oxide of, or protoxide of strontium (166); succinic acid (280); sugar of milk (280);

861. Talc (60); tamarinds (37); teasels (49); teeth, unmanufactured (166); terra-alba, aluminous (504); tica, crude (504);

862. Tin, in pigs, bars, or blocks, and grain-tin (329);

863. Tonquin, tonqua, or tonka beans (267); tripoli (419);

864. Umbrella sticks, crude, to wit, all partridge, hair-wood, pimento, orange, myrtle, and other sticks and canes, in the rough, or no further manufactured than cut into lengths suitable for umbrella, parasol, or sun-shade sticks or walking-canes (810-374);

865. Uranium, oxide of (60);

866. Vanilla beans or vanilla plants (264); Venice turpentine (73);

867. Wafers (402); wax, bay or myrtle, Brazilian and Chinese (166-272); whalebone, unmanufactured (69);

868. Yams (51); yeast-cakes (166);

869. Zaffer (504).

870. **Sec. 6.** That for all purposes the standard for vinegar shall be taken to be that strength which requires thirty-five grains of bicarbonate of potash to neutralize one ounce troy of vinegar, and all import duties that now are, or may hereafter be, imposed by law on vinegar imported from foreign countries shall be collected according to said standard (536).

871. **Sec. 7.** That for a term of two years from and after the passage of this Act, and no longer, machinery and apparatus designed only for, and adapted to be used for steam towage on canals, and not now manufactured in the United States, may be imported by any State, or by any person duly authorized by the legislature of any State, free of duty, subject to such regulations as may be prescribed by the Secretary of the Treasury; and also that for the term of two years from and after the passage of this Act, and no longer, steam plow machinery, adapted to the cultivation of the

soil, may be imported by any person for his own use, free of duty, subject to such regulations of the Secretary of the Treasury as before provided (743).

872. **Sec. 8.** That all imported goods, wares, and merchandise which may be in the public stores or bonded warehouses on the first day of August, eighteen hundred and seventy-two, shall be subjected to no other duty upon the entry thereof for consumption than if the same were imported respectively after that day; and all goods, wares, and merchandise remaining in bonded warehouses on the day and year this Act shall take effect, and upon which the duties shall have been paid, shall be entitled to a refund of the difference between the amount of duties paid and the amount of duties said goods, wares, and merchandise would be subject to if the same were imported respectively after that day.

873. **Sec. 9.** That where fire-arms, scales, balances, shovels, spades, axes, hatchets, hammers, plows, cultivators, mowing machines, and reapers manufactured with stocks or handles made of wood grown in the United States are exported for benefit of drawback under section four of the Act of August fifth, eighteen hundred and sixty-one, and entitled "An Act to provide increased revenue from imports, to pay interest on the public debt, and for other purposes," such articles shall be entitled to such drawback, under that Act, in all cases when the imported material exceeds one-half of the value of the material used (181).

874. **Sec. 10.** That from and after the passage of this Act all lumber, timber, hemp, Manilla, and iron and steel rods, bars, spikes, nails, and bolts, and copper and composition metal, which may be necessary for the construction and equipment of vessels built in the United States for the purpose of being employed in the foreign trade, including the trade between the Atlantic and Pacific ports of the United States, and finished after the passage of this Act, may be imported in bond, under such regulations as the Secretary of the Treasury may prescribe; and upon proof that such materials have been used for the purpose aforesaid, no duties shall be paid thereon : *Provided*, That vessels receiving the benefit of this section shall not be allowed to engage in the coastwise trade of the United States more than two months in any one year, except upon the payment to the United

States of the duties on which a rebate is herein allowed: *And provided further,* That all articles of foreign production needed for the repair of American vessels engaged exclusively in foreign trade, may be withdrawn from bonded warehouses free of duty, under such regulations as the Secretary of the Treasury may prescribe.*

875. **Sec. 11.** That the proviso in section four of an Act entitled "An Act to protect the revenue, and for other purposes," approved July twenty-eighth, eighteen hundred and sixty-six, is hereby modified and amended so as to read as follows: *Provided,* That from and after the date of the passage of this Act, imported salt in bond may be used in curing fish, taken by vessels licensed to engage in the fisheries, under such regulations as the Secretary of the Treasury shall prescribe; and upon proof that said salt has been used in curing fish, the duties on the same shall be remitted (597).

(Section 12 to Section 30 inclusive do not relate to import duties.)

Sec. 31. That on and after the first day of July next the Act entitled "An Act imposing taxes on distilled spirits and tobacco, and for other purposes," approved July twentieth, eighteen hundred and sixty-eight, be, and the same is hereby, amended as follows:

876. That section sixty-one be amended by striking out all after the second paragraph, and inserting in lieu thereof the following words: "On all chewing and smoking tobacco, fine-cut, cavendish, plug, or twist, cut or granulated, of every description; on tobacco twisted by hand or reduced into a condition to be consumed, or in any manner other than the ordinary mode of drying and curing, prepared for sale or consumption, even if prepared without the use of any machine or instrument, and without being pressed or sweetened; and on all fine-cut shorts and refuse scraps, clippings, cuttings, and sweepings of tobacco, a tax of twenty cents per pound" (632).

(Sections 32 to 45 inclusive do not relate to import duties.)

877. **Sec. 46.** That all Acts and parts of Acts inconsistent with the provisions of this Act are hereby repealed: *Provided,* That all the provisions of said Act, shall be in force for levying and collecting all taxes properly assessed, or liable

---

* Decision of June 20, 1872, specifies the regulations.

to be assessed, or accruing under the provisions of former Acts, the right to which has already accrued, or which may hereafter accrue, under said Acts, and for maintaining, continuing, and enforcing liens, fines, penalties, and forfeitures incurred under and by virtue thereof. And this Act shall not be construed to affect any act done, right accrued, or penalty incurred under former Acts, but every such right is hereby saved ; and all suits and prosecutions for acts already done in violation of any former Act or Acts of Congress relating to the subjects embraced in this Act may be commenced or proceeded with in like manner as if this Act had not been passed : *Provided,* That whenever the duty imposed by any existing law shall cease in consequence of any limitation therein contained before the respective provisions of this Act shall take effect, the same duty or tax shall be, and is hereby, continued until such provision of this Act shall take effect; and where any Act is hereby repealed, no duty or tax imposed thereby shall be held to cease in consequence of such repeal until the respective corresponding provisions of this Act shall take effect.

878. **Sec. 47.** (This section does not relate to import duties.)

SCHEDULE

OF

U. S. IMPORT DUTIES

UNDER

EXISTING LAWS AND DECISIONS.

EXPLANATION.

The articles in the following schedule are alphabetically arranged under the *noun*, the qualifying word following, and each article bears reference to the paragraphs of the Digest prescribing the rate of duty, which paragraphs are consecutively numbered. Those articles marked "according to material" are classed under manufactures.

The term "Reg. of 1857," refers to the General Regulations of the Treasury Department issued 1857; "Rev. Reg." to the Revised Regulations issued 1869; and the Decisions, i. e. "dec. of——," to those rendered by the Department from 1857 to Aug. 1, 1872.

Articles not enumerated or provided for in the following schedule, are liable to duty under section 24 of the Act of March 2, 1861. All articles entitled to entry free of duty are described or specified. (See paragraph No. 166.)

Articles produced *east* of the Cape of Good Hope and imported from a place *west* thereof, are subject to the discriminating duty of ten per centum, *in addition* to the rates herein named; as are also those articles which would otherwise be admitted *free* of duty. (See paragraphs 782 and 581.)

A

Absynthe, (see liquors.)

Academies, articles specially imported for, (see apparatus)

Accordeous, (see musical instr's.)

Acid, acetic, acetous, and pyro-ligneous acid, of specific gravity of 1.047, or less, (788) ....5 cts. per lb. exceeding the specific gravity of 1.047, (788)..30 cts. per lb.

" arsenious, crude, (708).....   free.

" benzoic, (266)..................10 per ct.

" boraic, (804)..................   free.

Acid, carbolic, crystalized, used for medicinal purposes, (dec. of Oct. 18, 1869,) (32) ....10 per ct.

" carbolic, liquid, (788)...10 per ct.

" chromic, (14)...............15 per ct.

" citric, (231) ....10 cts. per lb.

" gallic, (788)..............$1 per lb.

" muriatic, (708)... ....   free.

" nitric, yellow and white, (32)........................10 per ct.

" nitric, not chemically pure, (708) ....   free.

" oxalic, (708)..............   free.

Acid, picric. and nitro picric, (708) free.
"   rosalic, so-styled, (dec. of
     Sept. 24, 1869,) (166)...20 per ct.
"   succinic, (860)............... free.
"   sulphuric or oil of vitriol,
     (804) .... free.
"   sulphuric, fuming, (Nord-
     hausen,) (788).........1 ct. per lb.
"   tannic, (788). ....$1 per lb.
"   tartaric, (788)........15 cts. per lb.
Acids, of every description,
     used for chemical and manu-
     facturing purposes, not other-
     wise provided for, (120) ...... free.
Acids, of every description,
     used for medicinal purposes
     or in the fine arts, not other-
     wise provided for, (32).......10 per ct.
     Provided, that carboys con-
     taining acids shall be subject
     to the same duty as if empty,
     (708)
Aconite, root, leaf, and bark, (708) free.
Acorns and acorn coffee, (see
     coffee substitutes.)
Adamantine spar, as emery
     stone, (Reg. of 1857, p. 586)
     (786)
Adzes, (458-776)...90 per ct. of 45 per ct.
Agaric, (708)..................... free.
Agates, (see precious stones.)
"   unmanufactured, (804) free.
Agriculture, Department of, or
     the U. S. Botanic Garden;—
     plants, trees, shrubs, roots,
     seed-cane, and seeds import-
     ed for, (733)..................... free.
Alabaster, ornaments of. (71)....30 per ct.
Alba, canuella, bark, (712)...... free.
Albata, (see German silver.)
Albumen, (708)........ .... free.
Alcohol, (see liquors.)
"   amylic, or fusel oil,
     (522)..... ....$2 per gall.
Alcornoque, (120).................. free.

Ale, por er and beer, in bottles,
     *(424) ....35 cts. per gall.
Ale, porter and beer, otherwise
     than in bottles, (424) .20 cts. per gall.
Alkaline silicates, (689).......½ ct per lb.
Alkanet root, (708)................ free.
Alkekengi, (708)..................... free.
Almonds, (510)..................6 cts. per lb.
"   shelled, (510) ...10 cts. per lb.
"   shells, (804)........... free.
Aloes, (see gums.)
Alpaca, hair of the, (see wool.)
"   "   manufactur-
     ed, (see dress goods, clothing,
     and manufs. of worsted.)
Alum, patent alum, alum sub-
     stitute, sulphate of alumina,
     and aluminous cake, (232)
             60 cts. per 100 lbs.
Aluminium or aluminum, (804) free.
Amber, gum, (804)................. free.
Ambergris, (122)................... free.
Amelines of worsted, as manu-
     factures of worsted, (three
     decs. of Sept. 21, 1857.)
American Fisheries, all articles
     the produce of such fisheries,
     (153)..................... free.
American manufactures, (see
     United States.)
Amethyst, (see precious stones.)
Ammonia, (267)........... ....20 per ct.
"   acetate or pyrolignite
     of, (789)..... ..25 cts. per lb.
"   carbonate of, (267)..20 per ct.
"   crude, (708)........... free.
"   muriate of, (32)......10 per ct.
"   sal, (32)..... ....10 per ct.
"   sulphate of, (dec. of
     Feb. 11, 1871) (267).20 per ct.
Anatomy, preparations of, (739) free.
Anchors or parts thereof, (432-
     776)........ 90 per ct. of 2¼ cts. per lb.

---

*"The 35 cts. per gallon obviously includes duty on the bottles, as when not bottled pays but 20 cts. per gallon."—(Decision of January 22, 1869.)

"If it becomes sour on the voyage of importation, is subject to the regular duty for such articles, and if an abatement is claimed for damage resulting from 'souring,' it does not change the classification."—(Decision of May 3, 1869.)

"Under existing laws there are no restrictions as to the size of the packages in which beer, ale, and porter may be imported."—(Decision of March 30, 1868.)

"One doz. pint bottles considered one and one-eighth gallon."—(Decision of November 5 and 21, 1868.)

Anchors so broken, rusty or old as to be unfit for use and fit only to be remanufactured, (dec. of March 6, 1869,) (677-776).. ....90 per ct. of $8 per ton.

Anchovies, preserved in oil or otherwise, (540).................50 per ct.

Andirons, of cast iron, (441-776) ....90 per ct. of 1½ ct. per lb.

Angelica root, (806)................ free.

Aniline, chemical preparation, (dec of July 17, 1863,) (166).20 per ct.

Aniline, arseniate of, (808)...... free.

Aniline dyes and colors, by whatever name known, (dec. of March 22, 1870,) (687) 50 cts. per lb. and 35 per ct.

Animal carbon, (bone black) (505)...............................25 per ct.

Animals, alive, (695)..'...........20 per ct.

Animals, for breeding purposes, from beyond the seas, (under regulations,) (dec. of Feb. 3, 1871,) (695)?......... .... free.

Animals, teams of. including harness and tackle, actually owned by persons immigrating and in actual use, (under regulations,) (695)?............. free.

Animals brought into the U. S. temporarily, for exhibition or competition for prizes, as provided for in 695 and 807?..... free.

Annatto, (808)..................... free.

" extracts of, (808)...... free.

Anodyne, Hoffman's,(522)..50 cts. per lb.

" other, (see medicines.)

Antimony, crude, and regulus of, (512)..............10 per ct.

" ore of, and crude sulphuret of,(808). free.

Antiquity, collections of, specially imported and not for sale, (121-128-715) .... free.

Anvils, (430-776) 90 per ct. of 2½ cts. per lb.

Apparatus, (see boats, machinery and instruments.)

Apparatus, all philosophical and scientific, instruments and preparations, (dec.of October 29, 1857,) books,‡(dec.of Jan. 10, 1870,) maps,‡ charts,‡ statues, statuary, (dec. of March 12, 1870,) busts and casts of marble, bronze, alabaster or plaster of Paris; paintings,drawings,etchings, specimens of sculpture, cabinets of coins, medals, regalia,* gems and all collections of antiquities, specially imported for the use of any society or institution incorporated or established for philosophical, educational, scientific, literary, or religious† purposes, or encouragement of the fine arts, and not intended for sale, (121-730-815) free.

Apparel, (see clothing and effects.)

Appeal from decision of collector, (see par. 568)

Apple sauce, (79-365)............35 per ct.

Apples, (37)......................10 per ct.

" bitter, (713).............. free.

Aprons, silk, (486).................60 per ct.

Aqua fortis, (808)................... free.

Arabic, gum, (719)................:..... free.

Archill, (see orchill.)

Argentine, (see German silver.)

Argal dust, (808)..................... free.

Argols, crude, (see tartar.)

Arms, fire and side, except swords, (108-114-391-399-679-776).........90 per ct. of 35 per ct.

Aromatic cachous, (see cosmetics.)

Arrack, (see liquors.)

Arrow root, (514)..............30 per ct.

Arsenic, (708).......... .... free.

" in all forms, (267).....20 per ct.

‡Books, maps and charts specially imported, not more than two copies in any one invoice.—(See paragraph 815.)

*As to what is ruled as "regalia," see decisions of September 30, 1861; August 25, 1868; September 1, 1869; January 3, 1870; June 25, 1870; Jan. 25, 1870, and Nov. 14, 1865.

†Paragraph 569 provides that "all philosophical apparatus and instruments imported for the use of any society incorporated for *religious* purposes," shall be subject to a duty of fifteen per centum ad valorem.

Art, works of, (see apparatus and paintings.)

Articles, all, raw or unmanufactured, not otherwise provided for, (166)................10 per ct.

Articles imported for the use of the United States, (709)...... free.

Asbestos, (505)......................25 per ct.
    " not manuf'd, (708)... free.

Ashes, of wood and beet root, (742)...................... free.
    " of lead, (dec. of January 27, 1870,) (166)........10 per ct.

Asphaltum, (505)... ....25 per ct.

Assafœtida, (32-271)..............20 per ct.

Australia, gum, (719) .... free.

Augers,
Awls, } (458-776) 90 per ct. of 45 per ct.
Axes,

Axles or parts thereof, (432-776,) 90 per ct. of 2½ cts. per lb.

Axles or parts thereof, cast steel, (dec. of Oct. 6, 1864,) (458-776) 90 per ct. of 45 per ct.

B

Bacon, (16)......................2 cts. per lb.

Baggage, (see effects.)

Bagging, (see cotton bagging.)
    " waste, (see rags.)

Bags,‡ Amer. manuf. (see United States.)

Bags and cotton bags, and bagging, and all other like manufactures, not herein otherwise provided for, except bagging for cotton, composed wholly or in part of flax, hemp, jute, gunny cloth, gunny bags, or other material, (783)...........40 per ct.

Bags, gunny, (see gunny bags.)

Bait, fish for, (718)................ free.

Baize, as bocking.

Ballast, stone, unmanufactured, (dec. of April 6, 1869,) (166)...................10 per ct.
    " stone manufact'd, (dec. April 6, 1869,)(166).20 per ct.

Balls, bagatelle, ivory or bone, (542-781)..90 per ct. of 50 per ct.
    " billiard, ivory or bone, (1-542-781) 90 per ct. of 50 per ct.
    " India rubber, solid, from ½ to 2½ inches in diameter, classed as toys, (dec. of June 20, 1870,) (543-779) 90 per ct. of 50 per ct.
    " India rubber, larger than above, (dec. of June 20, 1870.) (77-364-779, see also 66)...90 per ct. of 35 per ct.

Balm of Gilead, (809) .... free.

Balmorals, wool or worsted,* (614-775) valued at 40 cts. or less per lb.
    90 per ct. of $\begin{cases} 20 \text{ cts. per lb.} \\ \text{and 35 per ct.} \end{cases}$
valued above 40 cts. and not above 60 cts. per lb.
    90 per ct. of $\begin{cases} 30 \text{ cts. per lb.} \\ \text{and 35 per ct.} \end{cases}$
valued above 60 cts. and not above 80 cts. per lb.
    90 per ct. of $\begin{cases} 40 \text{ cts. per lb.} \\ \text{and 35 per ct.} \end{cases}$
valued above 80 cts. per lb.
    90 per ct. of $\begin{cases} 50 \text{ cts per lb.} \\ \text{and 35 per ct.} \end{cases}$

Balmorals, if cotton chief value, (470-774)
    90 per ct. of $\begin{cases} 24 \text{ cts. per lb.} \\ \text{and 35 per ct.} \end{cases}$

Balmorals, any other material except wool, worsted or cotton, (470)...24 cts. per lb. and 35 per ct.

Balmoral skirts and skirting, (see clothing.)

Balsam, as cosmetic, (270)......50 per ct.
    " Canada or fir, (809).... free.
    " copavia, (809)........... free.
    " Peruvian, (809).......... free.
    " Tolu, (809)................ free.
    " used for medical purposes, (73)............30 per ct.

Bamboo reeds, (see reeds.)
    " unmanufac'd, (811)..... free.

---

‡" Grain bags, imported from Canada, filled with flaxseed, reported by appraiser as a 'not unusual' covering, are not liable to duty as bags."—(Dec. of April 10, 1868.)
*As to what shall be classed balmorals, see dec. of December 22, 1866.

Bananas, (see damage on fruit,)
(696)..............................10 per ct.

Barbary, gum (719)..... .... free.

Barilla, (impure carbonate of
soda) (123)........................ free.

Bark, cork (see cork bark.)

Barks, viz: aconite (708), calisaya (712), Canella alba (712),
cascarilla (712), all cinchona
barks (712), croton (712),
hemlock (720), Lima (712),
oak (726), Peruvian (852),
pomegranate (712), quilla
(712), sassafras (855), and all
other barks not otherwise
provided for (712)............... free.

Barks, all medicinal, crude, not
otherwise provided for, (827) free.

Barley, (16)..................15 cts. per bus.

" pearl or hulled, (297) 1 ct. per lb.

Barrege, (according to material.)

Barrels, Amer. manuf., (see
United States.)

" empty, (769).......... ..30 per ct.

Barytes, (234)...................½ ct. per lb.

" acetate or pyrolignite
of, (789)....... ..25 cts. per lb.

" combinations of, with
acids or water, (509)
3 cts. per lb.

" nitrate of, (504).......20 per ct.

" sulphate of, (234)...½ ct. per lb.

Baskets, and all other articles
composed of grass, ozier, palm
leaf, whalebone, or willow, not
otherwise provided for, (74-
362) .. ..35 per ct.

same of straw, (74-362-779)
90 per ct. of 35 per ct.

" of wood, (107-390)......35 per ct.

Bassoons, (see musical insts.)

Bayonets, (see guns.)

Bay rum, (see rum)

Bdellium, gum, (719)............. free.

Beads and bead ornaments,
(540)..............................50 per ct.

Beads, amber (804)............... free.

Beams, iron, (see iron beams.)

Beans, castor, (see seed)

Beans, for seed, (771).............20 per ct.

" St. Johns, (855)........... free.

" tonqua, (863).............. free.

" vanilla, (866)..... ... . free.

" used as vegetables, not
otherwise provided
for, (50). ....10 per ct.

Beds, feather, (56)................20 per ct.

" feathers and downs for,
(811)..................... free.

Bedscrews, (see screws.)

Bedsides, (see mats.)

Bed-ticking, (see cottons.)

Beef, (16)...... ....1 ct. per lb.

Beer, (see ale.)

Bees, (125)........................... free.

Beeswax, (33-272)................20 per ct.

Beets, (50).............................10 per ct.

Belladonna, root and leaf, (713) free.

Bells and bell metal, old and
broken and fit only to be remanufactured,† (123-714)..... free.

Bells, bell metal, (see notes to
manufs. of brass) (98-
383-777)..90 per ct. of 35 per ct.

" other, according to ma-
terial.

Beltings, wool, worsted, or mohair, (see trimmings.)

Belts or felts, endless, for paper
or printing machines, (615-
775) 90 per ct. of { 20 cts. per lb.
and 35 per ct.

Belts, other, (according to material.)

Benzine or benzole, (see oils,
illuminating.)

Benzoin or benjamin, gum,(719) free.

Benzoates, (75)..... ....30 per ct.

Berlin blue, (see paints.)

Berries, flowers, nuts, plants,
vegetables, and other articles
in a crude state, used exclusively in dyeing or in composing dyes, not otherwise provided for, (122-124-713)... . free.

Berries, as fruit, not otherwise
provided for, (37)...10 per ct.

---

†"Which ordinarily is composed of 78 parts of copper and 22 parts of tin."—(Decision of March 4, 1864.) Bells for churches subject to duty.—(Reg. of 1857, p. 554.)

Berries, juniper, (722).......... free.
" laurel, (722). .... free.
Bessemer metal, as steel, (680)
Beverages, spirituous, (see liquors.)
Beverages, as granulated effer-
vescent preparations, of citrate of soda, lemonade, ginger beer, &c., (dec. of Aug.
11, 1870,) (166)..................20 per ct.
Binding, cotton, (481-774).......
90 per ct. of 35 per ct.
" leather, (103-387-781)
90 per ct. of 35 per ct.
" silk, (486)......... .....60 per ct.
" wool, worsted or mo-
hair,(see trimmings.)
Birds, singing, or other, (dec. of
Mch. 30, 1872,) (125) free.
" stuffed, (811) .... free.
Biscuits, (166)...................20 per ct.
Bismuth, (125) .... free.
" subnitrate of, (dec. of
March 6,1867,)(108-
280)................ ....40 per ct.
Bits, polished, as saddlery,(dec.
of Sept. 18. 1869,) (85-
370-776)...90 per ct. of 35 per ct.
" except for saddlery, as
manufactures of steel,
(458-776) . ...
90 per ct. of 45 per ct.
Bitter apples, (713).............. free.
Bitters, (see liquors and medicines.)
Bitumen, as pitch, (63)...........20 per ct.
Bituminous and mineral sub-
stances in a crude state, not
otherwise provided for, (60,
see also 777)............................20 per ct.
Blacking, of all descriptions,
(166-272) ....30 per ct.
Black lead (plumbago) (852)... free.
" " powder (see lead)
Black, Frankfort, bone, and lamp,
(see paints.)
Bladders, manufs. of, (see manufs.)
" crude, (812)............ free.
" manufactured in part,
(dec. of June 28,
1868,) (166)...... ...20 per ct.
Blades, sword, (678-776)
90 per ct. of 35 per ct.

Blanc fixe, (see paints.)
Blanketing. machine. (dec. of
March 31, 1870,) (615-775)
90 per ct. of { 20 cts. per lb.
and 35 per ct.
Blankets,*(dec of May 13, 1871,)
(614-775) valued at 40 cts. or
less per lb.
90 per ct of { 20 cts. per lb.
and 35 per ct.
valued above 40 cts. and not
above 60 cts. per lb.
90 per ct. of { 30 cts. per lb.
and 35 per ct.
valued above 60 cts. and not
above 80 cts. per lb.
90 per ct. of { 40 cts. per lb.
and 35 per ct.
valued above 80 cts. per lb.
90 per ct. of { 50 cts. per lb.
and 35 per ct.
Blankets, gentionella, as manuf.
of wool, (dec. of Oct.23,1857.)
Bleeching powder, (chlorate of
lime) (819).............. .... free.
Blocks, viz : last, wagon, oar,
gun, heading, and all like
blocks or sticks. rough hewn
or sawed only, (765)..........20 per ct.
Same, otherwise than rough-
hewn or sawed. (Reg.
of 1857, p. 498) (107-
390).................... 35 per ct.
Blood, dried, (824)................ free.
" dragons, (716)............. free.
Blue, fig and wash, (419).......25 per ct.
" other, (see paints.)
Bluegalls, (see nutgalls.)
Blue mass, (dec. of March 28,
1870) (60).......................20 per ct.
Boards, (see lumber.)
Boats, life, and life-saving apparatus, specially imported
by societies incorporated or
established to encourage the
saving of human life, (724).. free.
Bobbinet, cotton, (481-774)
90 per ct. of 35 per ct.
Bocking, printed, colored, or
otherwise, (620-775)
90 per ct. of { 25 cts. per sq. yd.
and 35 per ct.

* For what is known by the term "blanket," see Reg. of 1857, p. 555.

Bodkins (according to material.)

Bolts, brass, (see notes to manufs. of brass) (98-383-777)
90 per ct. of 35 per ct.

" for railroads, (see note to R. R. chairs) (435-776)
90 per ct. of 2½ cts. per lb.

" wrought iron, (435-776)
90 per ct. of 2½ cts. per lb.

" other, of iron, (444-776)
90 per ct. of 35 per ct.

Bone or ivory drop black, (see paints.)

Bone dust and bone ash for manufacture of phosphates and fertilizers, (714)........... free.

Bone, manfs. of (see manfs.)

Bones burned or steamed (812) free.

" crude and not manufactured; bones ground or calcined, (812)...... free.

Bonnets and hoods, for men, women and children, of chip, grass, palm leaf, willow, or any other vegetable substance, or of whalebone or other material not otherwise provided for, (298).....................40 per ct.

" of hair, (685) ....30 per ct.

" of silk, (486)..... ......60 per ct.

" of straw, (298-779).....
90 per cent of 40 per ct.

——braids, plaits, flats, laces, trimmings, tissues, willow sheets and squares, used for making or ornamenting hats, bonnets, and hoods, composed of chip, grass, palm leaf, willow or any other vegetable substance, whalebone, or of other material, not otherwise provided for, (299).............30 per ct.

of hair, (685)........... ....30 per ct.

of straw, (299-779)........... ..
90 per ct. of 30 per ct.

of sparterre, (858)............... free.

Books,* all, bound or unbound, (544, see also 778)...25 per ct.

" blank copying (dec. of March 1, 1858) (544) 25 per ct.

" in use, (see effects.)

" metal clasps, &c.. (Reg. of 1857, p. 554, 556, 557 and 558.)

" maps and charts for library of Congress, (814)..................... free.

" moveable picture (dec. of March 5, 1864,) (544)....................25 per ct.

" printed and manufactured more than twenty-five years at the date of importation, (813).... .... free.

" specially imported, (see apparatus.)

Boots and shoes, india rubber, (179-779)......90 per ct. of 30 per ct.

The same, leather, (103-387-781)........... 90 per ct. of 35 per ct.

The same, felt leather, being in part wool. (dec of Oct. 21, 1864) (618-775)
90 per ct. of { 50 cts. per lb. and 40 per ct.

The same silk, (dec. of Feb. 10, 1871) (84-369)...........35 per ct.

Borax or tincal, crude, (812)... free.

" " refined, (234)..
10 cts. per lb.

Botany, specimens of (see specimens.)

Bottles, glass, not cut. (496-780)
90 per ct of 35 per ct.

" " cut, (497-780)
90 per ct. of 40 per ct.

---

* " Books exported and bound abroad are liable to duty on their full value on their return. The assessment of duty cannot be restricted to the value of the binding done abroad."—(Dec. May 19, 1870.)

" Books and tracts imported for distribution are subject to duty."—(Dec. of May 14, 1863.)

" A distinction is made between books imported in good faith to be *used* by Sunday Schools, and books imported for distribution among the scholars thereof. In the one case. the books remain the property of the schools; in the other, they become the property of the scholars."—(Dec. of March 11, 1868.)

The Duty on **Books** should read 90 per ct. of 25 per ct.

Bottles, containing wines, brandy and other spiritu-
ous liquors, (650-780)
90 per ct. of 3 cts. each.
" or jars, glass, filled with
sweetmeats or pre-
serves, (503-780)
90 per ct. of 40 per ct.
" containing other arti-
ticles, (29-780)
90 per ct. of 30 per ct.
Bougies (according to material.)
Bouillons (see trimmings.)
Boxes, musical,† (see musical
instruments.)
Boxes, fancy, of gold and silver,
(110-394-566-777)
90 per ct. of 35 per ct.
"   " japaned, (110-394-
566-777)
90 per ct. of 35 per ct.
"   " paper, (110-394-
778)
90 per ct. of 35 per ct.
"   " shell, (83-368)...35 per ct.
"   " tin.(110-394-566-
777)
90 per ct. of 35 per ct.
"   " wood, (110-386-
390 394).........35 per ct.
" packing, of wood,(769) 30 per ct.
Box-wood, (164).................... free.
Bracelets, if jewelry, (dec. of
Nov. 20, 1869,(70) 25 per ct.
" jet, gold mounted,
(dec. of Dec. 3,
1863) (92-377).....35 per ct.
" hair, (76-363-685).. 30 per ct.
Braces, (see suspenders.)
" other.(according to ma-
terial.)
Brackets, (according to material.)
Brads, (see tacks.)
Braids, cotton, (481-774)
90 per ct. of 35 per ct.
" for bonnets, hats, &c.,
(see bonnets.)
" hair, (76-363-685).......30 per ct.
" silk, (486)..................60 per ct.

Braids, wool, worsted or mohair
(see trimmings.)
Brandy, (see liquors.)
Brass, in bars or pigs,* (33-230-
777).........90 per ct. of 15 per ct.
" manufs. of, (see manufs.)
" old, and fit only to be remanufactured, (dec. of
July 26, 1870) (33-230-
777)........90 per ct. of 15 per ct.
" sheathing metal, (see
metal, sheathing.)
" sheet, (98-383-777)
90 per ct. of 35 per ct.
Brazil paste, (818)................ free.
" pebbles, for spectacles,
rough, (818)............. free.
Brazil wood and brazilletto,(see
dyewoods.)
Bread, (166)...................20 per ct.
Breakage, (see par. 650)
Breccia, in blocks or slabs, (127) free.
Brick, (53)..........................20 per ct.
" fire, (53).....................20 per ct.
Bridles, (see saddlery.)
Brilliants, see cottons, (dec. of
Dec. 31, 1862) (575)
Brine, (127) .... free.
Brimstone, crude, (714)......... free.
" in rolls, or refined,
(515)............$10 per ton.
Bristles, (523)................15 cts. per lb
" imitation of, made of
whalebone or other
similar substances,
(Reg. of 1857, p.558)
(166) ....20 per ct.
Britannia ware, (98-361-777)
90 per ct. of 35 per ct.
" metal, old, and fit only
to be remanufac-
tured, (852)......... free.
Bromine, (713)..................... free.
Bronze metal and powder, (see
metal and powder.)
" liquor, (see note to manufactures of copper,)
(33-777)90 per ct. of 10 per ct.
" manufs. of (see manufs.)

---

† " A bird musical box, being a gold snuff box with a musical attachment, held to
be manufactured of gold, and liable to duty accordingly."—(Dec. of May 18, 1859.)
*See note to manufactures of brass.

Brooms, if bone, horn, ivory,
gutta percha, leather,
or metal, chief value,
(78-364-777-779-781)
90 per ct. of 35 per ct.
" other than above, (78-
364)....................35 per ct.
Brown, Spanish, (see paints.)
Brown Hollands, (see linens.)
Brushes, if bone, horn, ivory,
gutta percha, leather,
or metal, chief value,
(524-777-779-781)
90 per ct. of 40 per ct.
" other than above,
(524)................ 40 per ct.
Buchu leaves, (714)............... free.
Buckles, (according to material.)
Buckwheat, (42 lbs. to bu)
(dec. of July 31, 1868) (166) 10 per ct.
Bugles, (see musical instruments.)
" glass, as beads, (dec. of
Jan. 18, 1865) (540,
see also 780)............50 per ct.
" other, (see trimmings.)
Bugs, dried, (824)................ free.
Building stones, (see stones.)
Bulbs, (see plants.)
Bullion, gold and silver, (127). free.
Bullrushes,(dec:of Nov.5,1866,)
(166-344)......$5 per ton and 10 per ct.
Bunting, (616.775)
90 per ct. of { 20 cts. per sq. yd.
and 35 per ct.
Burlaps, (see linens.)
Burning fluid, (234)......50 cts per gall.
Burr stones, manuf'd or bound
up into millstones in any
manner, (dec. of Feb. 15,
1869,) (53)......... ....20 per ct.
Burr stones, in blocks, rough
or unmanuf'd and not

bound up into millstones,
(dec. of Dec. 11, 1858)
(127-714)....................... free.
Busts, specially imported, (see
apparatus.)
Butter,* (16)....................4 cts per lb.
Buttons and button moulds of
all kinds, except as below,
(dec. of Oct. 18,1864,) (78)..30 per ct.
Buttons, horn, ivory, bone, or
gutta percha, (78-779-781)
90 per ct. of 30 per ct.
Buttons, brass, (see note to manufactures of brass,) (78-777)
90 per ct. of 30 per ct.
Buttons, cuff or sleeve, of glass,
cannot be classed as buttons,
(dec. Nov. 27, 1868,) (503, see
also 780) ....40 per ct.
Buttons and ornaments for
dresses and outside garments,
made of silk, or of which silk
is chief value, no wool, worst-
ed, or goat's hair, (688).......50 per ct.
Buttons or barrel buttons, or
buttons of other forms for
tassels or ornaments, of wool,
worsted or mohair, (see trimmings.)
———lasting, mohair cloth,
silk, twist, or other manufacture of cloth, woven or made
in patterns of such size, shape
and form, or cut in such manner as to be fit for buttons,
exclusively, not combined
with India rubber, (475).....10 per ct.
———above, wool, worsted
or cotton, (475-774-775)
90 par ct. of 10 per ct.
Butts, cast iron, (442-776)
90 per ct. of 2½ cts. per lb.
" other (according to ma-
terial.)

C

Cabinet ware, (see furniture.)
Cabinets, of coins, medals, and
all other collections of antiquities,(121-128-130-148-715) free.
Cables, (see chain cables, and
cordage)

Cachous, aromatic, (see cosmet-
ics.)
Cadmium, (128) .... free.
Calamine, (128)............... ..... free.
Calcium, chloride of, (166).....20 per ct.

* Butter become valueless in a public store, claimed to be admitted to entry as
"soap grease," not allowed.—(Dec. of March 26, 1868.)

Calf skins, (see skins.)

Calisaya, bark, (712)............   free.

Calomel, (54-273)..................30 per ct.

Cambrics, (see cottons.)

Calx, (lime) (42)...................10 per ct.

Cameos, (see precious stones.)

Cameos, in frames. (Reg. of
1857, p. 559,) (166)..............20 per ct.

Camphor, crude, (819)...........   free.

"   refined, (790)......5 cts. per lb.

Canals, machinery for. (see machinery.)

Candles and tapers, stearine
and adamantine, (301).....5 cts per lb.

Candles and tapers, spermaceti,
paraffine and wax, pure or
mixed, (301).................8 cts. per lb.

Candles and tapers, all other
(301) ....2½ cts. per lb.

Candlesticks, (according to material.)

Candy of sugar,(see confectionery.)

Canella Alba, bark, (712).......   free.

Canes and sticks, for walking,
finished, (79-365)...............35 per ct.

Canes and sticks, for walking,
in the rough, or no further
manuf'd than cut into suita-
ble lengths, (810-864).........   free.

Cannetille, (see trimmings.)

Cannon, iron, (444-776)
90 per ct. of 35 per ct.

"   brass, (see note to manufactures of brass,)
(98-383-777)..........
90 per ct. of 35 per ct.

Cantharides, or Spanish flies
(715).......................   free.

Canvas, (see linens.)

"   or duck for sails, (484) 30 per ct.

"   "   "   if cotton, (484-
774)......90 per ct. of 30 per ct

"   floor cloth or oil-cloth
foundations, of flax,
jute or hemp, (783) 40 per ct.

Cape of Good Hope, goods of
the produce east, imported
from places west, subject to
extra duty of (782).......... 10 per ct.

Cape, gum, (719)...................   free.

Capers, all, not otherwise provided for, (79-365)............35 per ct.

Caps, leggins, socks, stockings, wove shirts and drawers, and all similar articles made on frames, of whatever material composed, worn
by men, women or children,
not otherwise provided for,
except as below, (91-367) ...35 per ct.

cotton, (81-367-480-774)
90 per ct. of 35 per ct.

fur, (80-366)....................35 per ct.

hair, (685) ....30 per ct.

leather, (81-367-781)
90 per ct. of 35 per ct.

silk, or silk chief value, (dec.
of Oct. 19, 1868,) (486-
578)............ ....60 per ct.

wool, worsted, or goats'
hair, not knit, (dec. of Oct.
14, 1865,) (618-775)
90 per ct. of $\left\{\begin{array}{l}\text{50 cts. per lb.}\\\text{and 40 per ct.}\end{array}\right.$

worsted or goats' hair, knit
or made on frames. (81-
367-775).......90 per ct. of 35 per ct.

wool, knit, (613-775)
90 per ct. of $\left\{\begin{array}{l}\text{50 cts. per lb.}\\\text{and 35 per ct.}\end{array}\right.$

Carbon, animal, (bone black,)
(505)....................... ......25 per ct.

Carboys, empty, as manuf. of
glass, (496-780)
90 per ct. of 35 per ct.

"   of American manufac-
ture, (see United
States.)

"   containing acids shall
be subject to the same duty
as if empty, (708)

Carbuncles, (see precious stones.)

Card cases, of whatever material composed ex-
cept as below, (83-
368)................ ...35 per ct.

"   if bone, cotton, gutta
percha,horn,ivory,
leather,paper,skins,
worsted or wool,
chief value.(83-368-
774-775-777-778-779-
781)
90 per ct. of 35 per ct.

Cards, blank, (104-381-778)
90 per ct. of 35 per ct.

Cards, playing, costing not over
25 cts. per pack, (539-
778)
90 per ct. of 25 cts. per pack.

" playing, costing over 25
cents per pack, (539-
778)
90 per ct. of 35 cts. per pack.

" printed picture, (dec. of
Dec. 26, 1862,) (544-
778).....90 per ct. of 25 per ct.

" wool and cotton, part
iron, (444-776)
90 per ct. of 35 per ct.

" wool and cotton, part
steel, (458-776)
90 per ct. of 45 per ct.

Carmine, (see paints.)

Carnelian, (see cornelian.)

Carpets, Aubusson and Axminster, (620-775)
90 per ct. of 50 per ct.

" woven whole for rooms,
(620-775)
90 per ct. of 50 per ct.

" Brussels, printed on the
warp or otherwise,
(469-775)
90 per ct. of 50 cts. per sq. yd.

" Brussels, tapestry, printed on the warp or oth-
erwise, (620-775)
90 per ct. of { 28 cts. per sq. yd.
and 35 per ct.

" Brussels, wrought by
· the Jacquard ma-
chine, (620-775)
90 per ct. of { 44 cts. per sq. yd.
and 35 per ct.

" felt, classed as drugget,
(dec. of Oct. 26,
1868,) (620-775)
90 per ct. of { 25 cts. per sq. yd.
and 35 per ct.

" hemp or jute, (620)
8 cts. per sq. yd.

" Saxony, Wilton, and
Tournay velvet,
wrought by the Jac-
quard machine, (620-
775)
90 per ct. of { 70 cts. per sq. yd.
and 35 per ct.

Carpets, treble Ingrain, three-ply,
and worsted chain Ve-
nitian, (620-775)
90 per ct. of { 17 cts. per sq. yd.
and 35 per ct.

" velvet, patent and ta-
pestry, printed on
the warp or other-
wise, (620-775)
90 per ct. of { 40 cts. per sq. yd.
and 35 per ct.

" yarn Venetian and two-
ply ingrain, (620-
775)
90 per ct. of { 12 cts. per sq. yd.
and 35 per ct.

" flax, or other material
not otherwise provi-
ded for, (620).........40 per ct.

" of wool or cotton, not
otherwise provided
for, (620-774-775)
90 per ct. of 40 per ct.

(See provision as to mats.)

Carriages, & parts of, (83-368)..35 per ct.

same, if iron, steel,
metals, or leather,
chief value, (83-368-
776-777-781)
90 per ct. of 35 per ct.

" hardware and furni-
ture for, (see sad-
dlery.)

Cars, (see R. R. cars)

Carvers, as cutlery.

Cascarilla, bark, (712)........... free.

Cassimere, (see manufs. of wool.)

Casks, (see United States.)

Casks, empty, (769)...............30 per ct.

Cassava, or cassada, tapioca, (740) free.

Cassia and cassia vera, (661).10 cts. per lb.

" ground, (662)......... 20 cts. per lb.

" buds, (662) ....20 cts. per lb.

" fistula, (827)................ free.

Castings of iron, not otherwise
provided for, (443-776).......
90 per ct. of 30 per ct.

Castor or castoreum, (715).... ... free.

Castors, liquor stands, &c., plated, with or without bottles,
(dec. of May 17, 1859.)

Castors, (according to material.)

Catechu, or cutch, (715)......... free.

Catches, (according to material.)

Catgut or whipgut, unmanufactured, (715)...................... free.

Catgut, strings of, or gut cord,
for musical instruments
(819)....................... free.

Catsup, (79-273)...................40 per ct.

Cattle, (see animals.)

Cedar, (see lumber and woods.)

" boards, unmanufactured,
for cigar boxes, or used
otherwise than cabinet
wood, (dec. of Jan. 28,
1870,) (69)...............20 per ct.

Cement, Roman, (65)...... ....20 per ct.

Chains, as jewelry, (dec. of Nov.
20, 1869,) (70)........25 per ct.

" cable, or parts thereof,
(430-776)
90 per ct. of 2½ cts. per lb.

" cable, so broken, rusty,
or old as to be unfit
for use, (dec. of Mar.
6, 1869,) (677-776)
90 per ct. of $8 per ton.

Provided, that no chains made
of wire, or rods of a diameter
less than ½ an inch, shall be
considered a chain cable, (202)

Chains, curb, polished as saddlery, (dec. of Dec. 16,
1861,) (85-370-776)
90 per ct. of 35 per ct.

" fence, halter, trace and
other, made of wire
or rods, not less than
¼ inch in diameter,
(431-776)
90 per ct. of 2½ cts. per lb

" as above, less than ¼
inch in diameter and
not under No. 9, wire
gauge, (431-776)
90 per ct. of 3 cts. per lb.

" as above, under No. 9,
wire gauge, (431-776)
90 per ct. of 35 per ct.

" hair, (685)...............30 per ct.

" watch, silk, (486).......60 per ct.

" other, (according to material.)

Provided, That all wire rope
and wire strand or chain
made of iron wire, either
bright, coppered, galvanized,
or coated with other metals,
shall pay the same rate of
duty that is now levied on the
iron wire of which said rope
or strand or chain is made;
and all wire rope and wire
strand or chain made of steel
wire, either bright, coppered,
galvanized, or coated with
other metals, shall pay the
same rate of duty that is now
levied on the steel wire of
which said rope or strand or
chain is made, (777)

Chairs, (see furniture.)

Chalk, billiard, (540)..............50 per ct.

" red and French, (494)..20 per ct.

" unmanufactured, (715).. free.

" all, not otherwise provided for, (494)..........25 per ct.

Champagne, (see liquors.)

Chamomile flowers, (819)........ free.

Chandeliers, (according to material.)

Charcoal, (819)................. ...... free.

Charges when dutiable, (see par.
602)

Charts, (544-778) 90 per ct. of 25 per ct.

" specially imported, (see
apparatus and books.)

Chemisettes, silk, (486)..........60 per ct.

Cheese, (16)............... .....4 cts. per lb.

Chemical preparations, (see.
salts and preparations.)

Cheroots, (see segars.)

Chessmen and chess balls, ivory
or bone, (542-781)
90 per ct. of 50 per ct.

same, if wood, (107-390).....35 per ct.

Chesnuts, (178)...............2 cts. per lb.

Chicory root, ground or unground (761) 1 ct. per lb.

" " burnt or pre-
pared, (517) 5 cts. per lb.

Chimney pieces, of slate, (491).40 per ct.

China, porcelain, and Parian
ware, plain white, and not
decorated in any manner,
(490)...........................45 per ct.

China, porcelain, and Parian ware, gilded, ornamented, or decorated in any manner, (489)...............................50 per ct.

China root, (819)...................   free.

Chinese blue, (see paints.)

"   wax, (see wax.)

Chisels, as manufs. of steel,(458-776)...............90 per ct. of 45 per ct.

Chlobarium, chemical prep. (dec. of Dec. 3, 1870,) (166).20 per ct.

Chlorometers, part glass, (503).40 per ct.

Chloroform, (518)..................$1 per lb.

Chocolate, (773)...............5 cts. per lb.

Chocolate, prepared as confectionery, (see confectionery.)

Chrome yellow, (see paints.)

Chronometers, box or ship's, and parts thereof,* (34)......10 per ct.

Cicuta, (see conian.)

Cider, (166)...........................20 per ct.

Cigars and cigarettes, (see segars.)

Cinchona bark and root, (712-819).....................................   free.

Cinnamon, (657)..............20 cts. per lb.

"   chips,(dec.of Aug.19, 1870,) (657)..20 cts. per lb.

Citron, as fruit, (37)...............10 per ct.

"   preserved,(dec. of Sept. 26, 1860,) (see fruits preserved.)

Civit, crude, in natural pod, (724)...............................   free.

Clasps, (according to material.)

Clapboards, (see lumber.)

Clay, china, as kaoline, (decs. of May 5. 1863, and March 28, 1870,) (492-780) 90 per ct. of $5 per ton.

"   unwrought, pipe clay and fire clay, (492-780) 90 per ct. of $5 per ton.

"   prepared, (dec. of July 9, 1863,) (492-780) 90 per ct. of $5 per ton.

Cliffstone, unmanuf'd, (715, see also 494).........................   free.

Clippings, metal, (decs. of July 18, 1863, and Feb. 11, 1871) (166-776-777)...90 per ct. of 20 per ct.

Cloaks, (see clothing)

Clocks and parts of (83-368)...35 per ct.

Same if iron, steel, or other metal. chief value, (83-368-776-777)......90 per ct. of 35 per ct.

Cloth, bolting, (125)...............   free.

"   button, (see buttons.)

"   colored, cotton, for bookbinding,(June 16,1870) (481-774).90 per ct. of 35 per ct.

"   corset, (see corsets.)

"   crinoline, (see hair cloth.)

"   floor, of cork, india rubber. &c., (dec. of Oct. 2, 1865,) (787).........30 per ct.

"   grass, (484)..................30 per ct.

"   gunny, (see gunny cloth.)

"   hemp manilla, (Reg. of 1857, p. 574,) (166)...20 per ct.

"   hair, (see hair cloth.)

"   India rubber, (77-364-779, see also 66) 90 per ct. of 35 per ct.

"   Italian, (see dress goods.)

"   oil, (see oil cloth.)

"   seer sucker, so-styled, (dec.of April 13,1870,) (487).........................50 per ct.

"   water proof, not otherwise provided for,(621-775)......90 per ct. of 45 per ct.

"   woolen, (see manufactures of wool.)

Clothing,ready-made,and wearing apparel of every description, and balmoral skirts and skirting, and goods of similar description, or used for like purposes, composed wholly or in part of wool, worsted, the hair of the alpaca, goat, or other like animals. made up or manufactured wholly or in part by the tailor, seamstress, or manufacturer, except knit goods,† (618-775)

90 per ct. of {50 cts. per lb. and 40 per ct.

---

*"Empty chronometer boxes, liable to duty as manufactures of wood at 35 per cent." (Decision of August 3, 1853.)

†For classification of "clothing" or "articles worn," see Reg. of 1857, pages 560, 570, 581, 583.

Clothing, if knit, (see knit goods.)
cotton chief value, (84-369-774)...........90 per ct. of 35 per ct.
of silk, or silk chief value, except as above, (578).....60 per ct.
Clothing, ready-made, and wearing apparel of every description, of whatever material composed, except as above, made up or manufactured wholly or in part by the tailor, seamstress or manufacturer, (84-369)..............................35 per ct.
Clothing, such as articles worn by men, women, or children, of whatever material composed, made up, or made wholly or in part by hand, not otherwise provided for, (72-360)..35 per ct.
Cloves, (659)....................5 cts. per lb.
Clove stems, (690)...........3 cts per lb.
Coaches, furniture and hardware for, (see saddlery.)
Coal,§ anthracite, (715)..........   free.
"   bituminous, and shale, 80 lbs. to bus. and 28 bus. to ton,(754).75 cts. per ton.
"   all other, 80 lbs. to bus. 28 bus. to ton, (459) 40 cts. per ton.
"   slack or culm,† such as will pass through a half inch screen, 80 lbs. to bus. and 28 bus. to ton, (754).....40 cts. per ton.
"   culm of, other than above, (459). ....25 per ct.
Coatings, (see linens.)
Cobalt, (504)....................20 per ct.
"   oxide of, (504)..........20 per ct.
"   ore of, (821)...............   free.
Cobourgs as maufs. of worsted, (decs. of Sept. 21, 1857.)
Cocculus indicus, (715)...........   free.
Cochineal, (128)...................   free.

Cochineal, lake, (see paints.)
Cocoa or cocoa crude, (821).....   free.
"   leaves, fiber and shells of (821)........................   free.
"   ground or prepared, (773) 2 cts. per lb.
"   nuts, (847)..................   free.
"   wine,(if exclusively used medicinally, (Reg. of 1857, p.561) (108-280)40 per ct.
Codilla, (see hemp, tow of.)
Codfish, (see fish.)
Coffee, of all kinds,‡ (753, see also 782)....................   free.
Coffee, acorn, (dec. of Nov. 17, 1863,) and dandelion root, raw or prepared,and all other articles used or intended to be used as coffee, or a substitute for coffee, and not otherwise provided for, (303)..3 cts. per lb.
Coffee, extract of, (Reg of 1857, p. 566,) (166)................. 20 per ct.'
Cognac ether, (see oils.)
Coins, gold and silver, (130)...   free.
"   copper, (640)..............45 per ct.
"   (see cabinets.)
Coir, (821) ....free.
Coke, (459) ....25 per ct.
Colleges, articles specially imported for, (see apparatus.)
Colcothar, dry, or oxide of iron, (821) ... .   free.
Collodion, fluid, (519)..........$1 per lb.
Colocynth, (bitter apples) (713)   free.
Cologne water and other perfumery, of which alcohol forms the principal ingredient,(decs. of June 6 and April 8, 1868,(520) $3 per gal. and 50 per ct.
Coloquinitida, (bitter apples) (713)...........................   free.
Coloring for brandy,* (304, see also 594)........................50 per ct.

§"Coal brought by vessels, propelled by steam, may be retained on board; if landed, liable to duty."—(Reg. of 1857, p. 561.)

†As to what may be entered as "culm of coal," see decisions of March 10, 1870, and May 20, 1870.

Coal stores of American vessels free ; provided, that none shall be unloaded, (820.)

‡"Coffee (Java) imported from Rotterdam via London, in vessels of the Netherlands, liable to the discriminating duty under paragraph 782, after Oct. 1, 1872.—(Decision of February 8, 1869)

*"So-styled 'Prune wine for fining liquors,' does not on examination bear similitude to brandy coloring, and should be classed as non-enumerated manufactured article at 20 per cent," (166.)—(Dec. of August 10, 1870.)

Colors, (see aniline and paints.)

Colts foot, (crude drug,) (821).   free.

Colombo root, (715)..............   free.

Combs of all kinds, except as below, (86-371).......35 per ct.

" iron, steel or other metal, chief value, (86-371-776-777)
90 per ct. of 35 per ct.

" india rubber or gutta percha, (86-371-779)
90 per ct. of 35 per ct.

" bone, ivory or horn, (86-371-781)
90 per ct. of 35 per ct.

" curry, as manufactures of iron, (444-776)
90 per ct. of 35 per ct.

Comfits, (see fruits preserved.)

Comforters, (see caps.)

Compasses, (according to material.)

Composition of glass or paste, (see precious stones.)

Composition tops, (see furniture.)

Compounds, (see liquors and medicines.)

Confectionery, sugar candy,not colored, (422½)..........10 cts. per lb.

Confectionery, all other, not otherwise provided for, made wholly or in part of sugar, and on sugars, after being refined, when tinctured, colored, or in any way adulterated, valued at 30 cts. per lb. or less, (422½)..........15 cts. per lb.

Confectionery, all,valued above 30 cts. per lb , or when sold by the box, package,or otherwise than by the pound (422½)
50 per ct.

Conian cicuta, or hemlock seed and leaf, (715)............   free.

Contrayerva root, (821).........   free.

Copal gum, (see gums.)

Copper, bottoms, (640-777)
90 per ct. of 45 per ct.

" for U. S. Mint, (130-709)..............   free.

" in rolled plates called brazier's, (640-777)
90 per ct. of 45 per ct.

Copper, in plates, bars, ingots, pigs, and in other forms not manufactured, not otherwise provided for, (640-777) 90 per ct. of 5 cts. per lb.

" in sheets, rods & pipes, (640-777)
90 per ct. of 45 per ct.

" manfs. of, (see manfs.)

" old, fit only for remanufacture, (640-777)
90 per ct. of 4 cts. per lb.

" old, from American vessels' bottoms, compelled by marine disaster to repair in foreign ports, (822)   free.

" ore, on each pound of fine copper contained therein, (640-777) 90 per ct. of 3 cts. per lb.

" regulus of, and on all black or coarse copper, on each pound of fine copper contained therein, (640-777) 90 per ct. of 4 cts. per lb.

" sheathing, (see metal sheathing.)

" subacetate of (verdigris) (741)............   free.

" sulphate of, or blue vitriol, (790).....4 cts. per lb.

Copperas, green vitriol or sulphate of iron, (14-288)................½ ct. per lb.

Copybooks, (see books)

Coral, marine, unmanf'd, (148)   free.

" cut or manuf'd, (decs. of April 23. 1858, and Nov. 2, 1864, (86).....30 per ct.

Cordage or cables, tarred, (483)
3 cts. per lb.

Cordage, untarred Manilla,(483)
2½ cts. per lb.

Cordage, all other untarred, (483)..... ....3½ cts. per lb.

Cord, sash, as manfs. of hemp, (dec.of Nov. 11, 1869,) (484) 30 per ct.

Cord and cords and tassels, metal, (see trimmings.)
if cotton, (86-371-774)
90 per ct. of 35 per ct.

Cord and cord and tassels, if
silk, (486)................. .....60 per ct.
if wool, worsted or mohair,
(see trimmings.)
Cordials, (see liquors and medicines.)
Cork bark, manf'd, (see manufs.)
Corks, (dec. Mar. 1, '71,) (787) 30 per ct.
Cork wood or cork bark, unmanufactured, (715)...........   free.
Cork wood, pictures of, (dec. of
Jan. 4, 1870,) (787).. ......30 per ct.
Cornelian, (see precious stones.)
    " rings, as jewelry, (dec.
        of Mar. 29, 1871,)
        (70)....................25 per ct.
    " unmanuf'd, (715)......   free.
Corn, Indian or maize, (56 lbs.
    to bu.) (16)........10 cts. per bu.
    " meal, (34)...................10 per ct.
Cornplasters, (see plasters.)
Corsets, or manufactured cloth,
woven or made in patterns of
such size, shape, and form,
or cut in such manner as to
be fit for corsets, (664.)
valued at $6 per doz. or less,
                    $2 per doz.
valued over $6 per doz ......35 per ct.
if cotton chief value, (774)
    90 per ct. of the above duties.
Corset wire, (see wire or steel.)
Cosmetics, essences, extracts,
toilet waters, hair oils, pomades, hair dressings, hair
restoratives, hair dyes, tooth
washes, dentifrices, tooth
pastes, aromatic cachous, or
other perfumeries or cosmetics, by whatsoever name or
names known, used or applied as perfumes or applications to the hair, mouth or
skin, (270, see also 594).....50 per ct.
Cotton bagging, or other manufactures, not otherwise herein
provided for, suitable for the
uses to which cotton bagging
is applied, composed in whole

or part of hemp, jute, flax,
gunny bags, gunny cloth, or
other material,* (674, see also
783.)
valued at 7 cts. or less per
sq. yd...................2 cts. per lb.
valued at over 7 cts. per sq.
yd..........................3 cts. per lb.
if cotton chief value, (774)
    90 per ct. of the above duties.
Cotton bottoms, (see linens.)
Cotton grown in the U. S., exempt from internal tax after
the year 1867, (630.)
Cotton, raw, (630)................   free.
Cotton, unginned, containing
the seed, (dec. of Feb. 18,
1865,) (630).....................   free.
Cotton, manufactures of, except
as follows, (see manufactures)
Cottons, (except jeans, denims,
drillings, bed tickings, ginghams, plaids, cottonades, pantaloons stuff, and goods of
like description,) not exceeding 100 threads to the square
inch, counting the warp and
filling, and *exceeding* in
weight 5 ounces per sq. yd.
(574-774)
if unbleached,
    90 per ct. of 5 cts. per sq. yd.
if bleached,
    90 per ct. of 5½ cts. per sq. yd.
if colored, stained, painted,
or printed,
    90 per ct. of { 5½ cts. per sq. yd.
                  { and 10 per ct.
As above, weighing *less* than
5 ozs. per sq. yd. (dec. of
Oct. 28, 1868) (23-339-774)
if unbleached,
    90 per ct. of 2½ cts. per sq. yd.
if bleached,
    90 per ct. of 3 cts. per sq. yd.
if printed, painted, colored
or stained,
    90 per ct. of { 3½ cts. per sq. yd.
                  { and 10 per ct.

*"Cotton bagging is commercially known and understood to apply exclusively to articles used and suitable for the baling of cotton, without reference to material, and this the phraseology of the law clearly indicates."—(Decision of May 20, 1863.)

"Certain so-called 'Dundee Bagging,' reported by appraisers as suitable for the use to which cotton bagging was applied, subject to duty as 'cotton bagging.'"—(Decision of July 23, 1870.)

On finer and lighter goods of
like description, not ex-
ceeding 200 threads to the
square inch, counting the
warp and filling, (dec. of
Oct. 19, 1868) (574-774)

if unbleached,
    90 per ct. of 5 cts. per sq. yd.

if bleached,
    90 per ct. of 5½ cts. per sq. yd.

if colored, stained, painted,
or printed,
    90 per ct. of $\begin{cases} 5\frac{1}{2} \text{ cts. per sq. yd.} \\ \text{and 20 per ct.} \end{cases}$

On goods of like description,
exceeding 200 threads to
the square inch, counting
the warp and filling, (574-
774)

if unbleached,
    90 per ct. of 5 cts. per sq. yd.

if bleached,
    90 per ct. of 5½ cts. per sq. yd.

if colored, stained, painted,
or printed,
    90 per ct. of $\begin{cases} 5\frac{1}{2} \text{ cts. per sq. yd.} \\ \text{and 20 per ct.} \end{cases}$

Cottons, viz.: jeans, denims,
drilling, bed tickings, ginghams, plaids, cottonades,
pantaloon stuffs, and goods
of like description, or for
similar uses, and not exceeding 100 threads to the square
inch, counting the warp and
filling, and exceeding 5 oz. to
the square yard, (575-774)

if unbleached,
    90 per ct. of 6 cts. per sq. yd.

if bleached,
    90 per ct. of 6½ cts. per sq. yd.

if colored, stained, painted,
or printed,
    90 per ct. of $\begin{cases} 6\frac{1}{2} \text{ cts. per sq. yd.} \\ \text{and 10 per ct.} \end{cases}$

On finer or lighter goods of
like description, not ex-
ceeding 200 threads to the
square inch, counting the

warp and filling, (dec. of
Oct. 6, 1869) (575-774)

if unbleached,
    90 per ct. of 6 cts. per sq. yd.

if bleached,
    90 per ct. of 6½ cts. per sq. yd.

if colored, stained, painted,
or printed,
    90 per ct. of $\begin{cases} 6\frac{1}{2} \text{ cts. per sq. yd.} \\ \text{and 15 per ct.} \end{cases}$

On goods of lighter description, exceeding 200 threads
to the square inch, counting the warp and filling,
(575-774)

if unbleached,
    90 per ct. of 7 cts. per sq. yd.

if bleached,
    90 per ct. of 7½ cts. per sq. yd.

if colored, stained, painted,
or printed,
    90 per ct. of $\begin{cases} 7\frac{1}{2} \text{ cts. per sq. yd.} \\ \text{and 15 per ct.} \end{cases}$

Provided, that upon all plain
woven cotton goods, not
included in the foregoing
schedule,* (575-774)

if unbleached, valued at over
16 cts. per sq. yd.,
    90 per ct. of 35 per ct.

if bleached, valued at over
20 cts. per sq. yd.,
    90 per ct. of 35 per ct.

if colored, valued at over 25
cts. per sq. yd.,
    90 per ct. of 35 per ct.

Jeans, denims, and drillings,
valued at over 20 cts. per
sq. yd., unbleached,
    90 per ct. of 35 per ct.

All other cotton goods of
every description, the value
of which shall exceed 25
cts. per sq. yd.,
    90 per ct. of 35 per ct.

Provided further, that no cotton goods having more
than 200 threads to the sq.
inch, counting the warp

---

* "The terms of the law imposing duty according to the count of threads, should be held to apply in all cases where such count can be ascertained by means of the *glass* commonly used for such purpose, and in all cases where the value of the goods is par-tially or wholly determined between the manufacturer and the purchaser according to the number of threads to the square inch, &c."—(Decision of June 3, 1866.)

and filling, shall be admitted to a less rate of duty than is provided for goods which are of that number of threads (575.)

Cotton, thread of, on spool, containing on each spool not exceeding 100 yds. of thread,* (576-774)

90 per ct. of { 6 cts. per doz. and 30 per ct.

exceeding 100 yds., for every additional 100 yds. on each spool, or fractional part thereof, in excess of 100 yards,

90 per ct. of { 6 cts. per doz. and 35 per ct.

Cotton thread, yarn, warps, or warp yarn, not wound upon spools, whether single or advanced beyond the condition of single by twisting two or more single yarns together, whether on beams or in bundles, skeins, or cops, or in any other form, (707-774)

valued at not over 40 cts. per lb.,

90 per ct. of { 10 cts. per lb. and 20 per ct.

valued at over 40 cts. and not over 60 cts. per lb.,

90 per ct. of { 20 cts. per lb. and 20 per ct.

valued at over 60 cts. and not over 80 cts. per lb.,

90 per ct. of { 30 cts. per lb. and 20 per ct.

valued at over 80 cts. per lb.,

90 per ct. of { 40 cts. per lb. and 20 per ct.

Court plaster, (86-371) ....35 per ct.
Covering of goods, (see par. 602).
Covers, (see mats).
Cowage down, (823).......... free.

Cow hides, (see hides).
Cowrie, gum, (719).......... free.
Cow or kine pox, or vaccine virus, (823). .. .. free.
Crackers (bread) (166) ....20 per ct.
 "   fire, (see firecrackers).
Cranks, mill, wrought iron, (430-776)...90 per ct. of 2 cts. per lb.
Crapes, silk, (487)............50 per ct.
Crash, (see linens.)
Cravats, (see clothing.)
Crayons, of all kinds, (86)....30 per ct.
Cream of tartar, (see tartar).
Crinoline wire, (see wire of steel).
Crinoline cloth, (see hair cloth).
Crockery ware, (see earthenware).
Crocus colcottra, (505)........25 per ct.
Croton, bark, (712)........... free.
Cryolite, (see kryolite).
Crystals for watches, glass,(693-780, see also 503) 90 per ct. of 25 per ct.
Crystals, yellow, as aniline dyes.
Cubebs, (823)............... free.
Cubic niter, (725)... .... free.
Cudbear, (715).............. free.
Curls, hair, (76-363-685)......30 per ct.
 "   "   human (316)......30 per ct.
Currants, zante or other, (796)
1 ct. per lb.
Curry & curry powders, (823). free.
Cutch or Catechu, (715)...... free.
Cutlasses, (swords,) (679-776)
90 per ct. of 45 per ct.
Cutlery,† of all kinds, except pen, jack, and pocket knives, (dec. of March 30, 1865,) (86-371-455-776)...90 per ct. of 35 per ct.
Cuttlefish bone, (sepia) (715).. free.
Cyanite, or Kyanite (823)..... free.

---

* "Cotton thread, spools containing 200 yards each, how duty assessed."—(Decision of May 6, 1869.)

† It is the custom of this port to class the following articles as "cutlery": razors, scissors, garden scissors, pruning shears, table knives and forks, carvers, steels, fleams, lancets, pallettes, daggers, dirks, and bread, cook's, butcher, shoe, farrier's, bowie, budding, pruning, and fruit knives. (See note to paragraph 566)

D

Daggers, as cutlery.

Damage on fruit, viz : oranges, lemons, pineapples, grapes, limes, bananas, plaintains, shaddocks, and mangoes ; no allowance shall be made for loss by decay on the voyage, unless the said loss shall exceed twenty-five per cent. of the quantity, and the allowance then made shall be only for the amount of loss in excess of twenty-five per cent. of the whole quantity, (696.)

Damage on voyage of importation, (see art. 3 of the Appendix.)

Damage from rust, (see par. 224.)

Damar, gum, (719)............ free.

Damasks, (see linens.)

Dandelion root, (see coffee substitutes.)

Dates, (796)..............1 ct. per lb.
"   preserved, (see fruits preserved.)

Deals, (see lumber.)

Decanters, glass, not cut, (496-780)...... ...90 per ct. of 35 per ct.
cut, (497-780)..90 per ct. of 40 per ct.

Decoctions of logwood and other dyewoods, (274)......10 per ct.

Deer carcasses, (dec. of February 13, 1868) (166)..........10 per ct.

Demijohns, part glass, (503, see also 780)..................40 per ct.

Denims, (see cottons.)

Dentifrice, (see cosmetics.)

Diamond dust or bort, (716)...   free.

Diamonds, cut, (see precious stones.)
"   rough or uncut, (824)...........   free.
"   glazier's, set or not set, (824).......   free.

Diaper, (see linens.)

Dice, ivory or bone, (542-781)
                90 per ct. of 50 per ct.

Dirks, as cutlery.

Disks, (see plates.)

Discriminating duty, (see pars. 561 and 782.)

Dishes, (according to material.)

Distilled spirits, (see liquors.)

Divi divi, (131).............   free.

Dolls, if copper chief value, see note to manfs. of copper, (dec. of January 21, 1870) (640-777)
                90 per ct. of 45 per ct.
"   wholly or part of wool, (dec. of January 21, 1870) (613-775)
                90 per ct. of { 50 cts. per lb. and 35 per ct.
"   if bone, cotton, horn, ivory, gutta-percha, leather or metal chief value, (87-372-774-777-779-781) 90 per ct. of 35 per ct.
"   of all kinds, except as above, (dec. of Feb'y 4, 1870) (87-372)....35 per ct.

Dominoes, (97-380-781)
                90 per ct. of 35 per ct.
"   if toys, (543-781)
                90 per ct. of 50 per ct.

Downs, of all descriptions, for beds or bedding, (811)......   free.

Dragon's blood, (716)........   free.

Draughts, bone or ivory, (542-781)..........90 per ct. of 50 per ct.

Drawbacks, (see pars. 744 and 873.)

Drawers, (see caps.)

Drawings, (166).............20 per ct.
"   specially imported, (see apparatus.)

Dress goods, women's and children's, and real or imitation Italian cloths composed wholly or in part of wool, worsted, the hair of the alpaca, goat, or other like animals, (617-775.)

valued at not above 20 cts. per sq. yd.
                90 per ct. of { 6 cts. per sq. yd. and 35 per ct.

valued at above 20 cts. per sq. yd.

90 per ct. of $\begin{cases} 8 \text{ cts. per sq. yd.} \\ \text{and } 40 \text{ per ct.} \end{cases}$

Provided, that on all goods weighing four ounces and over per sq. yd. the duty shall be

90 per ct. of $\begin{cases} 50 \text{ cts. per lb.} \\ \text{and } 35 \text{ per ct.} \end{cases}$

Dressings for the hair, (see cosmetics.)

Dress ornaments, (see buttons and trimmings.)

Drillings, (see cottons.)

Drills, (see linens.)

Drop black, as paint, (dec. of July 11, 1859) (239)........25 per ct.

Druggets, printed, colored, or otherwise, (620-775)

90 per ct. of $\begin{cases} 25 \text{ cts. per sq. yd.} \\ \text{and } 35 \text{ per ct.} \end{cases}$

Drugs, for dyeing, (see berries.)

Drugs & medicines, crude, not otherwise provided for, (60) 20 per ct.

Duck, (see linens.)
" cotton, (dec. of Dec. 15, 1858,) (484-774)
90 per ct. of 30 per ct.
" sail,* (484)............30 per ct
" " cotton, (484-774)
90 per ct. of 30 per ct.

Dung salts, containing less than 30 per cent of potash, (dec. of Aug. 2, 1870) (160)........   free

Dutch metal (see metals.)
" pink, (see paints.)

Dutiable, charges when, (see par. 602.)

Duties, discriminating, (see pars. 561 & 782.)

Dyes, (see aniline, berries, and cosmetics.)

Dye, tyrian, (dec. of July 8, 1861) (166)................20 per ct.

Dyewoods, extract and decoction of, (274)..............10 per ct.

Dyewoods, all, in sticks, (127).   free.

E

Earth, fuller's (493-780)
90 per ct. of $3 per ton.

Earthenware, brown, and common stoneware, not ornamented, (488)..............25 per ct.

Earthenware, stoneware, or crockeryware, white, glazed, edged, printed, painted, dipped, or cream colored, composed of earthy or mineral substances, not otherwise provided for, (490)............40 per ct.

Earths, ochrey, (see paints.)

East India, gum, (719)........   free.

Ebony, (see woods and manufs. of wood.)

Effects, personal, and household, not merchandise, of citizens of the U. S. dying abroad, (155)..............   free.

Effects, personal, or baggage, in transit. (573)

Effects, personal, and wearing apparel, in actual use, not merchandise, professional books, implements, instruments, and tools of trade, occupation or employment of persons arriving in the U. S. *Provided,* that this exemption shall not include machinery, or other articles to be used in any manufacturing establishment or for sale,† (162-816-817)......   free.

---

* "The usual width of 'sail duck' is 24 inches, if over that being much too wide for strength, and is really intended for tents, cot bottoms, awnings, &c., and consequently falls under paragraph No. 482."—(Decision of January 28, 1864.)

† " Duty must be demanded on all watches, but one, brought by a single passenger." —(Decision of July 14, 1868.)

Effects, household, books, libraries or parts of libraries, in use of persons or families from foreign countries, if used abroad by them not less than one year and not intended for any person or persons, nor for sale* (817)................ free.

Eggs, (717). .... free.

" silkworm, (739)........ free.

Elecampane root, (825)........ free.

Embroideries, articles embroidered with gold, silver or other metal, except copper be a component part of chief value, (see note to manufactures of copper,) (71-359-777)
90 per ct. of 35 per ct.

if articles of ornament, (71-359-777)................35 per ct.

Embroideries, cottons, used as balmorals, (dec. of Feb. 2, 1866,) (470-774)
90 per ct. of { 24 cts per lb. and 35 per ct.

Embroideries, cotton & worsted reps, (dec. of April 20, 1865,) see manufactures of worsted.

Embroideries, wool covers, (dec. of April 20, 1865,) (613-775)
90 per ct. of { 50 cts. per lb. and 35 per ct.

Embroideries, part wool, except clothing, (613-775)
90 per ct. of { 50 cts. per lb. and 35 per ct.

Embroideries, part wool, if clothing, (618-775)
90 per ct. of { 50 cts. per lb. and 40 per ct.

Embroideries,† manufactures of cotton, linen, worsted or silk if embroidered or tamboured, in the loom or otherwise, by machinery or with the needle, or other process, not otherwise provided for, (100-385) 35 per ct.

if cotton chief value, (100-385-774)........90 per ct. of 35 per ct.

if worsted part value (100-385-775).....90 per ct. of 35 per ct.

Emeralds, (see precious stones.)

Emery, manufactured, ground or pulverized,(237) 1 ct. per lb.

" ore or rock, not pulverized, not ground, (786)............$6 per ton.

" grains, (786).......2 cts. per lb.

Emetic, tartar, (262)......15 cts. per lb.

Enamelled white, (see paints.)

Engravings, colored, or not, bound or unbound, (dec. of January 25, 1861.) (544-778)
90 per ct. of 25 per ct.

Envelopes, paper, (110-394-778)
90 per ct. of 35 per ct.

Epaulets, metal, (see trim'ngs.)

Ergot, (825)................ free.

Escutcheons, (accd'g to material.)

Esparto, or Spanish grass, and other grasses and pulp of, for manufacture of paper, (717-851)..................... free.

Essences, (see cosmetics, medicines and oils.)

Ethers of all kinds, not otherwise provided for, and etherial preparations or extracts, fluid, (519)... ....$1 per lb.

Ethers, fruit, (see oils.)

Ether, cognac, (see oils.)

" nitric, sp'ts of, (522)..50 cts. per lb.

Extracts, (see cologne, cosmetics, and medicines.)

Eyelets, if iron or any other metal chief value, (665-777)
90 per ct. of 6 cts. per M.

" all other, (665)...6 cts. per M.

Eyes, hooks and, (according to material.)

---

* " Household effects to be entitled to entry free of duty should be in use abroad for more than one year, and arrive with the owner, or within a reasonable time before or after his arrival. Five or six months cannot be considered a reasonable time."—(Decisions of October 24, 1868, and September 23, 1869.)

† " It has been the practice to classify under these sections (paragraphs 100 and 385) such goods as are commercially known as 'embroideries,' and not manufactures of any material, to which some embroidery may be added."—(Decision of April 20, 1865.)

F

Fans, common palm leaf,* (826)   free.
"   if bone, cotton, ivory, horn, leather, gutta-percha or metal chief value, (89-374-774-776-777-779-781)
    90 per ct. of 35 per ct.
"   paper, (89-374-788)
    90 per ct. of 35 per ct.
"   silk, (89-374)...........35 per ct.
"   all other material, (89-374).
    35 per ct.
Farina, (826)............... free.
Feathers, ostrich, vulture, cock, and other ornamental feathers, crude or not dressed, colored or manufactured,(538)..25 per ct.
When dressed, colored, or manufactured, (538)......50 per ct.
Feathers, for beds or bedding, (811)...................... free.
Feathers, artificial and ornamental, or parts thereof, of whatever material composed, not otherwise provided for, (540)..............50 per ct.
Feldspar, (56)...............20 per ct.
Feeding bottles, glass, India rubber, and wood, (dec. of October 13, 1868,) (503-780)
    90 per ct. of 40 per ct.
Felt, adhesive, for sheathing vessels, no part wool, (134)............... free.
"   roofing, (dec. of April 1, 1858,) (166).........20 per ct.
"   hair worked into felt, (dec. of Aug. 25, 1857,) (685)...............30 per ct.
Felts, (see belts.)
Fertilizers, (see guano & phosphates.)
Fibrin, in all forms, (718).... free.

Fiddles and fifes, (see musical instruments.)
Figs, (796)..............2¼ cts. per lb.
"   preserved, (see fruits preserved.)
Fig blue, (419)...............25 per ct.
Filberts, (530).........3 cts. per lb.
Filé, or gespinst, (see trim'gs.)
Files, file blanks, rasps, and floats, all kinds, (454-776.)
not over 10 inches in length,
   90 per ct. of { 10 cts. per lb. and 30 per ct.
over 10 inches in length,
   90 per ct. of { 6 cts. per lb. and 30 per ct.
Fire-arms, (108-391-776)
    90 per ct. of 35 per ct.
Finishing powder, (see powders.)
Fire-crackers, box of 40 packs, not over 80 to each pack, and in the same proportion for any greater or less number,† (798)...............$1 per box.
Fire-screens, if wood chief value, (89-374).35 per ct.
"   if iron or other metal chief value, (89-374-776)
    90 per ct. of 35 per ct.
Firewood, (828).... free.
Fish, herring, pickled or salted,‡ (dec. of Feb. 13, 1871) (15).........$1 per bbl.
"   mackerel, (15)........$2 per bbl.
"   salmon, pickled, (15)..$3 per bbl.
"   salmon, prepared, (dec. of July 11, 1866,) (113-397)......35 per ct.
"   salmon, preserved, (114) 30 per ct.
"   all other, pickled, in bbls. (15)............$1.50 per bbl.

* "Palm leaf fans, is a fan made from the leaf of the palm tree, the natural stem of the leaf being the handle, and the leaf simply bound to prevent cracking and breaking. Those having artificial handles of wood, bone, &c., with cords and tassels, and attached to the leaves by means of rivets, pay as other fans."—(Decision of June 7, 1870.)

† Paragraph 563 repeals so much of the Act of August 6, 1846 or any other Act, as requires the sale of fire crackers or prohibits their deposit in bonded warehouse.

‡ "Fish in kegs or kits, 8 to a bbl. of 25 lbs. each. A barrel is well understood, according to commercial usage, to weigh 200 lbs."—(Decision of March 29, 1867. See also decision of February 10, 1869.)

Fish, all other, foreign caught,
otherwise than in bbls.
or half bbls. or whether
fresh, smoked, or dried,
salted, or pickled, not
otherwise provided for,
(15).... ....½ ct. per lb.

" for bait, (718)........... free.

" fresh, for daily or immediate consumption,(134-
718)...... .... free.

" pickled in foreign salt of
American catch, (dec. of
Jan. 22, 1869,) (153).... free.

" prepared, (see prepared
meats, &c.)

" preserved in oil, (except
sardines and anchovies,)
(71)................30 per ct.

" shell, (739)............. free.

Fisheries, American, all articles
the produce of such fisheries,
(153)................... free.

Fish glue or isinglass, (840).... free.

" hooks, (see hooks.)

" skins, (see skins.)

Fish joints, wrought iron, (see
note to R. R. chairs,) (433-776)
90 per ct. of 2 cts. per lb.

Flageolets (see musical inst's.)

Flannels, (614-775),
valued at 40 cts. or less per lb.

90 per ct. of { 20 cts. per lb.
and 35 per ct.

valued above 40 cts. and not
above 60 cts. per lb.

90 per ct. of { 30 cts. per lb.
and 35 per ct.

valued above 60 cts. and not
above 80 cts. per lb.

· 90 per ct. of { 40 cts. per lb.
and 35 per ct.

valued above 80 cts. per lb.

90 per ct. of { 50 cts. per lb.
and 35 per ct.

Flannels, plaid, (Reg. of 1857,
p. 567,) (613-775)

90 per ct. of { 50 cts. per lb.
and 35 per ct.

Flannels, shirting, (dec. of Nov.
16, 1863,) (613-775)

90 per ct. of { 50 cts. per lb.
and 35 per ct.

Flasks, (according to material.)

Flat irons, or sad irons, of cast
iron, (441-776)
90 per ct. of 1½ ct. per lb.

Flats, for bonnets, hats, &c.,
(see bonnets.)

Flax, hackled, known as "dress-
line" (669).......$40 per ton.

" not hackled or dressed,
(669).............$20 per ton.

" straw of, (668)........$5 per ton.

" tow of, (671)....... .$10 per ton.

" manufs. of, (see manufs.)

Fleams, as cutlery.

Flies, Spanish,(see cantharides.)

Flint & ground flintstones, (828) free.

Flints, (828).................. free.

Floats, (see files.)

Flocks, mungo,shoddy or waste,
(37-275).............20 per ct.

Same if wool, (612½-775)
90 per ct. of 12 cts. per lb.

Flocks, pulverized wool, (Reg.
of 1857, p. 567,) (612½-
775)..90 per ct. of 12 cts. per lb.

Flour, rye, (47) ....10 per ct.

" wheat, (166)..........20 per ct.

" root, (854)............ free.

Flowers, artificial and ornamental, or parts
thereof,of whatever
material composed,
not otherwise pro-
vided for, (540)...50 per ct.

" chamomile, (819)..... free.

" orange & buds, (849).. free.

" dried & prepr'd, (824) free.

" medicinal, crude, not
otherwise provided
for, (827)......... free.

" used in dyeing, (see
berries.)

" all other, not other-
wise provided for,
(166).............10 per ct.

Flues, steam, gas, and water,
wrought iron,* (438-776)
90 per ct. of 2¼ cts. per lb.

Fluid, burning, (234)....50 cts. per gall·

Flutes, (see musical inst's.)

---

* Decision of May 23, 1870, imposes a duty of 3½ cts. per lb. on "Flues" under the
term "Tubes;" 1 ct. extra being imposed on Tubes by Par. 577.

Foil, gold or silver, (511-777)
　　　90 per ct. of 40 per ct.
" tin, (329-777)
　　　90 per ct. of 30 per ct.
" copper chief value, (see
　　note to manufs. of cop-
　　per,) (640-777)
　　　90 per ct. of 45 per ct.
Foils for fencing, (458 776)
　　　90 per ct. of 45 per ct.
Foliæ digitalis, (718).......... free.
Forks, (according to material.)
" table, as cutlery.
Fossils, (828)..... .... free.
Fountains, (see paintings.)
Fowls, land and water, (dec. of
　March 30, 1872) (125)....... free.
Frankfort black, (see paints.)
Frames and sticks for umbrel-
　las, (see umbrellas.)
Free goods, (see foot note to
　par. 166.)
Freestone, (682)........ $1.50 per ton.
Freight, when dutiable, (see
　par. 602.)
French green (see paints.)
Fringes, silk, (486)...........60 per ct.
" cotton chief value (481-
　　774)...90 per ct. of 35 per ct.
" wool, worsted or mo-
　　hair, (see trim'ngs.)
" other, (according to
　　material.)
Fruit ethers, (see oils.)
" juice, (526).............25 per ct.
" pic, (dec. of Mar. 8, 1860,)
　　(86-371).............35 per ct.
Fruits, green, ripe, or dried, not
　otherwise provided
　for, (37)............10 per ct.
" tropical and semi-tropi-
　　cal, for the purpose of
　　propagation or culti-
　　vation, (829) .... free.
" pickled, (79-365)......35 per ct.
" preserved in their own
　　juice, (dec. of March
　　8, 1860,) (526).......25 per ct.

Fruits, comfits or sweetmeats,
　preserved in sugar,
　brandy, or molasses,
　not otherwise provi-
　ded for, (86-371)....35 per ct.
" bottles and jars contain-
　　ing preserves or
　　sweetmeats pay sep-
　　arate duty, (see bot-
　　tles.)
" if fancifully arranged in
　　glace style, as confec-
　　tionery, (dec. of Feb.
　　27, 1865.)
Fulminates, fulminating pow-
　ders, and all articles used for
　like purposes, not otherwise
　provided for, (324)........30 per ct.
Fullers, earth, (493-780)
　　　90 per ct. of $3 per ton
Furniture, coach and harness,
　(see saddlery.)
" house or cabinet, in
　　pieces or rough,
　　and not finished,
　　(768)...........30 per ct.
" finished, (768)......35 per ct.
" springs, (see springs.)
" tops for, of composi-
　　tion or scagliola,
　　(86-114-371-399) 35 per ct.
" slate tops for, (491) 40 per ct.
" marble tops for, (319) 50 per ct.
Fur, manufs. of, (see manufs.)
" waste, (dec. of April 24,
　　1863,) (37-275)........20 per ct.
Furs, dressed, on the skin, (546) 20 per ct.
" not dressed, on the skin,
　　(718)................. free.
" hare's, not on skin, not
　　dressed, (dec. of Oct. 31,
　　1863,) (166)..... .....10 per ct.
" hatters', not on the skin,
　　(546)................20 per ct.
Fusel oil, (see alcohol.)
Fustic (see dyewoods.)

G

Gaiters, (see boots.)

Galanga or galangal, (830)..... free.

Galloons, cotton, (86-371-774)
90 per ct. of 35 per ct.

" metal, (see trim'ngs.)

" silk, (486).........60 per ct.

" wool, worsted or mo-
hair, (see trim'ngs.)

Gambia, or gambier, as cutch,
(dec. of May 3, 1864,) (715)... free.

Gamboge, gum, (719)........ free.

Game, prepared, (see prepared
meat, &c.)

Games, (dec. of Nov. 27, 1868,)
wood, (543)........50 per ct.

" paper, (543-778)
90 per ct. of 50 per ct.

Gannister, ground, mixed with
fire clay and used for the same
purpose,(dec. of July14, 1869,)
(492-780)....90 per ct. of $5 per ton.

Garancine (830)............. free.

Garbanum, gum, (719)....... free.

Garnets, (see precious stones.)

Garters, as suspenders.

Gas retorts and flues, (see retorts and flues.)

Gauze, Chamberg, (dec. of Feb.
16, 1867,) (485)............60 per ct.

Gelatine and all similar preparations, (94-379)........ .....35 per ct.

Gems, (see precious stones.)

" specially imported, (see
apparatus & cabinets.)

Gentian-root, (830)........... free.

German silver, manufactures of,
(see manufactures.)

German silver, albata, or argentine, unmanuf'd, (71-359-777)
90 per ct. of 35 per ct.

Gespinst, (see trimmings.)

Gilt ware, (see plated ware.)

Gimlets, as manuf. of steel, (458-
776)..........90 per ct. of 45 per ct.

Gimps, cotton, (86-371-774)
90 per ct. of 35 per ct.

" silk, (486)............60 per ct.

Gimps, wool, worsted or mohair, (see trim'ngs.)

" other, (according to material.)

Gin, (see liquors.)

Ginger, essence of, (772)......35 per

" ground, (772)......3 cts. per lb

" preserved or pickled,
(772)............ .....35 per ct.

" root, fresh or green,(dec.
of May 9, 1870,) (830).   free

Ginghams, see cottons, (dec. of
Oct. 6, 1869.)

Ginseng, root, (830)........... free.

Glass, fluted, rolled, or rough
plate, (not including crown,
cylinder, or common window
glass,) (500-780.)

not above 10x15 inches square
90 per ct. of ¾ ct. per sq. ft.

above 10x15 and not above
16x24
90 per ct. of 1 ct. per sq. ft.

above 16x24 and not above
24x30
90 per ct. of 1½ ct. per sq. ft.

all above 24x30,
90 per ct. of 2 cts. per sq. ft.

Provided, that all fluted,rolled,
or rough plate glass, weighing over 100 lbs. per 100 sq.
feet, shall pay an additional duty on the excess at
the same rates above im-
posed, (500-780)

Glass, all cast polished plate
glass, unsilvered, (501-780)

not above 10x15 inches square
90 per ct. of 3 cts. per sq. ft.

above 10x15 and not above
16x24,
90 per ct. of 5 cts. per sq. ft.

above 16x24 and not above
24x30,
90 per ct. of 8 cts. per sq. ft.

above 24x30 and not above
24x60,
90 per ct. of 25 cts. per sq. ft.

all above 24x60,
90 per ct. of 50 cts. per sq. ft.

Glass, all cast polished plate glass, silvered, or looking-glass plates,* (502-780)

not above 10x15 inches square
    90 per ct. of 4 cts. per sq. ft.

above 10x15 and not above 16x24,
    90 per ct. of 6 cts. per sq. ft.

above 16x24 and not above 24x30,
    90 per ct. of 10 cts. per sq. ft.

above 24x30 and not above 24x60,
    90 per ct. of 35 cts. per sq. ft.

all above 24x60,
    90 per ct. of 60 cts. per sq. ft.

Provided, that no looking-glass plates or plate glass, silvered, when framed, shall pay a less rate of duty than that imposed upon similar glass not framed, but shall pay in addition 30 per ct. upon such frames (502)

Glass, all unpolished cylinder, crown, and common window glass,† (498-780)

not above 10x15 inches square
    90 per ct. of 1½ ct. per lb.

above 10x15 and not above 16x24,   90 per ct. of 2 cts. per lb.

above 16x24 and not above 24x30,
    90 per ct. of 2½ cts. per lb.

all above 24x30,
    90 per ct. of 3 cts. per lb.

Glass, cylinder & crown glass, polished, (499-780.)

not above 10x15 inches square
    90 per ct. of 2½ cts. per sq. ft.

above 10x15 and not above 16x24,
    90 per ct. of 4 cts. per sq. ft.

above 16x24 and not above 24x30,
    90 per ct. of 6 cts. per sq. ft.

above 24x30 and not above 24x60,
    90 per ct. of 20 cts. per sq. ft.

all above 24x60,
    90 per ct. of 40 cts. per sq. ft.

Glass, colored, for manufacture of buttons and imitation of precious stones, (dec. of Dec. 3, 1859) (497-780)
    90 per ct. of 40 per ct.

" broken in pieces, which cannot be cut for use, and fit only to be re-manufactured (719)....   free.

" manuf's of, (see manuf's.)

" porcelain and Bohemian, cut or not, (Reg. of 1857, p. 568) (503-780)
    90 per ct. of 40 per ct.

Glassware, (see manufactures of glass.)

Globes, glass, (see manuf. of glass.)

"   wood, (107-390)......35 per ct.

" wood and metal, but metal chief value, (98-383-777)
    90 per ct. of 35 per ct.

Gloves, cotton, lined with wool waste, (dec. of Dec. 31, 1868) (613-775)
    90 per ct. of { 50 cts. per lb. and 35 per ct.

" cotton, (81-367-774)
    90 per ct. of 35 per ct.

" cotton, edged at the wrist with a small stripe or stripes of col'd worsted yarn, knit in for the purpose of ornament, (dec. of Jan 29, 1871) (81-367-774)
    90 per ct. of 35 per ct.

" hair, (685)..........30 per ct.

" kid, or other leather, (543-781)..........50 per ct.

" linen, (81-367).. .....35 per ct.

" silk, (486)..........60 per ct.

" woollen cloth, (dec. of Nov. 7, 1866) (618-775)
    90 per ct. of { 50 cts. per lb. and 40 per ct.

---

*"The term 'Looking Glass Plates' means any kind of silvered glass used as looking glasses, although not in fact *plate* glass."—(Dec. of July 2, 1863.)

†"No decision of the Treasury Department has recognized as 'window glass' any other than the broad, crown or cylinder glass; glass ground on one side must be taken as a manufacture of glass."—(Reg. of 1857, p. 568.)

Gloves, worsted, knit or made on frames, (81-367-775) 90 per ct. of 35 per ct.
" wool, knit, (see knit goods.)
" wool or worsted, not knit, (618-775) 90 per ct. of { 50 cts. per lb. and 40 per ct.
Glue, (57)..... ....20 per ct.
" fish, (840)............. free.
" stock, (see hide cuttings.)
Glycerine, (268).............30 per ct.
Goat, hair of the (see wool.)
" " " manuf'd, (see dress goods, clothing, and manufactures of worsted.)
Goats, (see animals.)
Goat skins, (see skins.)
Goblets, (see manf's of glass.)
Gold, bullion, (127)........... free.
" dust, (739).... .... free.
" leaf, pkge of 500 leaves, (240-777) 90 per ct. of $1.50 per pkge.
" leaf, half gold, as gold . leaf, (dec. of April 2, 1863.)
" manuf's of (see manuf's.)
" ore, (153)............. free.
" sweepings of (739) ..... free.
Gomline as albumen, (Reg. of 1857, p. 569) (708)......... free.
Gouges, as manufac's of steel, (458-770)......90 per ct. of 45 per ct.
Gowns, (see clothing.)
Granite, (see stones.)
Grapes, (see damage on fruit) (696).............20 per ct.
" sugar, or pulp of, (Reg. of 1857, p. 581) (166) 20 per ct.
" juice of, (526).......25 per ct.
Grass, Sisal (672).........$15 per ton.
" " manufac's of (see manufac's.)
Grass, Spanish, or Esparto, and other grasses and pulp of, for manufacture of paper (717-851)...................... free.
Grass, manuf's of (see manuf's.)

Grease (43). ....10 per ct.
" for use as soap stock only, not otherwise provided for, and soap stocks (831-857)...... free.
Green, French, mineral and Paris, (see paints.)
Greenstone, as marble.
Grenadines, silk (dec. of Oct. 12, 1866) (485)....60 per ct.
" cotton, (see cottons.)
Gridirons, manufac's of iron (444-770)......90 per ct. of 35 per ct.
Grindstones, (see stones.)
Ground beans, (see peanuts.)
Guano and other animal manures, and substances expressly used for manure (160-719)...................... free.
Guano, French imitation, (Reg. of 1857, p. 567) (166)......20 per ct.
Guava jelly, (see jellies.)
Guiac, gum (719)............. free.
Guitars, (see musical instr's.)
Gums, viz.: amber (804), aloes (708), Arabic, Australia, benzoin or benjamin, Barbary, bdellium, copal, Cape, cowrie, damar, East India, garbanum, gamboge, guiac, Jeddo, mastic, myrrh, olebanum, sandarac, Senegal, shellac, tragacanth, and all gums not otherwise provided for (719) free.
Gum perdu, (Reg. of 1857, p. 569) (704)................$1 per lb.
Gum resins, all, not otherwise provided for, (267)........20 per ct.
Gum substitute or burnt starch (38)...... ....10 per ct.
Gun barrels, (see guns.)
" blocks, (see blocks.)
" locks, (see guns.)
. " cotton or coton azotique, (dec. of Aug. 5, 1858) (324)................30 per ct.
Gunny bags and gunny cloth,* of hemp, jute or flax (484) valued at 10 cts. or less per sq. yd................3 cts. per lb.
valued over 10 cts. per sq. yd..................4 cts. per lb.

* If suitable for the uses to which cotton bagging is applied, pays as "cotton bagging."

Gunny bags and gunny cloth, old or refuse, fit only for re-manufacture (832)......... .. free.

same for manf. of paper (851) free.

Gunpowder, and all explosive substances used for mining, blasting, artillery, or sport-ing purposes, (548)

valued at 20 cts. or less per lb .....6 cts. per lb. and 20 per ct.

valued above 20 cts. per lb.
10 cts. per lb. and 20 per ct.

Guns, (dec. of April 12, 1865) (108-391-776)
90 per ct. of 35 per ct.

" bayonets, and locks for, (dec. of Aug. 20, 1870) (458-776)
90 per ct. of 45 per ct.

Guns, barrels, moulds for, steel, not in bars, (dec. of Aug. 20, 1870) (458-776)....90 per ct. of 45 per ct.

Gun wads, sporting, of all de-scriptions, (dec. of Nov. 16, 1869) (690-775-778)
90 per ct. of 35 per ct.

Gut and worm-gut, manuf'd or unmanuf'd, for whip and other cord, (833)............ free.

Guts, salted (833)............ free.

" and all integuments of animals not otherwise provided for (812).... free.

Gutta percha, crude, (719)..... free.

" manufac's of (see manufactures.)

Gypsum, (see plaster of Paris.)

H

Hackles, part steel, (458-776)
90 per ct. of 45 per ct.

Hair, of the alpaca, goat, &c., (see wool.)

same manf'd (see dress goods, clothing, and manufactures of worsted.)

Hair cloth, not otherwise pro-vided for, (70-375-685)......30 per ct.

Hair cloth of the description known as hair seating, (684)

18 ins. wide or over, 40 cts. per sq. yd.

less than 18 ins. wide, 30 cts. per sq. yd.

Hair cloth known as crinoline cloth, (685)...............30 per ct.

Hair of all kinds, cleaned, but unmanuf'd, not other-wise provided for, (39-775)......90 per ct. of 10 per ct.

" curled, except of hogs, for beds or mattresses, (58-775) 90 per ct. of 20 per ct.

" curled, of hogs, for beds and mattresses, and not fit for bristles, (834).... free.

" dressings, dyes, &c., (see cosmetics.)

Hair of all kinds, (except hu-man hair) uncleaned and unmanufactured, (141) free.

" horse & cow, not cleaned and dressed, (720)...... free.

" horse, long, used for weav-ing, cleaned or un-cleaned, drawn or un-drawn, (141)......... free.

" all horse, cattle, cleaned or uncleaned, drawn or undrawn, but unmanu-factured, (834)........ free.

" hogs', (523-775)
90 per ct. of 1 ct per lb.

" manuf's of, (see manuf's.)

" nets, (see nets.)

" human,* raw, uncleaned, and not drawn, (316)..20 per ct.

" human, cleaned or drawn, but not manufactured, (316)............... 30 per ct.

" human, when manufac-tured, (316)..........40 per ct.

" seating, (see hair cloth.)

Hames, (see saddlery.)

---

* Paragraph 775 which reduces hair of *animals* 10 per ct., I have interpreted not to include human hair.

Hammers, blacksmith's, (432-776)
 90 per ct. of 2¼ cts. per lb.
" brass, (see note to manufs. of brass,) (98-383-776)
 90 per ct. of 35 per ct.
" iron, (444-776)
 90 per ct. of 35 per ct.
" part steel, (458-776)
 90 per ct. of 45 per ct.
Hams, (16)...............2 cts. per lb.
Hand-bills or show-bills, lithographed, (dec. of October 9, 1861) (544-778)
 90 per ct. of 25 per ct.
Handkerchiefs, cotton, printed, as cottons,* (dec. of Sept. 10, 1861.)
" linen, (dec. of Sept. 22, 1868) (see linens.)
" silk, (486).....60 per ct.
Handles for umbrellas, (see umbrellas.)
Hardware, coach and harness, (see saddlery.)
Harmonicons, (see mus. inst's.)
Harness, (see saddlery.)
Harps, (see musical inst's.)
Hassocks, (see mats.)
Hat bands, silk and cotton, but commercially known as silk hat bands, as silk trimmings, (dec. of March 10, 1870) (486) 60 per ct.
Hat bodies, cotton, (90-375-774)
 90 per ct. of 35 per ct.
" wool, (613-775)
 90 per ct. of { 50 cts. per lb. and 35 per ct.
Hatchets, as manf. of steel, (458-776).....90 per ct. of 45 per ct.
Hats, of chip, grass, palm leaf, willow, or any other vegetable substance, or of whalebone, or other material, not otherwise provided for, (298)...40 per ct.

Hats, fur, (80-366)...........35 per ct.
" hair, (685).............30 per ct.
" leather (298-781)
 90 per ct. of 40 per ct.
" silk, (486)... ....60 per ct.
" straw, (298-779)
 60 per ct. of 40 per ct.
" wool,† (614-775)
 valued at 40 cts. or less per lb.
 90 per ct. of { 20 cts. per lb. and 35 per ct.
 valued above 40 cts. and not above 60 cts. per lb.
 90 per ct. of { 30 cts. per lb. and 35 per ct.
 valued above 60 cts. and not above 80 cts. per lb.
 90 per ct. of { 40 cts. per lb. and 35 per ct.
 valued above 80 cts. per lb.
 90 per ct. of { 50 cts. per lb. and 35 per ct.
" woollen cloth, (618-775)
 90 per'ct. of { 50 cts. per lb. and 40 per ct.
" wool or worsted knit, (see knit goods.)
Hatters' irons, of cast iron, (441-776)........90 per ct. of 1½ ct. per lb.
Hatwire, (see wire of steel.)
Hay, (dec. of April 8, 1868) (166)....................20 per ct.
Heading blocks, (see blocks.)
Head nets, (see nets.)
Healds, old, the worn out harness of cotton looms, (dec. of March 5, 1870,) (166)........10 per ct.
Hellebore root, (835)......... free.
Hemlock bark, seed and leaf, (715-720)................... free.
Hemp, Indian, (crude drug) (838)..................... free.
Hemp, Manilla, and other like substitutes for hemp, not otherwise provided for, (670).....$25 per ton.

---

* "Handkerchiefs, pocket, although hemmed or otherwise prepared for use, are articles carried and not worn."—(Reg. of 1857, p. 570.)

† "The term 'hats of wool' applies only to hats the bodies of which are composed of wool that has undergone no process of manufacture, except felting or fulling, but not hats of cloth of wool."—(Decision of Sept. 1, 1860.)

Hemp, Russia, unmanf'd, (dec.
Jan. 5, 1871) (670) $25 per ton.
"   sunn, (672)........$15 per ton.
"   tow of, (671). .....$10 per ton.
"   manfs. of, (see manfs.)
Henbane leaf, (720). .... free.
Herring, (see fish.)
Hessians, (see bags and cotton
bagging, and dec. of Dec. 27,
1862.)
Hide cuttings, raw, with or
without the hair on, for glue
stock, (835)......... ...... free.
Hide rope, (835)............. free.
Hides, raw or uncured, whether
dry, salted, or pickled, (836) free.
Hides, tanned, (see leather.)
Hinges, wrought or cast iron,
(434-442-776)
90 per ct. of 2½ cts. per lb.
"   other, (according to
material.)
Hods, (according to material.)
Hoes, iron, (444-776)
90 per ct. of 35 per ct.
"   part steel, (458-776)
90 per ct. of 45 per ct.
"   steeled, (dec. of March
13, 1866) (458-776)
90 per ct. of 45 per ct.
Hoffman's anodyne (522) 50 cts. per lb.
Hogsheads, (see casks.)
Hollands, brown, (see linens.)
Hollow ware, glazed or tinned,
embracing castings of iron
only, (dec. of July 12, 1861,)
(442-776)...90 per ct. of 3½ cts. per lb.
Hones and whetstones, (837)... free.
Honey, (524)..........20 cts. per gall.
Hoods, (see bonnets.)
Hoofs, (720)................. free.

Hooks, fish, (458-776)
90 per ct. of 45 per ct.
"   reaping, (458-776)
90 per ct. of 45 per ct.
Hooks and eyes, (according to
material.)
Hoop iron, (see iron.)
Hoops, iron, (444-776)
90 per ct. of 35 per ct.
"   iron, not advanced beyond hoop iron ex-
cept cut into lengths
as hoops, duty as
hoop iron, (dec. of
Nov. 10, 1868.)
"   wood, split, not finished,
(dec. of May 23, 1867)
(166)..............20 per ct.
"   wood, (107-390)......35 per ct.
Hops, (315)..............5 cts. per lb.
Hop roots, for cultivation, (837) free.
Horn, manufs. of, (see manufs.)
"   strips, (837)............ free.
Horns and horn tips, (720) ... free.
Horses, (see animals.)
Hose, leather, (103-387-781)
90 per ct. of 35 per ct.
"   india rubber, (66-779)
90 per ct. of 20 per ct.
Hosiery, (see caps.)
Household effects, (see effects.)
Hubs, for wheels, rough hewn
or sawed only, (765)..20 per ct.
"   otherwise than rough,
hewn or sawed, (Reg.
of 1857, p. 498) (107-
390)..............35 per ct.
Huckabacks, (see linens.)
Hyoscyamus or henbane leaf,
(720)..................... free.
Hydrometers, part glass, (503,
see also 780)...... .....40 per ct.

I

Ice, (142)....,.............. free.
Implements of trade,(see effects.)
Indian hemp, (crude drug) (838) free.
India rubber, crude, and milk
of, (721)...... free.
"   "   balls, (see balls.)

India rubber, in strips, unmanufactured,(dec.
of July 8, 1861)
(721)......... free.
"   "   manufactures of,
(see manufs.)

Indigo, (142)................. free.
" carmined, (504).......20 per ct.
" extract of, as carmined, (dec. of April 4, 1865,) (504)...............20 per ct.

Indio or malacco joints, (see joints.)

Ink and ink powder, (91-376)...35 per ct.
" printers', (91-376) ....35 per ct.

Ink stands, (according to material.)

Insertings, cotton, (481-774) 90 per ct. of 35 per ct.
" thread, (67-286)..30 per ct.

Instruments and apparatus, musical, (see musical inst's.)

Instruments and apparatus, surgeons', (accord'g to material.)

Instruments and apparatus, mathematical, (according to material.)

Instruments and apparatus, philosophical, (98-283-777) 90 per ct. of 40 per ct.

Instruments and apparatus, philosophical part steel, (98-283-566-777) 90 per ct. of 40 per ct.

Instruments and apparatus, specially imported, (see apparatus and effects.)

Integuments, all, of animals, not otherwise provided for (812)................ ..... free.

Insulators for use exclusively in telegraphy, except those made of glass, (784)........25 per ct.

Inventions, models of, (see models.)

Iodine, crude, (721).......... free.
" resublimed, (242)..75 cts. per lb.
" salts of, (14)..........15 per ct.

Ipecac, (721)................. free.

Iridium, (840)................. free.

Iris or orris root, (142)........ free.

Iron, acetate or pyrolignite of, (789) ....25 cts. per lb.

Iron, band, hoop and scroll, from 1/2 to 6 inches in width, not thinner than 1/8 of an inch, (429-776) 90 per ct. of 1 1/4 ct. per lb.
under 1/8 inch in thickness, and not thinner than No. 20, wire gauge, 90 per ct. of 1 1/2 ct. per lb.
thinner than No. 20, wire gauge, 90 per ct. of 1 3/4 ct. per lb.

" bar, rolled or hammered, comprising flats not less than one inch or more than 6 inches wide, nor less than 3/8 of an inch or more than two inches thick,* (426-776) 90 per ct. of 1 ct. per lb.
less than 3/8 of an inch or more than two inches thick, or less than one inch or more than six inches wide, 90 per ct. of 1 1/2 ct. per lb.

" round, not less than 3/4 of an inch nor more than 2 inches in diameter,(426-776)...90 per ct. of 1 ct. per lb.
less than 3/4 of an inch or more than 2 inches in diameter, 90 per ct. of 1 1/2 ct. per lb.

" round, in coils.†

" square, not less than 3/4 of an inch, nor more than two inches square, (426-776)....90 per ct. of 1 ct. per lb.
less than 3/4 of an inch or more than two inches square 90 per ct. of 1 1/2 ct. per lb.

Provided, That all iron in slabs, blooms,‡ loops, or other forms, less finished than iron in bars, and more advanced than pig iron, except castings,

*" Instructions relative to classification of scrap or bar iron." (See dec. of Feb. 1, 1870.)

† "That round iron in coils, 3-16 of an inch or less in diameter, whether coated with metal or not so coated, and all descriptions of iron wire and wire of which iron is a component part, not otherwise specially enumerated and provided for, shall pay the same duty as iron wire, bright, coppered or tinned," (paragraph 680.)

‡ " Certain so styled iron in muck bar or bloom, which by reason of its having been sunk in St. Lawrence Bay, for two years, had become corroded, and in fact only fit to be remanufactured, was refused admission to entry as old scrap iron. The department held that its character was not changed."—(Decision of April 5, 1869.)

shall be rated as iron in bars, and pay a duty accordingly, (426)

Provided further, That none of the above iron in bars, rounds or squares shall pay a less rate of duty than (426-776)..... 90 per ct. of 35 per ct.

Iron bars for railroads, and inclined planes, made to pattern and fitted to be laid without further manufacture, (427-577-776.)
90 per ct. of 70 cts. per 100 lbs.

" beams, as rolled or hammered, not otherwise provided for, (dec. of Dec. 2. 1868,) (430-776),
90 per ct. of 1¼ ct. per lb.

" boiler, or other plate, not less than 3-16 of an inch in thickness, (427-776)
90 per ct. of 1½ ct. per lb.

" boiler plate, not otherwise provided for, (5-196) 90 per ct. of $25 per ton.

" carbonate of, Reg. of 1857, p. 559, (166)..... ...20 per ct.

" casting (see castings.)

" coated or galvanized with any metal by electric batteries, (800-776)
90 per ct. of 2 cts. per lb.

other than by electric batteries, (428-777)
90 per ct. of 2½ cts. per lb.

" filings of, (444-776)
90 per ct. of 35 per ct.

" galvanized for roofing purposes, (dec. of Dec. 28,1870),(see iron coated or galvanized.)

" liquor (40)..... ....10 per ct.

" malleable, in castings, not otherwise provided for, (432-776)
90 per ct. of 2½ cts. per lb.

Iron manufs. of, (see manufs.)

" moisic, made from sand ore by one process (801)
$15 per ton.

" nitrate of,(chem. salt,)(66) 20 per ct.

" octagonal shape, (dec. of March 6, 1869,)(430-776)
90 per ct. of 1¼ ct. per lb.

" ore, (dec. of January 20, 1868,) (60-776). ....20 per ct.

" oxide of, or dry colcothar, (821)..... .... free.

" pieces of, new, (dec. of Dec. 17, 1868,) (426-776)
90 per ct. of 1 ct. per lb.

" pig, (675-776)
90 per ct. of $7 per ton.

" reduced by hydrogen, (dec. of June 7, 1870,) (108-280)..... ....40 per ct.

" rolled or hammered, not otherwise provided for, (430-776)
90 per ct. of 1¼ ct. per lb.

" scrap, cast, of every description,* (676-776)
90 per ct. of $6 per ton.

" scrap, wrought, of every description, (677-776)
90 per ct. of $8 per ton.

Provided, that nothing shall be deemed scrap iron except waste or refuse iron that has been in actual use, and fit only to be remanufactured, (677.)

" sheet, common or black, not thinner than No. 20 wire gauge,† (427-776)
90 per ct. of 1¼ ct. per lb.

thinner than No. 20, and not thinner than No. 25 wire gauge,
90 per ct. of 1½ ct. per lb.

thinner than No. 25 wire gauge,
90 per ct. of 1¾ ct. per lb.

---

* " Instructions relative to classification of scrap or bar iron."—(See dec. of Feb. 1, 1870.)

† " Iron bands on sheet iron to be considered as tare, being of but trifling value and of the poorest iron, and are thought to be no more liable to duty than iron hoops around casks or boxes."—(Decision of January 4, 1865.)

Iron, sheet, smooth or polished, by whatever name designated, (427-776)
90 per ct. of 3 cts. per lb.

" sheet, bessemer, as steel in sheets,* (dec. of Jan. 12, 1869.)

" slit rods, (see rods.)

" sulphate of, (14-288)...½ ct. per lb.

" sulphuret of, (dec. of Oct. 29, 1860,) (60).........20 per ct.

" vessels of, cast, not otherwise provided for, (441-776) 90 per ct. of 1½ ct. per lb.

" washers, wrought, ready punched, (433-776)
90 per ct. of 2 cts. per lb.

" wire, (see wire.)

" " rope (see wire rope.)

Iron, wrought, for ships, steam engines, and locomotives, or parts thereof, weighing each 25 pounds or more, (430-776)
90 per ct. of 2 cts. per lb.

Isinglass, or fish glue, (840).... free.

Istle or tampico fibre man'fs. of, not suitable for cotton bagging, (dec. of May 12, 1869, (484)..................30 per ct.

Istle or tampico fibre, (840)..... free.

Italian cloth, (see dress goods).

Ivory and vegetable ivory, unmanufactured, (721)........ free.

same, manufs. of, (see manufs.)

Ivory black, (see paints.)

" nuts, (721).............. free.

J

Jackets, woollen, (dec. of Oct. 21, 1861,) (618-775)
90 per ct. of { 50 cts. per lb. and 40 per ct.

" cardigan, (dec. of Oct. 26, 1869,) (614-775)
90 per ct. of { 50 cts. per lb. and 35 per ct.

Julap, (841)............... free.

Japanned wares, all kinds, not otherwise provided for, (92-278-777).......90 per ct. or 40 per ct.

if articles of ornament.....40 per ct.

Jars, filled, (see bottles.)

" other, (according to material.)

Jeans, (see cottons.)

Jeddo, gum, (719)........... free.

Jellies, all kinds, (542).......50 per ct.

bottles or jars containing jellies pay a separate duty, (see bottles.)

Jet, manufac'd and imitation thereof, (92-377).......35 per ct.

" unmanufac'd, (722)........ free.

Jewelry,† (70)..............25 per ct.

" imitation of, (dec. of July 28, 1863,) (70)25 per ct.

" of jet, or imitation of jet, (decs. of Sept. 7, 1866, & Dec. 3, 1863,) (92-377)...35 per ct.

Jewels, watch, (694)........10 per ct.

Joints, fish, wrought iron, (see note to R.R. chairs,) (433-776)
90 per ct. of 2 cts. per lb.

Joints, malacca or indio, not further manufactured than cut into suitable lengths for the manufactures into which they are intended to be converted (839)............... free.

Josstick or josslight, (841)..... free.

* " Metal converted, cast or made from iron by the Bessemer or pneumatic process, of whatever form or description, shall be classed as "steel."—(Paragraph 680.)

† "The term jewelry embraces the manufacture of personal ornaments in gold, silver and precious stones."—(Decs. of Nov. 20, 1869, and March 1, 1871.)

Juice, lime and lemon, (42)....10 per ct.
"   fruit, (526) ....25 per ct.
Junk, old, (143)..............   free.

Jute,* (672)..............$15 per ton.
"   butts, (841)...........   free.
"   manufs. of, (see manufs.)

K

Kallidunger, (see dung salt.)
Kaoline (492-780)
          90 per ct. of $5 per ton.
Kelp, (alkaline matter of sea-
  weeds,) (144)...............   free.
Kermes, mineral, (43).......10 per ct.
Kerosene oil, (see oils, illumin-
  ating.)
Kerosene oil,residuum of,under
  20° Beaumé, (dec. of Oct. 3,
  1871,) (166)................20 per ct.
Kettles, cast of iron, (441-776)
          90 per ct. of 1½ ct. per lb.
"   other, (according to
      material.)
Keys, watch, gold and silver,
  (70)................25 per ct.
"   other, (according to ma-
      terial.)
Kieserite, (dec. of June 7, 1870,)
  (66)......................20 per ct.
Kine pox, (see cow pox.)
Kirshwasser, (see liquors.) ·
Knees, ship, (843)............   free.
Knit goods, wholly or in part
  of wool, worsted, the hair of
  the alpaca, goat, or other
  like animals, (dec. of June 4,
  1870,) (618-775)
valued at 40 cts. or less per lb.
  90 per ct. of { 20 cts. per lb.
                 { and 35 per ct.

valued above 40 cts. and not
  above 60 cts. per lb.
  90 per ct. of { 30 cts. per lb.
                 { and 35 per ct.
valued above 60 cts. and not
  above 80 cts. per lb.
  90 per ct. of { 40 cts. per lb.
                 { and 35 per ct.
valued above 80 cts. per lb.
  90 per ct. of { 50 cts. per lb.
                 { and 35 per ct.
Knives, butcher, (dec. of Aug.
  22, 1868,) bread, bowie, budding, cooks', farriers', fruit,
  pruning, shoe, and table, as
  cutlery, which see, (86-371-
  776)..........90 per ct. of 35 per ct.
Knives, beam, curriers', drawing, (dec. of March 30, 1865,)
  fleshers, hay, putty, (dec. of
  March 16, 1868,) straw, and
  tanners', as manfs. of steel,
  (458-776)......90 per ct. of 45 per ct.
Knives, pen, jack and pocket,
  (455-776)......90 per ct. of 50 per ct.
Knobs and knockers, (accord-
  ing to material.)
Knots, metal, (see trimmings.)
Kreosote, (108-280)...........40 per ct.
Kryolite, (723)..............   free.
Kyanite, or cyanite, (823).....   free.

---

* For tare on jute, see department letter of May 8, 1866, and decision of May 19, 1870.

L

Labels, blank, (dec. of May 28, 1869,) (544-778)
  90 per ct. of 25 per ct.

" printed and figured paper, (dec. of Oct. 15, 1870,) (544-778)
  90 per ct. of 25 per ct.

" other, (according to marial.)

Lace, (see laces.)

Lacets, silk, part metal, (dec. of Nov. 29, 1861,) (487) 50 per ct.

Lacings, boot and shoe, (dec. of June 15, 1864,) (72-360-774)
  90 per ct. of 35 per ct.

Lacquered ware, metal, (98-383-777)......90 per ct. of 35 per ct.

  same wood, (107-390)......35 per ct.

Lac S. crude, seed, button, stick, shell or dye, (724).. .... free.

Lac spirits and sulphur, (145).. free.

Lactarine, (708) .... free.

Ladles, (according to material.)

Lampblack, (see paints.)

Lamps, (accord'g to material.)

Lancets, as cutlery.

Lance wood, (see woods.)

Lanterns, (accord'g to material.)

Lanterns, magic, if toys, (dec. of Nov. 12, 1864,) tin, iron or other metal, chief value, (543-777)..... .....90 per ct. of 50 per ct.

Lappets, cotton, (decs. of May 18, 1866, and Dec. 22, 1866,) (470-774)
  90 per ct. of { 24 cts. per lb. and 35 per ct.

Lappings, according to material, (dec. of July 12, 1859.)

Lard, (16)...............2 cts. per lb.

Laces, cotton, (481-774)
  90 per ct. of 35 per ct.

" metal, (see trimmings.)

" silk, (486)............60 per ct.

" silk and cotton, known as silk lace, (dec. of Mar. 4, 1868,) (486)...60 per ct.

" thread, (67-286)........30 per ct.

" for bonnets, hats, &c., (see bonnets.)

Laces, wool, worsted or mohair, (see trimmings.)

" other, (according to material.)

Last blocks, (see blocks.)

Lasting for buttons, (see buttons.)

" other, (according to material.)

Latches, (accord'g to material.)

Laths, (766).....15 cts. per 1000 pieces.

Laudanum, (dec. of Nov. 21, 1871,) (108-280)...........40 per ct.

Lava, unmanufactured, (724).. free.

Lava gas burners, (dec. of June 15, 1858) (490)...........40 per ct.

Lawns, (see linens & cottons.)

Lead, acetate or pyrolignite of, brown, (789)......5 cts. per lb.

" acetate of, white, (780)
  10 cts. per lb.

" ashes of, (dec. of Jan. 27, 1870) (166)..........10 per ct.

" black or plumbago, (852) free.

" black, powder or British lustre, (dec. of Nov. 16, 1869) (166)........ 20 per ct.

" chromate of, (see paints.)

" dross, as ore, (dec. of Jan. 16, 1865) (462, see also 777)............1¼ ct. per lb.

" in pigs and bars, (dec. of Jan. 6, 1870) (460-777)
  90 per ct. of 2 cts. per lb.

" in sheets, pipe, or shot, (460-777)
  90 per ct. of 2¼ cts. per lb.

" manufs. of, (see manufs.)

" molten, old bullets, as lead in pigs or bars, (dec. of Mar. 24, 1864) (460-777)
  90 per ct. of 2 cts. per lb.

" nitrate of, (14)......3 cts. per lb.

" old scrap, fit only to be remanufactured, (dec. of Jan. 6, 1870) (460-777)
  90 per ct. of 1½ ct. per lb.

Lead ore, (462, see also 777)
      1½ ct. per lb.
"   red, (see paints.)
"   sugar of, as acetate of,
   (dec. of June 22, 1869.)
"   white, (see paints.)
Leaf, (see metal, gold, and
  silver.)
Leakage, (see par. 650.)
Leather, bend or belting, and
  Spanish, or other
  sole, (757)........15 per ct.
"   upper of all kinds, and
   skins dressed and
   finished, of all kinds,
   except calf skins and
   skins for morocco,
   (759-758-760)......20 per ct.
"   old scrap, (842) ..... free.
"   manufs. of, (see man'fs.)

Leaves, aconite (708), buchu
  (714), belladonna
  (713), hemlock (715),
  henbane (720), palm
  (154), rose (738),
  senna (739), and all
  not otherwise pro-
  vided for, (842)....   free.
"   for dyes, (see berries.)
"   medicinal, crude, not
   otherwise provided
   for, (827).........   free.
Leeches, (724)............... free.
Leggins, (see caps.)
Lemon juice, (42)...........10 per ct.
"   "   concentrated,
   (Reg. of 1857, p.
   574,) (42).....10 per ct.
"   peel, (44)............10 per ct.
"   peel, not preserved, candied or otherwise pre-
   pared, (726)........   free.
Lemons, (see damage on fruit)
  (696)............ ......20 per ct.
Levant, wormseed, (742)...... free.
Lichens, all, prepared or not
  prepared, (724)............ free.

Licorice, (see liquorice.)
Life boats, (see boats.)
Lignumvitæ, (see woods.)
Lima, bark, (712)............   free.
Lime, (42)...................10 per ct.
"   acetate or pyrolignite of,
   (507)..............25 per ct.
"   borate of, (812)........   free.
"   chloride of, (bleaching
   powders,) (819).......   free.
"   citrate of, (715)........   free.
"   hydrocarbonate, (dec. of
   July 27, 1866,) (495) 1 ct. per lb.
"   sulphate of, (see plaster
   of Paris.)
"   white, (see paints.)
Limes, (see damage on fruit,)
  (696).............. ...10 per ct.
"   in salt and water, as
   pickles, (dec. of July
   20, 1870,) (79-365)....35 per ct.
"   juice of, (42).........10 per ct.
"   "   concentrated.
   (Reg. of 1857,
   p. 574,)(42)..10 per ct.
Limestone, (see stones.)

Linens, viz :

burlaps, all, and like manufactures of flax, jute, or
  hemp, or of which flax, jute
  or hemp shall be the component material of chief
  value, excepting such as
  may be suitable for bag-
  ging for cotton, (783).....30 per ct.
bagging for cotton, (see cot-
  ton bagging.)
bagging and bags not suitable for baling cotton, (see
  bags.)
brown or bleached linens,
  blay linens, brown hol-
  lands, coatings,* damasks,*
  and drills,† (decs. of March

---

* Decision of March 9, 1870, classifies "brown damasks" under paragraphs 26 and 343 of the digest. This decision also covers goods commercially known as "bleached damasks."

* Decision of April 21, 1868, classifies "brown or bleached drills and coatings," under paragraphs 26 and 343, and "linen drills and coatings, not brown or bleached," under paragraph 452.

† Certain so styled drills liable to 35 per ct. Drills are usually 26 or 27 inches wide. —(Decision of January 10, 1870.)

Linens — Continued.

14 and 18, 1867, July 13 & 18, 1871; Jan. 29, 1872) (26-343.)

value 30 cts. or less per sq. yard.................30 per ct.

value above 30 cts. per sq. yard. ....35 per ct.

brown and bleached linens, canvas, (except canvas for sails, and for oil cloth foundations or floor cloth) cotton bottoms, crash, diaper, ducks, (except sail duck,) handker'fs, (dec. of March 8, 1872), huckabacks, lawns, paddings, or other (fabrics woven,) manufactures of flax, jute or hemp, or of which flax, jute or hemp shall be the component material of chief value, not otherwise provided for, (482, see also 783.)

value 30 cts. or less per sq. yard....·.............35 per ct.

value above 30 cts. per sq. yard..................40 per ct.

linen if embroidered, (see embroideries.)

Lines, (see thread.)

Liniments, (see medicines.)

Linseed cake, (oil cake,) (849)...   free.

"   meal, (166)..........20 per ct.

"   (see seeds.)

Lint, cotton, (481-774)
90 per ct. of 35 per ct.

"   linen, (482).............40 per ct.

Liqueurs, (see liquors.)

Liquorice paste or in rolls, (527-781)
90 per ct. of 10 cts. per lb.

"   juice, (244-781)
90 per ct. of 5 cts. per lb.

"   root, (724)........   free.

Liquor stands, (see castors.)

Liquors, viz : Brandy, Cordials, Wines, &c.

Brandy, and other spirits manufact'd or distilled from grain or other material,* (651)...............$2 per pf. gall.

Provided, That each and every gauge or wine gallon of measurement shall be counted as at least one proof gallon, (651)

Cordials, liqueurs, arrack, absynthe, kirshwasser, ratafia, and other similar spirituous beverages, (except vermuth, which shall pay the same duty as on wines of the same cost, 794) or bitters containing spirits,* (652)...............$2 per pf. gall.

None of the above shall pay a lower rate or amount of duty than that fixed for first proof; and none under first proof shall pay a less rate of duty than 50 per cent, (423½)

Preparations or compounds of which distilled spirits is a component part of chief value, pay not less than distilled spirits, (594)

Wines, all, imported in casks, containing not more than 22 per ct. of alcohol,† (648) valued at 40 cts. or less per gall....... .... 25 cts. per gall.

valued at over 40 cts. and not over $1 per gall.
60 cts. per gall.

valued at over $1 per gall.
$1 per gall. and 25 per ct.

Wines, of all kinds, imported in bottles, and not otherwise provided for, the same rate per gallon as if in casks, but all bottles contaning one quart or less than one quart, and more than one pint, shall be held

---

* The department authorizes the adoption of the practice of stating in entries of distilled spirits, the actual number of wine gallons, with the duty assessed thereon according to the number of degrees proof at 2 cts. a degree of each gallon, instead of stating the number of proof gallons at two dollars per gallon, as now practised, as it is more simple and correct, in that it does away with fractional statements of gallons.— (Dept. letters of Feb. 24, 1871, and Oct. 23, 1871.)

† "The cost of boxes, bottles, transportation, and all charges until on shipboard, shall be included in determining the value per gallon.—(Decisions of Jan. 4, 1865, and March 15, 1866.)

166   U. S. IMPORT DUTIES UNDER

Liquors, &c.— Continued.

to contain one quart, and all bottles containing one pint or less shall be held to contain one pint, (649.)

Wines, champagne and all sparkling, in bottles, containing each not more than one quart and more than one pint, (650). $6 per doz. bottles.

containing not more than one pint each, and more than one half pint,
$3 per doz. bottles.

containing one half pint each, or less $1.50 per doz. bottles.

in bottles containing more than one quart each, shall pay, in addition to $6 per doz. bottles, on the quantity in excess of one quart per bottle at the rate of $2 per gall.

Provided, That all imitations of brandy, or spirits, or of wines, shall be subject to the highest rate of duty provided for the genuine article intended to be represented, and in no case less than $1 per gall. (423.)

Provided, That any liquors containing more than 22 per cent. of alcohol, which shall be entered under the name of wine, shall be forfeited to the United States, (650.)

Provided, That wines, brandy, and other spirituous liquors imported in bottles, shall be packed in packages containing not less than one dozen bottles (of not more than one quart each for wine, except champagne and sparkling wines, 594) in each package, and all such bottles shall pay an additional duty of 90 per ct. of 3 cts. for each bottle,* (650-780.)

Liquors, &c.— Continued.

Allowance for breakage, (see 650.)

Proof spirit shall be held and taken to be that alcoholic liquor which contains one-half its volume of alcohol of a specific gravity of seven thousand nine hundred and thirty-nine ten thousandths (.7939) at 60° Fahrenheit, (631-651.)

Provided, That any brandy or spirituous liquors imported in casks of less capacity than 14 gallons, shall be forfeited to the United States,† (652.)

For regulations for branding, marking or certifying casks, vessels and cases containing distilled spirits in bond, see 585.

Litharge, (see paints.)

Lithographs, colored or not, (dec. of Jan. 25, 1861,) (544-778).........90 per ct. of 25 per ct.

Litmus and all lichens, prepared or not prepared, (724).   free.

Loadstones, (see stones.)

Locks, brass, (see note to manfs. of brass), (98-383-777)
90 per ct. of 35 per ct.

"   iron, (444-776)
90 per ct. of 35 per ct.

"   with steel springs, (dec. of Oct.3,1864,) (458-776)
90 per ct. of 45 per ct.

Logs and round unmanufactured timber, not otherwise provided for, (dept. letter, Jan. 10, 1871, (843)......free.

Logwood, extract or decoction of, (274).............10 per ct.

Looking glasses, (see glass.)

Lotions, (see cosmetics.)

Lozenges, (see medicines.)

* "The importation of wines together with assorted spirituous liquors, or of an assortment of spirituous liquors in a case or package, is not prohibited by sec. 21 of the Act of July 14, 1870, provided the package contains not less than one dozen bottles of liquor."—(Dec. of Feb. 15, 1871.)

† "The restricted quantity which may be imported in a package, applies only to brandy and other spirituous liquors, and that 'Wine,' other than that put up in bottles, may be imported in any capacity."—(Decision of February 14, 1868.)

Lumber, * *viz :*

boards sawed, plank, deals, and other lumber of hemlock, white wood, sycamore, and basswood, (763)

   $1 per M feet board measure.

all other varieties of sawed lumber, (764)

   $2 per M feet board measure.

clapboards, pine, (767)......$2 per M.

  "   spruce,.(767) $1.50 per M.

Provided, That when lumber of any sort is planed or finished, in addition to the

Lumber — Continued.

rates above provided, there shall be levied and paid, for each side so planed or finished, 50 cts. per thousand feet; and if planed on one side, and tongued and grooved, $1.00 per thousand feet; and if planed on two sides and tongued and grooved $1.50 per thousand feet.

Lutes, (see musical instruments.)

Lye, of wood ashes, (742)...... free.

M

Maccaroni. (844)............. free.

Mace, (658)......... .. ..25 cts. per lb.

Machinery, according to material, except as specified below.†

Machinery and apparatus for steam towage on canals may be imported as provided for in 871........... free.

Machinery for the manufacture of beet sugar, and for that purpose only, (dec. of Dec. 8, 1869,) (608½)........ free.

Machinery for repairs, may be imported as provided in paragraph 639 and dec. of May 12, 1870........... free.

Machinery, models of, (see models.)

Machinery,steam plow, adapted to the cultivation of the soil, may be imported as provided for in 871.................. free.

Mackerel, (see fish.)

Madder, and munject ground or prepared, (844).. free.

  "   root, (724)......... ... free.

  "   extract of, all, (844).... free.

Magic lanterns, (see lanterns.)

Magnesia, acetate of, or pyrolignite of, (507)

      50 cts. per lb.

  "   calcined, (246) 12 cts. per lb.

  "   carbonate of, (246)

      6 cts. per lb.

  "   Henry's, (dec. of Sept. 30, 1868,) (269)...........50 per ct.

  "   sulphate of, (Epsom salts,) (237)....1 ct. per lb.

Magnets, (844)............... free.

Mahogany, (see woods.)

Mails, (according to material.)

Maize, Indian, (see corn.)

Malacca, (see joints.)

Mallets, wood, (107-390)......35 per ct.

Malt, (see note to paragraph 602,) (60)...........20 per ct.

  "   extract of, (108-280)....40 per ct.

Manganese, (43)............10 per ct.

  "   oxide or ore of, (844)........... free.

Mangoes, (see damage on fruit,) (696)...... ....10 per ct.

---

* The produce of the Forest of Maine upon the St. John and the St. Croix Rivers and its tributaries, free of duty. (See paragraphs 590½ and 591½. Circular of April 14, 1870, prescribes the regulations.)

† "Machinery composed of iron and steel, if the value of each be stated separately on the invoice, the duty applicable to each *per se* should be separately levied."—(Decisions of Oct. 10, 1864, June 5, 1865, and Oct. 25, 1870, and dept. letter of Jan. 10, 1867.)

Machinery of American manufacture, old and broken up, and so imported to pay as scrap iron.—(Reg. of 1857, p. 577, see also decision of Nov. 9, 1869.)

Manilla, (see hemp.)

Manna, (724)................. free.

Mantillas, silk, (486).........60 per ct.

Mantles, slate, (491).........40 per ct.

Manufactures of, viz : *

Articles, all, in whole or in
part, not enumerated or
provided for in this schedule, (166 and foot-note
thereto)..................20 per ct.

Bladders, (320)........... 30 per ct.

Bone or bone chief value, not
otherwise provided for, (97-
380-781).....90 per ct. of 35 per ct.

Brass or bronze, or either
chief value, not otherwise
provided for,† (98-383-777)
90 per ct. of 35 per ct.

Copper, or copper chief value,
not otherwise provided
for,† (640-777)
90 per ct. of 45 per ct.

Cork bark, (787)...........30 per ct.

Cotton, or cotton chief value,
not otherwise provided for,
(481-774).....90 per ct. of 35 per ct.

Fur, not otherwise provided
for, (80-366)..............35 per ct.

Manufactures of — Continued.

Flax, (except fabrics woven
as provided for under
" linens " and " bags,") or
flax chief value, not otherwise provided for,‡ (482)...40 per ct

German silver, (see manufs.
of gold.)

Glass, all plain and mould
and press glass, not cut,
engraved or painted, not
otherwise provided for, and
not commercially known
as glassware, (496 780)...35 per ct.

if commercially known as
glassware,
90 per ct. of 35 per ct.

Glass, cut, engraved, painted,
colored, printed, stained,
silvered, or gilded, (not including plate-glass silvered,
or looking-glass plates,) or
of which glass shall be a
component material not
otherwise provided for, and
not commercially known
as glassware, (497-503-780) 40 per ct.

if commercially known as
glassware,
90 per ct. of 40 per ct.

---

* Articles manufactured from two or more materials, the duty shall be assessed at the highest rates at which any of its component parts may be chargeable.—(See paragraph 1.)

* Articles partially manufactured shall be termed as wholly manufactured.—See Reg. of 1857, p. 498, and Decisions of March 31, 1859, and March 1, 1871.)

† The Treasury Department decided July 14, 1869, that "the act of 24th February, 1869, providing that all manuf's of copper or of which copper shall be a component of chief value, not otherwise herein provided for, requires that all articles made of the composition usually known as brass—copper being the component of chief value, should be subject to the duty of 45 per ct. ad valorem. The fact that brass and many other articles of which copper forms the principal part, have other distinctive names never known as manufactures of copper in commerce, does not affect the question of the duty imposed by the act;" and further decided July 19, 1869, that "the language of the act of 24th February, 1869, embraces every manufacture of which copper is the component of chief value, whether the copper be the simple metal, or in the form of an alloy or combination, chemical or otherwise, with any other articles."

† The District Court of the United States, Southern District of New York, decided, (Internal Rev. Record of March 4, 1871,) That " Dutch Metal " 75 per ct. of which was copper, was liable only to "ten" per centum ad valorem, under section 19, Act of March 2, 1861, and not as a manufacture of which copper is of chief value at 45 per ct. under act of February 24, 1869, it being a manufacture of which "brass" forms the chief value; that brass is recognized in commerce as also in the 22d section of the act of March 2, 1861, and 13th section of the Act of July 14, 1862, (paragraphs 98 and 383 of the Digest,) as a distinct metal from copper, although brass as known in commerce contains generally 60 per ct. of copper   Under the ruling of said court, all articles, not otherwise provided for, of which the brass of commerce is the component of chief value, is a manufacture of brass and not a manufacture of copper, within the meaning of the act of February 24, 1869. The Treasury Department will appeal this case to the Supreme Court.

‡ Such as cannot be measured by the square yard, and not otherwise provided for, are embraced in this provision, (dec. of July 2, 1862.)

Manufactures of *— Continued.

Gold, silver, German silver, or plantina, or of which either of these metals shall be a component part, not otherwise provided for, (511-777)... 90 per ct. of 40 per ct.

Grass, not otherwise provided for, (74-362)..........35 per ct.

Grass, sisal, (see manufs. of jute.)

Gutta percha, (dec. of July 22, 1871,) (547-779) 90 per ct. of 40 per ct.

Hair, not otherwise provided for, in the Act of July 14, 1870, except human hair, (685)................30 per ct.

Hemp, (except fabrics woven as provided for under "linens" and "bags,") or hemp chief value,not otherwise provided for,‡ (484)...30 per ct.

Horn, or horn chief value, not otherwise provided for,(97-380-781)......90 per ct. of 35 per ct.

India rubber, articles wholly of, (not fabrics) not otherwise provided for, (66-779) 90 per ct. of 20 per ct.

India rubber, (fabrics) wholly or in part of, (except silk & India rubber) not otherwise provided for, (77-364) 90 per ct. of 35 per ct.

India rubber and silk,or India rubber and silk, and other materials, (except wool) (321)................50 per ct.

if India rubber, cotton, worsted, or leather chief value, (321-774-775-781) 90 per ct. of 50 per ct.

Iron, or iron chief value, (not part steel) not otherwise provided for, (98-383-444-776, see also 224) 90 per ct. of 35 per ct.

Ivory, or ivory chief value, not otherwise provided for, (97-380-781)...90 per ct. of 35 per ct.

" vegetable, (97-380)...35 per ct.

Manufactures of — Continued.

Jute, (except fabrics woven as provided for under "linens" and "bags") or sisal grass, not otherwise provided for,‡ (484)......30 per ct.

Lead, or lead chief value, not otherwise provided for,(98-383-777).....90 per ct. of 35 per ct.

Leather, or leather chief value, not otherwise provided for, (103-387-781) 90 per ct. of 35 per ct.

Marble, not otherwise provided for, (319)..........50 per ct.

Metals not enumerated or otherwise provided for, or such metals chief value, (98-383-777) 90 per ct. of 35 per ct.

Ozier,not otherwise provided for, (74-362)..............35 per ct.

Palm leaf, not otherwise provided for,(74-362) ....35 per ct.

Paper, not otherwise provided for, (104-381-778) 90 per ct. of 35 per ct.

Papier mache, (105-388-778) 90 per ct. of 35 per ct.

Pewter,or pewter chief value, not otherwise provided for, (98-383-777)..90 per ct. of 35 per ct.

Platina, (see manufs. of gold.)

Shell, (dec. of April 27, 1872,) (97-380)................35 per ct.

Silk, or silk chief value, not otherwise provided for, (487).............. .....50 per ct.

if embroidered, (see embroideries.)

Silk and India rubber, (see manufs. of India rubber and silk.)

Silver, (see manufs. of gold.)

Slate, (except roofing slates) (491)..................40 per ct.

Spelter, or spelter chief value, not otherwise provided for,) (98-383-777)..90 per ct. of 35 per ct.

Steel, or steel component part, not otherwise provided for, (458-776, see also 224)...... 90 per ct. of 45 per ct.

‡ Such as cannot be measured by the square yard, and not otherwise provided for, are embraced in this provision, (dec. of July 2, 1862.) * See notes on page 168 marked *

Manufactures of *—Continued.

Straw, not otherwise provided for, (74-362-779)
          90 per ct. of 35 per ct.

Teuteneque, o r teuteneque chief value, not otherwise provided for, (98-383-777)
          90 per ct. of 35 per ct.

Tin, or tin chief value, not otherwise provided for,(98-383-777).....90 per ct. of 35 per ct.

Whalebone, not otherwise provided for, (74-362)....35 per ct.

Willow, not otherwise provided for, (74-362).........35 per ct.

Wood, (dec. of June 2, 1863) (101-107-386-390).........35 per ct.

Wool, of every description, made wholly or in part of wool, not otherwise provided for, in the act of March 2, 1867, and woollen cloths and woollen shawls, (613-775)

90 per ct. of { 50 cts. per lb. and 35 per ct.

Worsted, the hair of the alpaca, goat, or other like animal, wholly or in part of, of every description (except such as part wool) not otherwise provided for, (614-775)

valued at 40 cts. or less per lb.

90 per ct. of { 20 cts. per lb. and 35 per ct.

valued above 40 cts. and not above 60 cts. per lb.

90 per ct. of { 30 cts. per lb. and 35 per ct.

valued above 60 cts. and not above 80 cts. per lb.

90 per ct. of { 40 cts. per lb. and 35 per ct.

valued above 80 cts. per lb.

90 per ct. of { 50 cts. per lb. and 35 per ct.

if embroidered, (see embroideries.)

Manure, (see guano)

Manuscripts, (148)........... free.

Maps, (544-778)   90 per ct. of 25 per ct.
"   specially imported, (see apparatus & books.)

Marble, manfs. of, (see manfs.)

Marble, white statuary, brocatella, sienna and verd antique, in block, rough or squared, (549)
          $1 per cubic ft. and 25 per ct.

Marble, veined, and marble of all other descriptions, in block, rough or squared, not otherwise provided for, (549)
          50 cts. per cu. ft. and 20 per ct.

Marble, all sawed, dressed, or polished, marble slabs, and marble paving tiles, 30 per ct. ad valorem, and 25 cts. per superficial sq ft. not exceeding two inches in thickness; if more than two inches in thickness 10 cts. per ft. in addition to the above rates for each inch or fractional part thereof in excess of two inches in thickness: (683)

Provided, That if exceeding six inches in thickness, shall be subject to the duty imposed on marble blocks, (683)

Marbles as toys, (dec. of Nov. 12, 1864,) (543)...........50 per ct.

Marmalade, (see fruits preserved.)

Marrow crude, (844).........   free.
"   for toilet soap perfumed, (dec. of Mar. 3, 1858) (270)......50 per ct.

Marsh mallows, (844)........   free.

Masks, paper, for adults, (dec. of Nov. 2, 1866,) (104-381-778)..........90 per ct. of 35 per ct.

Masks, paper, other, as toys, (543-778)......90 per ct. of 50 per ct.

Matches, (107-390)...........35 per ct.
"   cotton wax and paper, (dec. of Mar. 8, 1870, (99-384-774-778) 90 per ct. of 35 per ct.

Mastic, gum, (719)...........   free.

---

*See notes on page 168 marked *

Matico leaf, (844)............ free.
Mats, cocoanut, (60-280)......30 per ct.
" dunnage, (dec. of Mar.
    31, 1863.)
" of flags. jute or grass,
    (dec. of April 5, 1867)
    (60-280).............30 per ct.
" India-rubber, (dec. of
    May 5, 1870,) (620-
    779)......90 per ct. of 45 per ct.
" palm leaf, (dec. of June
    2, 1870,) (74-362).....35 per ct.
" straw, (74-362-779)
    90 per ct. of 35 per ct.
" all other, (not exclu-
    sively of vegetable ma-
    terial) screens, has-
    socks and rugs, (620) 45 per ct.
    if gutta percha, India
    rubber,skins,leather,
    or metal,chief value,
    (620-777-779-781)
    90 per ct. of 45 per ct.
" wool lining, (613-775)
    90 per ct. of { 50 cts. per lb.
                  { and 35 per ct.
Provided, That mats, rugs,
screens, covers, hassocks,
bedsides, and other por-
tions of carpets or car-
peting shall be subject
to the rate of duty im-
posed on carpets or car-
peting of like character
or description. (620)
Matting, coir, (60-338).......25 per ct.
" China, and other floor,
    (60-280).........30 per ct.
" straw, (60-280-779)
    90 per ct. of 30 per ct.
Meal, corn, (34).............10 per ct.
" oat, (756)............¼ ct. per lb.
Meats,(see prepared meats,&c.)
Medals, gold or silver, (148)..... free.
" specially imported,(see
    apparatus and cabi-
    nets.)
Medicinal balsoms, (73)..... .30 per ct.
" barks, flowers, leaves,
    plants, roots, and

seeds, in a crude
    state, not otherwise
    provided for, (827)   free.
Medicinal water, (see mineral
    waters.)
Medicines and drugs, crude,
    not otherwise provided for,
    (60)......... ....20 per ct.
Medicines, not crude or patent,
    as medicinal prep. not other-
    wise provided for, (108-280) 40 per ct.
Medicines, patent, viz: pills,
    powders, tinctures, troches
    or lozenges, syrups, cordials,
    bitters, anodynes, tonics,
    plasters, liniments, salves,
    ointments, pastes, drops,
    waters, essences, spirits, oils,
    and other medicinal prepara-
    tions or compositions, recom-
    mended to the public as pro-
    prietary medicines, or pre-
    pared according to some pri-
    vate formula or secret art, as
    remedies or specifics for any
    disease or diseases or affec-
    tions whatever effecting the
    human or animal body, (269) 50 per ct.
    If spirits be of chief value
    pay as spirits, (594)
Meerchaum, crude or raw, (844)   free.
Melado, (see molasses.)
Melodeons, (see mus. instrs.)
Mercurial preparations, (see
    preparation.)
Mercury or quicksilver, (578-
    777)........ .90 per ct. of 15 per ct.
Merinos, printed, of worsted
    and cotton, see manfs. of
    worsted and dress goods,
    (dec. of Sept. 21, 1857.)
Metal, bell, (see bells.)
" britannia, and pewter,
    old, and fit only to be
    remanufactured, (852)   free.
" Bessemer, as steel.
" bronze and dutch in
    leaf, (see notes to
    manfs. of brass,)(35-
    777)....90 per ct. of 10 per ct.
" sheathing or yellow*

---

* "Sheathing metal imported per British Brig 'Chesapeake,' intended to be used in sheathing the bottom of the said brig, and no portion of which is intended to be landed or used for any other purpose, held to be liable to duty."—(Decision of Sept. 15, 1863, and January 6, 1870, see also dec. of January 11, 1870.)

copper not chief value
(see note to manufs.
of copper,) (328-777)
90 per ct. of 3 cts. per lb.

Metal, sheathing brass, old and
fit only for remanuf.
(dec. of July 26, 1870,)
(33-230-777)
90 per ct. of 15 per ct.

" sheathing zinc, (dec. of
Oct. 28, 1857,) (328-
777)..90 per ct. of 3 cts. per lb.

" silver plated, in sheets
or other form, (114-
399-777) 90 per ct. of 35 per ct.

" type (67-400-777)
90 per ct. of 25 per ct.

" yellow, (see metal, sheathing.)

Metals, unmanuf'd, not otherwise provided for, (60-777)
90 per ct. of 20 per ct.

" manuf'd, (see manufs.)

Mica and mica waste (844)....   free.

Milk (166)...................20 per ct.

" preserved or condensed
(797). ....20 per ct.

" sugar of (860).........   free.

Mill irons and cranks, of
wrought iron (430-776)
90 per ct. of 2 cts. per lb.

Millstones, (see burrstones.)

" not burrstones, (dec.
Dec. 14, 1859,) (166) 20 per ct.

Mills, coffee, &c., (according to
material.)

Mineral and bituminous substances, in a crude state, not
otherwise provided for, (60
see also 777) ....20 per ct.

Mineral, blue and green, (see
paints.)

Mineral, kermes, (43)........10 per ct.

Mineralogy, specimens of, (see
specimens.)

Mineral or medicinal waters,
all, *not artificial* (from
springs impregnated with
minerals) (844)............   free.

Mineral or medicinal waters, *if
artificial*, in bottles or jugs
containing one quart or less,
(550).....3 cts. each and 25 per ct.

More than one quart, 3 cts.
for each additional quart or
fractional part thereof and
25 per ct., (dec. of Feb. 1,
1869,) (550)

Not in bottles or jugs, (dec.
of Aug. 20, 1870,) (108)....30 per ct.

Mint, copper for U. S. (130-709.)   free.

Mirrors, (see glass.)

Mitts, as gloves.

Models of invention, and other
improvements in the arts;
Provided, that no article shall
be so deemed which can be
fitted for use, (150)........   free.

Mohair (see wool, and manufs.
of worsted.)

Moisic iron (see iron.)

Molasses,* (645).........5 cts. per gall.

Concentrated molasses, concentrated melado, and tank
bottom syrup of sugar cane
juice, and melado, (646) 1½ ct. per lb.

Provided, that if any of the
same be entered under the
name of 'molasses,' shall be
forfeited to the U. S. (750)

Monuments of red granite,
(dec. of Feb. 8, 1868,) (166) 20 per ct.

Mops, wood and cotton, cotton
chief value, (107-390-481-774)
90 per ct. of 35 per ct.

Morocco skins, (see skins.)

Morphia, and on all salts of
(706)................ ..$1 per oz.

Mortars,(according to material.)

" agate, as stoneware,
(Reg. of 1857, p. 553.)

Mosaics, (see precious stones.)

" in a setting or frame,
(Reg. of 1857, p.
575,) (166).... ....20 per ct.

" of slate, as ornaments
for mantels, &c.(dec.
of Jan. 24, 1870,)
(491).............40 per ct.

---

* Concentrated molasses and concentrated melado is defined in Reg. of 1857, p. 562. No allowance
can be made for damage to molasses soured on the voyage of importation.—(Decision of June 1,
1866.) Molasses on board a Spanish brig from Cuba is liable to the regular duties and the discriminating duty under Par, 561.—(Decision of April 8, 1868.)

Moss, crude, (724)............ free.
" for beds or mattresses (845) free.
" Iceland, (724).......... free.
" prepared, as artificial flowers, (decs. of June 30, 1863, and Jan. 20, 1866,) (540)..........50 per ct.
Moulds, button, (see buttons.)
Moulds, lunar caustic, (dec. of Jan. 19, 1869,) (166).........20 per ct.
Muffs, foot, dressed sheep skins, with wool on, and leather, (dec. of Nov. 15, 1870,) (103-387-781) 90 per ct. of 35 per ct.
Muffs, fur, (80-366)..........35 per ct.
Mules, (see animals.)
Mundic, iron pyrites or arsenical pyrites, (dec. of Dec. 7, 1869,) (60 see also 777)..........20 per ct.
" copper pyrites, on the copper therein, (ibid) (640-777) 90 per ct. of 5 cts. per lb.
Mungo, (see flocks.)
Mungeet, (see madder.)
Murexide, (846)............. free.
Muslin, (see cottons.)
Music, printed with lines,

bound or unbound, (43-280-778)..........90 per ct. of 20 per ct.
Musical instruments,* brass chief value, (see note to manufs. of brass,) (60-280-777)......... 90 per ct. of 30 per ct.
Musical instruments, of all kinds, (60-280)............30 per ct.
If horn, bone, ivory, leather, iron, steel, or any other metal chief value, (60-280-776-777-781) 90 per ct. of 30 per ct.
Same if toys (543-776-777-781)........90 per ct. of 50 per ct.
Same if toys, wood, (543)...50 per ct.
Same, strings for, gut, (819). free.
Same, strings for, silk, (487) 50 per ct.
Same, strings for, silk and metal, silk not chief value, (dec. of April 5, 1858,) (98-383-777) .90 per ct. of 35 per ct.
Musk, crude, in natural pod, (846)................ free.
" as perfume, (270).....50 per ct.
Muskets, (see guns.)
Mustard, when enclosed in glass or tin, (795) 14 cts. per lb.
" ground, in bulk, (795) 10 cts. per lb.
Myrrh, gum (719)....... .... free.

N

Nails, board, wrought iron, (435-776) 90 per ct. of 2½ cts. per lb.
" brass, (see note to manfs. of brass,) (98-383-777) 90 per ct. of 35 per ct.
" composition and zinc, (98-383-777) 90 per ct. of 35 per ct.
" china heads, (dec. of May 28, 1866,) (490, see also 776)......45 per ct.

Nails, gold, silver, and German silver, (511-777) 90 per ct. of 40 per ct.
" iron, cut, (436-776) 90 per ct. of 1½ ct. per lb.
" horseshoe, (436-776) 90 per ct. of 5 cts. per lb.
" other, (according to material.)
Naphtha, (see oils, illuminating.)
Natron as soda ash.

* Parts of musical instruments, or articles appertaining thereto and which cannot be used for any other purpose, come within the provision of musical instruments —(Reg. of 1857, p. 575.)

Natural history, specimens of,
(see specimens.)

Necklace of pearl and diamonds, set in gold, (dec. of
March 1, 1870,) (70). ......25 per ct.

Needles, for sewing, darning,
knitting, and all
other descriptions,
(61-392-776)
90 per ct. of 25 per ct.

"   crochet, (dec. of Nov.
22, 1864,) (61-392-
776-781)
90 per ct. of 25 per ct.

"   for knitting or sewing
machines, (456-776)
90 per ct. of $ \begin{cases} \$1 \text{ per } 1,000 \\ \text{and } 35 \text{ per ct.} \end{cases} $

"   sail, (dec. of Feb. 13,
1865,) (61-392-776)
90 per ct. of 25 per ct.

Nets, head, wool, worsted or
mohair,(see trimmings.)

"   head or hair, of silk and
gum elastic,(dec. of Dec.
17,1866,) (72-360).....35 per ct.

"   spot, silk and cotton, but
commercially known as
silk lace, (dec. of March
4, 1868,) (486).......60 per ct.

Newspapers (544-778)
90 per ct. of 25 per ct.

Nickel, (691-777)
90 per ct. of 30 cts. per lb.

"   oxide and alloy of, with
copper, (692, see also
777)...........20 cts. per lb.

Nippers, (according to material.)

Niter cubic, as nitrate of soda.

Nitric ether, spirits of, (522)
50 cts. per lb.

Nitro-benzole, (dec. of Aug. 22,
1868,) (251)...............50 per ct.

Noils, (see wool noils.)

Non enumerated, articles (see
articles, and manufs.)

Nutgalls, (152) ....   free.

Nutmegs, (657)..........20 cts. per lb.

Nuts, all kinds, (except of metal,) not otherwise pro-
vided for, (178)...2 cts. per lb.

"   cocoa (847)............   free.

"   Brazil or cream (847)...   free.

"   palm, (727)............   free.

"   used in dyeing, (see berries.)

"   wrought iron, (433 776)
90 per ct. of 2 cts. per lb.

Nux vomica, (847)...........   free.

O

Oakbark, (726)......... ......   free.
Oakum, (143) ....   free.
Oar blocks, (see blocks.)
Oatmeal, (756)............¼ ct. per lb.
Oats, (16) (32 lbs. to bu.)..10 cts. per bu.
"   for seed, (dec. of Jan. 24,
1860,) (16).... ...10 cts. per bu.
"   ground for provender, (dec.
of Feb.26,1870,)(16)10 cts. per bu.
Objects of art, (see apparatus
and paintings.)
Ochres and ochrey earths, (see
paints.)
Odors, (see cosmetics.)
Oenanthic ether, (see oils.)
Oilcake, linseed, (849)........   free.

Oilcloth foundations or floor
cloth canvas, made of flax,
jute, or hemp, or of which
flax, jute, or hemp shall be the
component material of chief
value, (783)...............40 per ct.

Oilcloths, for floors, stamped,
painted or printed, (621-779)

valued at 50 cts. or less per
sq. yd.......90 per ct. of 35 per ct.

valued at over 50 cts. per sq.
yd.........90 per ct. of 45 per ct.

Oilcloth, silk, (621-779)
90 per ct. of 60 per ct.

Oilcloth, all other, (621-779)
90 per ct. of 45 per ct.

Oils, fixed or expressed.

" all expressed, not otherwise provided for, (62).....20 per ct.
" almonds, (848).......... free.
" bay or laurel, (250)..20 cts. per lb.
" castor, (529)....... ...$1 per gall.
" croton, (529)............$1 per lb.
" laurel or bay, (250)...20 cts. per lb.
" mace, (848)............. free.
" mustard, not salad, (250) 25 cts. per gall.
" olive, in flasks or bottles, and salad,* (529).....$1 per gall.
" olive, not salad, (250) 25 cts. per gall.
" olive, for perpetual lamp of a synagogue, (dec. of April 28, 1868,) (529) $1 per gall.
" salad, (529)..........$1 per gall.

Oils, Essential or essence.

" all essential, not otherwise provided for, (251)....50 per ct.
" almonds, (848)... .... free.
" amber, crude, (848)...... free.
" amber, rectified, (848).... free.
" ambergris, (848)......... free.
" anise, or aniseseed, (848). free.
" anthos or rosemary, (848) free.
" bay leaves, (251)... $17.50 per lb.
" bergamot, (848) .... free.
" cajeput, (848)............ free.
" carraway, (848)........ free.
" cassia, (848)............ free.
" cedrat, (848)............. free.
" chamomile, 848)........ free.
" cinnamon, (848)......... free.
" citronella or lemon grass, (848)................ free.
" cloves, (529)............$2 per lb
" cognac or oenanthic ether, (529) .. ..$4 per oz.
" cubebs, (251)..........$1 per lb.
" fennel, (848)...... .... free.
" jasmine or jessamine, (848) free.
" juglandium, (848)... ... free.

Oils, Essential or essence—Continued.

" juniper, (848).......... free.
" lavender, (848)... ...... free.
" lemons, (251).......50 cts. per lb.
" orange, (251) ....50 cts. per lb.
" origannm, or red thyme, (848)... .... free.
" roses, ottar of, (848)...... free.
" thyme, white, (848)...... free.
" thyme, red, (848)........ free.
" valerian, (848).......... free.

Oils or essences.

" aniline, crude, (708)..... free.
" animal, all, (698).... ...20 per ct.
" amylic, alcohol, (fusil oil.) (522)............. $2 per gall.
" bay rum or essence, (792) 50 cts. per oz.
" bene, (848) .... free.
" cenne, or sesame seed, (848) .... free.
" civit, (848)............. free.
" coal, crude, (578)..15 cts. per gall.
" cocoanut, (727)......... free.
" cod liver, fit for med. purposes, (dec. of Jan. 8, 1869,) (108-280).......40 per ct.
" cod liver, crude, (698)....20 per ct.
" cotton seed, (702)..30 cts. per gall.
" fish, (foreign fisheries,) (698)...............20 per ct.
" flaxseed, 7¼ lbs. to gall. (699)..........30 cts. per gall.
" for cosmetics, (see cosmetics.)
" fruit, ethers, essences or oils of apple, pear, peach, apricot, strawberry and raspberry, made of fusil oil or of fruit, or imitations thereof, (238) $2.50 per lb.
" fusil, (522)............$2 per gall.
" harleam, (269)..........50 per ct.
" hempseed, (14-280) 23 cts. per gall.

* "Olive oil fit for use as salad oil, duty $1 per gallon, under the special provision for salad oil; whether olive oil is salad depends upon its quality, and not upon the character of the package in which imported."—(Decision of November 28, 1870.)

Oils or essences—Continued.

" illuminating, and naphtha, benzine, and benzole, refined or produced from the distillation of coal, asphaltum, shale, peat, petroleum, or rock oil, or other bituminous substances used for like purposes, (578)..40 cts. per gall.

" lemon grass, (848)...........free.

" linseed, 7½ lbs. to gall. (699)...........30 cts. per gall.

" medicinal, not otherwise provided for, (see medicines.)

" mineral, (dec. of March 2, 1859,) (578).....40 cts. per gall.

" neat's foot, (698)........20 per ct.

" peanuts, expressed, (dec. of Jan. 18, 1859,) (62)..20 per ct.

" palm, (727).............   free.

" petroleum, crude, (578) 20 cts. per gall.

" poppy, (848) ....   free.

" rum essence, (792)...50 cts. per oz.

" rapeseed, (14-289)..23 cts. per gall.

" red beets, or vegetables, (as distilled spirits.)

" rock, crude, (578)..20 cts. per gall.

" seal, (698).............20 per ct.

" sesame or sesamum seed or bene, or cenne, (848)...   free.

" spermaceti, (foreign fisheries,) (698)........20 per ct.

" vegetable, if essential, (dec. of April 21, 1858,) (251).....   ....50 per ct.

" vegetable, if expressed, (dec. of April 21, 1858,) (62)...   ....20 per ct.

" whale, (foreign fisheries,) (698).............20 per ct.

Ointments, (see medicines.)

Olebanum, gum, (719)........   free.

Olives, green or prepared, (849)   free.

Onions, (50)............ ...10 per ct.

Opium, (704).............$1 per lb.

" extract of, (705) .....$6 per lb.

" prepared for smoking, and all other preparations of opium, not otherwise provided for, (dec. of Nov. 21, 1871,) (705).......$6 per lb.

" if it be deposited in bonded warehouse, (see regulations in 705, and dec. of Jan. 6, 1871.)

Orange buds and flowers, (849)   free.

" peel, (44)............10 per ct.

"   " not preserved, candied, or otherwise prepared, (726)   free.

" mineral, red lead, (dec. of Aug. 23, 1862,) (525) ....3 cts. per lb.

Oranges, (see damage on fruit,) (696)...................20 per ct.

Orchill, or archill, in the weed or liquid, (726) ....   free.

extract of (persis) (852)....   free.

Ore, specimens of, not otherwise provided for, (166)...10 per ct.

Ore, (see gold, silver and iron.)

Organs, (see mus. instrs.)

Orleans, (see roncou.)

Ornaments, alabaster and spar, (71)..........30 per ct.

"   bend, (540, see also 780-781)......50 per ct.

"   dress, (see buttons and trimmings.)

"   for bonnets, hats, &c. (see bonnets.)

Orpiment, (849).............   free.

Orris or iris root, (142)......   free.

Osier, (see willow.)

Osmium, (849).............   free.

Osnaburgs, (see linens.)

Ottar of roses, (see oils.)

Oxiding paste, (849) ....   free.

Oysters, as shellfish, (739)....   free.

P

Packthread, (see thread.)

Padding, (see linens.)

" wool, (613-775.)

90 per ct. of { 50 cts. per lb. and 35 per ct.

Paddy, (557).......... .... 1¼ ct. per lb.

Pader as steel, (dec. of March 18, 1872)

Paintings* and statuary,† not otherwise provided for, (45) 10 per ct.

Paintings, Geneva, enameled, (dec. of Mar. 3, 1858,) (166)..20 per ct.

Paintings, on glass or glasses, (decs. of March 29, 1859, and Aug. 20, 1860,) (503)..... 40 per ct.

Same for churches, (dec. of Jan. 25, 1870,) (121)....... free.

Paintings, specially imported, (see apparatus.)

Paintings, statuary, fountains, and ot' er works of art, the production of American artists, if fact of such production be verified as prescribed in 728...................... free.

The same if for presentation to national or other institutions, under regulations as prescribed in 625-729, and dec. of Jan. 5, 1870.. free.

Paints and painters' colors, dry or ground in oil, and moist water colors, used in the manufacture of paper hangings and colored papers and cards, not otherwise provided for, (239)...........25 per ct.

Paints, water colors, (118-402)..35 per ct.

Paints and colors, if not water colors :

Berlin blue, (419)..........25 per ct.

Blanc fixe, (509).......3 cts. per lb.

Paints and colors, if not water colors— Continued.

Bone or ivory drop black, (505)....................25 per ct.

Carmine, dry, (239).......25 per ct.

Carmine lake, dry or liquid, (509)..................35 per ct.

Chinese blue, (419).........25 per ct.

Chrome yellow, (chromate of lead,) (239).............25 per ct.

Cochineal lake, (reg. of 1857, p. 561,) (239)............25 per ct.

Dutch pink, (239).........25 per ct.

Drop black, as paint, (dec. of July 11, 1859,) (239)......25 per ct.

Enameled white, (509)...3 cts. per lb.

Frankfort black, (419)......25 per ct.

French green, dry or moist, (509) .... 30 per ct.

Indian red, (505)...........25 per ct.

Ivory drop black, (505).....25 per ct.

Lampblack, (59)...........20 per ct.

Lead, red or white, and litharge, dry or ground in oil, (525)................3 cts. per lb.

Lime white, (509).......3 cts. per lb.

Mineral blue, dry or moist, (509) ....30 per ct.

Mineral green, dry or moist, (509)................. ....30 per ct.

Ochres and ochrey earths, not otherwise provided for, dry, (249)....... .....¼ ct. per lb.

Same, ground in oil, (249) 1¼ ct. per lb.

Oxide of zinc, dry or in oil, (14-295)..............1¾ ct. per lb.

Paris green, dry or moist, (509)..................30 per ct.

---

* "Paintings, within the meaning of the law, must be an object of taste, recognized as a painting in the usual acceptation of the term; and not paintings on glass, porcelain, or similar materials, or on plates, goblets, or any other utensil, or capable of being converted into breastpins, ear-dops, or other ornaments to be worn on the person."—(Circular of April 15, 1857, and decision of March 23, 1870.)

* Portraits "done in silk" are not to be considered as paintings.—(Reg. of 1857, p. 581.)

* Paintings, statuary and photographic pictures, imported for exhibition only, are free of duty, as provided in the act of March 5, 1872.

† The term "statuary" is defined in paragraph 580 of the Digest, and Decision of Dec. 15, 1869.

Paints and colors, if not water colors—
Continued.

Paris white, dry, (495)....1 ct. per lb.
"   "   ground in oil,
(253).....1½ ct. per lb.
Prussian blue, dry or moist,
(509)..................30 per ct.
Rose pink, (239)...........25 per ct.
Satin white, (509).......3 cts. per lb.
Spanish brown, (505).......25 per ct.
Ultramarine, (666)......6 cts. per lb.
Umber, (14).....   .....½ ct. per. lb.
Vandyke brown, (68)......20 per ct.
Venetian red, (239).......25 per ct.
Vermillion, (239)..........25 per ct.
Whiting, dry, (495)......1 ct. per lb.
"   ground in oil, (495)
2 cts. per lb.
Wood lake, (239) ....25 per ct.
Palings, (see proviso to lumber,) (766)................20 per ct.
Palladium, (850) .. ..   free.
Pallettes, as cutlery.
Palm leaf, unmanufact'd, (155)   free.
"   "   manufactured, (see
manufs.)
"   nuts and palm nut kernels, (727)..........   free.
Pamphlets, bound or unbound,
(544-778).....90 per ct. of 25 per ct.
Pans, frying, wrought iron, tinned, (dec. of July 14,
1869,) (444-776)
90 per ct. of 35 per ct.
"   of cast iron, (441-776)
90 per ct. of 1½ ct. per lb.
"   glazed or tinned, (442,
776)..90 per ct. of 3½ cts. per lb.
Pantaloon stuff, (see cottons.)
Paper, all kinds, not otherwise
provided for, (111-395,
778)....90 per ct. of 35 per ct.
"   clippings of, (see rags.)
"   manufs. of, (see manufs.)
"   printing, unsized, used
for books and newspa-
pers exclusively, (419,
778) ....20 per ct.

Paper, all, sized or glued, suitable only for printing
paper.* (793)........25 per ct.
"   rags, waste, wood, &c.,
for manuf. of paper,
(see rags and wood.)
"   sheathing, (48-778)
90 per ct. of 10 per ct.
"   stock, crude, (see rags.)
"   stock, pulp, (dec. of
April 6, 1858, (166)..20 per ct.
Papers, illustrated or not, (544-
778)..........90 per ct. of 25 per ct.
Papier mache, manufs. of, (see
manufs.)
Paraffine, (253)..........10 cts. per lb.
Parasols and frames, (see umbrellas.)
Parchment, (112)............30 per ct.
Parianware, (see china.)
Paris white and green, (see
paints.)
Paste, Brazil, (818)...........   free.
"   or composition of glass,
(see precious stones.)
"   oxiding, (849).........   free.
Pastel or woad, (163).........   free.
Pastes. (see cosmetics and medicines.)
Patent medicines, (see medicines.)
"   size, (504)...........20 per ct.
Pattern cards, if invoiced, subject to duty, (dec. of December 20, 1862.)
Patterns for slippers, paper, engraved, (dec. of January 19,
1869,) (544-778)
90 per ct. of 25 per ct.
If wool, in whole or part,
(dec. of August, 15, 1868,)
(613-775)
90 per ct. of { 50 cts. per lb.
{ and 35 per ct.
Paving tiles, (see tiles.)
"   stones, (see stones.)
Peanuts or ground beans, (530)
1 ct. per lb.
"   shelled, (530).....1½ ct. per lb.

* Under this provision there will be entitled to entry such paper as is generally used for printing, distinguished from that used for writing and other such purposes; fine glazed paper, such as is used for books, magazines and illustrated weekly papers, will be admitted at this rate of duty.

Pearl ash, as bicarbonate of soda, (dec. of May 10, 1866,) (178-290)...............1½ ct. per lb.

Pearl, mother of, (shell,) un-manufac'd, (739)........... free.

Pearl, mother of, manufs. of, (see manfs. of shell.)

Pearls, (see precious stones.)
" on strings used as beads, (dec. of Dec. 11, 1858,) (540).....50 per ct.
" and pearl shells, of American fisheries, (dec. of Feb. 8, 1869,) (153)............... free.

Peas, as seed, (dec. of April 30, 1870,) (771)...........20 per ct.
" as vegetables, (50).....10 per ct.
" split, (dec. of April 30, 1870,) (166)........ ..20 per ct.

Pebbles, for spectacles, rough, (818)..................... free.
Same, not rough, (503, see also 780)................40 per ct.

Pebbles, Brazil, for spectacles, (818) rough.............. free.

Pellitory root, (852)......... free.

Pelts, as skins.

Pencils, wood, filled with lead or other materials, .537) 50 cts. per gro. & 30 per ct.
Same, if lead chief value, (537-777)
90 per ct. of { 50 cts. per gross and 30 per ct.
" slate, not covered with wood, (491).......40 per ct.
" hair, (90-375, see also 685)..............35 per ct.
" lead, not covered with wood, (325-777) 90 per ct. of $1 per gro.

Penknives, (see knives.)

Pens, metallic, (554-777)
90 per ct. of { 10 cts. per gro. and 25 per ct.

Pen tips and pen holders, or parts thereof, wood, (554)..35 per ct.
Same, if gutta percha, bone, ivory, horn or metals chief value. (554-777-779-781) 90 per ct. of 35 per ct.

Pepper bird, (dec. of July 11, 1862,) black, white, and red or cayenne, (653).......5 cts. per lb.
The same, when ground, (654).... ....10 cts. per lb.

Pepper dust, (dec. of April 21, 1866,) (653)...........5 cts. per lb.

Peppers, haytien. in salt and water, (dec. of Oct. 30, 1857,) (166)....... ....20 per ct.

Percussion caps, (see note to m'fs, of copper,) (525-777)..40 per ct.

Perclines, silk, (486)..... ...60 per ct.

Perfumery, (see cologne and cosmetics.)

Periodicals, bound or unbound, (544-778).....90 per ct. of 25 per ct.

Persis, (see orchil.)

Personal effects, (see effects.)

Peruvian bark, (852).... ... free.

Pestles, (according to material.)

Petroleum, oil, (see oils, illumi-nating.)

Petroleum, redium of, or tar, under 20° Beaume, (dec. of Oct. 3, 1871,) (166)............20 per ct.
When over 20° Beaume, (ibid,) (578)...20 cts. per gall.

Pewter and britannia metal, old, and fit only to be re-manf'd, (852)........ free.
" manfs. of, (see manufs.)

Plumglein, (852)......... ... free.

Philosophical instruments, (see instruments)

Phosphates, crude or native, for fertilizing purposes, (732).. free.

Phosphorus, (chem. salt) (66)..20 per ct.

Photographic baths and dip-pers, (dec. of February 23, 1861,) (503, see also 780,)....40 per ct.

Photographic views, (dec. of Dec. 16, 1858,) (166, see also 778).....................20 per ct.

Photographs, (dec. of May 16, 1870) (166, see also 778)....20 per ct.

Pianos, (see musical instrs.)

Pickets, (see proviso to lum-ber,) (766)............. ...20 per ct.

Pickles, all, not otherwise pro-vided for, (79-365)..... ...35 per ct.

Pictures, (see paintings, engravings, &c.)

Pills, (see medicines.)

Pimento, (653).. ....5 cts. per lb.
" ground, (654) ...10 cts. per lb.

Pinchers, iron, (444-776)
90 per ct. of 35 per ct.
" part steel, (458-776)
90 per ct. of 45 per ct.
" shoe, case-hardened iron, (dec. of Feb. 3, 1871.) (444-776)
90 per ct. of 35 per ct.

Pine apples, (see damage on fruit,) (696).............20 per ct.

Pine apple slips, for seed, (dec. of March 5, 1869,) (771, see also 829).. ....20 per ct.

Pink, dutch and rose, (see paints.)

Pinksauces, (cosmetic,) (270)..50 per ct.

Pins, hair, of iron wire, (686-776).....90 per ct. of 50 per ct.
" if jewelry, or imitation of, (70)...............25 per ct.
" solid head or other, (98-396-776)..90 per ct. of 35 per ct.
" other, (according to material.)

Pipe cases, pipe stems, tips, mouth pieces and metallic mountings for pipes, and all parts of pipes or pipe fixtures, and all smokers' articles, (553).................75 per ct.
if gutta percha, bone, ivory, horn, skins, leather, or metal chief value, (553-776-777-779-781) 90 per ct. of 75 per ct.

Pipe bowls, common clay, (dec. of March 6, 1870,) (552)
$1.50 per gro. and 75 per ct.

Pipes, clay, common or white, (551) . ...35 per ct.
" clay, colored, (dec. of Oct. 19, 1864,) (552)
$1.50 per gro. and 75 per ct.
" meerschaum, wood, porcelain, lava. and all other tobacco smoking pipes and pipe bowls, not otherwise provid'd for, (552)
$1.50 per gro. and 75 per ct.

Pipes, if gutta percha, bone, ivory, horn, skins, leather or metal chief value, (552-776-777-779-781)
90 per ct. of { $1.50 per gro. and 75 per ct.
" steam, gas, and water, cast iron, (442-776)
90 per ct. of 1½ ct. per lb.

Pistols, (108-391-776)
90 per ct. of 35 per ct.

Pitch, (63)........ ....20 per ct.
" burgundy, (818)........   free.

Plaids, (see cottons.)

Plaits for bonnets, hats, &c. (see bonnets.)

Planes, part steel, (458-776)
90 per ct. of 45 per ct.
" irons, (steel.) (458-776)
90 per ct. of 45 per ct.

Planks, (see lumber.)

Plantains, (see damage on fruit,) (696).............10 per ct.

Plants for dyes, (see berries.)
" for botanic garden, (see agriculture dept).
" bulbous roots, (309)....30 per ct.
" and fruits, tropical and semi-tropical, for the purpose of propagation or cultivation, (829).................   free.
" medicinal, crude, not otherwise provided for, (827).... ....   free.
" trees, shrubs, not otherwise provided for, for fruit, shade, lawn and ornamental purposes, (770)...............20 per ct.
" tea, (740)...... ....   free.
" vanilla or beans, (866)..   free.

Plagues, (dec. of July 27, 1860,) (166)......................20 per ct.

Plaster of Paris, calcined, (63) 20 per ct.
"   " when ground, (45-283)...20 per ct.
"   " manufs. of, (490)......40 per ct.
"   " unground, (155)   free.

Plasters, (see medicines.)

Plasters, part wool, (dec. of
Feb. 12, 1869,) (613-
775)
90 per ct. of { 50 cts per lb.
and 35 per ct.
Plated and gilt ware, all kinds,
(112 396-777)
90 per ct. of 35 per ct.
if articles of ornament,
(112-396-777)........35 per ct.
Plates, engraved, of copper,
(640-777)
90 per ct. of 45 per ct.
" engraved, of steel, wood
or any other material,
(323).... ....25 per ct.
if steel or other metal
chief value, (223-
776-777)
90 per ct. of 25 per ct.
" fashion, engraved on
steel or on wood, col-
ored, plain, (dec. of
Feb. 2, 1871,) (718)...   free.
" fish, wrought iron, (see
note to R. R. chairs,)
(433-776)
90 per ct. of 2 cts. per lb.
" glass, or disks, un-
wrought, for optical
instruments, (38, see
also 780) ....10 per ct.
" landscape (dec. of Aug.
20, 1860,) (503, see
also 780)...........40 per ct.
" stereotype, (66-399-776)
90 per ct. of 25 per ct.
Platina, unmanuf'd, * (155)...   free.
" manfs. of (see manf's.)
Pliers, iron (444-776)
90 per ct. of 35 per ct.
" part steel, (458-776)
90 per ct. of 45 per ct.
Ploughs, part steel, (458-776)
90 per ct. of 45 per ct.
" steam (see machin-
ery.)
Plumbago or black lead, (852)   free.
Plums, (697) ....2¼ cts. per lb.
" green (dec. of Oct. 30,
1868,) (37)....... .. 10 per ct.

Plush, hatters, cotton and silk,
cotton chief value, (58-
384-774)..90 per ct. of 25 per ct.
" other (according to ma-
terial.)
Pocket books, leather or metal
chief value, (83-368-
777-781)
90 per ct. of 35 per ct.
" all other (83-368).....35 per ct.
Polishing powders, (see powders.)
" stones, (see stones.)
Polypodium (852)...........   free.
Pomatum and pomades, (see
cosmetics.)
Pomegranates, (37).........10 per ct.
Pongees, silk, (480).........60 per ct.
Poplins, (see dress goods.)
Porcelain ware, (see china.)
Pork, (16)................1 ct. per lb.
Porter, (see ale.)
Posts, rough hewn or sawed
only, (765)..........20 per ct.
" otherwise than rough
hewn or sawed (Reg.
of 1857, p. 408,) (107-
390)................35 per ct.
Potash, (dec. of May 10, 1866,)
(166)........ ....20 per ct.
" acetate of, (789)..25 cts. per lb.
" bichromate of, (254) 3 cts. per lb.
" calcined, as bicarbon-
ate of soda, (dec. of
July 13, 1869,) (178-
290).... ....1¼ ct. per lb.
" chlorate of, (790)..3 cts. per lb.
" chromate of, (14)..3 cts. per lb.
" hydriodate, iodate, and
iodide of, (254) 75 cts. per lb.
" hydrate of, as bicar-
bonate of soda, (dec.
of July 13, 1869,)
(178-290). .....1¼ ct. per lb.
" muriate of, (735)....   free.
" nitrate of, (see saltpetre.)
" prussiate of, yellow,
(254) ....5 cts. per lb.

* "Platina unmanufactured extends to and comprehends platina imported either in ingots or in the form of sheets, or in the form of wire, or in any shape or form not constituting an article suitable for use without further manufacture."—(Reg. of 1857, p. 581.)

Potash, prussiate of, red, (254)
.10 cts. per lb.

Potatoes, (756)........ 15 cts. per bu.

Pots, cast iron, (441-776)
90 per ct. of 1¼ ct. per lb.

Poultry, dressed, (dec. of Feb.
13, 1868,) (166)....10 per ct.

"   prepared, (see pre-
pared meats, &c.)

Powder, bronze, (see note to
manufs. of brass,)
(53-777) 90 per ct. of 20 per ct.

"   bleaching, (chlorate of
lime,) (819)........ free.

"   curry (see curry.)

"   finishing, (504)......20 per ct.

"   gun, (see gunpowder.)

"   hair, skin, and tooth,
(see cosmetics and
medicines.)

"   ink, (91-376)........ 35 per ct.

"   polishing, all kinds,
(419).......... . 25 per ct.

Precious stones, such as diamonds cut, cameos, mosaics,
(dec. of Jan. 26, 1861,) pearls,
rubies, &c., not set,
(466)....... .... 10 per ct.

When set, (70)............25 per ct.

Imitation of above, composition of glass or paste, not
set, (497-503, see also 780) 40 per ct.

When set, (dec. of June 16,
1868,) (70-371)........ 30 per ct.

Precipitate red, (65). ....20 per ct.

Preparations of anatomy, (739) free.

"   chemical, not oth-
erwise provided
for, (166)......20 per ct.

"   medicinal, (108-
280)..........40 per ct.

Preparations, medicinal, if patent, (see medi-
cines.)

"   mercurial, not
otherwise pro-
vided for, (60) 20 per ct.

"   philosophical, (see
apparatus.)

"   spirits chief value,
(see liquors.)

Prepared vegetables, meats, fish,
poultry, and game, sealed or
unsealed, in cans or otherwise, (113-397).... ......35 per ct.

Presents,* (see paintings.)

Preserves, (see fruits preserved.)

Printed matter, all, (544-778,)
90 per ct. of 25 per ct.

Prints, as engravings, (544-778)
90 per ct. of 25 per ct.

Proprietary medicines, (see medicines.)

Protest against collector's decision, and appeal to Sec'y
of Treas'y, (par. 558.)

Prunes, (796).............1 ct. per lb.

Prussian blue, (see paints.)

Pulp, dried, (55)............20 per ct.

"   rag, (Reg. of 1857, p.
581,) (104 381-778,)
90 per ct. of 35 per ct.

"   for manuf. of paper, (717) free.

Pulu, vegetable substance for
beds, (845)......... .... free.

Pumice and pumice stones, (155) free.

Pumpkins, (50)..... ....10 per ct.

Punches, shoe, (458-776,)
90 per ct. of 45 per ct.

Purses, according to material,)
(see Reg. of 1857, p. 581.)

Putty, (254)..............1½ ct. per lb.

Pyrite or sulphuret of iron,
(dec. of Oct. 29, 1860,) (166)..20 per ct

Q

Quadrants, (according to material.)

Quassia wood, (see woods.)

Queensware, (see earthenware.)

Quickgrass root, (853)........ free.

Quicksilver, (578-777,)
90 per ct. of 15 per ct.

Quilla, bark, (712)........... free.

Quills, prepared or unprepared, (853) free.

Quinine, (257) ....45 per ct.

"   sulphate of, (790).....20 per ct.

"   other salts of, (257)..45 per ct.

"   amorphous, (Reg. of
1857, p. 553,) (257) 45 per ct.

Quoits, or curling stones, (823) free.

---

* "Articles imported 'as presents,' other than such as are exempted by law from duty, are liable
to duty."—(Reg. of 1857, p. 600.)

R

Rags, cotton, linen, jute, and hemp, and paper waste, or waste or clippings of any kind, including waste rope and waste bagging, fit only for the manuf. of paper.* (dec. of Dec. 7, 1869,) (737, see also 742).... free.

" other than wool, paper stock, crude, of every description, including all grasses, fibers, waste, shavings, clippings, old paper, rope ends, waste rope, waste bagging, gunny bags and gunny cloth, old or refuse, to be used in making and fit only to be converted into paper, and unfit for any other manufacture and cotton waste, whether for paper stock or other purposes, (851)....... free.

" woolen, (612½-775,) 90 per ct. of 12 cts. per lb.

" other than as above, (179).... ....10 per ct.

Railroad chairs. wrought iron,† (433-776,) 90 per ct. of 2 cts. per lb.

" bars, of iron, (see iron bars.)

" bars, of steel, or part steel, (see steel.)

" iron, for repairs, subject to regulations in 169 and dec. of Mar. 22, 1870..... free.

" ties, wood, (854)..... free.

Raisins, (796)..........2½ cts. per lb.

Rakes, iron, (444-776) 90 per ct. of 35 per ct.

" part steel, (458-776) 90 per ct. of 45 per ct.

Rasps, (see files.)

Ratafia, (see liquors.)

Ratans, (see reeds.)

Raw or unmanufac'd articles, not otherwise provided for, (166).....................10 per ct.

Razors, as cutlery, (dec. of Feb. 13, 1865.)

Red lead, (see paints.)

Red precipitate, (65).........20 per ct.

Reeds and ratans, unmanufac'd, (854)............ .... free.

" for umbrellas, canes, &c., (see umbrellas, and canes.)

Regalia, (see apparatus.)

Re-importations, (see U. S.)

Rennets, raw or prepared, (854) free.

Repairs on vessels, (see vessels.)

Reps, embroidered, (see embroidery.)

" other, (according to material.)

Residuum of petroleum, (see petroleum.)

Resinous substances used for same or similar purposes as gum copal, (178).......10 cts. per lb.

Resins, crude, not otherwise provided for, (738).. free.

" gum, all, not otherwise provided for, (267) 20 per ct.

Resin of scammony, (see scammony.)

Retorts, gas, (488)......... 25 per ct.

Retorts or vases of platinum for chemical uses, or parts of, (155-734)................. free.

Return cargo, (see U. S.)

Rhubarb, (738) .... free.

Ribbons, cotton, (481-774) 90 per ct. of 35 per ct.

---

* "40 per cent. of woolen rags, in bundles of rags for the manufacture of paper, is too large a proportion to be admitted free of duty. The importer should, where no evidence of fraud appears, be made to separate the free from the dutiable rags on entry."—(Decision of December 28, 1868.)

† "Wrought iron fish plates, fish joints or splice bars should be classified by assimilation, by virtue of section 20, act of July 30, 1842, as wrought iron railroad chairs at 2 cents per lb.; all spikes and bolts for like use, at two and one-half cents per lb."—(Dec. of November 14, 1868.)

Ribbons, silk or part silk, (dec.
    of April, 21, 1870,)
    (485) .... 60 per ct.
Ribs for umbrellas, &c., (see
    umbrellas.)
Rice, cleaned, (557)....... 2½ cts. per lb.
    " uncleaned, (557).....2 cts. per lb.
Rifles, (see guns.)
Ringlets, hair, (76-363-685)...35 per ct.
    " human hair, (316)..30 per ct.
Rings, as jewelry, (70)........25 per ct.
    " for saddlery, (see sad-
        dlery.)
    " other, (according to ma-
        terial.)
Rivets, wrought iron, (435-776)
        90 per ct. of 2½ cts. per lb.
    " other, (according to ma-
        terial.)
Robes, buffalo, dressed, (dec. of
        Sept. 28, 1863,) (546-
        759)................ 20 per ct.
    " other, (see clothing.)
Rocou, (see roncou.)
Rods, iron wire, in coils, as
        rolled or hammered
        iron, (dec. of March
        14, 1870, see also foot
        note to iron, round,
        in coils,) (430-776)
        90 per ct. of 1¼ ct. per lb.
    " slit, (430-776)
        90 per ct. of 1½ ct. per lb.
    " other, (according to ma-
        terial.)
Roncou, rocou, annatto or Or-
    leans, (808)............... free.

Root or rooots.

    Aconite, (708), alkanet,
    (708), angelica,(806),bella-
    donna, (713), china, (819),
    cinchona, (819), colombo,
    (715), contrayerva, (821),
    elecampane, (825), galan-
    ga, (830), gentian, (830),
    ginger, (830), ginseng,
    (830), hellebore, (835),hop,
    for cultivation, (837), iris
    or orris, (142), liquorice,
    (724), madder, (724), pelli-
    tory, (852), quick grass,
    (853), sassafras, (855)..... free.
    " beet, for manuf. of paper,

Root or roots—Continued.
    (dec. of Dec. 15, 1858,)
    (717)................. free.
    " bulbous, (309).........30 per ct.
    " chickory, (see chickory.
    " dandelion, (see coffee sub-
        stitutes.)
    " flour, (854) .... free.
    " medicinal, crude, not
        otherwise provided,
        (827) .... free.
Rope, bale, of hemp, (dec. of
        April 21, 1858,) (484) 30 per ct .
    " hide, (835)............. free.
    " wire, (see wire rope.)
    " waste, (see rags.)
Rosaries, as beads, (dec. of Feb.
    1, 1865,) (540).............50 per ct.
Rose leaves, (738)........... free.
Rosepink, (see paints.)
Rosewood, (see woods.)
Rosin, (65) ....20 per ct.
Rottenstone, (157)........... free.
Rubies, (see precious stones.)
Rugs, railway, so styled, ac-
        cording to material, (see
        decs. of Jan. 18, 1870,
        and June 6 and 28, 1870.)
    " travelling, part wool,
        (dec. of Sept. 21,1859,)
        (613-775)
        90 per ct. of { 50 cts. per lb.
                      { and 35 per ct.
    " other, (see mats.)
Rules, (according to material.)
Rum, (see liquors.)
    " essence, (see oils.)
    " bay or bay water, wheth-
        er distilled or com-
        pounded, of first proof,
        (791)..............$1 per gall.
        in proportion for any
        greater strength
        than first proof.
Runners, for umbrellas, &c.,
    (see umbrellas.)
Rust on iron and steel, (see par.
    224.)
Rye, (56 lbs. to bu.) (16)...15 cts per bu.
    " flour, (47) ....10 per ct.
    " shorts, (dec. of June 3,
        1870,) (47)..........10 per ct.

S

Sabres, (swords,) (679-776)
90 per ct. of 45 per ct.
Saddlery, coach and harness
furniture, and hardware of
all kinds, (dec. of Dec. 16,
1861,) (85-370-777)
90 per ct. of 35 per ct.
If copper chief value, see
note to manufs. of copper.
Saddles, (85-370-781)
90 per ct. of 35 per ct.
Sadirons, cast iron, (441-776)
90 per ct. of 1¼ ct. per lb.
Safflower, (855).... .... free.
" extract of (855). ... free.
Saffron, (855)...... .... free.
" cake, (855)........... free.
Sago, crude, (855)... .... free.
Sago and sago flour, (855).... free.
Sails, (see canvas and duck.)
Sal acetosella, chem. salt, (dec.
of Aug. 27, 1857,) (66)....20 per ct.
Salacine, (855).............. free.
Salep or saloup, (855)........ free.
Saleratus, (178-290) .. ..1½ ct. per lb.
Salmon, (see fish.)
Salt in bulk,* (755)....8 cts. per 100 lbs.
" in bags, sacks, barrels or
other packages, (755)
12 cts. per 100 lbs.
" rock, (dec. of June 12,
1863,) (755)...8 cts. per 100 lbs.
" dung, (see dungsalt.)
Saltpetre, crude,† (803)....1 ct. per lb.
" refined and partially
refined, (803)..2 cts. per lb.
Salts, black, (811)............ free.
" epsom, (237)...... 1 ct. per lb.
" glauber, (237)......½ ct. per lb.
" Rochelle, (790).... 5 cts. per lb.
" other, (see the base.)
" and preparations of salts,
not otherwise provided
for, (66)............20 per ct.
Salves, (see medicines.)
Samples of goods having no
intrinsic value as merchan-

disc and cannot be so used,
(dec. of June 11, 1868.)..... free.
Sand, (166).................10 per ct.
" french, (dec. of April 27,
1858,) (60)..........20 per ct.
" magnetic, iron, (dec. of
Jan. 20, 1868,) (60)...20 per ct.
Sandal-wood, (see woods.)
Sandarac, gum, (719). .... free.
Sandstones, (see stones.)
Santonine, (790)............$3 per lb.
Sarcop hagus, red granite, dec.
of Feb. 8, 1868,) (166)......20 per ct.
Sardines, pres'd in oil or other-
wise, (540)..............50 per ct.
Sarsaparilla, (267)...........20 per ct.
" crude, (739)..... free.
Sassafras, bark and root (855) free.
Satin white, (see paints.)
" wood, (see woods.)
Saucepans, (see pans.)
Sauces, all kinds, except catsup, not otherwise provided
for, (79-365)........ ....35 per ct.
Sauerkraut, (855)............ free.
Sausages, (113-397)..........35 per ct.
" bologna, (812)...... free.
" skins (855)...... .. free.
Saw logs, (see logs.)
Saws back, all, (453-776)
not over 10 inches in length,
90 per ct. of { 75 cts. doz,
and 30 per ct.
over 10 inches in length,
90 per ct. of { $1 per doz.
and 30 per ct.
" circular, (458-776)
90 per ct. of 45 per ct.
" cross-cut, (450-776)
90 per ct. of { 10 cts. per
lineal foot.
" hand, all, (452-776,)
not over 24 inches
in length,
90 per ct. of { 75 cts. per doz.
and 30 per ct.
" over 24 inches in length,
90 per ct. of { $1 per doz.
and 30 per ct.

---

* Salt for curing fish, used by vessels licensed to engage in the fisheries, (875.)

† Respecting the drawback on saltpetre, see paragraphs 744 and 421, and Dec. of August 19, 1868.
Rule for classification specified in Dec. of July 1, 1872.

Saws, mill, pit and drag, (10-
451-776.)
   not over 9 inches wide,
      90 per ct. of { 12¼ cts. per
                lineal foot.
   over 9 inches wide,
      90 per ct. of { 20 cts. per
                lineal foot.
Scales, (according to material.)
Scammony, or resin of, (739)   free.
Scantling, (see lumber.)
Scarfs, silk, (486)............60 per ct.
  " other, (see clothing.)
Schools, articles specially imported for, (see apparatus.)
Scilla or squills, (739)........   free.
Scissors, as cutlery.
  " garden, as cutlery.
Scrapers, part steel, (458-776)
         90 per ct. of 45 per ct.
Screens, (see fire screens and
mats.)
Screws, iron, (commonly called
wood screws,) (439-
776.)
   2 inches or over in
length,
         90 per ct. of 8 cts. per lb.
   less than 2 inches in
length,
         90 per ct. of 11 cts. per ct.
  " bed, (434-776)
         90 per ct. of 2¼ cts. per lb.
  " brass, (see note to
manfs. of brass,)(439-
776)...90 per ct. of 35 per ct.
  " iron or other metal,
except as above,
(439-776)
         90 per ct. of 35 per ct.
Sculpture, (see paintings, and
apparatus.)
Scythes, (dec. of March 30,
1865,) (458-776)
         90 per ct. of 45 per ct.
Sealing wax, (114-399).......35 per ct.
Seating, (see hair cloth.)
Seaweed, not otherwise provided for, (739)......   free.

Seaweed, used for beds and
    mattresses, (845)...   free.
Seed lac, (see lac.)

SEEDS, viz:

agricultural purposes, not
otherwise provided for,
(771)................... 20 por ct.
all, not otherwise provided
for, (739)...........   free.
annatto (808), anise and star
anise (856), canary (856),
caraway (739), cardamon
(739), chia (856), conium
cicuta or hemlock (715),
coriander (739), cummin
(739), fennel (739), fenugreek (739), of forest trees
(856), mustard, brown and
white (846), sesamum (856),
sugar cane (856), and other
seeds not otherwise provi-
ded for, (739)............   free.
castor* or beans, (50 lbs. to
bu.) (516)..... .....60 cts. per bu.
cotton, (dec. of May 5, 1863,)
(771)....................20 per ct.
flax or linseed,(56 lbs. to bu.)
(701) ....20 cts. per bu.
  Provided, That no drawback shall be allowed on
oil cake made from im-
ported seed, (701).
garden, flower and all other,
for horticultural and agricultural purposes, not
otherwise provided for,
(770-771)...............20 per ct.
hemp, (700)..............½ ct. per lb.
horticultural purposes, not
otherwise provided for,
(771)...................20 per ct.
manufacturing purposes, not
otherwise provided for,
(186)...................   free.
medicinal, crude, not otherwise provided for, (827)...   free.
oil, of like character to hempseed and rapeseed, except
linseed or flaxseed, (700)
             ½ ct. per lb.
rape, (700).... ....½ ct. per lb.

---

* "An allowance can be made for weight of the pods as tare."—(Decision of Feb.
23, 1870.)

Segars, cigarettes and cheroots,* (dec. of Dec. 15, 1868,) (635-637)......$2.50 per lb. and 25 per ct. *Internal Rev. tax*, in addition, (638-634.)

segars and cheroots......$5 per M.

cigarettes weigh'g not over 3 lbs. per M.........$1.50 per M.

cigarettes, weigh'g over 3 lbs. per M......$5 per M.

Provided, That cigars shall be packed in boxes, not before used for that purpose, containing respectively, 25, 50, 100, 250 or 500 cigars each, (decs. of Aug. 14, 1868, and Feb. 1, 1869,) (636-638.)

Provided further, That no cigars shall be imported unless the same are packed in boxes of not more than 500 in each box, and no entry of any imported cigars shall be allowed of less quantity than 3,000 in a single package, (592)

Provided further, That all cigars on importation shall be placed in public store or bonded warehouse, and shall not be removed therefrom until the same shall have been inspected, and a stamp affixed to each box indicating such inspections, with the date thereof, (592)

Seines, (483)............6½ cts. per lb.

Senegal, gum, (719).......... free.

Senna, in leaves, (739)........ free.

Sepia or cuttle fish bone, (715) free.

Serges, (according to material.)

Sextants,(accord'g to material.)

Shaddocks, (see damage on fruit) (696)............10 per ct.

Shafts, cast steel, (dec. of Oct. 6, 1864,) (458-776) 90 per ct. of 45 per ct.

Shale, (see coal.)

Shawls, silk, (486)..........60 per ct.

Shawls, woollen, (dec. of Jan. 28, 1862,) (613-775) 90 per ct. of { 50 cts. per lb. and 35 per ct.

" other material, (see clothing.)

Shears, as cutlery.

" hedge or garden, (dec. of March 26, 1869,) (458 776) 90 per. ct of 45 per ct.

" pruning, as cutlery.

" sheep, (dec. of March 30, 1865,) (458-776) 90 per ct. of 45 per ct.

Sheathing, metal and paper, (see metal, and paper.)

Sheep, (see animals.)

" skins, (see skins.)

Sheeting, Russia and other, of flax or hemp, brown and white, (484)..............35 per ct.

Sheets for bonnets, hats, &c., (see bonnets.)

Shellac, gum, (719).......... free.

Shellfish, (739)............. free.

Shells,all kinds,unmanuf'd,(739) free.

" polished, (dec. of April 4, 1872,) (739)....... free.

" manuf'd, (see manuf's.)

Shingle bolts, (160).......... free.

Shingles, all, (766).......35 cts. per M.

Ship timber, (see timber.)

" knees, as ship timber.

Shirting, flannel, (see flannels.)

Shirts, imitation merino,† (81-367-774) 90 per ct. of 35 per ct.

" bosoms for, not tamboured, linen, (dec. of May 18, 1859,) (482) 40 per ct.

" other material, (see caps.)

Shoddy, (see flocks.)

Shoes, horse, iron, (444-776) 90 per ct. of 35 per ct.

" " part steel, (458-776) 90 per ct. of 45 per ct.

" other, (see boots.)

---

* "No tare allowed for the mouth pieces of Russian cigarettes."—(Decision of Sept. 15, 1869.)

† "Cotton shirts, merino finish, this article, it seems, is composed wholly of cotton, and by raising a nap and some further application or process, a fine woolly surface and a close imitation of merino are produced."—(Decision of Sept. 4, 1860.).

Shooks, (see staves.)
"   sugar box, (769).. ...20 per ct.
Shovels, iron, (444-776)
                90 per ct. of 35 per ct.
"   brass, (see note to
          manf's of brass,)
          (98-383-777)
                90 per ct. of 35 per ct.
"   part steel, (458-776) .
                90 per ct. of 45 per ct.
Shot, cast-iron, (443-776)
                90 per ct. of 30 per ct.
Show bills, (see handbills.)
Shrimps, (739).............   free.
Shrubs, (see plants.)
Sickles, iron, (444-776)
                90 per ct. of 35 per ct.
"   part steel, (458-776)
                90 per ct. of 45 per ct
Sidearms, except swords, (114-
    399-776)......90 per ct. of 35 per ct.
Sieves, wood and iron, iron
    chief value, (107-390-444-776)
                90 per ct. of 35 per ct.
same, wood chief value, (107-
    390-444).................35 per ct.
Silesias, as cottons, (dec. of
    April 26, 1866.)
Silicates, alkaline, or of soda,
    (689)...................½ ct. per lb.
Silla or squills, (739) ....   free.
Silk, all dress and piece, (decs.
    of Sept. 25, 1866, and
    Jan. 29, 1867,) (485)....60 per ct.
"   cocoons, (160)...........   free.
"   floss, (dec. of March 21,
        1870,) (485)............35 per ct.
"   and India rubber, manuf's
        of, (see manuf's.)
"   in the gum not more ad-
        vanced than singles,
        tram, and thrown or
        organzine, (dec. of June
        19, 1866,) (485).......35 per ct.
"   manufs. of, (see manufs.)
"   organzine, not in the
        gum, (dec. of Oct. 5,
        1864,) (487)......... ...50 per ct.

Silk, raw, or as reeled from the
    cocoon, not being dou-
    bled, twisted, or ad-
    vanced in manuf. any
    way,* (160)...........   free.
"   scraps, or strips of, (dec.
        of March 17, 1870,)
        (487).... ....50 per ct.
"   sewing, in the gum, or
        purified, (485)........40 per ct.
"   single and tram, (dec. of
        Dec. 27, 1862,) (487)....50 per ct.
"   spun, for filling in skeins
        or cops, (485-577)......35 per ct.
"   waste, (160).............   free.
Silkworm eggs, (739).........   free.
Silver, bullion, (127).........   free.
"   leaf, p'kge of 500 leaves,
        (240-777)
                90 per ct. of 75 cts. per pkge.
"   nitrate of, (med. prep.)
        (108-280)...........40 per ct.
"   manufs. of, (see manufs.)
"   old, (127).............   free.
"   ore, (153).............   free.
"   sweepings of, (739).....   free.
Sirups, (see medicines and mo-
    lasses.)
Sisal grass, (as jute.)
Size, gold, (830)............   free.
"   patent, (504)............20 per ct.
Skates, costing 20 cts. or less
    per pair, (449-776)
                90 per ct. of 8 cts. per pair.
"   costing over 20 cts. per
        pair, (449-776)
                90 per ct. of 35 per ct.
Skeletons, and other prepara-
    tions of anatomy, (739)......   free.
Skins, asses', raw, unmanufac-
    tured, (836).........   free.
"   asses, (72)............:...30 per ct.
"   raw or uncured, whether
        dried, salted, or pickled,
        (836)..............   free.
"   bird, dressed with feath-
        ers on, (dec. of June
        30, 1870,) (759)........20 per ct.
"   calf, tanned, or tanned
        and dressed, (758)... 25 per ct.

* "When re-reeled in a country other than that of production, is subject to duty."—
Decisions of March 28, and June 19, 1866.)

Skins, calf, glazed, (dec. of Oct.
26, 1857,) (758).......25 per ct.
" dressed with alum only,
(dec. of March 8, 1870,)
(759)...............20 per ct.
" fish, (56-759)..........20 per ct.
" fox, white, (dec. of July
31, 1869,) as fur skins.
" fur, dressed, (546-759)..20 per ct.
" fur, all kinds, not dressed
in any manner, (dec. of
June 30, 1870,) (718)..   free.
" goat, raw, (dec. of Aug.
29, 1870,) (719)........   free.
" goat, angora, raw, without the wool, unman-
ufactured, (836).......   free.
" goose and swan, dressed
with feathers on, (dec.
of Aug. 16, 1870,) (759) 20 per ct.
" goldbeaters* and moulds,
(830)................   free.
" japanned,patent or enamelled, (759)..........20 per ct.
" lamb, dressed, as furs,
(dec. of Aug 5, 1870,)
(546-759)............20 per ct.
" mink, as fur skins, (dec.
of Sept. 28. 1859.)
" morocco, (759)..........20 per ct.
" for morocco, tanned, but
unfinished, (760)......10 per ct.
" prepared for rugs, (dec.
of March 5,1866,)(620) 45 per ct.
" pulled of the hair, as undressed, (dec. of Oct.
15, 1868,) (718)... .....   free.
" sausage, (855)..........   free.
" shark, (857)...........   free.
" sheep, with wool on, (see
wool on the skin.)
" sheep, dressed with wool
on, (decs. of June 30, &
Aug. 5, 1870,) (759)..20 per ct.
" swan, (see skins-goose.)
" tanned and dressed, all
kinds, wholly or par-
tially, (dec of Mar. 3,
1870,) (759)..........20 per ct.
" vicunia, as wool on the
skin, (dec. of Jan. 31,
1859.)

Skirting, Paris, as balmorals,
(dec. of May 5, 1865.)
Skivers, as skins.
Slate, manufs. of, (see manufs.)
" split in the quarry, not
skipped or trimmed,
(dec. of June 5, 1869,)
(60)................20 per ct.
Slates, (491)...............40 per ct.
" patent,iron plates coated
with mineral powder,
&c. (dec. of January 9,
1860,) (98-383-776)
90 per ct. of 35 per ct.
" porcelain, (dec. of March
23, 1870,) (490).......45 per ct.
" porcelain, decor'd, (dec.
of Mar. 23, 1870,)(489) 50 per ct.
" roofing, (dec. of Feb'y 9,
1870,) (115-398).. ....35 per ct.
Sledges, blacksmiths', (432-776)
90 per ct. of 2½ cts. per lb.
Slippers, as boots and shoes.
" patterns, (see patt'ns.)
Smalt, (504).............20 per ct.
Smoker's articles, (see pipes.)
Snails, (857)...............   free.
Snuff, and snuff flour, (425-632-
633,) 50 cts. per lb. and int.
rev. tax of 32 cts. per lb.
Soap, fancy, perfumed, honey,
transparent, and all de-
scriptions of toilet and
shaving soap, (555)
10 cts. per lb. and 25 per ct.
" all other, (555)
1 ct. per lb. and 30 per ct.
" castile, (555)
1 ct. per lb. and 25 per ct.
" windsor, (555)
10 cts. per lb. and 25 per ct.
" stocks and stuffs, (831-
857)............ ..   free.
Socks, (see caps.)
Societies, articles specially imported for. (See apparatus.)
Soda, acetate or pyrolignite of,
crude or refined, (dec.
of Aug. 4, 1869,) (789)
25 cts per lb.

* "An article styled gold beaters' skins but not made of the same material nor adapted to the same uses, was held to be dutiable as a manufacture of bladder at 30 per centum ad valorem."—(Decision of Feb. 9, 1869.)

Soda, all carbonates of, by whatever name designated, not otherwise provided for, (66)..... ....20 per ct.
" ash, (790)............¼ ct. per lb.
" bicarbonate of, (178-290) 1½ ct. per lb.
" carbonate of, (178)...¼ ct. per lb.
" caustic, (178-290)....1½ ct. per lb.
" hyposulphate of, (66)...20 per ct.
" nitrate of, or cubic niter, (725)................ free.
" sal, (790)............¼ ct. per lb.
" salts of, (dec. of Aug. 3, 1869,) (66)...........20 per ct.
" silicate of, (689)......½ ct. per lb.
Sounds, hake, as fish glue, (dec. of Oct. 23, 1866,) (840)...... free.
Souvenirs, all, (82-368).........35 per ct.
if cotton, wool, worsted, metals, paper, india rubber, straw, gutta percha, skins, bone, ivory, horn, or leather, chief value (82-368-774 to 781)...90 per ct. of 35 per ct.
Spades, iron, (444-776) 90 per ct. of 35 per ct.
" part steel, (458-776) 90 per ct. of 45 per ct.
Spanish brown, (see paints.)
" flies, (see cantharides.)
" grass, (see grass.)
Spar, ornaments of, (71)......30 per ct.
Spars, hewn and sawed, (53)..20 per ct.
" dressed or planed, (107-390, see also proviso to lumber). ....35 per ct.
" if ship timber, (843).... free.
Sparterre for bonnets, hats, &c., (see bonnets.)
Spatulas, as cutlery.
Specimens of natural history,* botany and mineralogy, when for cabinets as objects of taste or science, and not for sale, (739)..................... free.
Spectacles, brass, (see note to manufs. of brass), (98-383-777) 90 per ct. of 35 per ct.

Spectacles, glasses or pebbles, for, (503, see also 780)...........40 per ct.
if rough, (818)... free.
" gold and silver, (511-777) 90 per ct. of 40 per ct.
" part steel, (dec. of Nov. 5, 1864,) (458-776) 90 per ct. of 45 per ct.
Spelter, manf'd in blocks or pigs, (465-777) 90 per ct. of 1½ ct. per lb.
" in sheets, (465-777) 90 per ct. of 2¼ cts. per lb.
" manfs. of, (see manfs.)
Spices, all kinds, not otherwise provided for, (663)....20 cts per lb.
when ground or prepared, (663)................30 cts. per lb.
Spiegel, as pig iron, (dec. of Jan. 21, 1864,) (675-776) 90 per ct. of $7 per ton.
Spikes, brass, (see note to manfs. of brass) (98-383-777), 90 per ct. of 35 per ct.
" for railroads, (see note to R. R. chairs,) (435-776) 90 per ct. of 2½ cts. per lb.
" iron, wrought, (435-776) 90 per ct. of 2¼ cts. per lb.
" iron, cut, (436-776) 90 per ct. of 1½ ct. per lb.
Spirits, spirituous beverages and compounds, (see liquors.)
Spirits lac, (see lac spirits.)
Splicebars, (see note to R. R. chairs,) (433-776) 90 per ct. of 2 cts. per lb.
Spokeshaves, part steel, (458-776)...... ......90 per ct. of 45 per ct.
Spokes, wood, (107-390)......35 per ct.
Sponges, (267)..............20 per ct.
Spoons, (according to material.)
Sprigs, (see tacks.)

* "The term 'specimens of natural history' comprehends only articles imported for the cabinet of the naturalist, and has no application to living animals."—(Reg. of 1857, p. 554.)

Springs, wire, spiral, for furniture, (624-776)

90 per ct. of $\begin{cases} 2 \text{ cts. per lb.} \\ \text{and 15 per ct.} \end{cases}$

Spunk, (859)................. free.

Spurs, as saddlery.

" of clay, (dec. of Aug. 8, 1868,) (490)..........40 per ct.

Spy glasses, (according to material.)

Squares, iron, marked on one side, (457-776)

90 per ct. of $\begin{cases} 3 \text{ cts. per lb.} \\ \text{and 30 per ct..} \end{cases}$

" all other, of iron or steel, (457-776)

90 per ct. of $\begin{cases} 6 \text{ cts. per lb.} \\ \text{and 30 per ct.} \end{cases}$

" brass, (see note to manfs. of brass,)(98-383-777)
90 per ct. of 35 per ct.

" wood, (107-390).....35 per ct.

Squills or silla, (739).......... free.

Squirrel tails, dressed, (dec. of June 8, 1867,) (346-759)....20 per ct.

Starch, of potatoes or corn, (556)
1 ct. per lb. and 20 per ct.

" of rice or other material, (556)
3 cts. per lb. and 20 per ct.

" burnt or gum substitute, (38)..............:.10 per ct.

Stars, metal, (see trimmings.)

Statuary, (see apparatus and paintings.)

Stavebolts, (160)............. free.

Stavesacre, crude, (859). ..... free.

Staves for pipes, hhds. or other casks, (285).........10 per ct.

" hewn or sawed, (53)...20 per ct.

" shaved, grooved and fitted for setting up into bbls. known as shooks, (dec. of Feb. 16, 1870) (107-390)...... .....35 per ct.

Steam engines, iron for, (see iron.)

Steel, in bars, billets, coils, ingots and sheets, (decs. of June 19, 1866 and Feb. 12,1870,)(446-776)

valued at 7 cts. or less per lb.
90 per ct. of $2\frac{1}{4}$ cts per lb.

valued at above 7 cts.' and not over 11 cts. per lb.
90 per ct. of 3 cts. per lb.

valued at above 11 cts. per lb.
90 per ct. of $\begin{cases} 3\frac{1}{4} \text{ cts. per lb.} \\ \text{and 10 per ct.} \end{cases}$

" as cross cuts, as steel in sheets, (dec. of Aug. 19, 1868.)

" bars, slightly tapered, (dec. of Sept. 17, 1863,) (448-776)
90 per ct. of 30 per ct.

" blooms, see dec. of May 8, 1868,) (458-776)
90 per ct. of 45 per ct.

" cast, forgings in the rough (dec. of October 6, 1864) (458-776)
90 per ct. of 45 per ct

" cast in coils, (decs. of June 19, 1858, and Nov 22, 1861,) (448-776)
90 per ct. of 30 per ct.

" in any form, not otherwise provided for, (448-776)
90 per ct. of 30 per ct.

" manfs. of, (see manfs.)

" plough, (dec. of Oct. 20, 1860,) (448-776)
90 per ct. of 30 per ct.

" railway bars, (680-776)
90 per ct. of $1\frac{1}{4}$ ct. per lb.

" railway bars, in part of steel, (680-776)
90 per ct. of 1 ct. per lb.

" scrap, (dec. of Aug. 4, 1870,) (448-776)
90 per ct. of 30 per ct.

" spring, German, dec. of Sept. 10, 1858,) (448-776)....90 per ct. of 30 per ct.

Provided, That metal converted, cast, or made
from iron by the Bes-
semer or pneumatic
process, of whatever
form or description,
shall be classed as
"steel." (680)

Steel, wire, (see wire.)
" wire rope, (see wire rope.)
Steels, as cutlery.
Stereoscopic views on glass
(decs. of Feb. 15, 1865, and
May 9, 1870,) (166, see also
780).... ....20 per ct.
same on paper (166-778)
90 per ct. of 20 per ct.
Stereoscopes, (according to material.)
Stereotype plates, (see plates.)
Sticks,(see canes,and umbrellas.)
Stick lac, (see lac.)
Stockings, (see caps.)
Stones, ayr, as whetstones, (dec.
Sept. 24,1869,) (837).. free.
" ayr, for polishing, (Reg.
of 1857, p. 586,) (155) free.
" bezoar, (811) .... free.
" bristol, (166)...........10 per ct.
" burr, (see burrstones.)
· " building or monumen-
tal, except marble,
(682)....... ...$1.50 per ton.
" curling or quoits, (823) free.
" filtering, unmanufact'd
(166).................10 per ct.
" filtering, manf'd, (166) 20 per ct.
" free, (682).......$1.50 per ton.
" glass cutters, as grindstones, (dec. of Dec.
23, 1868.)
" granite, (682).....$1.50 per ton.
" " polished, (dec.
of March 25,
1871,) (166)...20 per ct.
" grind, finished,*(681) $2 per ton.
" grind, rough or unfin-
ished, (681)......$1.50 per ton.
" green, an inferior kind
of marble, but dutiable
as marble, (dec. of
Nov. 16, 1868.)

Stones, lithographic, not engraved, (842) .... free.
" loud, (842)............ free.
" mill, (see burrstones and
millstones.)
" lime, for making lime,
(dec. of May 8, 1866),
(60)................20 per ct.
" oil, (whetstones) (837).. free.
" paving, (45).........10 per ct.
" polishing, (155)........ free.
" precious, (see precious
stones.)
" pumice, (155)......... free.
" rag, (166)............10 per ct.
" rotten, (157).......... free.
" sand, (682) ..... $1.50 per ton.
" tomb, (decs. of June 28
and 29, 1859,) (319)..50 per ct.
" touch, (166).........20 per ct.
" whet, (837)........... free.
Stoneware, above the capacity
of 10 galls. (348)20 per ct.
" other, (see earthen-
ware.)
Storax, or styrax, (859)....... free.
Stoves and stove plates, of cast
iron, (441-776)
90 per ct. of 1½ ct. per lb.
Straw, unmanuf'd, (859)...... free.
" manfs. of, (see manfs.)
" twisted, for bonnets,
hats, &c. (Reg. of
1857, p. 586,) (see
bonnets.)
Stretchers for umbrellas, &c.,
(see umbrellas.)
Strings for musical insts., (see
mus. insts.)
" all other, of whip gut
or catgut, (60-280)..30 per ct.
" gut and worm gut,(833) free.
Strontia, chem. prep. (166) ...20 per ct.
" acetate or pyrolignite
of, (789)......25 cts. per lb.
" muriate of, (166)....20 per ct.
" nitrate of, (166) .....20 per ct.
" oxide of, or protoxide
of strontium, (860) free.
Strychnia (strychnine) (790)
$1 00 per oz.

---

*"Line of distinction between wrought or finished and rough unwrought or un-
finished grindstones."—(Dec. of September 11, 1870.)

Strychnia, salts of, (536)...$1 50 per oz.

Studs, gold, silver, or set with precious stones, or imitation of, (dec. of Nov. 20, 1869,) (70)........25 per ct.

" other than above,according to material, (Reg. of 1857, p. 587,(dec. of Nov. 20, 1869.)

Styrax or storax, (859)........ free.

Substances (see bituminous, mineral, resinous, vegetable, and guano.)

Succory root, (see chickory.)

Sugar, all, not above No. 7, Dutch standard in color,* (746½).....1¾ ct. per lb.

" above No. 7, and not above No. 10, (747) 2 cts. per lb

" above No. 10, and not above No. 13, (747½) 2¼ cts. per lb.

" above No. 13, and not above No. 16, (748) 2¾ cts. per lb.

" above No. 16, and not above No. 20, (749) 3¼ cts. per lb.

" above No. 20, and on all refined loaf, lump, crushed, powdered & granulated, (750) 4 cts. per lb.

Sugar, box-shooks (see shooks.)

" of lead and milk (see lead, and milk.)

" refined, tinctured, &c. (see confectionery.)

Sulphur, flour of, (533) $20 per ton and 15 per ct.

Sumac,† (266) ....10 per ct.

Sunshades and frames, (see umbrellas.)

Suspenders, cotton and india rubber, (77-364-481-774-779) 90 per ct. of 35 per ct.

" linen, (72-360)....35 per ct.

" silk, (486).........60 per ct.

" silk and India rubber, (321).......50 per ct.

if india rubber chief value, (321-779) 90 per ct. of 50 per ct.

" woollen, (618-775) 90 per ct. of { 50 cts. per lb. and 40 per ct.

Sweetmeats, (see fruits pres'd.)

Sweepings of gold or silver, (739)..................... free.

Swords, (679-776) 90 per ct. of 45 per ct.

" blades for, (678-776) . 90 per ct. of 35 per ct.

Syrup, (see molasses.)

T

Tables, (see furniture.)

" cloths for, (according to material.)

Tacks, brads and sprigs, cut, (437-776) not over 16 ozs. to the 1000, 90 per ct. of 2¼ cts. per 1000. over 16 ozs. to the M. 90 per ct. of 3 cts. per lb.

" steel, (458-776) 90 per ct. of 45 per ct.

Tacks, other, (according to material.)

Taggers' iron, (536-776) 90 per ct. of 30 per ct.

Tailors' irons, (441-776) 90 per ct. of 1½ ct. per lb.

Tails of squirrels, (see squirrel tails.)

Talc, mineral, (861)........... free.

Tallow, (14)................1 ct. per lb.

Tamarinds, (Reg. of 1857, p. 587,) (861)...... free.

* " Foreign sugars cannot be refined while in bond."—(Dec. of Nov. 29, 1870.)

*Standard samples to be furnished by the Secretary of the Treasury.—(Par. 422.)

* As to how sugar shall be sampled, (see par. 750.)

† " Grinding sumac, a dutiable charge."—(Dec. of Jan. 30, 1866.)

Tamarinds, preserved, (dec. of
Aug. 28, 1858)
(see fruits pre-
served.)
Tamboured articles, (see embroideries.)
Tambourines, (see mus. insts.)
Tampico fibre, (see istle.)
Tankfootings, as melado, (dec.
of Dec. 17, 1868.)
Tankbottom syrup, (see molasses.)
Tannin, (see acid tannic.)
Tanning, articles for, crude,
not otherwise provided for,
(122)...................... free.
Tapers, (see candles.)
Tape, cotton, (481-774)
90 per ct. of 35 per ct.
 "   linen, (482)........ ...40 per ct.
 "   silk, (487).... ....50 per ct.
 "   measuring, linen, (482)...40 per ct.
 "   "   leather, (103-
387-781)
90 per ct. of 35 per ct.
Tapioca, (740)............... free.
Tar, (67)..... ....20 per ct.
 "   petroleum,(see petroleum.)
Tares, vegetables, (50)........10 per ct.
 "   black, (811)........... free.
Tarlatine, (see cottons.)
Tartar or argols, crude, (708).. free.
 "   cream of, (dec. of Jan.
5, 1870,) (233)...10 cts. per lb.
 "   emetic, or tartrate of
antimony, (262) 15 cts. per lb.
 "   partially refined, (dec.
of Aug. 9, 1871,) (233)
6 cts. per lb.
Tassels, (see cords and tassels.)
Teaplants, (740).... free.
Teapots, (accord'g to material.)
Teas, all kinds, (753-782, see
also 585).................. free.
Teasels, (861) .... free.
Teeth, manf'd, (39-286).......20 per ct.
 "   unmanf'd, (861)........ free.
Telescopes, (according to material.)
Terra alba, (504)............20 per ct.
 "   "   aluminous, (861)... free.

Terra japonica, as cutch, (dec.
of May 3, 1864,) (715)..   free.
 "   de sienna and umbra, as
ochrey earths, (see
paints.)
Teutenague, manf'd in blocks
or pigs, (465-
777)
90 per ct. of 1½ ct. per lb.
 "   in sheets, (465-
777)
90 per ct. of 2¼ cts. per lb.
 "   manf'd, (see mfs.)
Thermometers, (according to
material.)
Thimbles, (according to material.)
Thread, cotton, (see cotton
thread.)
 "   flax or linen, (482)...40 per ct.
 "   metal, (see trim'ngs.)
 "   pack, (482)..........40 per ct.
Tica, crude, (861)............. free.
Tickings, (see cottons.)
Ties, cotton, (dec of July 31,
1868,) (444-776)
90 per ct. of 35 per ct.
 "   cotton, old and unfit for
use, as scrap iron, (dec.
of Mar. 20, 1868.)
 "   railroad, wood, (854)..... free.
Tiles, encaustic, (88-373)......35 per ct.
 "   marble, (see marble.)
 "   paving and roofing, not
otherwise provided for,
(53)................20 per ct.
 "   slate, (491)............40 per ct.
Timber, hewn and sawed, (53) 20 per ct.
 "   round, unmanuf'd, not
otherwise provided
for, (843)........... free.
 "   used in build'g wharves
(53)...............20 per ct.
 "   ship, (dec. of Apr. 24,
1871,) (843)........ free.
 "   squared or sided, not
otherwise provided
for, (see proviso to
lumber) (762)
1 ct. per cub. ft.
Tin, in bars, blocks or pigs, &
grain tin, (862)........ free.

Tin, liquor, (166)............20 per ct.
" manuf's of, (see manuf's.)
" muriate of, (329)........30 per ct.
" nitrate of, (66)..........20 per ct.
" oxide of, (329)..........30 per ct.
" in plates or sheets, (dec. of
    Apr. 24, 1865,) (799-777)
        90 per ct. of 15 per. ct.
" plates, after reaching that
    condition,be subsequent-
    ly galvanized or coated
    with any metal by elec-
    tric batteries, (dec. of
    June 1, 1870,) (800-777)
        90 per ct. of 2 cts. per lb.
    same, otherwise than by
    electric batteries, (428-
    777). .90 per ct. of 2½ cts. per lb.
" roofing, continuous and
    fastened together, ready
    for use, (dec. of Dec. 13,
    1869,) (98-383-777)
        90 per ct. of 35 per ct.
" salts of, (329)...........30 per ct.
" tagger and terne, (799-777)
        90 per ct. of 15 per ct.
Tincal, (see borax.)
Tinctures, (see medicines and
    cosmetics)
Tippets, fur, (80-366)........35 per ct.
" other material, (see
    clothing.)
Tips, (see horns.)
" for umbrellas, &c., (see
    umbrellas.)
Tires and parts thereof for loco-
    motives, (430-776)
        90 per ct. of 3 cts. per lb.
" and parts, cast steel, (dec.
    Oct. 6, 1864,) (458-776)
        90 per ct. of 45 per ct.
Tobacco manf'd, of all descrip-
    tions, and stemmed
    tobacco, not other-
    wise provided for,
    (425-633-876)...50 cts. per lb.
    &int.rev. tax of 20 cts. per lb.
" in leaf, unmanf'd and
    not steamed, (425)
        35 cts. per lb.
" stems, (578)......15 cts. per lb.
" unmanf'd, (4).......30 per ct.
Toilets, (see cosmetics.)

Toilet vials, (see bottles.)
Ton deemed, 2240 lbs. (168)
Tongues, (166)..............20 per ct.
Tonics, (see liquors and medi-
    cines.)
Tongs, iron, (444-776)
        90 per ct. of 35 per ct.
" brass,(see note to man-
    uf's of brass;) (98-383-
    777)
        90 per ct. of 35 per ct.
Tools of trade, (see effects.)
Tooth paste, washes, &c., (see
    cosmetics.)
" picks, (accord'g to ma-
    terials.)
Topaz, (see precious stones.)
Tops for furniture, (see furni-
    ture.)
Toys, (decs. of Feb. 4, 1870;
    Nov. 27, 1868, and Nov. 12,
    1864,) (543) ....50 per ct.
    if cotton, metals, paper,
    india-rubber, gutta-per-
    cha,straw,leather,skins,
    bone, ivory or horn,
    chief value,(543-774-776
    to 781)... 90 per ct. of 50 per ct.
" whole or part wool, (dec.
    of Jan. 21, 1870,) (613-
    775)
    90 per ct. of { 50 cts. per lb.
                { and 35 per ct.
" copper chief value, (see
    note to manf's of cop-
    per,) (dec. of Jan. 21,
    1870,) (640-777)
        90 per ct. of 45 per ct.
Tragacanth, gum, (719).......free.
Traps, iron, (444-776)
        90 per ct. of 35 per ct.
" part steel, (458-776)
        90 per ct. of 45 per ct.
Trays, japanned, (92-278-777)
        90 per ct. of 45 per ct.
" plated, (112-396-777)
        90 per ct. of 35 per ct.
" wood, lacquered, (107-
    (390)..............35 per ct.
" gold or silver, (511-777)
        90 per ct. of 40 per ct.
Trees, (see plants.)
Tresses, metal, (see trim'ngs.)

Trimmings, bead, silk and metal,(dec. of Jan. 30, 1865,) (487).....50 per ct.

"   cotton, (481-774) 90 per ct. of 35 per ct.

"   crape, silk chief value, (dec. of Feb. 16, 1865,) (487)..50 per ct.

"   for bonnets, hats, &c.,(see bonnets)

"   silk, (dec. of March 10, 1870,) (486)..60 per ct.

"   viz: epaulets, galloons,laces,knots, stars, tassels,tresses, and wings, of gold, silver, or other metal, (see note to manfs. of brass,) (88-373-777)..........35 per ct.

if *not* articles of ornament, (88-373-777) 90 per ct. of 35 per ct.

"   viz: bouillons or cannetille, and metal threads, filé or gespinst, (785)..25 per ct.

if *not* articles of ornament,(785-777) 90 per ct. of 25 per ct.

"   viz: webbings, beltings, bindings, braids, galloons, fringes, gimps, cords, cords and tassels,dress trimmings, head nets, buttons or barrel buttons, or buttons of other forms for tassels or ornaments, wrought by hand or braided by machinery, made of wool, worsted, or mohair, or of which either is a component material, (619-775)

90 per ct. of { 50 cts. per lb. { and 50 per ct.

Tripod, bronze, not statuary & pay according to material, (Reg. of 1857, p. 559.)

Tripoli, (polishing powder)(863)   free.

Troches, (see medicines.)

Trowels, part steel, (458-776) 90 per ct. of 45 per ct.

Trusses (according to material.)

Tubes, steam, gas, and water, wrought-iron, (see note to flues,) (438-577-776) 90 per ct. of 3½ cts. per lb.

"   other, (according to material)

Tumblers,* glass, not cut, (496-780) 90 per ct. of 35 per ct.

"   glass, cut, (497-780) 90 per ct. of 40 per ct.

Turbans, silk, (486)..........60 per ct.

Turmeric, (161)............. free.

Turpentine, spirits of, (533) 30 cts. per gall.

"   Venice, (866).... free.

Turtles, (740)................. free.

Tweezers,(accord'g to material.)

Twills, worsted and cotton, as manf. of worsted, (three decs. of Sept. 21, 1857.)

Twine,† flax or linen, (482)....40 per ct.

"   any other material, (dec. of Nov. 28, 1863,) (116-400)....35 per ct.

if cotton, or paper chief value, (116-400-774-778) 90 per ct. of 35 per ct.

Twist, for buttons,(see buttons,)

"   silk, or silk and mohair, (dec. of Oct. 28, 1868) (179)................40 per ct.

"   silk for fringes, not commercially known as silk twist, (dec. of Oct. 28, 1868,) (487)......50 per ct.

Type metal, (67-400-777) 90 per ct. of 25 per ct.

Types new, (67-400-777) 90 per ct. of 25 per ct.

"   old, and fit only to be remanuf'd, (161)....... free.

---

* "Glass tumblers smoothed by cutting or grinding or with engraved sides, are subject to duty as 'glass cut.'"—(Reg. of 1857, p. 563.)

† Decision of November 28, 1863, defines the difference between "twine" and "yarn."

U

Ultra marine, (see paints.)

Umber, (see paints.)

Umbrellas, parasols and sunshades, silk, or alpaca, (802) 60 per ct.

cotton, chief value, (802-774)
90 per ct. of 45 per ct.

other material, (802)........45 per ct.

ribs and stretchers, frames, tips, runners, handles, or other parts thereof, when made in whole or chief part of iron, steel, or any other metal, (802-776-777)
90 per ct. of 45 per ct.

bamboo reeds, and sticks of patridge, hair wood, pi mento, orange, myrtle, and other sticks, in the rough,or no further manufactured than cut into lengths suitable for umbrella, parasol or sunshade sticks, (810-864).... free.

frames and sticks for umbrellas, parasols, and sunshades, other than above, when finished or unfinished, (89-374)...........35 per ct.

if iron, steel, bone, ivory or horn, chief value,(89-374-776-781)....90 per ct. of 35 per ct.

Uncnumerated articles, unmanufactured, (see 166 and footnote thereto.)

if manf'd (see manufactures.)

United States, articles imported for the use of, *Provided*, That the price of the same did not include the duty, (709).. free.

articles the growth, produce, and manufacture of the U. S. when returned *in the same condition as exported: Provided*, That proof of the identity of such articles be made under regulations; and if such articles were subject to int. tax at the time of exportation, such tax shall be proved to have been paid before exportation, and not refunded,* (710) free.

if no internal tax has been assessed or paid, or upon which such tax has been paid and refunded by allowance or drawback,shall pay a duty equal to the tax imposed by int. rev. laws upon such articles.† (605)

casks, barrels, or carboys, and other vessels,and grain bags, the manufacture of the U. S. if exported, containing American produce, and declaration be made of intent to return the same empty, under such regulations as shall be prescribed by Sec'y of the Treasury, (dec. of June 18, 1872,)(805) free.

Uranium, oxide of, (865)......... free.

V

Vaccine virus, (see cowpox.)

Vandyke brown, (see paints.)

Varnish, (dec. of Dec. 15, 1869), (263).

valued at $1.50 or less per gallon
50 cts. per gall. and 20 per ct.

valued at above $1.50 per gall. 50 cts. per gall. and 25 per ct.

Vases, (see retorts.)

"   other according to material, (Reg. of 1857, p. 589.)

Vegetable substances used for beds and mattresses, (845).. free.

if used for cordage, not otherwise provided for, (27-344)........ ....$15 per ton.

---

† "This being a customs duty, is payable in coin."—(Rev. Reg. part 4, p. 35.)

* "Dutiable merchandise imported into the United States and afterwards exported, although it may have paid duty on the first importation, is liable to duty on every subsequent importation into the United States."—(Rev. Reg. part 4, p. 57.)

Vegetable substances —
  if not otherwise provided for,
  (dec. of Nov. 5, 1866,)
  (166-344) 10 per ct. and $5 per ton.
Vegetables, not otherwise provided for, (50)..10 per ct.
  "   desiccated or com-
        pressed, (dec. of
        Aug. 30, 1859,)
        (113-397)..... ..35 per ct.
  "   prepared, (see pre-
        pared meats, &c.)
  "   used for dyeing,
        (see berries.)
Veils, silk, (486).............60 per ct.
Vellum, (parchment) (118)....30 per ct.
  "   cloth, cotton, (dec. of
      March 16, 1863,)
      (481-774)
             90 per ct. of 35 per ct.
Velvet, cotton, (481-774)
             90 per ct. of 35 per ct.
  "   printed or painted,
        (118-401-774)
             90 per ct. of 35 per ct.
  "   silk and cotton, cotton
        chief value, (481-774)
             90 per ct. of 35 per ct.
  "   silk, or silk chief value,
        (485)..............60 per ct.
Veneers, as woods-cabinet,(dec.
  of June 21, 1859.)
Verdegris, (subacetate of copper,) (741)............... ...   free.
Venetian red, (see paints.)
Vermicella, (844)............   free.
Vermilion, (see paints.)
Vermuth, (see liquors.)
Vessels, cast iron, not otherwise provided for,
  (441-776)
             90 per ct. of 1½ ct. per lb.
  "   other (according to
        material.)

Vessels, repairs on *.........50 per ct.
Vestings, silk, (486)..........60 per ct.
  "   silk and cotton, but
        sold as a pure silk
        article, (dec. of Jan.
        6, 1871,) (486).....60 per ct.
  "   wool, (613-775)
        90 per ct. of { 50 cts. per lb.
                      { and 35 per ct.
  "   other, (according to
        material.)
Vests, (see clothing.)
Vials, (see bottles.)
Vices, part steel, (458-776)
             90 per ct. of 45 per ct.
Vinegar, (536)..........10 cts. per gall.
        That for all purposes
        the standard for
        vinegar shall be
        taken to be that
        strength which re-
        quires thirty - five
        grains of bi-carbon-
        ate of potash to
        neutralize 1 ounce
        troy of vinegar.(870)
  "   concentrated, (see
        acid, acetic.)
  "   raspberry, (dec. of
        May 31, 1867,)
        (526)...........25 per ct.
Violins, (see mus. instr's.)
Violin boxes, when empty, according to material, (dec. of
  May 21, 1859.)
Virus, (see cowpox.)
Vitriol, oil of, (sulphuric acid.)
        (804)...............   free.
  "   blue or Roman, (sul-
        phate of copper,)(790)
                        4 cts. per lb.
  "   green, (14-288)...... ¼ ct. per lb.
  "   white, (69)...........20 per ct.

W

Wadding, (according to mate-
  rial.)
Wads, (see gun wads.)
Wafers, (867)...............   free.
Wagon blocks, (see blocks.)

Waiters, (see trays.)
Walnuts, all kinds, (530)..3 cts. per lb.
  "   in salt and water,
        (dec. of Sept. 30,
        1858,) (166)......20 per ct.

---

* See sec. 23 of Act of July 18, 1866, U. S. Statutes at Large, vol. 14, p. 178; also sec. 2 of Act of June 6, 1872, p. 118 of the Digest, and Reg. of 1857, p. 565-566.

* "That round iron coils, three-sixteenths of an inch or less in diameter, whether coated with metal or not so coated, and all descriptions of iron wire, and wire of which iron is a component part, not otherwise specifically enumerated and provided for, shall pay the same duty as iron wire, bright, coppered, or tinned," (paragraph 680.)

Wire, over No. 25, wire gauge, (5-197-776)

90 per ct. of $\begin{cases} \text{4 cts. per lb.} \\ \text{and 15 per ct.} \end{cases}$

Provided, that wire covered with cotton, silk, or other material, shall pay 5 cts. per lb. in addition to the foregoing rates, (197-427,) (see foot note to iron.)

" steel, not less than ¼ of an inch in diameter, (446-776)

valued at 7 cts. or less per lb.
90 per ct. of 2¼ cts. per lb.

valued at above 7 cts. and not above 11 cts.
90 per ct. of 3 cts. per lb.

valued at above 11 cts. per lb.
90 per ct. of $\begin{cases} \text{3½ cts. per lb.} \\ \text{and 10 per ct.} \end{cases}$

" steel, less than ¼ of an inch in diameter, (447-776.)

not less than No. 16, wire gauge,
90 per ct. of $\begin{cases} \text{2¼ cts. per lb.} \\ \text{and 20 per ct.} \end{cases}$

less than No. 16, wire gauge,
90 per ct. of $\begin{cases} \text{3 cts. per lb,} \\ \text{and 20 per ct.} \end{cases}$

" of steel, or steel commercially known as crinoline, corset, and hat steel wire, (680-776)
90 per ct. of $\begin{cases} \text{9 cts. per lb.} \\ \text{and 10 per ct.} \end{cases}$

" springs for furniture, (see springs.)

" rope and wire strand or chain made of iron wire, either bright, coppered, galvanized, or coated with other metals, shall pay the same rate of duty that is now levied on the iron wire of which said rope or strand or chain is made, without the 10 per cent reduction; &

all wire rope and wire strand or chain made of steel wire, either bright, coppered, galvanized, or coated with other metals, shall pay the same rate of duty that is now levied on the steel wire of which said rope or strand or chain is made, without the 10 per cent. reduction. (777)

" telegraph, galvanized, as wire, bright, coppered or tinned, (580,) (see also dec. of Sept. 18, 1869.)

" other, (according to material.)

Woad or pastel, (163)........ free.

Wood, box, cedar, ebony, granadilla, lignum-vitæ, lance, mahogany, rose, satin, and all cabinet woods, unmanf'd, (164) .... free.

" Brazil, brazilletto, and all other dyewoods, in sticks, (127)........ free.

" ebony, green, a dye, (dec. of Oct. 30, 1857,) (127)........... .. free.

" fire, (828)............ free.

" manufs. of, (see manfs.)

" poplar and other woods for the manuf. of paper, (742)........... free.

" quassia, (736)........ free.

" sandal, (739) .... free.

. " unmanuf'd, not otherwise provided for, (dec. of May 5, 1868, and Reg. of 1857, p. 498,) (69)...........20 per ct.

Wool,† hair of the alpaca, goat, and other like animals, unmanufactured, shall be divided, for the purpose of fixing the duties, into *three classes,*

Class 1 *and* 2.—Clothing and combing wools, hair of the alpaca, goat, and other like animals, (specified in 609

---

† "Decisions of April 9, 1868; Oct. 21, 1868; Feb. 26, 1869; April 20, 1870, relate to 'Dutiable value and classification by race or blood.'"

and 610) the value whereof at the last port or place whence exported to the U. S., excluding charges in such port, shall be 32 cts. or less per lb. (612-775,)

90 per ct. of $\left\{\begin{array}{l}\text{10 cts. per lb.}\\\text{and 11 per ct.}\end{array}\right.$

exceeding 32 cts. per lb.

90 per ct. of $\left\{\begin{array}{l}\text{12 cts. per lb.}\\\text{and 10 per ct.}\end{array}\right.$

Class 3.—Carpet wools, and all other similar wools, (specified in 611) the value whereof at the last port or place whence exported into the U.S.,excluding charges in such port. shall be 12 cts. or less per lb. (612-775,)

90 per ct. of 3 cts. per lb.

exceeding 12 cts. per lb.,   .

90 per ct. of 6 cts. per lb.

Provided, if the above be imported other than in the ordinary condition, or mixed with dirt, &c., to evade the duty, pays twice the amount it would be otherwise subjected to. (612)

Provided, further, when wool is imported of different qualities in same package, it is appraised at the average aggregate value; when invoiced at the same

price, whereby the average price shall be reduced more than 10 per ct. below the value of the bale of the best quality, the whole appraised according to best quality; and no package shall be liable to a less rate in consequence of being invoiced with wool of lower value. (612)

Provided, further, that wool of Class 1, imported *washed,* shall be twice the amount of duty as when imported *unwashed,* and that wool of all Classes imported *scoured* shall be three times the amount of duty as when imported *unwashed,* (dec. of Sept. 21, 1869.) (612)

Wool, manf's of, (see manf's)
"   noils, being short pieces and knots of wool, classed as wool, (dec. of April 19, 1869.)
"   on the skin,* same rate as wool .(667)
"   pickings.(dec. of May 29, 1868,) (612-775)

90 per ct. of $\left\{\begin{array}{l}\text{10 cts. per lb.}\\\text{and 11 per ct.}\end{array}\right.$

Wormseed, levant, (742)...... free.

Worsted, manf's of, (see manf's)

X

Xylonite or xylotile, (742).....   free.

Xylonite, partially manf'd, as knife handles, (dec. of April 7, 1871,) (166). .20 per ct.

Y

Yams, (868)................   free.

Yarn, carpet, of wool waste, cows' hair, &c., as woollen yarn, (dec. of Jan. 9, 1869.)
"   coir, (821)...........   free.

Yarn, cotton, (see cotton thread)
"   flax, (dec. of May 8, 1863) (482).................40 per ct.
"   hemp, (483)........5 cts. per lb.
"   jute† (484)...........25 per ct.

*"The wool should be properly classified for duty according to its grade by the standard samples, and that the skins be also entered for duty under the proper classification."—Circular of Dec. 27, 1870. Decisions of April 22, 1872 and June 24, 1872, prescribe the number of pounds to be estimated to the skin.

†"Jute yarn in balls, reported by appraisers that said article was commercially known as twine, bought, sold, and used as such, liable to duty as twine."—(Decision of July 8, 1870.)—*See foot-note to twine.*

Yarn, tow of flax, (dec. of July 10, 1861,) (482)......40 per ct.

"   flax or linen, for carpets, not exceeding No. 8 Lea, (482)

valued at 24 cts. or less per lb........30 per ct.

valued at above 24 cts. per lb....... 35 per ct.

"   woollen and worsted, (614-775) valued at 40 cts. or less per lb.

90 per ct. of $\begin{cases} 20 \text{ cts per lb.} \\ \text{and } 35 \text{ per ct.} \end{cases}$

Yarn, woollen and worsted, valued above 40 cts. and not above 60 cts. per lb,

90 per ct. of $\begin{cases} 30 \text{ cts. per lb.} \\ \text{and } 35 \text{ per ct.} \end{cases}$

valued above 60 cts. and not above 80 cts. per lb.

90 per ct. of $\begin{cases} 40 \text{ cts. per lb.} \\ \text{and } 35 \text{ per ct.} \end{cases}$

valued above 80 cts. per lb.

90 per ct. of $\begin{cases} 50 \text{ cts per lb.} \\ \text{and } 35 \text{ per ct.} \end{cases}$

Yeast cakes, (868)............ free.

Yellow crystals, as aniline dyes.

Z

Zaffer, (869)............... free.

Zinc, acetate or pyrolignite of, (789).........25 cts. per lb.

"   corrugated, (dec. of Oct. 28, 1857,) (98-383-777) 90 per ct. of 35 per ct.

"   manf'd in blocks or pigs (465-777) 90 per ct. of 1½ ct. per lb.

"   in sheets, (dec. of Nov. 11, 1870,) (465-777) 90 per ct. of 2¼ cts. per. lb.

Zinc, manfs. of, (see manfs.)

"   old and fit only to be re-manf'd, (dec. of June 30, 1869,) (60-777) 90 per ct. of 20 per ct.

"   oxide of, (see paints)

"   sulphate of, (69)... ....20 per ct.

"   valerianate of, (Reg. of 1857, p. 589,) (108-280) 40 per ct.

APPENDIX.

Invoices,' when in order.

(Act March 3, 1801, Act March 2, 1799, sec. 61, and Act June 30, 1864, sec. 27, from Rev. Reg. part 4, p. 8, &c.)

ARTICLE 1. Invoices of all goods imported into the United States, subject to a duty *ad valorem*, are required to be made out in the currencies, weights, and measures of the place or country from which the importation shall be made; and shall contain a true statement of the actual cost of such goods. Invoices of free goods or of goods paying strictly a specific duty, can be made out in the currency of the United States, or that of any country where its value is fixed by our laws. All invoices must be verified by the shipper before the U. S. Consul or Commercial Agent nearest the place of shipment. (Dec. of Feb. 17, 1870.) Where the value of the foreign currency is fixed by law, (for which see table of Foreign Moneys,) the value is to be taken in estimating the duties; where the value is not fixed by law, the invoice must be accompanied by a consular certificate showing its value in Spanish or United States silver dollars.

Entry without Invoice.

(Sec. 19, Act of July 18, 1866, from Rev. Reg., part 4, pages 13 and 14.)

ART. 2. When the value of an importation does not exceed *one hundred dollars*, the collector may, in his discretion, admit the same to entry by appraisement, without an invoice. The same may be done in the case of perishable goods of any value, when the collector and naval officer are satisfied that the importation is not fraudulent; and in case of goods found derelict at sea, or taken from a wreck, or landed from a vessel in distress, and disposed of under Sec. 60, act of March 2, 1799.

Small parcels containing objects of affection or presents, not intended for sale, and not exceeding *two hundred dollars* in value, will be admitted to entry upon appraisement, without invoice.

Abatement of duties for damage during the voyage of importation.

(Sec. 59, Act of March 2, 1799, from Rev. Reg. part 4, page 63.)

ART. 3. No abatement of duties on merchandise, on account of damage occurring during the voyage of importation, can be allowed, unless proof to ascertain such damage shall be lodged in the custom house within ten working days after the landing of such merchandise.*

Samples of Goods.

(Regulations of 1857, p. 582.)

ART. 4. Samples of Goods having no intrinsic value as merchandise, and cannot be so used, free of duty. (Dec. of June 11, 1868.)

Re-appraisement.

(Sec. 17, Act of August 30, 1842, from Rev. Reg., part 4, p. 40.)

ART. 5. If the importer be dissatisfied with the decision of the appraisers, (decision of February 17, 1870,) he may, if he have complied with the legal requirements, give notice of such dissatisfaction, in writing, to the collector. This notice must be given within *twenty-four hours* after being notified by the collector of the advance by the appraisers.

---

* Bill of lading, proof of sound shipment. (Dec. of March 17, 1868.)

In case of a re-appraisement, a merchant appraiser will act with the United States Appraiser General. An original appraisement unappealed, (decision of March 29, 1870,) as well as the decision of the merchant appraisers on appeal, is final and conclusive against the importer.*

As no re-appraisement is authorized by law in cases of allowance for damage, the return of the appraiser in the premises, as to the fact of damage, or the character or extent thereof, when submitted to the collector, is final and conclusive as to the damage which can be allowed.—(Decision of January 4, 1870.)

Duties Payable in Coin.
(Decision of October 15, 1868.)

ART. 6. All duties must be deposited in coin as prescribed by law. A deposit of the equivalent in currency is not allowable.

Excess of Weight.
(Decision of June 10, 1868.)

ART. 7. Regulations of 1857, art. 379, forbidding any allowance to be made for any increase of weight caused by contraction of moisture on the voyage of importation, refers only to the moisture contracted as one of the ordinary incidents of the voyage of importation, and not to cases of accidental and unusual leakage and shipment of water.—(See Circular of November 30, 1853, p. 7.)

Lien for Duties.
(Decision of April 20, 1868.)

ART. 8. It has been decided by the Supreme Court of the United States, in the case of Harris vs. Dennie, (3 Peters, 302,) that the U. S. have no general lien upon goods imported for duties due from the importer, but only a specific one for those upon the particular goods. In this opinion the Department concurs: and collectors are advised that they have no right to permit one importation of merchandise to pass out of their custody, when the duties are unpaid, with the view of holding a lien for the payment thereof upon some other goods of the same importation.

Rates of Drawback Allowed on the Products of Sugar and Molasses.
(Decision of March 20, 1871.)

ART. 9. The following rates of drawback will be allowed on the exportation of the articles hereinafter named, manufactured wholly of materials on which duty was paid under the tariff now in force :

ON THE PRODUCTS OF SUGAR.

On refined crystalline sugar, $2\frac{3}{4}$ cents per pound.
On refined soft B and C lower grade sugar, 2 cents per pound.
On syrup of sugar, (sugar-house molasses,) 5 cents per gallon.

ON THE PRODUCTS OF MOLASSES.

On New England rum, $5\frac{1}{4}$ cents per gallon.
On syrup from molasses, 4 cents per gallon.
On sugar from molasses, 1 cent per pound.
All allowances under the above rates to be subject to the legal deduction of 10 per cent.

Nitrate of soda has been placed upon the free list. No drawback will be allowed on gunpowder manufactured in part from that article, in cases, where the nitrate of soda was imported since the present tariff went into effect.

No drawback is now allowed on copal varnish, unless manufactured of materials imported under the former tariff.

---

* "Question of classification and not of valuation, are not subjects for re-appraisement."—(Decision of September 30, 1868, see also decision of April 10, 1868.)

FOREIGN MONEYS.
VALUE AS FIXED BY THE LAWS OF THE UNITED STATES.
(From Rev. Reg., Part IV., page 9.)

	$	FRACTIONAL PARTS.		WHEN FIXED.
Dollar, rix, of Bremen......	0 78¾	72 grotes	5 swares	Mar. 3, 1843
Dollar, thaler, of Bremen of 72 grotes.	71	72 "	5 "	"
Dollar, specie, of Denmark	1 05	6 marks	16 skillings	May 22, 1846
Dollar, specie, of Norway	1 06	6 " .	16 "	"
Dollar, specie, of Sweden..	1 06	48 skillings	12 'ore	"
Dollar or Thaler of Prussia and the Northern States of Germany.......	69	30 groschen	12 pfenning	"
Dollar, pillar, of Spain, and Dollar of Mexico, Peru and Bolivia, when shown by assay to be of the weight and fineness required by law............	1 00			
Dollar of Chili and Central America, and the same re-stamped in Brazil, when of the weight and fineness required by law.	93			
Ducat of Naples.............	80	100 grani		May 22, 1846
Florin, silver, of the empire of Austria and city of Augsburg...............	48½	60 kreutzers	4 pfennings	"
Florin, new, of Austria....	48 $\frac{19}{100}$			March 2, 1861
Florin of the Southern States of Germany........	40	60 kreutzers	4 "	May 22, 1846
Florin, or Guilder, of the Netherlands.................	40	100 centimes		March 2, 1799
Franc, five piece, when of the required weight and fineness	93			March 3, 1843
Franc of France	18 $\frac{6}{10}$	100 "		May 22, 1846
Franc of Belgium.............	18 $\frac{6}{10}$	100 "		"
Liva of Sardinia, (Kingdom of Italy)..............	18 $\frac{6}{10}$	4 reali	20 soldi	"
Livre Tournois of France	18½			March 2, 1799
Marc Banco of Hamburg..	35	16 shillings	12 pfennings	March 3, 1843
Mark of the German Empire.........	23			Dec June 20, '72
Milrea of Portugal.........	1 12	1000 reas		March 3, 1843
Milrea of Maderia...........	1 00	1000 "		"
Milrea of the Azores.......	83½	1000 "		"
Ounce of Sicily..............	2 40	30 tari	20 grani	May 22, 1846
Pagoda of India.............	1 94	36 fanams	48 jittas	March 2, 1799
Pagoda, Star, of Madras..	1 84	36 "	48 "	March 2, 1801
Pound Sterling of Great Britain and of Jamaica...	4 84	20 shillings	12 pence	July 27, 1842 and dec. of Oct. 30, 1857
Pound of British Provinces, of Nova Scotia, New Brunswick, Newfoundland and Canada..........	4 00	20 "	12 '	May 22, 1846

FOREIGN MONEYS—CONTINUED.

	$	FRACTIONAL PARTS.		WHEN FIXED.
Rial of·Plate of Spain......	10	34 maravedis		March 2, 1799
Rial of Velium of Spain...	05	34 "		"
Rouble of Russia............	75	100 kopecks		March 3, 1843
Rupee of British India.....	44½	16 annas	12 pice	"
Tael of China................	1 48	10 mace	100 candarems	March 2, 1799
Tael of Shanghai..........	1 35			Dec.Oct.11,'70

"Switzerland having adopted the Franc of France as the standard of value of the Swiss 'franc federal' equivalent to eighteen cents and six-tenths of a cent, no consular certificate of value in the U. S. currency will be required to invoices of Swiss goods, made out in the franc federal." (Rev. Reg. Part 4, p. 10.)

FOREIGN WEIGHTS AND MEASURES.

REDUCED TO U. S. STANDARD.

ALGERIA.

Onguyah........... ....4 grammes.
Hollah, (liquid)..................16·66 litres.
Psa, (dry)................. 48   "
French system in general use.

ARGENTINE CONFEDERATION.

Quintal ....,........101·44 lbs. av.
Arroba....... ....25·35   "
Fanega............... . ... .1·5 imp. bu.

AUSTRIA.

Centner, 100 Pfund.....123·50 lbs. avdp.
Mark, (gold and silver)..........9 oz. troy.
Eimer, (40 mass)........14·94 wine galls.
Metze................ ....1·75 bu.
Klafter.........................67 cubic feet.

BELGIUM, (AS FRANCE.)

BOLIVIA.

Libra, (ounce)....... ....1·014 lbs. avdp.
Quintal................. ......101·44   "
Arroba of 25 lbs.. ....25·36   "
   "   of wine or spirits.6·70 imp. galls.
Gallon..................................0·74
Vara ....·.........0·927 yards
Square Vara.................0·859 sq. yds.

BRAZIL.

Libra ....1·012 lbs. av.
Arroba................. ....32·38   "
Quintal... ....129·54   "

Alqueire, (of Rio)..... ....1 imp. bu.
Oitava............................55·34 grains.
   In parts of the empire same as Portugal.
   The French system is compulsory in 1872.

CANADA, (AS GREAT BRITAIN.)

CAPE OF GOOD HOPE,(AS GREAT BRITAIN.)

CEYLON, (AS GREAT BRITAIN.)

CHILI, (AS BOLIVIA.)

CHINA.

Leang or Tael..................1·33 oz. av.
Picul... .... 133 lbs. av.
Catty....... ....1·75   "
Chih ....14·10 inch.
Chang.. ....11·75 feet.

COLOMBIA, (AS FRANCE.)

COSTARICA, (AS SPAIN.)

DENMARK.

Lod...... ....227 grains troy.
Pound....... ....1·102 lbs. av.
Ship last...................................2 tons.
Tonde or bbl. of grain & salt.3·8 imp. bu.
   "   "   coal..............4·7   "
Foot................................1.03 eng. ft.
Viertel......... ....1·7 imp. gall.

EQUADOR, (AS FRANCE.)

ENGLAND, (SEE GREAT BRITAIN.)

EGYPT.

Killow...........................0·9120 imp. bu.
Almud...........................1·151 imp. gall.
Oke of 400 drams...........2·833 lbs. av.
Gasab of 4 diraas.....................3 yards.
Feddan al risach.............3·208 sq. yds.

FRANCE.

Gramme...................14·434 grains troy.
Kilogramme......................2·205 lbs. av.
Quintal Metrique............220·46   "
Tonneau.....................2204·60   "
Litre................................2·11 pints.
Hectolitre........................26·40 galls.
   "   (dry)........................2·84 bus.
Metre................................3·28 feet.
Kilometre.......................1093 yards.
Metre Cube, (stere).........35·31 cubic ft.

GERMANY.

The following are in general use through-
out all of Germany.
Centner, (100 lbs.).......110·5 lbs. avdp.
Ship Last, of timber.............80 cub. ft.
Scheffel, of grain............ ..1·5 imp. bu.
Klafter.............................6 feet.
Schock................... ....60 pieces.
Toune, (weight)............ 227 lbs. avdp.
   "   (measure of coal.............6 bus.
Loth ....225 gr. troy.
Eimer................................18·14 galls.

GREAT BRITAIN.

Ale or beer gallon.................1·22 gall.
Wine gallon........ ⅓ less than imp. gall.
Imp. gallon.............................1·20 gall.
   "   bushel.............................1·03 bu.
   "   quarter.................. ....8·25 "
   "   yard...............................36 inches.

GREECE.

Oke......... ....2·80 lbs. avdp.
Cantar ....,...............123·20   "
Livre........................ .....1·05   "
Baril, (wine)...............16·33 imp. gall.
Kilo..........................0·114 imp. quarter.
Pike........................⅘ eng. yard.

HONG KONG, (AS CHINA.)

INDIA.

Maund of Bengal, } ...2·054 lbs. avdp.
   of 40 seers   {
Maund of Bombay.............28 lbs. avdp.
   "   Madras.............25   "

Candy, of 20 maunds...............24·3 bus.
Tola...................................180 grains.
Guz of Bengal........ ....36 inches.

ITALY, (AS FRANCE.)

JAPAN.

Picul or ton... ....133 lbs. avdp.
King=160 nomme..........1·33   "
Shaku=10 sung...... ....11·75 inches.

JAVA.

Amsterdam Pond............1·09 lbs. advp.
Pecul..............................133   "
Catty................... ....1·33   ·'
Chang........ ....4 yards.

LIBERIA.

British weights and measures generally
used.

MEXICO, (AS SPAIN.)

NETHERLANDS, (AS FRANCE.)

NORWAY AND SWEEDEN.

Swedish Skalpond........0·936 lbs. avdp.
Norwegian Pund............1·100   "
Swedish Fot...............11·7 eng. inches.
Norwegian Fod.........12·02   "
Swedish Kanna .... 4·6 imp. pints.
Norwegian Kaude..........3·3   "

PARAGUAY, (AS ARGENTINE CONFEDER-
ATION.)

PERSIA.

Batman...............................13·5 lbs. avdp.
Collothun.....................1·809 imp. gall.
Artata.....................1·809 imp. bu.
Zer...... ....38 inches.

PERU, (AS BOLIVIA.)

PORTUGAL.

French system compulsory after Oct. 1,
1868.
The chief old measures now in use, are
Libra..........................1·012 lb. avdp.
Almunde of Lisbon............3·7 imp. gall.
   "   Oporto...........5·6   "
Alquiere....... ....0·36 imp. bu.
Moio.......................2·78 imp. quarter.

POLAND, (AS RUSSIA.)

PRUSSIA (AS GERMANY.)

RUSSIA.

Berkowitz.....................360 lbs. avdp.
Pood (63 to a ton)............36   "
Chetvert.........................5·77 imp. bus.
Oxhuft.........................58·5 wine galls
Anker.............................9·75   "
Vedro .... 2·75 imp. galls.
Arsheen...........................28 inches.
Ship last.............................2 tons.
Pound ....0·9 lbs. avdp.
Tchetvert ....0·7 imp. quarter.
Verst.............................3500 feet.

SIAM.

Tael.........................1·33 ozs. avdp.
Pical, Catty and Chang....same as Java.

SPAIN.

Quintal, (100 lbs.).......101·44 lbs. avdp.
Libra.. ....1·014   "
Arroba for wine............3·5 imp. galls.
  "   for oil ....2·75   "

Square Vara...............1·09 vara=1 yard
Fanega...............................1·5 imp. bu.

SWEDEN, (SEE NORWAY.)

SWITZERLAND.

French system used with some changes of names and subdivisions.

TURKEY.

Oke of 400 drams.......2·8326 lbs. avdp.
Almund......................1·151 imp. gall.
Killow.......................0·9120 imp. bu.
Okes=1 Cantar or Kintal 125 lbs. avdp.
39·44 Okes...............................1 cwt.
180 Okes=1 Tcheke.........511·380 lbs.
1 Kilo=20 okes.......0·36 imp. quarter.
816 kilos..................100   "
Andaze, (cloth measure)........27 inches.

URUGUAY, (AS ARGENTINE CONFEDERATION.)

VENEZUELA, (AS FRANCE.)

STANDARD WEIGHT OF GRAIN.

(SEC. 33, ACT OF JULY 18, 1866, FROM U. S. STATUTES AT LARGE, VOL. 14, P. 187.)

That for the purpose of estimating the duties on importations of grain, the number of bushels shall be ascertained by weight, instead of by measure, and the following shall respectively be estimated as a bushel:

Wheat..60 lbs. to the bushel.
Corn...56 "   "   "
Rye ....56 "   "   "
Barley.. 48 "   "   "
Oats ....32 "   "   "
Peas..60 "   "   "
Buckwheat..42 "   "   "

RATES OF TARE.

PRESCRIBED BY TREASURY DEPARTMENT, PER CIRCULAR OF JANUARY 24, 1863.

Almonds.................................in bales............................... 2½ per cent.
"   ....in bags.............................. 2   "
"   .... in frails.............................. 8   "
Alum................................in casks 10   "
Barytes... 3   "
Cheese............................. in casks or tubs................. 10   "
Cassia..............................in mats......................... 9   "
Coffee, Rio......................in single bags................... 1   "
"   "   ....in double bags................... 2   "
"   all other ....actual tare.
Cinnamon............................in bales........................ 6 per cent.
Cocoa................................in bags.......................... 2   "
"   ....in ceroons...................... 8   "
Chicory............................in bags............................ 2   "
Copperas............................in casks.........................10   "
Currants............................in casks.........................10   "
Hemp, Manilla....................in bales................... 4 pounds per bale.
"   Hamburg, Leghorn, Trieste................ 5   "   "   "
Indigo................................in ceroons...............10 per cent.
Melado...11   "
Nails.................................in bags........................ 2   "
"   ....in casks........................ 8   "
Ochre, dry.........................in casks...................... 8   "
"   oil..........................in casks.......................12   "
Peruvian Bark....................in ceroons.....................10   "
Paris White.......................in casks 10   "
Pepper..............................in bags.......................... 2   "
"   ....in double bags................. 4   "
Pimento.............................in bags......................... 2   "
Raisins...............................in casks.......................12   "
"   ....in boxes........................25   "
"   ....in half boxes.................27   "
"   ....in quarter boxes.............29   "
"   ....in frails......................... 4   "
Rice..................................in bags.......................... 2   "
Spanish Brown, dry.............in casks.......................10   "
"   "   oil...............in casks.......................12   "
Sugar................................in hhds.......................12½   "
"   ....in tierces......................12   "
"   ....in bbls.........................10   "
"   ....in boxes.......................14   "
"   ....in bags.......................... 2   "
"   .... in mats........................ 2½   "
Salt, fine...........................in sacks................... 3 pounds per sack.
"   coarse or ground alum..in sacks .... 2 pounds each.
Teas from China or Japan...........................duty on net lbs. per invoice.
"   all others......................................actual weight by tare.
Tobacco, leaf.....................in bales................10 pounds per bale.
"   "   ....in bales, with extra covers..12   "   "   "
Whiting.............................in casks...................10 per cent.

"The tares, as above, is that uniformly allowed in all ports in the United States when the actual tare is not claimed by the importer at the time of entry."—(Decision of January 17,1870.)

POUNDS STERLING

REDUCED TO CUSTOM HOUSE STANDARD

AT

$4.84, as Fixed by Law.

£	$ cts.	£	$ cts.	£	$ cts.	£	$ cts.	£	$ cts.
1	24	28	135 52	74	358 16	120	580 80	166	803 44
2	48	29	140 36	75	363 00	121	585 64	167	808 28
3	73	30	145 20	76	367 84	122	590 48	168	813 12
4	97	31	150 04	77	372 68	123	595 32	169	817 96
5	1 21	32	154 88	78	377 52	124	600 16	170	822 80
6	1 45	33	159 72	79	382 36	125	605 00	171	827 64
7	1 68	34	164 56	80	387 20	126	609 84	172	832 48
8	1 94	35	169 40	81	392 04	127	614 68	173	837 32
9	2 18	36	174 24	82	396 88	128	619 52	174	842 16
10	2 42	37	179 08	83	401 72	129	624 36	175	847 00
11	2 66	38	183 92	84	406 56	130	629 20	176	851 84
12	2 90	39	188 76	85	411 40	131	634 04	177	856 68
13	3 15	40	193 60	86	416 24	132	638 88	178	861 52
14	3 39	41	198 44	87	421 08	133	643 72	179	866 36
15	3 63	42	203 28	88	425 92	134	648 56	180	871 20
16	3 87	43	208 12	89	430 76	135	653 40	181	876 04
17	4 11	44	212 96	90	435 60	136	658 24	182	880 88
18	4 36	45	217 80	91	440 44	137	663 08	183	885 72
19	4 60	46	222 64	92	445 28	138	667 92	184	890 56
£1	4 84	47	227 48	93	450 12	139	672 76	185	895 40
2	9 68	48	232 32	94	454 96	140	677 60	186	900 24
3	14 52	49	237 16	95	459 80	141	682 44	187	905 08
4	19 36	50	242 00	96	464 64	142	687 28	188	909 92
5	24 20	51	246 84	97	469 48	143	692 12	189	914 76
6	29 04	52	251 69	98	474 32	144	696 96	190	919 60
7	33 88	53	256 52	99	479 16	145	701 80	191	924 44
8	38 72	54	261 36	100	484 00	146	706 64	192	929 28
9	43 56	55	266 20	101	488 84	147	711 48	193	934 12
10	48 40	56	271 04	102	493 68	148	716 32	194	938 96
11	53 24	57	275 88	103	498 52	149	721 16	195	943 80
12	58 08	58	280 72	104	503 36	150	726 00	196	948 64
13	62 92	59	285 56	105	508 20	151	730 84	197	953 48
14	67 76	60	290 40	106	513 04	152	735 68	198	958 32
15	72 60	61	295 24	107	517 88	153	740 52	199	963 16
16	77 44	62	300 08	108	522 72	154	745 36	200	968 00
17	82 28	63	304 92	109	527 56	155	750 20	201	972 84
18	87 12	64	309 76	110	532 40	156	755 04	202	977 68
19	91 96	65	314 60	111	537 24	157	759 88	203	982 52
20	96 80	66	319 44	112	542 08	158	764 72	204	987 36
21	101 64	67	324 28	113	546 92	159	769 56	205	992 20
22	106 48	68	329 12	114	551 76	160	774 40	206	997 04
23	111 32	69	333 96	115	556 60	161	779 24	207	1001 88
24	116 16	70	338 80	116	561 44	162	784 08	208	1006 72
25	121 00	71	343 64	117	566 28	163	788 92	209	1011 56
26	125 84	72	348 48	118	571 12	164	793 76	210	1016 40
27	130 68	73	353 32	119	575 96	165	798 60	211	1021 24

POUNDS STERLING REDUCED TO CUSTOM HOUSE STANDARD.

£	$ cts.	£	$ cts.	£	$ cts.	£	$ cts.	£	$ cts.
212	1026 08	267	1292 28	322	1558 48	377	1824 68	432	2090 88
213	1030 92	268	1297 12	323	1563 32	378	1829 52	433	2095 72
214	1035 76	269	1301 96	324	1568 16	379	1834 36	434	2100 56
215	1040 60	270	1306 80	325	1573 00	380	1839 20	435	2105 40
216	1045 44	271	1311 64	326	1577 84	381	1844 04	436	2110 24
217	1050 28	272	1316 48	327	1582 68	382	1848 88	437	2115 08
218	1055 12	273	1321 32	328	1587 52	383	1853 72	438	2119 92
219	1059 96	274	1326 16	329	1592 36	384	1858 56	439	2124 76
220	1064 80	275	1331 00	330	1597 20	385	1863 40	440	2129 60
221	1069 64	276	1335 84	331	1602 04	386	1868 24	441	2134 44
222	1074 48	277	1340 68	332	1606 88	387	1873 08	442	2139 28
223	1079 32	278	1345 52	333	1611 72	388	1877 92	443	2144 12
224	1084 16	279	1350 36	334	1616 56	389	1882 76	444	2148 96
225	1089 00	280	1355 20	335	1621 40	390	1887 60	445	2153 80
226	1093 84	281	1360 04	336	1626 24	391	1892 44	446	2158 64
227	1098 68	282	1364 88	337	1631 08	392	1897 28	447	2163 48
228	1103 52	283	1369 72	338	1635 92	393	1902 12	448	2168 32
229	1108 36	284	1374 56	339	1640 76	394	1906 96	449	2173 16
230	1113 20	285	1379 40	340	1645 60	395	1911 80	450	2178 00
231	1118 04	286	1384 24	341	1650 44	396	1916 64	451	2182 84
232	1122 88	287	1389 08	342	1655 28	397	1921 48	452	2187 68
233	1127 72	288	1393 02	343	1660 12	398	1926 32	453	2192 52
234	1132 56	289	1398 76	344	1664 96	399	1931 16	454	2197 36
235	1137 40	290	1403 60	345	1669 80	400	1936 00	455	2202 20
236	1142 24	291	1408 44	346	1674 64	401	1940 84	456	2207 04
237	1147 08	292	1413 28	347	1679 48	402	1945 68	457	2211 88
238	1151 92	293	1418 12	348	1684 32	403	1950 52	458	2216 72
239	1156 76	294	1422 96	349	1689 16	404	1955 36	459	2221 56
240	1161 60	295	1427 80	350	1694 00	405	1960 20	460	2226 40
241	1166 44	296	1432 64	351	1698 84	406	1965 04	461	2231 24
242	1171 28	297	1437 48	352	1703 68	407	1969 88	462	2236 08
243	1176 12	298	1442 32	353	1708 52	408	1974 72	463	2240 92
244	1180 96	299	1447 16	354	1713 36	409	1979 56	464	2245 76
245	1185 80	300	1452 00	355	1718 20	410	1984 40	465	2250 60
246	1190 64	301	1456 84	356	1723 04	411	1989 24	466	2255 44
247	1195 48	302	1461 68	357	1727 88	412	1994 08	467	2260 28
248	1200 32	303	1466 52	358	1732 72	413	1998 92	468	2265 12
249	1205 16	304	1471 36	359	1737 56	414	2003 76	469	2269 96
250	1210 00	305	1476 20	360	1742 40	415	2008 60	470	2274 80
251	1214 84	306	1481 04	361	1747 24	416	2013 44	471	2279 64
252	1219 68	307	1485 88	362	1752 08	417	2018 28	472	2284 48
253	1224 52	308	1490 72	363	1756 92	418	2023 12	473	2289 32
254	1229 36	309	1495 56	364	1761 76	419	2027 96	474	2294 16
255	1234 20	310	1500 40	365	1766 60	420	2032 80	475	2299 00
256	1239 04	311	1505 24	366	1771 44	421	2037 64	476	2303 84
257	1243 88	312	1510 08	367	1776 28	422	2042 48	477	2308 68
258	1248 72	313	1514 92	368	1781 12	423	2047 32	478	2313 52
259	1253 56	314	1519 76	369	1785 96	424	2052 16	479	2318 36
260	1258 40	315	1524 60	370	1790 80	425	2057 00	480	2323 20
261	1263 24	316	1529 44	371	1795 64	426	2061 84	481	2328 04
262	1268 08	317	1534 28	372	1800 48	427	2066 68	482	2332 88
263	1272 92	318	1539 12	373	1805 32	428	2071 52	483	2337 72
264	1277 76	319	1543 96	374	1810 16	429	2076 36	484	2342 56
265	1282 60	320	1548 80	375	1815 00	430	2081 20	485	2347 40
266	1287 44	321	1553 64	376	1819 84	431	2086 04	486	2352 24

POUNDS STERLING REDUCED TO CUSTOM HOUSE STANDARD.

£	$ cts.	£	$ cts.	£	$ cts.	£	$ cts.	£	$ cts.
487	2357 08	542	2623 28	597	2889 48	652	3155 68	707	3421 88
488	2361 92	543	2628 12	598	2894 32	653	3160 52	708	3426 72
489	2366 76	544	2632 96	599	2899 16	654	3165 36	709	3431 56
490	2371 60	545	2637 80	600	2904 00	655	3170 20	710	3436 40
491	2376 44	546	2642 64	601	2908 84	656	3175 04	711	3441 24
492	2381 28	547	2647 48	602	2913 68	657	3179 88	712	3446 08
493	2386 12	548	2652 32	603	2918 52	658	3184 72	713	3450 92
494	2390 96	549	2657 16	604	2923 36	659	3189 56	714	3455 76
495	2395 80	550	2662 00	605	2928 20	660	3194 40	715	3460 60
496	2400 64	551	2666 84	606	2933 04	661	3199 24	716	3465 44
497	2405 48	552	2671 68	607	2937 88	662	3204 08	717	3470 28
498	2410 32	553	2676 52	608	2942 72	663	3208 92	718	3475 12
499	2415 16	554	2681 36	609	2947 56	664	3213 76	719	3479 96
500	2420 00	555	2686 20	610	2952 40	665	3218 60	720	3484 80
501	2424 84	556	2691 04	611	2957 24	666	3223 44	721	3489 64
502	2429 68	557	2695 88	612	2962 08	667	3228 28	722	3494 48
503	2434 52	558	2700 72	613	2966 92	668	3233 12	723	3499 32
504	2439 36	559	2705 56	614	2971 76	669	3237 96	724	3504 16
505	2444 20	560	2710 40	615	2976 60	670	3242 80	725	3509 00
506	2449 04	561	2715 24	616	2981 44	671	3247 64	726	3513 84
507	2453 88	562	2720 08	617	2986 28	672	3252 48	727	3518 68
508	2458 72	563	2724 92	618	2991 12	673	3257 32	728	3523 52
509	2463 56	564	2729 76	619	2995 96	674	3262 16	729	3528 36
510	2468 40	565	2734 60	620	3000 80	675	3267 00	730	3533 20
511	2473 24	566	2739 44	621	3005 64	676	3271 84	731	3538 04
512	2478 08	567	2744 28	622	3010 48	677	3276 68	732	3542 88
513	2482 92	568	2749 12	623	3015 32	678	3281 52	733	3547 72
514	2487 76	569	2753 96	624	3020 16	679	3286 36	734	3552 56
515	2492 60	570	2758 80	625	3025 00	680	3291 20	735	3557 40
516	2497 44	571	2763 64	626	3029 84	681	3296 04	736	3562 24
517	2502 28	572	2768 48	627	3034 68	682	3300 88	737	3567 08
518	2507 12	573	2773 32	628	3039 52	683	3305 72	738	3571 92
519	2511 96	574	2778 16	629	3044 36	684	3310 56	739	3576 76
520	2516 80	575	2783 00	630	3049 20	685	3315 40	740	3581 60
521	2521 64	576	2787 84	631	3054 04	686	3320 24	741	3586 44
522	2526 48	577	2792 68	632	3058 88	687	3325 08	742	3591 28
523	2531 32	578	2797 52	633	3063 72	688	3329 92	743	3596 12
524	2536 16	579	2802 36	634	3068 56	689	3334 76	744	3600 96
525	2541 00	580	2807 20	635	3073 40	690	3339 60	745	3605 80
526	2545 84	581	2812 04	636	3078 24	691	3344 44	746	3610 64
527	2550 68	582	2816 88	637	3083 08	692	3349 28	747	3615 48
528	2555 52	583	2821 72	638	3087 92	693	3354 12	748	3620 32
529	2560 36	584	2826 56	639	3092 76	694	3358 96	749	3625 16
530	2565 20	585	2831 40	640	3097 60	695	3363 80	750	3630 00
531	2570 04	586	2836 24	641	3102 44	696	3368 64	751	3634 84
532	2574 88	587	2841 08	642	3107 28	697	3373 48	752	3639 68
533	2579 72	588	2845 92	643	3112 12	698	3378 32	753	3644 52
534	2584 56	589	2850 76	644	3116 96	699	3383 16	754	3649 36
535	2589 40	590	2855 60	645	3121 80	700	3398 00	755	3654 20
536	2594 24	591	2860 44	646	3126 64	701	3392 84	756	3659 04
537	2599 08	592	2865 28	647	3131 48	702	3397 68	757	3663 88
538	2603 92	593	2870 12	648	3136 32	703	3402 52	758	3668 72
539	2608 76	594	2874 96	649	3141 16	704	3407 36	759	3673 56
540	2613 60	595	2879 80	650	3146 00	705	3412 20	760	3678 40
541	2618 44	596	2884 64	651	3150 84	706	3417 04	761	3683 24

11

POUNDS STERLING REDUCED TO CUSTOM HOUSE STANDARD.									
£	$ cts.	£	$ cts.	£	$ cts.	£	$ cts.	£	$ cts.
762	3688 08	812	3930 08	862	4172 08	912	4414 08	961	4651 24
763	3692 92	813	3934 92	863	4176 92	913	4418 92	962	4656 08
764	3697 76	814	3939 76	864	4181 76	914	4423 76	963	4660 92
765	3702 60	815	3944 60	865	4186 60	915	4428 60	964	4665 76
766	3707 44	816	3949 44	866	4191 44	916	4433 44	965	4670 60
767	3712 28	817	3954 28	867	4196 28	917	4438 28	966	4675 44
768	3717 12	818	3959 12	868	4201 12	918	4443 12	967	4680 28
769	3721 96	819	3963 96	869	4205 96	919	4447 96	968	4685 12
770	3726 80	820	3968 80	870	4210 80	920	4452 80	969	4689 96
771	3731 64	821	3973 64	871	4215 64	921	4457 64	970	4694 80
772	3736 48	822	3978 48	872	4220 48	922	4462 48	971	4699 64
773	3741 32	823	3983 32	873	4225 32	923	4467 32	972	4704 48
774	3746 16	824	3988 16	874	4230 16	924	4472 16	973	4709 32
775	3751 00	825	3993 00	875	4235 00	925	4477 00	974	4714 16
776	3755 84	826	3997 84	876	4239 84	926	4481 84	975	4719 00
777	3760 68	827	4002 68	877	4244 68	927	4486 68	976	4723 84
778	3765 52	828	4007 52	878	4249 52	928	4491 52	977	4728 68
779	3770 36	829	4012 36	879	4254 36	929	4496 36	978	4733 52
780	3775 20	830	4017 20	880	4259 20	930	4501 20	979	4738 36
781	3780 04	831	4022 04	881	4264 04	931	4506 04	980	4743 20
782	3784 88	832	4026 88	882	4268 88	932	4510 88	981	4748 04
783	3789 72	833	4031 72	883	4273 72	933	4515 72	982	4752 88
784	3794 56	834	4036 56	884	4278 56	934	4520 56	983	4757 72
785	3799 40	835	4041 40	885	4283 40	935	4525 40	984	4762 56
786	3804 24	836	4046 24	886	4288 24	936	4530 24	985	4767 40
787	3809 08	837	4051 08	887	4293 08	937	4535 08	986	4772 24
788	3813 92	838	4055 92	888	4297 92	938	4539 92	987	4777 08
789	3818 76	839	4060 76	889	4302 76	939	4544 76	988	4781 92
790	3823 60	840	4065 60	890	4307 60	940	4549 60	989	4786 76
791	3828 44	841	4070 44	891	4312 44	941	4554 44	990	4791 60
792	3833 28	842	4075 28	892	4317 28	942	4559 28	991	4796 44
793	3838 12	843	4080 12	893	4322 12	943	4564 12	992	4801 28
794	3842 96	844	4084 96	894	4326 96	944	4568 96	993	4806 12
795	3847 80	845	4089 80	895	4331 80	945	4573 80	994	4810 96
796	3852 64	846	4094 64	896	4336 64	946	4578 64	995	4815 80
797	3857 48	847	4099 48	897	4341 48	947	4583 48	996	4820 64
798	3862 32	848	4104 32	898	4346 32	948	4588 32	997	4825 48
799	3867 16	849	4109 16	899	4351 16	949	4593 16	998	4830 32
800	3872 00	850	4114 00	900	4356 00	950	4598 00	999	4835 16
801	3876 84	851	4118 84	901	4360 84	951	4602 84	1000	4840 00
802	3881 68	852	4123 68	902	4365 68	952	4607 68	2000	9680 00
803	3886 52	853	4128 52	903	4370 52	953	4612 52	3000	14520 00
804	3891 36	854	4133 36	904	4375 36	954	4617 36	4000	19360 00
805	3896 20	855	4138 20	905	4380 20	955	4622 20	5000	24200 00
806	3901 04	856	4143 04	906	4385 04	956	4627 04	6000	29040 00
807	3905 88	857	4147 88	907	4389 88	957	4631 88	7000	33880 00
808	3910 72	858	4152 72	908	4394 72	958	4636 72	8000	38720 00
809	3915 56	859	4157 56	909	4399 56	959	4641 56	9000	43560 00
810	3920 40	860	4162 40	910	4404 40	960	4646 40	10000	48400 00
811	3925 24	861	4167 24	911	4409 24				

FRANCS

REDUCED TO CUSTOM HOUSE STANDARD

AT

$18\frac{6}{10}$ Cents, as Fixed by Law.

Francs.	$ cts.	Francs.	$ cts.	Francs.	$ cts.	Francs.	$ cts.
1	19	31	5 77	61	11 35	91	16 93
2	37	32	5 95	62	11 53	92	17 11
3	56	33	6 14	63	11 72	93	17 30
4	74	34	6 32	64	11 90	94	17 48
5	93	35	6 51	65	12 09	95	17 67
6	1 12	36	6 70	66	12 28	96	17 86
7	1 30	37	6 88	67	12 46	97	18 04
8	1 49	38	7 07	68	12 65	98	18 23
9	1 67	39	7 25	69	12 83	99	18 41
10	1 86	40	7 44	70	13 02	100	18 60
11	2 05	41	7 63	71	13 21	200	37 20
12	2 23	42	7 81	• 72	13 39	300	55 80
13	2 42	43	8 00	73	13 58	400	74 40
14	2 60	44	8 18	74	13 76	500	93 00
15	2 79	45	8 37	75	13 95	600	111 60
16	2 98	46	8 56	76	14 14	700	130 20
17	3 16	47	8 74	77	14 32	800	148 80
18	3 35	48	8 93	78	14 51	900	167 40
19	3 53	49	9 11	79	14 69	1000	186 00
20	3 72	50	9 30	80	14 88	2000	372 00
21	3 91	51	9 49	81	15 07	3000	558 00
22	4 09	52	9 67	82	15 25	4000	744 00
23	4 28	53	9 86	83	15 44	5000	930 00
24	4 46	54	10 04	84	15 62	6000	1116 00
25	4 65	55	10 23	85	15 81	7000	1302 00
26	4 84	56	10 42	86	16 00	8000	1488 00
27	5 02	57	10 60	87	16 18	9000	1674 00
28	5 21	58	10 79	88	16 37	10000	1864 00
29	5 39	59	10 97	89	16 55		
30	5 58	60	11 16	90	16 74		

MARK OF THE GERMAN EMPIRE

REDUCED TO CUSTOM HOUSE STANDARD

At 23 Cents,

As fixed by Treasury Department June 20, 1872.

M	$ cts.	M	$ cts.	M	$ cts.	M	$ cts.
1	.23	31	7.13	61	14.03	91	20.93
2	.46	32	7.36	62	14.26	92	21.16
3	.69	33	7.59	63	14.49	93	21.39
4	.92	34	7.82	64	14.72	94	21.62
5	1.15	35	8.05	65	14.95	95	21.85
6	1.38	36	8.28	66	15.18	96	22.08
7	1.61	37	8.51	67	15.41	97	22.31
8	1.84	38	8.74	68	15.64	98	22.54
9	2.07	39	8.97	69	15.87	99	22.77
10	2.30	40	9.20	70	16.10	100	23.00
11	2.53	41	9.43	71	16.33	200	46.00
12	2.76	42	9.66	72	16.56	300	69.00
13	2.99	43	9.89	73	16.79	400	92.00
14	3.22	44	10.12	74	17.02	500	115.00
15	3.45	45	10.35	75	17.25	600	138.00
16	3.68	46	10.58	76	17.48	700	161.00
17	3.91	47	10.81	77	17.71	800	184.00
18	4.14	48	11.04	78	17.94	900	207.00
19	4.37	48	11.27	79	18.17	1000	230.00
20	4.60	50	11.50	80	18.40	2000	460.00
21	4.83	51	11.73	81	18.63	3000	690.00
22	5.06	52	11.96	82	18.86	4000	920.00
23	5.29	53	12.19	83	19.09	5000	1150.00
24	5.52	54	12.42	84	19.32	6000	1380.00
25	5.75	55	12.65	85	19.55	7000	1610.00
26	5.98	56	12.88	86	19.78	8000	1840.00
27	6.21	57	13.11	87	20.01	9000	2070.00
28	6.44	58	13.34	88	20.24	10000	2300.00
29	6.67	59	13.57	89	20.47		
30	6.90	60	13.80	90	20.70		

RIX DOLLARS OF PRUSSIA

REDUCED TO CUSTOM HOUSE STANDARD

AT

69 Cents, as Fixed by Law.

R $	$ cts.	R $	$ cts.	R $	$ cts.	R $	$ cts.
1	69	31	21 39	61	42 09	91	62 79
2	1 38	32	22 08	62	42 78	92	63 48
3	2 07	33	22 77	63	43 47	93	64 17
4	2 76	34	23 46	64	44 16	94	64 86
5	3 45	35	24 15	65	44 85	95	65 55
6	4 14	36	24 84	66	45 54	96	66 24
7	4 83	37	25 53	67	46 23	97	66 93
8	5 52	38	26 22	68	46 92	98	67 62
9	6 21	39	26 91	69	47 61	99	68 31
10	6 90	40	27 60	70	48 30	100	69 00
11	7 59	41	28 29	71	48 99	200	138 00
12	8 28	42	28 98	72	49 68	300	207 00
13	8 97	43	29 67	73	50 37	400	276 00
14	9 66	44	30 36	74	51 06	500	345 00
15	10 35	45	31 05	75	51 75	600	414 00
16	11 04	46	31 74	76	52 44	700	483 00
17	11 73	47	32 43	77	53 13	800	552 00
18	12 42	48	33 12	78	53 82	900	621 00
19	13 11	49	33 81	79	54 51	1000	690 00
20	13 80	50	34 50	80	55 20	2000	1380 00
21	14 49	51	35 19	81	55 89	3000	2070 00
22	15 18	52	35 88	82	56 58	4000	2760 00
23	15 87	53	36 57	83	57 27	5000	3450 00
24	16 56	54	37 26	84	57 96	6000	4140 00
25	17 25	55	37 95	85	58 65	7000	4830 00
26	17 94	56	38 64	86	59 34	8000	5520 00
27	18 63	57	39 33	87	60 03	9000	6210 00
28	19 32	58	40 02	88	60 72	10000	6900 00
29	20 01	59	40 71	89	61 41		
30	20 70	60	41 40	90	62 10		

RIX DOLLARS OF BREMEN

REDUCED TO CUSTOM HOUSE STANDARD

AT

78¼ Cents, as Fixed by Law.

R. Dol.	$ cts.	R. Dol.	$ cts.	R. Dol.	$ cts.	R. Dol.	$ cts.
1	78¼	31	24 41	61	48 04	91	71 66
2	1 58	32	25 20	62	48 83	92	72 45
3	2 36	33	25 99	63	49 61	93	73 24
4	3 15	34	26 78	64	50 40	94	74 03
5	3 94	35	27 56	65	51 19	95	74 81
6	4 73	36	28 35	66	51 98	96	75 60
7	5 51	37	29 14	67	52 76	97	76 39
8	6 30	38	29 93	68	53 55	98	77 18
9	7 09	39	30 71	69	54 34	99	77 96
10	7 88	40	31 50	70	55 13	100	78 75
11	8 66	41	32 29	71	55 91	200	157 50
12	9 45	42	33 08	72	56 70	300	236 25
13	10 24	43	33 86	73	57 49	400	315 00
14	11 03	44	34 65	74	58 28	500	393 75
15	11 81	45	35 44	75	59 06	600	472 00
16	12 60	46	36 23	76	59 85	700	551 25
17	13 39	47	37 01	77	60 64	800	630 00
18	14 18	48	37 80	78	61 43	900	708 75
19	14 96	49	38 59	79	62 21	1000	787 50
20	15 75	50	39 38	80	63 00	2000	1575 00
21	16 54	51	40 16	81	63 79	3000	2362 50
22	17 33	52	40 95	82	64 58	4000	3150 00
23	18 11	53	41 74	83	65 36	5000	3937 50
24	18 90	54	42 53	84	66 15	6000	4725 00
25	19 69	55	43 31	85	66 94	7000	5512 50
26	20 48	56	44 10	86	67 73	8000	6300 00
27	21 26	57	44 89	87	68 51	9000	7087 50
28	22 05	58	45 68	88	69 30	10000	7875 00
29	22 84	59	46 46	89	70 09		
30	23 63	60	47 25	90	70 88		

LINEAL YARD

FROM

⅛ of an Inch to 100 Inches in Width

REDUCED TO

SQUARE YARDS.

Inches wide.	Sq. yds.	Inches wide.	Sq. yds.	Inches wide.	Sq. yds.	Inches wide.	Sq. yds.
⅛	.0035	21	.5833	48	1.3333	75	2.0833
¼	.0069	22	.6111	49	1.3611	76	2.1111
⅜	.0104	23	.6389	50	1.3888	77	2.1389
½	.0139	24	.6666	51	1.4166	78	2.1667
⅝	.0174	25	.6944	52	1.4444	79	2.1944
¾	.0208	26	.7222	53	1.4722	80	2.2222
⅞	.0242	27	.7500	54	1.5000	81	2.2500
1	.02775	28	.7777	55	1.5277	82	2.2778
2	.0555	29	.8056	56	1.5555	83	2.3056
3	.0933	30	.8333	57	1.5833	84	2.3333
4	.1111	31	.8611	58	1.6111	85	2.3611
5	.1389	32	.8689	59	1.6388	86	2.3889
6	.1667	33	.9167	60	1.6666	87	2.4167
7	.1944	34	.9444	61	1.6944	88	2.4444
8	.2222	35	.9722	62	1.7222	89	2.4722
9	.2500	36	1.0000	63	1.7500	90	2.5000
10	.2778	37	1.0277	64	1.7777	91	2.5278
11	.3055	38	1.0555	65	1.8055	92	2.5556
12	.3333	39	1.0833	66	1.8333	93	2.5833
13	.3611	40	1.1111	67	1.8611	94	2.6111
14	.3888	41	1.1389	68	1.8888	95	2.6389
15	.4166	42	1.1667	69	1.9166	96	2.6667
16	.4444	43	1.1944	70	1.9444	97	2.6944
17	.4722	44	1.2222	71	1.9722	98	2.7222
18	.5000	45	1.2500	72	2.0000	99	2.7500
19	.5278	46	1.2777	73	2.0278	100	2.7778
20	.5555	47	1.3055	74	2.0556		

www.ingramcontent.com/pod-product-compliance
Lightning Source LLC
Chambersburg PA
CBHW030326270326
41926CB00010B/1516